The Heroes' Wife

BY

Dora Griffin Bell

Bloomington, IN

Milton Keynes, UK

AuthorHouse™
1663 Liberty Drive, Suite 200
Bloomington, IN 47403
www.authorhouse.com
Phone: 1-800-839-8640

AuthorHouse™ UK Ltd.
500 Avebury Boulevard
Central Milton Keynes, MK9 2BE
www.authorhouse.co.uk
Phone: 08001974150

First published by AuthorHouse 5/5/2006

ISBN: 1-4259-2605-3 (e)
ISBN: 1-4259-2603-7 (sc)
ISBN: 1-4259-2604-5 (dj)

Library of Congress Control Number: 2006902364

Printed in the United States of America
Bloomington, Indiana

This book is printed on acid-free paper.

For the heroes' children —
James, Glyn Carol, Tom, Matt and Ann

Heroes do not go to war and put themselves in *harm's way* because they love war...they go because they hate war and love peace.

———————————

"Hero: Any man admired for his courage, nobility, or exploits, especially in war."

Webster's New World Dictionary, 1960.

———————

Prologue

In 1965 more than 10,000 American military men were representing the country in a bitter conflict in Southeast Asia. The nation's participation became a fact following the Tonkin Gulf Resolution of August 1964.

Although from time to time even I have felt a little "heroic" for the sacrifices I made during the Vietnam War, most of the time I have felt anything but heroic. Being the wife of one of the men who give their all and risked their lives for their country is not easy. Most of the time, we know we are not worthy of the task we face--that of supporting and being the alter ego of men who rightly deserve to be called heroes.

I began writing this book some thirty-eight years ago. At that time I kept a diary to cover the events of my first hero husband's shoot down in Vietnam. Eventually, I stopped writing in the diary, thinking I would never forget the things that were happening to us and to the other families in our military community. Fortunately, time has a way of erasing some of our most difficult moments, the pain, the loneliness, and the sadness, while most of the good memories remain with us forever. So, in writing this memoir I have had to approximate some events long past. I hope that I am not faulted for that.

It has been a difficult decision to include portions of the personal letters received from Jimmie Griffin during his two combat cruises to Vietnam. Some forty years have passed since the letters were written, but rereading them and copying portions was painful, even after so many years and a second happy marriage. And since I had no other way of knowing what those captives who survived the war experienced, I have included "What Did You Do in the War, Granddad?" written by my second husband, the hero who, during the thirty years of our time together, shared with me his memories of more than seven years in captivity in Hanoi.

I have been fortunate to be loved by two men who made great sacrifices for their country. So this book has been written, really, by three people: by myself, by my first husband in his letters, and by Jim Bell, the hero who came home to find that during his absence he had lost the most important thing of all--his family.

For many years, while seeing books written by the returned Vietnam POWs and their family members, I felt that anything I might write about my experiences would be redundant. In the beginning there seemed to be almost too many books about the Vietnam War, and I could not imagine my story being of interest to anyone. But early in 2003 something happened to make me realize that my story is, after all, a special one. And by sharing my experiences with spouses (and today some of them will be men) of military personnel in combat situations at this time, I hope to pass along some of the strength that carried me through those horrendous years.

I was awakened to the possibility that my story might still be meaningful for others one evening in the spring of 2003. I had undergone eye surgery a few days earlier, and so I had not taken great pains with personal grooming. As we sat down to dinner my husband said, "Dora, you're going to have to comb your hair."

My first thought was that he was gently ribbing me about my appearance, so I just nodded and continued eating. Near the close of the meal he again said, "Dora, you really need to comb your hair."

"Give me a break, Jim. You know I can't wash my hair or wear makeup until this eye heals. I'll do better in a couple of days," I replied.

"I'm trying to tell you that a TV crew is going to be here in about thirty minutes, and I know you'll want to fix up a little bit."

When I asked why a television crew would be coming to our house, he explained that Channel Seven wanted to get his views on what the American POWs in Iraq are going through. We'd lived in the Washington area almost twenty-eight years, and no one had called to interview him about his POW experiences, but now they were coming. "They may want to talk with you, too!"

So I did my best to rearrange my hair so it would not be too scraggly, and soon I sat in our living room watching while Jim poured out his heart to the reporter during a forty-five-minute videotaping. He was telling how it felt to face guns as he climbed out of the water, trying to untangle himself from his parachute as he cringed with the pain of a broken shoulder during his capture in Ha Long Bay near Haiphong. He told the reporter about the rats in their cells, the rocks in their rice, the primitive toilet arrangements, the fears they dealt with, the beatings, and the concern about their families back home. Then the camera was turned on me for a few questions about my first husband's capture and death and about our friends who played matchmaker to bring Jim and me together after the war.

Taping the interview took about an hour, and the reporter was gentle in her handling of questions. But when the tape was broadcast later that evening only about two minutes of it were aired.

Then the next day we received a call from Channel Nine, and their reporter also wanted to do an interview. He seemed unaware of the earlier broadcast, and this time, I was finally able to wash my hair before the crew arrived. The entire process was repeated as though the first had never taken place. I wondered who had given Jim's name to two television stations in one day. This time they had us bring out photos, and Jim showed a model of an RA5-C airplane like the one he was flying when he was shot down in October of 1965. Again the reporter spent a couple of minutes with me at the end, getting the story that I had been married to two men who were prisoners in Vietnam.

When the interview was aired on the evening news, again just a couple of minutes of footage, Washington anchor J.C. Hayward prompted the reporter, "And did Captain Bell have a wife?"

So the reporter briefly explained that Jim's first wife obtained a divorce and remarried during the war, and when he returned home friends had put him in touch with the widow of another POW: Me. "What a nice story! I'd like to hear more about that," J.C. replied. So, with that comment I decided that there may be others who would like to know about the things we go through, we wives of heroes.

→ 1 ←

Sanford, Florida
May 20, 1967

The sound of television from the next room awakens me on a lazy Saturday morning. The children have risen early to watch their favorite cartoons, while in my bedroom I stay buried beneath the covers thinking about the glorious days ahead. In less than four weeks the *USS Kitty Hawk* will be docking in San Diego, and my favorite navy pilot will be flying home after eight months of combat missions over Vietnam.

May is always warm and humid in central Florida, and the whine of the window air conditioner encourages me to lie there a while longer. As I close my eyes again, I can see Jimmie walking across the tarmac, wearing a khaki G-suit, swaggering like a toddler with a load in his pants. He is just over six feet tall, and his dark brown hair has yet to recede from the natural hairline. Tall, dark, and handsome is coming home to me.

Eventually Glyn Carol, newly turned six years old, and Jamey, ten, prepare their favorite breakfast of cinnamon toast and chocolate milk and make a cup of instant coffee for me. I awaken again as a tangly haired little angel quietly opens the door and peeps into my room.

"Here is your newspaper, Mom," Glyn Carol greets me at 8:30.

Resigned to my fate, I pull on a pair of faded tan shorts and an orange print shirt and stumble in to join them at the breakfast table. I scan the headlines about the war, learning that five planes were lost yesterday in raids marking the birthday of Ho Chi Minh. No names are given in the story, but I shiver as I remember that our squadron is still on line--in the combat zone.

Our quiet morning is interrupted when, with a slightly soprano chirp, Samson, our miniature schnauzer pup, announces that we have a visitor. Trying to quiet him, I look out the front window and see a black and white official navy sedan parked at the curb, and a man in uniform carrying a briefcase is coming up our front walk. My throat constricts, and my heartbeat quickens.

It is a dreaded moment I have imagined many times in the two years my husband has been flying combat missions in the Vietnam War. This scene has been experienced by more of my friends than I can count on the fingers of both hands. Arrival of the official car always bodes bad news for someone, bringing a representative from the Wing Commander's office and sometimes a chaplain—and word of a combat casualty. I have seen the car arrive at Rozelle's and Ann's and Mary's and Maggie's. This time the bad news is for me. All military fliers' wives fear this moment. None of us know just how we will handle it when the time comes.

A few weeks ago, when Jimmie had a nose-wheel collapse while landing aboard the aircraft carrier, I was notified by phone that a message about the event had come through garbled, but it appeared the message described the pilot as "injured." Dave Fall, our neighbor who is our squadron's liaison on the Air Wing, called me, and after a week of uncertainty the message was re-serviced. Jim had not only walked away without injury; he had handled the landing so smoothly that Jack Walters, his navigator who rides in the back seat, did not even realize the landing was unusual.

Now, seeing the Casualty Assistance Calls Officer at my door, I try to be optimistic. My first thought is that Jimmie has had another nose-wheel collapse, and this time has not handled it with such aplomb. And maybe this time the Wing decided not to handle it by telephone.

I duck behind the curtain, calling to the children to "Bring me a pair of shoes" and run my fingers through my hair.

Lieutenant Bob Watson rings the doorbell, and when I open the door he quickly steps inside. I must appear deathly pale, because, without sitting down or pausing, he gets straight to the point.

"Mrs. Griffin, I'm Bob Watson, and I'm afraid I have some bad news for you..."

I try to be courteous, but the lump in my throat is fighting inside me to postpone the message I am about to receive. At the same time my heart goes out to Lieutenant Watson. I know the men whose duty it is to bring such official news find it a difficult and unpleasant task at best. He gives me no time to suffer or wonder—--without pausing he tells me, "Your husband's airplane was shot down this morning over the city of Hanoi. The escort saw the plane break up—--it was threatened by a Mig, a SAM, and ground fire, and we're not sure what hit it, but two good chutes were seen. No rescue attempts were made because of the highly dangerous area. However, a few hours later Hanoi Radio announced that the North Vietnamese had captured Lieutenant Commander Griffin and Lieutenant Walters."

Bob has to get all of his message out, perhaps fearing I might faint or start crying. He seems not to take a breath until he has said it all. The children have entered the living room, and they join me on the sofa. Both are clinging tightly to my arms.

"Mom, is it Dad*?"* my son cautiously asks.

"He's all right, honey. He's all right. Let's listen to Mr. Watson," I say, trying to convince myself as much as the children.

Bob continues, describing the importance of the mission Jim was on, the speed of his aircraft, the altitude, and other statistics. I try to make mental notes of all the facts, so I ask him several times to repeat the details.

"You should receive a telegram in a few hours with all this information on it," he says. He gives me a copy of the telegram that has already been delivered to Pat Walters, the young wife of Jim's navigator. He said the facts will be identical. He seems not to know the reason for the delay in the arrival of my telegram. He tells me that Captain Fowler, the Wing Commander, will be arriving shortly.

At this point I remember that I am still barefoot, and I again ask the children to bring me a pair of shoes. Apparently, I will not have time to dress properly for this, the most weighty occasion of my life thus far.

Clare Daum, my thoughtful next-door neighbor whose husband also is a pilot in Jimmie's squadron, slips in through the kitchen door. She is the mother of two sets of toddler twins, her face is as pale as skim milk, but she has seen the official car and has come to help. She immediately takes charge in the kitchen, making coffee, returning to her own house to get her percolator when she is unable to find one in my kitchen. I have no idea who is watching Clare's children, perhaps Anne Perrella or another squadron wife.

I find two pairs of sandals have appeared at my feet just as Captain and Mrs. Fowler arrive. They also had dressed quickly, but they have rushed here to be with me. Some eighteen months ago, when the Fowlers went to tell Ann Johnson that her husband's plane was down, Ann met them at the door wearing a baggy bathrobe, her hair in curlers. After that, we all vowed that we would make a point of putting on makeup and a decent dress every morning before going out to get the newspaper, but I have failed to do that on this day. That is usually the tip-off to the casualty officer, waiting in a car at the curb. When someone comes out to get the morning paper, it means the family is up.

Now, as the information is given about the shoot down, I do not cry. I am too numb to cry, and once I hear that Jimmie is alive I concentrate on being calm and alert enough to ask questions. "Where was the plane? When did it happen?"

We have lost at least ten RA5-Cs from the Wing in combat during the past two years, four of them from our own squadron. Just six weeks ago we lost our commanding officer, Commander Charles Putnam. The squadron, RVAH-13, is nearing the end of its second combat cruise in two years. It has set impressive records in spite of so many losses. Months ago Jimmie and Jack completed their one-hundredth combat mission just as the monsoon season was ending, and they may have flown twenty or so more hops since then in the good weather. All of our planes have been performing beautifully and bringing back valuable reconnaissance information. These are not bombers, although the Vigilante originally was designated as an attack plane. The mission Jim and Jack were on probably would have been their last major flight in the combat zone before returning home in just a few weeks.

A few days ago, perhaps due to the difficulty of the task and the frequency of losses, the Fowlers put out the word that they would no longer make immediate personal calls on wives of men of the Wing when planes are downed, but today, they have thrown on their clothes and hurried to my house. Realizing this, I concentrate on not making the morning difficult for them. They stay with us for two hours, and we talk about the squadron's good record, the contents of the message on Jim, and other Wing news.

Throughout the discussion the children huddle beside me in their pajamas. Their faces are solemn, but they join me in asking questions. At one point Jamey, our self-appointed family artist, leaves the room and comes back to show me a cartoon he has drawn. It depicts a gigantic soldier, labeled "Me," with rifle in hand stomping the devil out of a North Vietnamese soldier who has grasped in his tight fist an American pilot, marked "Dad." We do not laugh, but we almost smile.

How wonderful that my son can express his agonizing thoughts so effectively.

Soon other squadron wives arrive—Anita Wallace, whose children are best friends with Jamey and Glyn Carol, joins Clare in the kitchen. After about a half hour Clare dresses Glyn and takes her next door so she can be "lost" in helping her two sets of twins eat breakfast. Glyn stays with Clare most of the day, and Jamey remains with me. Later he goes over to talk with his sister and reassure her.

I ask Captain Fowler, now drinking his second cup of coffee, whether Jimmie's parents have been notified in person as well. He says that they will be receiving a telegram and that he will see to it that a casualty officer calls on them if I give directions for reaching them. He gets on the phone to Memphis Naval Air Station, some ninety miles from the Griffins' rural home, relaying instructions to the base chaplain, while I tell him how to travel Highway 51 to Ripley, take another road to Nutbush, then a third through Toulon to Forked Deer.

Captain Fowler says he had not realized Jim was originally a country boy. In spite of the gravity of the situation, we smile again. As soon as I can think clearly I phone Willis Warren, a neighbor of the Griffins in Tennessee, asking him to intercept the navy representative who is en route to their house. I want him to be with them when they receive the news that their son's plane has gone down. I tell Willis I will call later in the day, after Mother Griffin has a chance to pull herself together. But as soon as the naval official leaves their house, she phones me.

I had not expected her to be able to talk for hours, but she is amazing. Just minutes after learning her son is in communist captivity, she calmly tells me that she has faith in God that Jimmie will be okay. She insists she will pack a suitcase immediately. "Billy and I will be down as soon as we can. We'll leave early in the morning and be at your house Monday," she says. Gene, her youngest son, and his wife

Christine will drive them down. "I will stay with you as long as you want me," she says. Now in her mid-fifties, Mother G is much stronger than I had imagined.

Sometime during the morning, I manage to make more phone calls. I get through to Jimmie's brother, John Chaney, in Salinas and his sister Barbara in San Diego. John is too upset to talk, and he gives the phone to his wife Lois. She gets the basic facts from me and seems reassured. Barbara is very upset when I talk with her. Both John and Barbara's families live in California, so they saw their brother after I last saw him, while the *Kitty Hawk* was off the West Coast preparing to get underway for this cruise. I realize that, up until now, I have not cried. Somehow, that would be a welcome release...but tears do not come just yet.

Next, I call my mother in Memphis. My father died during the first of Jimmie's two Vietnam cruises, so Mother is alone, but she knows it is important to me to get through the day without breaking down. Mother says she will phone my sister Charlotte in North Carolina. My other sister Agnes lives just three hours away in West Palm Beach, and when I call she offers to drive up to stay with us overnight.

It has been the custom, when one of the squadron wives loses her husband, that she not be left alone, especially the first night. There are many reasons for this—that she might have someone to talk to, to handle telephone calls that she might not feel like answering, or to deal with newspaper reporters. Anxious to be with family, I welcome Aggie's offer. She and her husband and youngest son can only stay the one night because they all work, but I feel great relief that some of my family will be with me this night. *After all, Jimmie is not dead! He is alive and a prisoner, so there is no need for the squadron wives to fear that I might be overcome with grief. I have so much to be thankful for!*

By now the chaplains have arrived, and Dave Fall, who lives across the street and is the wing liaison officer, comes in wearing shorts and a tee shirt and looks as though he might throw up any minute. People come and go all day---other wives from the squadron, our pastor, and friends from church. Someone keeps the coffee going and the dishes washed. Ann Fall brings over some food for lunch. I seem to be moving through the day by rote.

Several close friends, civilian and military, come by. As they express concern I think of the times I have made similar calls on wives of missing fliers as well as those families who learned right away that there was no hope of ever seeing their men again. At the time I went to their homes to give strength to those involved. Now, reexamining my motives, I wonder if instead of *giving* strength, I went to receive it from those who were in situations that required them to be at their strongest. With this in mind, I try to use what little fortitude I have left to pass it on to those who come to see us.

I know that the wives of other men in the squadron are unconsciously, or maybe consciously, afraid that at any moment they might see an official car in their own driveway! Early during our men's first deployment in the war we lost a plane and crew just two days after another plane piloted by our Operations officer had gone down.

My husband has been a leader in the squadron. He began the two cruises as Administration Officer, but after the loss of those first two aircraft he assumed the duties of Operations Officer. He is one of the finest officers turned out by the United States Naval Academy and, according to his fellow fliers, an outstanding pilot with many flying hours to his credit. He has always been a good moral influence, both among his civilian acquaintances and his friends in the navy. If this description sounds a bit glowing and prejudiced, I admit it. I am in love with the guy! However, my opinion is shared by many others who know him.

Jimmie has prepared me for this difficult day. He has given me years of devotion and instilled in me much respect for the navy and all that our country stands for. Because of this, I can take a deep breath and try to reassure all those who come to call that I am certain that Jimmie is well and that he was prepared for the rough times that lie before him.

When Reverend Bob Temple, our Methodist pastor, and his wife Nancy arrive, she hugs me and says, "I want you to know I took a shower and dressed just for you this morning." Others in the room get quiet. But I realize that Nancy is trying to lighten the atmosphere with a little humor. Saturday is their day off.

The dog greets everyone enthusiastically in the beginning of the morning, but he finally gets bored by the scene and retreats to the den to stay out of the way.

One bright spot in the morning comes when Joni Higgenbotham, wife of the squadron's new commanding officer, arrives. A striking platinum blonde, Joni is dressed in a bright yellow and black polka-dotted dress. Joni is a colorful person both in personality and her eye-catching attire. She is a former model and wears false eyelashes, elaborate hairdos, and, always, mini-dresses! Her appearance immediately makes me feel better.

Dave and Bob, who had left when the chaplains arrived, return just before noon. They both now are wearing uniforms. Dave calls me aside and says he has more news and would like to speak with me privately. The three of us go into the small study just off the living room where Samson is napping. Dave says that Hanoi Radio has broadcast an interview with Jimmie. *A live interview? He really is alive!!!*

Dave says he will try to get a transcript of the interview for me. Or, he says, I can request a copy of the tape made by the agency that monitored the broadcast. Bob tells me the interview was done in a Hanoi hospital. Jimmie was injured when he ejected from the plane, but the extent of his injuries is unknown. *Is this the reason my telegram has been delayed? Maybe the Pentagon is trying to ascertain as much as they can about Jimmie's injuries before sending me a telegram.* The radio broadcast, Dave says, gave the names of five men captured on May 19th during the Hanoi raids.

Dave and Bob leave, and those gathered in the living room ask me what further information I have received. I tell them Hanoi Radio has broadcast an interview with Jim. I do not mention the injuries.

There are still several people in the living room when I am called to the telephone. Dave, who has gone back to the office, has more information. He says Jim and Jack's names have been picked up by some of the wire services—in fact, their names were published today in several newspapers around the country. He asks if I object to having the Wing select a photograph of Jimmie for publication, because if we refuse to furnish one, the papers will just choose one themselves. I tell him I don't mind.

The crowd begins to thin out toward the end of the afternoon. Clare comes in and asks if the kids and I will have dinner with her in an hour or so. Until this moment I have given no thought to meal preparation although two people have brought over covered dishes during the afternoon. I gratefully accept and realize that Clare is not only a very special friend, she is a terrific neighbor and a devoted squadron wife.

About 6 o'clock the Falls, Ann and Dave, return, and they join Mary Putnam and me for a glass of sherry. Tiny Mary, with her big, sad brown eyes, has sat quietly through most of the afternoon. Just weeks earlier Mary's own husband, Charlie, who was then commanding officer of RVAH-13, was shot down over North Vietnam. She has received no word about his fate, but things don't look good. Putt's navigator, Frank Prendergast, was picked up offshore in Vietnam waters on March 9th. And now Mary has come to help *me* through this day!

After placing a note for other visitors who might come by while I am away, I walk next door to Clare's house. She has made lasagna and kept the children, hers and mine, busy through the afternoon. Now, watching her adorable twins eat, I can almost forget the gravity of what has happened to us. Jamey and Glyn Carol remain with Clare when I return home to find my house empty, so I make a quick decision to drive across town to see the other wife whose life has been changed by the day's tragic events.

Throughout the morning my thoughts have often been on Pat Walters, the pretty young wife of Jim's navigator (which in the Vigilante community we referred to as a back-seater), and Stan, their eighteen-month-old son. I had telephoned her after the Fowlers left my house to go to hers, and Pat showed surprising spirit for one so new to navy life. Now, I need to see her in person. Somewhat restored by Clare's lasagna dinner, I get in the car and turn on the radio to catch the 7 p.m. news as I drive toward Pat's house. With an eerie feeling, I listen to the newscaster announce coast to coast that Jimmie and Jack were among those captured by North Vietnam that day and that an interview with Jim has been aired by Hanoi Radio.

The Walters' house is across town on Jenkins Circle in Pinecrest, where Jimmie and I had previously lived in a small bungalow just down the street from Pat and Jack. Her house, like mine, has been the scene of callers throughout the day. Ann Marie Thompson and the Walters' minister are with her when I arrive.

Often, during the three years our husbands have flown together, Pat and I have shared the feeling that if our husbands ever went down in Vietnam, we hoped they would be together. I know that Jim feels he has the best damn navigator in the navy, and Pat says Jack thinks Jim is the best pilot. Both men grew up on farms, and we're sure the rugged country life with outhouses and water pumps and wells has been good preparation for the hardships they now face.

We talk about how lucky we are to learn immediately that our husbands are alive and captives. Of all our friends whose men have been shot down over enemy territory, none have been so fortunate as we. Pat and I have learned immediately that our guys are alive...prisoners! *Can that be a good thing?* We agree that it is much better than not knowing, and far better than being told they are dead.

The drive back to my house is difficult. I worry about how James and Glyn Carol are really feeling. I concentrate on breathing, and I drive very carefully, afraid of missing a stop sign or light. When I pull into my driveway, I find that my sister Agnes and her husband Lester have arrived from West Palm Beach. Someone has stayed with my house, and the children have returned home, so I am relieved.

It's still daylight when Ken and Mary McIntosh, who were neighbors when we first moved to Sanford and lived in Pinecrest, come by. Ken, who is one of the city's leading attorneys, says he will help me with any legal matters I might encounter. At this point, I can't even imagine what those legal problems might be.

While Aggie and Les, the McIntoshes, and I talk over coffee, there is a knock on the door. My telegram has arrived! After several attempts at reading it—the words keep running together—I hand it over to Ken and Lester:

> I REGRET TO CONFIRM ON BEHALF OF THE UNITED STATES NAVY THAT YOUR HUSBAND, LIEUTENANT COMMANDER JAMES LLOYD GRIFFIN, 595955/1310, USN, HAS BEEN PLACED IN A CAPTURED STATUS FOLLOWING THE LOSS OF HIS AIRCRAFT ON 19 MAY 1967 WHILE ON A BOMB DAMAGE ASSESSMENT MISSION OVER HANOI, NORTH VIETNAM. YOUR HUSBAND'S AIRCRAFT RECEIVED ENEMY GROUND FIRE, SURFACE- TO-AIR MISSILE, AND MIG THREATS IN THE VICINITY OF THE TARGET AREA. PRIOR TO REACHING THE

TARGET AT APPROXIMATELY 3500/4500 FEET, YOUR HUSBAND'S AIRCRAFT WAS OBSERVED TO BREAK UP AND DISINTEGRATE. TWO GOOD PARACHUTES WERE THEN OBSERVED DESCENDING OVER A POPULATED AREA. SEARCH AND RESCUE EFFORTS WERE NOT ATTEMPTED DUE TO THE HIGH- RISK AREA. IN VIEW OF THIS INFORMATION, YOUR HUSBAND WILL BE CARRIED IN A CAPTURED STATUS PENDING RECEIPT AND REVIEW OF A FULL REPORT OF THE CIRCUMSTANCES. YOU MAY BE CERTAIN THAT YOU WILL BE INFORMED OF ANY INFORMATION RECEIVED REGARDING YOUR HUSBAND OR ANY ACTION TAKEN RELATIVE TO HIS STATUS. INASMUCH AS YOUR HUSBAND IS PRESENTLY BEING CARRIED IN A CAPTURED STATUS, IT IS SUGGESTED, FOR HIS SAFETY, THAT YOU REVEAL ONLY HIS NAME, RANK, FILE NUMBER, AND DATE OF BIRTH, TO INQUIRIES FROM SOURCES OUTSIDE YOUR IMMEDIATE FAMILY. I WISH TO ASSURE YOU OF EVERY POSSIBLE ASSISTANCE TOGETHER WITH THE HEARTFELT SYMPATHY OF MYSELF AND YOUR HUSBAND'S SHIPMATES AT THIS TIME OF HEARTACHE AND UNCERTAINTY. IF I CAN ASSIST YOU, PLEASE WRITE OR TELEGRAPH THE CHIEF OF NAVY PERSONNEL, DEPARTMENT OF THE NAVY, WASHINGTON, D.C. 20370. MY PERSONAL REPRESENTATIVE CAN BE REACHED BY TELEPHONE AT OXFORD 42746 DURING WORKING HOURS AND OXFORD 42768 AFTER WORKING HOURS. FOR YOUR INFORMATION, A BROADCAST FROM HANOI VIA

INTERNATIONAL SERVICE IN ENGLISH ON 20 MAY 1967 STATED THAT "THE UPS HIGH COMMAND IN HANOI HELD A PRESS CONFERENCE HERE THIS MORNING ON THE GREAT VICTORY OF HANOI ARMED FORCES WHO YESTERDAY SHOT DOWN TEN U.S. PLANES AND KILLED OR CAPTURED A SIZABLE NUMBER OF AIR PIRATES, SMASHING ONE OF THE MOST FRENZIED AIR ATTACKS ON THE CAPITAL CITY." A LIST OF SOME OF THE "PILOTS" CAPTURED WAS THEN MADE PUBLIC AT THIS PRESS CONFERENCE AND YOUR HUSBAND WAS AMONG THOSE THAT WERE NAMED. HANOI ALSO REPORTED THAT YOUR HUSBAND HAD RECEIVED BURNS WHEN HE EJECTED FROM HIS AIRCRAFT AND THAT HE HAD BEEN GIVEN LOCAL TREATMENT.

Vice Admiral B.J. Semmes Jr.,
Chief of Naval Personnel

Now it is official. I have seen the words in print. But it could be much worse than it is. The McIntoshes soon leave, and Aggie and Lester raid the fridge for a snack while I put the children to bed. As I huddle with them together for their prayers, both Jamey and Glyn Carol finally are able to express their fears. But as we talk things out they seem to gain some confidence. They seem to understand as well as a six- and a ten-year-old can. The hardest question for me to answer is "Why did it have to be Dad?"

We talk about the fact that we know Daddy is alive, something that so many families have not known. We talk about their father's strength and character. *Maybe God needed him there in the prison so he can help some other prisoner.* We talk about the courage and faith we are going to need for the long difficulties ahead. *Am I asking too much of my children?*

Aggie and Les sit up with me, and we talk and talk, until I am exhausted. But I need to express my own concerns before I can put the day to rest. She asks me about a cartoon posted inside the door of the kitchen cupboard. Actually, it is a reproduction printed on the back of a "Plan of the Day" from USS *Kitty Hawk* that Jimmie sent to me several months ago. Depicted is a swimming duck beside the words, "Be like a duck... above the surface be calm and unruffled. Beneath the surface, paddle like hell!" I tell her this is what Jimmie would want me to do now.

During the afternoon the base doctor has come by and left me a couple of tranquilizers, so after a while I take the pills and go to bed. No sleep comes, but as I lie alone in the dark the tears trickle down my cheeks. I am not sure whether they are tears of joy or relief...or fear. There are too many things to think about, too many prayers to offer up.

→ 2 ←

May 21, 1967

I had intended to teach my Sunday school class as usual today, but the minister's wife offered to fill in for me, so my sister and the children and I have the morning at home to talk things over. In the afternoon several people stop by, bringing roses from their yards, food, and prayers. Aggie and Les leave to drive back to south Florida when they see that we are not going to be left alone. In the late afternoon Bea Coffee and Dave and Ann Fall arrive with a pitcher of daiquiris and cute little green glasses. When Pat Walters and Ann Marie Thompson arrive, Dave walks back across the street to return with a second pitcherful of drinks. This gathering breaks the tension, and we remind ourselves that we are celebrating the fact that our men came through alive!

At dinnertime Clare again feeds me and the children at her house, hamburgers this time, and I stay to talk awhile. Talking seems to be beneficial for both of us. I try to remember how the other wives in the squadron must feel. They are anxious for their own men's safety at the same time they are tearing their hearts out for us. I am sure that Clare is dealing with her feelings by doing things for us, preparing our dinner and taking care of Glyn Carol.

Back at home, almost thankful to have some time alone, I do a little housecleaning, and then I finally go to bed. I feel drained, but my heart is filled with joy that Jimmie and Jack are alive. *Alive!*

News stories published May 20, 1967:

San Francisco Chronicle

BUDAPEST—AP—The correspondent of the Hungarian news agency reported from Hanoi yesterday that three American pilots were wounded when their planes were shot down in Friday's air raid on the North Vietnamese capital.

They were listed as William R. Stark, 37, California; Jack N. Walters Jr., 28, from the carrier Kitty Hawk, and James L. Griffin, 35, Tennessee. Hanoi broadcasts identified Stark and Griffin as lieutenant commanders and Walters as a Navy lieutenant.

The report did not specify their injuries.

The Hungarian report said Griffin made a confession on the bed which was recorded on tape and played back at the news conference in Hanoi.

"On May 19, my plane received a hit over Hanoi when I was just trying to make a film of the effect of the bombs dropped by other planes of my squad," the agency said the statement read. "I'm deeply sorry to have joined this action. The Vietnamese by whom I was captured gave me humane treatment. They gave me first aid instantly and brought me to hospital where nothing was left undone to spare my life."

Ft. Lauderdale News

HONG KONG, (Reuters)—North Vietnam announced the names Saturday of five American airmen captured after being shot down during air raids over Saigon Friday, the North Vietnamese News Agency reported here.

Quoting a communiqué from the North Vietnamese high command, the agency said 10 U.S. aircraft were shot down Friday, six in the morning and four in the afternoon.

The report said four of the five captured airmen were from the U.S. Navy aircraft carrier Kitty Hawk and one from the carrier Enterprise.

Their names were announced as Lt. Joseph Charles Plumb of Indiana, Lt. Gareth Laverne Anderson, Lt. Jack N. Walters Jr., and Lt. Cmdr. James L. Griffin of Tennessee, all from the Kitty Hawk, and Lt. Cmdr. William R. Stark of California, from the Enterprise.

The report said Plumb, Anderson, and Stark were piloting F4B jets and Walters and Griffin RA5C reconnaissance planes.

The agency quoted Griffin as saying in a recorded statement he was ordered to fly a reconnaissance mission over Hanoi to prepare for a future attack on the city center.

***Orlando Sentinel* on May 21, 1967:**

SANFORD—Two local naval aviators are reported downed over Vietnam, and captured. They have been identified as Lt. Cmdr. James L. Griffin and Lt. Jack Walters Jr.

Further information was not available.

May 21

On Monday I drive the children to school, trying to resume our normal routine, but when I get back to my house Bob Watson, the CACO, is waiting to talk with me. He hands me a tape of the broadcast of Jimmie's voice in Hanoi, and we set up my tape player and try to listen to it. The broadcast begins with the high-pitched voice of a Vietnamese woman, and the entire tape is full of static and very difficult for me to understand. I thank him, and when he leaves I play the tape over and over. Slowly I manage to come up with what I think are the words Jimmie speaks on the tape. At least, I think it is his voice. I put the tape away to listen again when I am calmer.

During the morning rains come to cool the parched Florida landscape, and it feels like a cleansing of my spirit. There are many phone calls throughout the day, and the mail arrives, bringing a letter from Jimmie mailed just six days ago. Enclosed is a photo of him, seated at his desk on the ship. He looks great! I remind myself that he is still alive, and although he must not look so good at this moment, he will look good again someday.

The rain is coming down in torrents as the Griffins arrive after their eighteen-hour drive from Tennessee. Jimmie's younger brother Gene and his wife Christine have driven them down, and they all seem to be handling things fairly well. I am so amazed by Mother Griffin's fortitude. She seems to be holding up all the rest of them. She gives each of us a hug, and before she even sits down she reminds me of Jimmie's strong spirit and his ability to instill confidence in others. I think he must have acquired that trait from her because she seems invincible.

After dinner we leave Glyn and Jamey with Gene and Christine while I drive Mother and Dad Griffin across town to visit with Pat and with Jack's mother and father who have arrived from North Carolina. It is a unique assemblage—parents of two men who grew up on farms and who now have gone halfway around the world to do battle for their country. Jack's parents get on well with the Griffins. They seem to give strength to one another.

May 23

Mother Griffin remains with us, but the others leave today to return to Tennessee. Little Perry, Gene and Christine's baby, who was left in the care of Christine's mother, could not spare them for too long, and Dad G., who teaches industrial arts in a Tennessee high school, has end-of-year reports to complete. Just as they are loading the car for the trip north, Reverend Temple stops by. He can see that the Griffins feel positive that Jimmie will be returning to us in due time. We have a prayer together in the living room, and the two cars drive away, leaving Mother G. and me alone. We decide to take naps before the children get home from school.

We hear the postman flipping open the mailbox just as we are preparing mid-afternoon glasses of iced tea. And there, buried among the bills and junk mail, is a thin envelope, addressed in Jimmie's handwriting. The letter is postmarked "May 19," and I realize it will be the last letter he wrote before that fateful flight. Emogene sits quietly while I slit open the envelope.

Inside is one page, printed in block letters the way he did when he had no time to write a real letter. *Or maybe this time he realized the danger he faced and could not find the words to write more.* In crossword-puzzle style, he had penned:

Dearest Dora,

Always, Jimmie

Finally, the tears come, for both of us.

The next few days bring a flood of letters and phone calls from friends. We try to get back to normal as much as possible. In the afternoons after school is out I take Mother G. to watch Glyn Carol's dance class practice. It is reassuring to see that life goes on for my shy little daughter, brown eyes searching the audience, brown hair tied up in a ponytail. After the class we take her to attend a playmate's birthday party at Rainbow's Inn ice cream parlor in a Sanford shopping center. Mother G. and I leave to go grocery shopping for a while then return to the scene of the party to have chocolate sundaes while we wait for Glyn.

Letter received from RVAH-13 squadron commander on May 24th, 1967:

20 May 1967

Dear Dora,

What can I possibly say except that we all share your feelings at this time. We are all available at any time for anything that we in the squadron can possibly do for you and the children.

By the time you receive this, you will have all the details and, I'm sure, will be relieved that the news has come out of Hanoi that Jim has been captured. It's not a very big consolation, but we feel it is much better than the other possibilities.

Don't hesitate to call upon Joni for any assistance whatsoever. I'm sure that she can be a great source of strength at this time.

Ignore the statements purportedly made by Jim, as I'm sure that they have little, if any, basis in fact. The propaganda war is as real as the actual war, and each time Hanoi says they've downed four airplanes we may have lost one.

We shall bring Jim's personal effects back with us, and I intend to see that they are delivered personally so that you may keep them until he returns.

I know that you are as proud, if not more proud, of Jim as we are. He is a pillar of strength to the squadron, as you have been. I know that you will continue to be one of our finest.

We all share with you the deep sorrow at the extended separation and stand ready at all times to be of assistance.

My warmest regards,

Higg.

Letter received from Al Wattay:

Dear Dora and Children,

Just wanted to drop a few lines to say "Hi" and pass a few things on to you that you may be in need of at this trying time.

I took care of Jim's gear and have it all ready for shipment back to Sanford with the rest of the squadron gear. A few items I felt I should explain to you. I am enclosing two checks. The smaller is a rebate of Jim's mess bill and mess share...I hope the remainder of Jim's things reaches you satisfactorily and that you can get through it without too much trouble.

Dora, I can't express to you how very sorry we all are this happened. Personally, of course, I felt very close to Jim—and you—and still do. Living together out here and next door to each other in Sanford, certainly had an impact on me. I do feel the outlook is bright and I'll certainly look forward to seeing Jim back with us. My prayers are with you and Jim always. I'll be looking forward to seeing you in Sanford.

Very sincerely,

Al

Letter from Capt. Jim Holloway, Commanding Officer, *USS Enterprise*

(Former commanding officer of VA-83, Jimmie's first squadron, during 1956-58)

23 May 1967

Dear Dora,

I was so terribly saddened at the news that Jim's Vigilante had been shot down over Hanoi. It happened at the end of a long, grim day for TF-77. ENTERPRISE lost two crews, the B.H. RICHARD 2 pilots, and the KITTY HAWK an F-4 crew as well as Jim's RA-5, on that particular day, while striking Hanoi.

I was also immensely heartened to hear that Jim and his crewman had gotten out and were in good shape. We learned this only through the medium of Hanoi's announcement that they have been captured. I hope you understand why it was a good omen to have Hanoi announce that he was captured. It means that he is alive, in good shape, and accounted for. The fact that Hanoi announced his capture is important. In the release or exchange of prisoners, he cannot be held back as a hostage for later bargaining, as could a prisoner of whose existence we were not aware.

He is in the hands of the most civilized people in North Vietnam. Some prisoners such as Dieter Dengler, who were shot down over the wilds of central Indochina, fell into the hands of virtual savages, and their treatment was harsh. The best information that we in the Navy and Air Force have on captured airmen, as opposed to the sensation-seeking stories in the press, indicates that those held by Hanoi are being satisfactorily taken care of. There is absolutely NO evidence from any source that they have been mistreated. Five ENTERPRISE aviators from our last cruise are confirmed POWs and we have had three captured so far this year. I have read a letter written by Cdr. Jim Mulligan (he was XO of VA-36) to his wife, which she sent on to me, and his principal complaint, after missing his family, is boredom and the tedium of waiting.

Dora, I don't mean to infer by any stretch of the imagination that this is any bed of roses for you or for Jim. It is tough, and it is going to be difficult. I just want you to understand it's not as black as some people are going to paint it, and it's going to be OK in the end. I, for one, feel that the end IS in sight. The United States has reached the point where we must go all out or agree to some terms in the next 18 months, and I don't think we are going all out.

Keep your chin up and look to the future. Everything is going to be OK. You have the complete sympathy of Dabney and me at this trying time, and you know I stand ready to help in any way possible. Write me or wire me if there is anything I can do. I'll be in Washington this summer and keep in touch with you. I'll let you know anything I hear that concerns Jim.

All the best luck,

Jim

This is the last week of school for the children before summer vacation, and Glyn Carol has a kindergarten graduation and dance recital. At the PX, we purchase a movie camera, hoping to capture the weekend's events on film to save for Jimmie's return. Jamey will be our camera operator, and this gives him a sense of purpose while his sister performs on stage.

For the dance program, we brush Glyn's long brown locks and pull them into a ponytail then tease the ends to form a little bun on top of her head. Her dress for the tap number is a bright pink floral print, and the skirt has a liner that glows in ultra-violet light with a "Mammy" face on it. The little girls all dance and sing their hearts out. Then Glyn appears in a ballet number, dressed in an emerald green leotard and tights. Jamey records it all with the movie camera.

Pat Walters attends the program with us, and after the recital we see Bea Coffee and Pat Hanson, wife of Gerry Coffee's navigator. Bea's husband was captured some fifteen months earlier while I was in Tennessee for my father's funeral. After introductions, I explain to Jamey that they are "just two more of the prisoners' wives," and he seems to appreciate my attempt to keep things light. We may as well make the best of it. They all come by the house then for dessert, a cheesecake brought to us today by a church friend.

The next day Bea returns for an afternoon visit and gives me and Mother G. a new perspective by sharing her thoughts, her scrapbook, and six letters she has received from Gerry since his capture in 1966. Some of the letters seem to contain propaganda. I am not sure whether to believe Gerry wrote it all, but Bea assures us it is in his handwriting. I don't know how I will feel if we receive such a letter from Jimmie, but, oh how I would like to hear from him again!

Mother G. goes with us to church, and since I am teaching the fifth-grade class, she visits the adult women's class and meets Ophelia Bennett, a large, vivacious lady whose folksy manner is reminiscent of the *Grand Ole Opry*'s Minnie Pearl but whose singing voice can calm screaming babies. Ophie is Jimmie's favorite choir soloist, and we are comforted when at the close of the church service Ophie leads the choir in a musical "*Prayer for Peace.*"

Oh, God of love,
Oh, King of Peace,
Make wars throughout
the world to cease.

In the afternoon Glyn's grandmother enjoys watching the children in a swim demonstration. Our little six-year-old can really swim well now; she even breathes correctly, and she surprises even me by doing a back crawl the length of the pool! Jamey, her main swimming instructor, proudly demonstrates his underwater swimming skills as well.

For her kindergarten graduation on Monday, Glyn is to perform as Sambo in a musical number called "*Little Brave Sambo.*" Her teased hair is hopelessly tangled after the dance recital arrangement, so we decide to give her a haircut. *What will Jimmie think about his daughter's shorn locks?* Mother G. assures me that the shorter hair will encourage the ends to curl. And the new hairstyle turns out well. Glyn is adorable with her slightly curly bob, playing the part of Little Brave Sambo like a pro. Then, as the little graduates come forward to receive their diplomas, she becomes quite serious, all decked out in a white cap and gown. The show was stolen, however, by her former neighbor and playmate, Alex Wattay, when the "alumni" were called on stage. Alex's father is—or was—Jimmie's roommate on the *Kitty Hawk.*

I treat myself to a trip to the beauty parlor and a dress shop where I buy two new casual dresses. It does wonders for my sagging spirits and my looks. The yellow moygashal linen dress purchased last month to wear for Jimmie's homecoming has been pushed to the back of the closet. It will be reserved for his return, however long that may be.

On Thursday we get down to business. Pat and I meet with the station's legal officer. He answers our questions and recommends that we each make out our wills! I decide to get some advice from Ken McIntosh, and when I meet with him he suggests some changes to the sample will furnished to me by the navy. He agrees to take care of changes of title for the car and on our bank account. I am so relieved not to have to do these things myself.

On Friday evening Mother Griffin and I attend a tea for the squadron's enlisted wives at Gail Johnson's house. It is Mother G.'s first exposure to the camaraderie of a military wives' gathering. Unaware that the punch is spiked, she has two cups and declares it delicious. For that evening, Mother G. becomes "one of the girls." I think the experience is good for all of us.

Friends visit us almost every day, and we welcome them all, glad to have something to distract us from our concerns that we might receive more news that we do not want to hear.

Jamey also has completed his school year, and I have signed all the necessary legal documents for Ken, so we decide it is time to make an exit and go to Tennessee for a few days. The letters from Higg and Al are reminders that the *Kitty Hawk* is headed home, and I feel it is best that we not be here when the squadron returns from cruise. The wives have been so good to us, and the men need to focus on their own families rather than those of us who have had losses. Mother Griffin also is ready to return home, and I want to see my mother who waits in Memphis.

⇾ 3 ⇽

June 1967

Anticipating the return of the ship and the men of RVAH-13 who will reunite with their own families after a long and grueling combat cruise, I put Samson in the kennel for the first time and load up the car to drive to Tennessee. Emogene Griffin is anxious to return to her home, and the children seem to relax as they think about seeing their cousins and Grandpa Griffin at the farm in Forked Deer.

We are glad for the air conditioning as our Buick Skylark zips north on the interstate through Florida and northwest along Route 81, a path I've driven many times with the children. This time, for once, the sky does not open up with a blinding thunderstorm. The trip from Sanford to West Tennessee takes almost eighteen hours' driving time, so we stop at a small motel in Albany, Georgia, the city where the Sanford Naval Air Station will be moving within the year. We don't feel much like looking around the town or even thinking about the future move, so we eat a light supper and go to bed.

Summer heat has already made its mark, and the cornfields are teeming with parched, stunted crops. The air smells dusty the next day when we stop for Cokes and a bathroom break at a Texaco station in a tiny town in Alabama. The station manager ambles out to the car, and, after filling the tank, casually informs me that two of my tires are in bad shape. The Skylark is barely two years old, but he insists that I need new ones before we head further on our journey. In no shape to argue with him, I accept his advice, get out my Texaco card, and purchase the tires. At least he doesn't tell me I need a new engine!

I drive on, cutting across Mississippi, heading north at Columbus, then turning toward Jackson, Tennessee. From there we continue on the narrow blacktop road that leads past Frog Jump to the community of Forked Deer where both Jimmie and I were born. We cross over a bridge at the Forked Deer River at the exact spot where he and I had a frightening accident on our wedding day in 1955. We had left the wedding reception, riding in our new Chevrolet, when the car hit a pothole and spun around, throwing me onto the floor and taking out part of the bridge railing. I had a piece of wedding cake in my mouth, having no chance to really sample it during the reception, and Jimmie had glanced over at me and grinned, temporarily taking his attention off the road.

A slab of the bridge guardrail came through the car and made a major gash in the shoulder of my "going away suit," but we were only shaken up and dazed for a few hours before we started out again on our honeymoon journey. Our new car was left behind for major repairs as we headed west in the Griffin's older gray Mercury. The event altered our plans to spend a week in the Smoky Mountains; we stayed, instead, in Montgomery Bell State Park near Nashville.

Jimmie had brought along some champagne from a case we had received as a wedding present, and since there was no ice bucket in our room in the alcohol-free park, we celebrated our safe arrival by drinking the champagne warm. Now, I drive very carefully as we cross over that bridge over the Forked Deer River!

At the farm John and Lois and their children have already arrived from their home in California. They have three boys, ranging from two years older than Jamey to one year older than Glyn Carol, and a daughter a year younger. At once my two youngsters get lost among their Griffin cousins and Gene, their uncle, who is ten years Jamey's senior. Big old Pete, the shaggy dog that has guarded the yard for several years, lumbers over, tail wagging furiously. For a moment I worry that the kids will be upset because Samson is not with us, but they seem to understand that this is Pete's place, and our house in Florida belongs to Sam.

Summer at the farm in Forked Deer is always hot, and the house is not air conditioned, but somehow it never feels uncomfortably warm here. We can sit in the shade of the huge trees that surround the house, and there usually seems to be a breeze, albeit sometimes a warm one. Only the upstairs bedrooms get really hot during the day, but by evening they cool down enough that, especially with the help of an electric fan, sleep comes easily.

Dinner is the midday meal here, where through the years farm work was done in the fields from daybreak until noon and a hefty serving of calories was needed to stoke up the body for more work later in the afternoon. And summer dinners at the farm are bountiful—purple hull peas; fresh, ripe tomatoes; corn right out of the field; hot yeast rolls made by Mother G.; and sometimes peach or berry pie made from fruit stored in the gigantic freezer on the back porch. Always, there is plenty of iced tea. And after dinner—this is the early afternoon now and the hottest part of the day—we have a nap or at least "quiet time." There is no problem getting the kids to at least have quiet time, but, with so many cousins of all ages here, you have to be concerned if they get too quiet.

Family friends stop by, expressing their hopes for Jimmie's safety. These are the people with whom he grew up in this farming community. Just over the hill is the white house where my grandmother lived and where I was born. The house is now owned by a man named Sanford Mills, but to me it will always be "Grandmother Smith's house." Now both dead, my grandmother, for whom I was named, and Jimmie's grandmother began school together somewhere around 1880 here in this village. I'm not sure just where the schoolhouse was at that time, but now it is in a brick building just across the road from the entrance to the Griffin property. There was always some disagreement as to which of the women was older—both claimed the other had waited until age seven to begin school, "so she must be older."

Dora Burlison Smith, whose education probably ended somewhere around the beginning of her teens, took great pride in her appearance. She had a closet of silk dresses, and she wore lipstick and powder any time she thought a visitor would be stopping by. Mattie Hardy Griffin, called Mammy by her family, however, had most of her clothes made from attractive flour-sack fabric—a tradition among country women of her day—and to my knowledge she never wore lipstick in her life. But she did complete her education, and she was a champion of education for all of her family.

My grandmother had eight children, and you could always count on lots of joking and punches in the ribs when the family got together—and the men were known for "passing the bottle" on the porch while the women stirred the turnip greens in the kitchen. But Mammy Griffin was a church worker and a staunch supporter of temperance—make that Temperance with a capital T. My father-in-law, however, had been a buddy of my Uncle James, and they had had their fun together when they were young and single and out of Mammy's sight.

My father, the eldest of the Smith children, served in World War I, as did two of his brothers, but Billy Griffin, as my father-in-law is known, was too young. Born in 1904, he was just an infant when his dad was killed while cutting timber, and, though he was named James Fletcher after his father, he has always been called Billy. "Because he sounded like a little billy goat crying," his mother said. The families were both there during the Civil War, and between us, Jimmie and I had three Haywood County grandfathers who served as Confederate soldiers.

Billy Griffin wears a patch over one eye, having been diagnosed when he was just a kid with what we today call "lazy eye." In the 1930s, when he taught at the community schoolhouse and my sister Agnes was one of his students, the kids thought he had eyes in the back of his head. Actually he could see their reflection in his glasses while writing assignments on the blackboard. I've always thought the patched eye gives him a rakish, handsome look.

When the excitement at the Griffin house has seemed to distract Jamey and Glyn Carol from thoughts about their father, we go on to Memphis to spend a few days with my mother. My father died in February last year, and Jimmie, then on the first of his two cruises to Vietnam, agonized about not being able to be here with me. While we were here in Tennessee for the funeral, our squadron lost its third plane; Gerry Coffee, who had been transferred to the *Kitty Hawk* just days earlier, was shot down over North Vietnam. It is comforting that we know now that Gerry is a prisoner of war as well, but we do not know the fate of his navigator.

When we are in Memphis the children enjoy trips to the zoo, located just a mile or so from my mother's house. Jamey has always called it "Grandpa's zoo." The day is hot and clammy when we arrive at the park this time, and Monkey Island has the dank smell of the African jungle. As in past visits, Jamey and Glyn Carol enjoy feeding the ducks in the smelly pond that surrounds the monkeys, and they become ecstatic when the giraffe makes an appearance. This is a day for ice cream, and I don't worry about the extra sugar as we all enjoy cones of our favorite flavors.

After a few days with Mother we return to Forked Deer to accompany the family to church on Sunday. A rural congregation, Eureka Methodist Church does not have a full-time pastor. Rather, the preacher alternates between this church and one in the nearby community of Gates, and on the Sundays when there is no preaching, there still is Sunday school. I am glad that this day there is no worship service, but the congregation gathers before church school for songs and prayers. Leading the group is Wilder Pearson, Jim's childhood buddy who went to college with me at University of Tennessee while Jimmie was attending the Naval Academy. We sing hymns, accompanied on piano by Wilder's wife Norma, who was my suite-mate during those college days. Gracing the wall at the front of the sanctuary, just behind the altar, is a copy of the painting of Jesus in the Garden of Gethsemane, painted by Dorothy Jean Warren, another of his childhood friends. We are at home here.

It was on the steps of this church that I first recall meeting Jimmie, although my family tells me he came to my sixth birthday party and that my grandmother had to chase him and his friends out of the trees they had climbed in her apple orchard. But here, late in the summer just before I began college while visiting my grandmother, a handsome young man came over to confidently introduce himself. I had not spent many summers in Forked Deer during my teen years, having found a number of eligible young men in Covington, where I graduated from high school. This guy seemed different from the other local boys, and I now realize that was because he had gained some polish during his first year as a midshipman, and he no longer had a Tennessee drawl. That evening he phoned and asked me for our first date, and though I was distracted by the dozen or so young men I dated at university, none ever compared to Jimmie.

A week after he graduated from Annapolis we were married here in this church, and I walked down the aisle wearing a lace gown I had sewn myself. The Griffins probably had worried that I might wear my cousin's beautiful silk wedding dress, complete with cascading train. But I made my tea-length gown, and with it I wore a short veil and headpiece fashioned by a friend of their family. That was the wedding day that ended with the car crash on that nearby bridge, but somehow, we made it this far, and I must believe we will have more to come.

On the Griffin's property, Jimmie's brother John has begun construction on his vacation house, adjacent to the Griffin's family home. We call John's house "the barn" because it is red and, architecturally, it resembles a barn. It is obvious that this project is going to take years to complete since building it must take place during their summer visits from California. His boys are all playing carpenter, helping John with the construction during our visit, and my children hang around, watching their every move.

Since John and Lois have never been to Florida, they ask to accompany us to Sanford when we return home—"for a visit." I know they are concerned about me driving back alone, though I have driven this 800-mile trip several times in the past. They leave their children, Johnny, Rodney, Leigh Ann, and David, with the two sets of grandparents and, after a final stop to bid goodbye to my mother in Memphis, we head south at six o'clock in the evening.

We have chosen this odd hour to begin the journey to minimize the time we are traveling in the summer heat, and we plan to switch off drivers so we can drive straight through without stopping for the night. We have chosen a route that is different than the usual one I drive from Florida, and the Mississippi Highway Department has played a trick on us. They have just resurfaced the road we must take south out of Memphis, and there is no center line. That makes a difficult drive at night for drivers unfamiliar with this stretch of two-lane highway. John yawns a lot and sighs, "Oh, me," several times. I offer to take over the driving for a few hours so he can catch some z's. He takes me up on my offer, and I quickly see how hard it is to drive through the Mississippi countryside at night with no center line!

Although Jamey and Glyn nap, lying in the backseat across the lap of whichever adult has the backseat shift, the trip leaves the rest of us completely exhausted. It is early afternoon when we arrive in Sanford, and before driving to the house we take a quick detour by the kennel to pick up Samson. We have chosen this kennel because it is located in a rural area and has a yard where the puppies can socialize rather than be cooped up all the time. The children are devastated when we learn that Sam was so frightened to be separated from us that he demolished his bed on the first night of his stay. He has also destroyed all the toys we had left with him. The kids try to hug Samson when we put him in the car, but as we drive on toward our house we realize that Sam is covered in fleas! And, of course, so are we all!

During their visit, we take Lois and John to New Smyrna Beach, and ignoring our warnings about getting too much sun too soon, they both get fried in the blazing Florida sun. They stay a few days to meet some of our neighbors and to be sure the children and I are "going to be all right." We put them on the train back to Tennessee, and I return home to look at the empty mailbox as I turn into our driveway, realizing that a new phase in our lives has begun. There will be no more letters from Jimmie for a while.

The squadron members have been reunited with their families during our absence. I know it is difficult for them to talk with me, but in the days that follow, several of them stop by or phone. Dick Daum comes over from next door to chat, and I try to reassure him that I am, indeed, "all right." When shipments arrive from the *Kitty Hawk*, there are a couple of cruise boxes containing Jimmie's belongings. Now the waiting begins.

Neighbors are wonderful, and members of the church are solicitous. I remind them constantly how very lucky we are that we KNOW that Jimmie is alive. It is a matter of waiting...and keeping a stiff upper lip. The base swimming pool is a good distraction, and that is where I still feel a part of things. We go there almost every day, leaving home around 9 a.m. and staying until the hot sun chases us home before noon. Then, after a few hours' rest, we often return to the pool in the late afternoon. James helps Glyn with her swimming skills or plays in the water with his friends while I sit and chat with the other wives.

Each night the children and I have a conversation about their dad, always expressing concern but having confidence that he will be home again as soon as he can. Their prayers at bedtime are always the same, "God bless Daddy and Mommy and Samson, Amen."

When the house is quiet, I go into the little study and begin a new ritual. I have two huge boxes of letters from my husband, saved through the past few years. Each evening I will read one letter from Jimmie, who wrote almost every day on the two cruises to Southeast Asia. He has written me this often each time we have been apart, beginning during those days of courtship when I was in college. Although he is known by his squadron mates as Jim, he usually signed his letters to me as Jimmie. The letters now offer me comfort and hope, and there enough letters to get me through almost two years if I read only one each night.

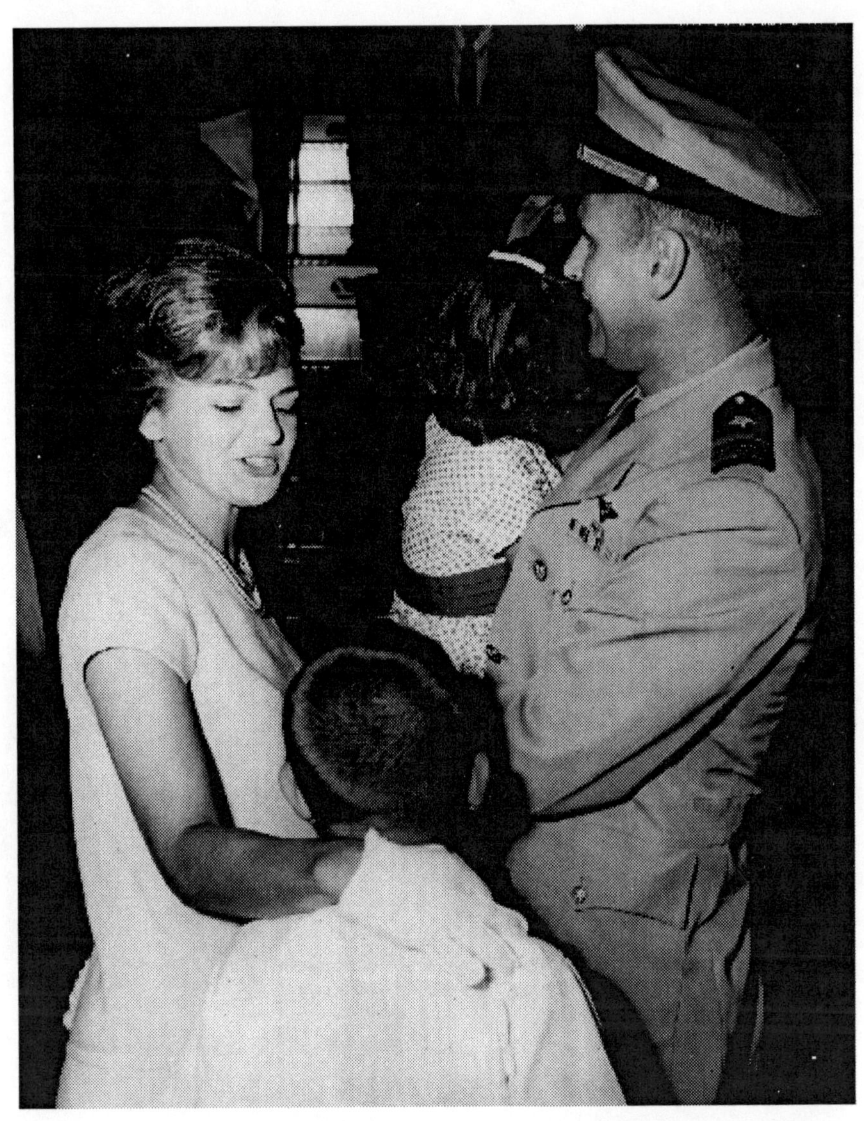

Jim and Dora Griffin with children, James and Glyn Carol, at end of first cruise to Vietnam in June, 1966.

Jim Griffin, Navy pilot, Sanford, Florida 1965

Dora and Jim Griffin at Sanford Wives Club dance 1966.

Jim Griffin awarded medals aboard USS Kitty Hawk 1966.

4

In two large boxes, I keep all the letters that Jimmie has written me over the past two years. He often wrote me every day, so I read one letter each day. The letters in the box begin with his first correspondence during what the navy calls a "shakedown cruise," when the squadrons and the ship personnel are settling in, preparing for the long at-sea period and missions ahead.

USS Kitty Hawk
Off San Diego
July 22, 1965

Hi Darling,

I know this is a hard way to start a letter, especially our first of many. But I guess you heard about RVAH-1's loss of its Skipper, Val Matula, and Carl Gronquist. You may have heard before I did, since Jack told me on the way out here, and we didn't find out what happened until last night.

They apparently were landing at night and the wire broke just as they were about stopped. The plane still had enough speed to go on over the side though. I don't know if they drowned or if the crash got them. Both were real fine people, though, and I'm sure the squadron will feel the loss. Please go see Barbara if you haven't already. I think Ann is still in Milan, Tennessee.

I'll try to call if I can get off here early enough that it won't be after midnight your time. This time difference got us all fouled up last night. In fact, I was starved by the time I got to eat.

The trip out here went pretty well, but it was a typical group grope thing. I took us 4 1/2 hours flying time, but we had to stop at Carswell AFB, Texas to refuel, and it took over three hours to get fuel. And on the ramp in that hot Texas sun it got really dry. Florida is cool compared to that place, and of course trying to get over into the ship last night was quite a grapple, too. Our rooms aren't the best, but I guess they will do for now.

I met a few people I know on here, including Sam McKee! He looks much the same as ever. I called Barbara this afternoon, and Bill is working tonight. So I'll go over Saturday and Saturday night to see them. We have some briefings this weekend, so I'll have to fit it in between them.

They have a very ambitious schedule starting out Monday morning, so we have to have most things under control before then. Have only about half the space they used to have, so I can already see what a flail this is going to be. It appears to be a fairly good ship, but the air group is about twice the normal size.

Our last troops should be arriving from Sanford now, so I'd better go meet them. Good night for now, Sweetheart. I love you and Jamey and Glyn Carol, too. Give a big hug and a kiss around for all. I miss you.

I love you,

Jimmie

USS Kitty Hawk
Tuesday afternoon
27 July '65

Hi Honey,

Looks like this letter writing is going to come in bits and pieces, whether I like it or not. We spent most all of yesterday climbing in and out of aircraft and last night, too. So far today, it's been no different. I have about five minutes now before I can go get late lunch, so if I start this, maybe I will finish it.

We're showing the ship how fast these RA-5C's can go down just prior to launch. I must have taxied three of them all over the deck yesterday before we finally got one airborne. If Sam McKee thought he had handling problems before, he realizes now he never had it so good. Actually, we are doing better than we were on the beach as far as numbers of launches go. They are scheduling us for about twice what our normal schedule used to run.

Wednesday night (late)

Guess my words were truer than I meant them to be. You probably read in the paper where the two A-6s ran together out here—about the time I was writing that first page in fact. You wouldn't know any of the people involved, but one of them we never did find. The other three are aboard and doing fine. We spent the afternoon searching for the fourth, but no luck. Then, we spent the night finishing our night refresher quals, and I'm glad that flail is over. In and out of airplanes like yoyos until about midnight!

I woke up this morning to find out "guess who?" is on the accident board. The new system has to have members from other commands. So all day today has been spent with interviews, and that's why I can't tell you anymore about the accident, cause I know too much. I had to take myself off the flight schedule for two days so we can get the investigation rolling. Just hope we are due to head back for the East Coast. We've had pretty good luck with our "birds" today and the schedule has come along rather well....

We got the "big" news (about the baby's arrival) from Pat this morning, and it sure helped brighten things up out here. Jack has been the brightest thing around here you ever saw, and now he's really putting the pressure on Renner since it was a boy! He called Pat tonight by the ship-to-shore phone, and of course that made him feel even better. I'm sure that did a few things for her, also. What do Jamey and Glyn have to say about it? You'll have to take some Polaroid shots to send to Jack.

...I'll try to write Jamey and Glyn if I get the chance, but I don't expect things to let up much these next two weeks. This AAR board fouls up my plans to go see John and Lois as well. Maybe they can come up for a while one afternoon. Tell Jamey and Glyn to take good care of little Stan until we get back.

Love and kisses to you all,
Nite Sweetheart,
Jimmie

USS Kitty Hawk
Off San Diego
1 August '65

Hi Honey,

Got a few minutes here before time for church, and then we fly again this afternoon. Didn't even get to sleep in late this morning, which really hurt the most. As a matter of fact, I guess that's my biggest complaint. Lack of sleep...I did end up rooming with Max, and we are right outside the wardroom door which is an advantage, but the room is small. Rooms up under the flight deck are nicer, but it's a long way down to the Ready Room, and it's a lot noisier up there. I don't know if we will swap or not.

Jack got diverted to the beach with Ray the other day, so Pat probably told you he called. Pat said everyone was surviving there okay. I'll try to call you from San Francisco, depending on what day I can get ashore. And provided my throat is well enough to talk by then.

...I love you, too! Jim

USS Kitty Hawk
Off San Diego
5 August '65

...Don't any of you sweat the rumors you hear, because they are minor compared to the ones floating around out here. The schedule remains as I told you right now, and I don't see any plans for a change. One of the boys in Jack's shop asked him if it were true that we were going to off load and fly our planes out of Da Nang. That one is about as "far out" as I heard.

Right now, we should see you the night of 12 August. But I hear the CO may have to stop for a conference at North Island, so it may be sometime the 13th before we get there. As soon as we decide where we are going to stop on the way, we will let you know. We will probably call from the place we refuel and pass the word as to who is coming and what time we will arrive at Sanford.....

I love you all...Jimmie

USS Kitty Hawk
Off San Diego
9 August '65

Dear James,

I don't know if you and Mother have a map or not, so I thought I would send this one along. We stay about where the green + is, and I guess that's where I'll be for Christmas. Hope Santa brings you and Glyn lots of nice toys and you have a very happy time.

I love you, Dad

USS Kitty Hawk
Off San Diego
24 September '65

Hi Darling and Jamey and Glyn,

Sure was nice talking to you tonight. I never did get a call through to Mother. The line was always busy in the afternoon, and then when I did get a line through, they apparently weren't home. We tried and tried but no answer. Can't figure where they were unless some of the relatives came down, and they all went up to the funeral home. (Jimmie's grandmother, called "Mammy," had just died.)

...Seems like a real blessing in itself with Mammy suffering the way she was. And later on, it will be so much better for Mother and Dad. Mom will probably go buggy trying to figure out what to do with herself now that she has no one at home to look after. Of course, she and Daddy both are getting old enough to start having problems of their own now, so the relief will probably be short-lived.

Well, we had a nice trip out this time. Flight went along just as planned without anyone having problems, and, actually, it was a pleasant trip. Had a whale of a thunderstorm in Carswell that almost washed us off the runway. Most of us got wet and it delayed our departure about an hour, but at least it cooled the hot Texas sun off a bit while we were there.

Had a funny one Monday morning that Jamey will get a laugh out of. We didn't have our bags to unpack Monday night, so I didn't have my alarm clock. Max had his, but it has a tendency to stop at 10:30. We were tired so went to bed about 10:00 p.m. Max woke up about midnight and saw the clock had stopped at 10:30, so he looked at his watch and reset the clock and set the alarm for 6:30.

Well, he had forgotten to set his watch up from Sanford time, and besides that, he had read his watch one hour wrong. So when the alarm went off at 6:30, he got up and shaved and dressed, and I told him to call me at seven when he had finished breakfast.

When he went in to breakfast, there was no one there except one steward who told him they didn't start serving until 6:00. He looked at his watch and saw it wasn't quite six, so he figured he had read it an hour wrong when he reset the clock. By then I was up and shaving when he came in, and he told me to get back in bed because the clock was one hour wrong. I finished shaving and got back in bed. He was dressed, so he decided to finish unpacking while waiting for breakfast to start.

We reset the clock back one hour to six and then a little later went back to see about chow. The steward must have thought Max was crazy, because he said he had told him once that breakfast didn't start till 6:00 a.m. Max looked at the ship's clock then and saw it was only a little after 4 a.m. He was so mad by then that he couldn't go back to sleep, so he just came back to the room and wrote letters until breakfast time.

So, first thing that morning, I went up and found my footlocker and got out my clock to use for an alarm.

We haven't bought a rug yet because they still think some of the rooms may have to be changed. I hope they settle all that soon, though, because I want to pick one up this time in port. Looks like it might be cheaper to buy a 9 x 12 and cut out enough of it to cover the whole floor. I just want a cheap one we can throw away when we are through with it anyway.

...Well, I'd better get a letter off to the folks. Sounds like Jamey has moved right along in Scouts—Good show! Have him send me a picture of him wearing his new medals.

Love to all, Jimmie

USS Kitty Hawk
Off California coast
27 September 1965

Hello Honey,

Don't seem to get back to this writing as often as I would like to. Spent all of yesterday and most of last night strapped to an airplane, so I just kinda collapsed last night. We got some good flying in yesterday, but the airplanes aren't holding up too well today. Sure was black out there last night, though. One of those proverbial ink wells with no moon and the usual California coast fog overcast. We catch up on all our instrument flying out here, which we never seem to do in Florida. I think they will cut us down to a reasonable schedule from here on, though.

The ship's schedule is moderately out now, but not too much for publication. Sticks pretty much to the original schedule, and we will get three or four days in Pearl Harbor. The airlift home (before leaving for Vietnam) may come through, but I wouldn't get any hopes up—especially the kids. We asked for three lifts to bring three groups back to Sanford for about two days each. Actually, it figures out to be one day going, two days at home, and one day coming back. The in-port period is 8 to 18 October, so it will be during that period.

We got one outfit to say they would furnish the flight crews if someone else would pay for it. Please don't spread the word around, because it still is in the doubtful stage, and I will let you know as soon as anything looks firm. Regardless, we will leave our airplanes out here and some of the crews will have to stay and fly here while the others are gone home. Everyone doesn't plan to come back there, even if we can arrange it.

Actually, a short two days does just prolong the departure and makes it harder to leave all over again. But I'll take two days with you, Honey, anytime I can get it...I guess what it really means is I love you, and when that's really true, all this other just comes naturally. So, I love you, I love you, I love you. Maybe that's why I haven't been down in the dumps the last few days like some others have.

I'm not happy at all about leaving, but I sure feel a lot more comfortable about leaving you in Sanford than I ever did in Norfolk. It's a lot harder, heart-wise, to leave now than it was then, though, and I guess that's because we're more used to being together now. And of course there are two kids instead of one. I've got to get Jamey and Glyn on my letter-writing schedule too this time.

Doesn't look like I'm going to have as much time to myself this cruise as we had in A-4's. A lot of things on ship have to be done by pilots only, and with the small number we have it gets right brutal schedule-wise. So I can almost assure you there won't be any letter-a-day basis, but I'll try to do what I can. We're having all kinds of drills and stuff now, too, to get ready for the ORI and even when we're not flying, we're suited up for one evolution or the other.

Sunday afternoon

Got called out before I finished writing last night. Have the Operations duty today, and that means I have to climb all the way to Pri Fly up in the tower for each launch and recovery. There are 214 steps up and 214 steps straight down. I guess I'm more out of shape than I thought. If my knees are this shaky after only five trips, I can imagine how I will be by midnight tonight. That was what got rid of 15 pounds for me on the Forrestal, though, so maybe it will have the same effect here. I'm beginning to wonder if it's supposed to produce a stronger heart, too, or just heart failure.

...Well, it's time to brief another flight, so I'll have to go.

I love you so very, very much,

A kiss for Jamey and Glyn, also,

Jimmie

USS Kitty Hawk
Off California Coast
5 October 1965

...The airlift looks like a good possibility, but we have our hands full now trying to set a cutoff point, since we didn't get quite as many seats as we need. Don't know how it will work out, so keep your fingers crossed...I could possibly be there the night of the 11th and leave on the 14th. That's what I hope for, but you might keep 8 October to 18 October open, just in case the dates are changed.

...My love to you all, I miss you much,

Love, Jimmie

USS Kitty Hawk
6 October '65

Hi Darling,

We have one of these late nights tonight and then an early, early tomorrow morning for the fly-off. Won't have a chance for much more than a note now, but I will call you tomorrow night.

Right now, we still are battling this airlift home. They didn't furnish us with enough seats to take care of everyone that wants to go. We have asked the Wing to see about a plane to carry the rest, but I expect it will be several days before that comes through. If they can't provide it, I would hope we will say for officers to stay here and let the enlisted men go back.

If things go as planned, I'll try to be home for the night of the 11th and leave to come back here on the 14th. I have to get a low pressure chamber check on the 15th, so that's why that period.

It's going to be a long night, so I'll just say I love you so very, very much. Really getting anxious to see you—and the kids, too.

Nite, Sweetheart,

I love you, Jimmie

The First Combat Cruise to Vietnam Begins

Aboard USS Kitty Hawk
Off California coast
Sunday 17 October '65

Hi Darling,

Kinda hard to figure out where to start on this one. I'm still bubbling over from the most wonderful week we have ever spent together. I guess the most accurate start is "I love you."

We got here about midnight Friday night, and things have been on the run ever since. We flew nonstop from Sanford to North Island which helped in some respects but made it rather rough on others, toward the bottom end especially. Somehow, they didn't get enough box lunches aboard, so Ray and I had to split the sandwich out of one. And after that whole piece of pie I had for lunch and then 12 hours on the plane, well that one slice of turkey got awful thin. So, naturally, Ray and I had to go out and get some food after we got here. Made Saturday morning come awful early.

Had an air force sergeant on the plane, and before we got there, he wished he had given us his box lunch. It was a little rough coming out and guess who the only one was that got sick out of one air force and 49 sailors on the plane. He had to fight it for about six hours, and I felt sorry for him, but I think he was suffering most from embarrassment.

We had test flights yesterday and today and finally got them all flown before we load them aboard tomorrow. I'm playing XO right now, and we've had personnel problems that kept me going till 1 a.m. last night. It's getting sea-going time now, and these guys are really coming up with the lu-lu's to get out of going on cruise. I wonder how many of them we won't be able to find when it comes time to go on Tuesday morning. Sometimes you wonder what kind of patriotic Americans we are raising. They had marches and demonstrated in downtown San Diego yesterday over the Vietnam policy.

...I felt real bad leaving you there Friday, but I was so filled with the love of the few days before that I didn't have to feel overly emotional. And you and Glyn and James all were just wonderful to keep your composure and make it as easy as possible. I thank

you so much, Honey, and will try to hold that with me until we get back.

Needless to say, I'll miss you very much, Darling, but I'll love you all the more more for it. I used to think there was a limit as to how much we could love each other, but now I'm sure there are no bounds...Feels good to look forward to more wonderful days ahead.

Always, your loving husband,
Jimmie

USS Kitty Hawk
Tuesday night
19 October 1965

Hi Honey,

Well, ready or not, we got out of old CONUS right on schedule today. One of the guys at chow tonight said, "Gee, you know this cruise is starting to drag already." I think that is true, though, as we've got training scheduled for about the next five days in a row to get ready for the ORI.

Was nice to talk to you last night—and Jamey, too. Wish Glyn hadn't been so sleepy, but I know how she felt. Would have been better if I had called in the middle of the afternoon. It will be about five hours difference in time when we get to Hawaii, so I will have to call early in the day there.

Just had a call that I thought was to go turn up my airplane, but will be a little later I guess. One disadvantage of not flying them is that we have to crank them up and get everything to working on deck every few days to keep the seals from drying out...It's a long way across this puddle. Actually, I guess the trip from San Diego to Hawaii almost compares to the one from Norfolk to Gibraltar.

And we don't have Bermuda and the Azores to fly beside along on the way.

Sure don't like the feel of this boat traveling the opposite way from you, Darling. I don't think the heart can get any fonder, but I've said that before, and it always did. So maybe we'll find a love this time that we never had before.

Good night, Sweetheart, I love you,

Jimmie

USS Kitty Hawk
21 October 1965

Dearest Dora, James, and Glyn,

...We have over 5,000 people on this ship right now, so I don't know if one plane can carry all the mail to shore. I knew we were overloaded, but I had no idea it was as many as all that. They have bunks put up just about everywhere they can find to put them now. And to beat all that, they brought aboard some VIP news reporters from California for the ride out to Hawaii. The wardroom is so crowded you have to get there early to get a seat. They are still feeding fairly good chow, however. At least I don't have any signs of losing any weight yet!

As many times as I run up and down these ladders, I should trim off a little bit, though. That's one disadvantage of these bigger boats. It's a lot longer way to get from one place to another.

Sammy McKee was telling me that he was aboard in Bremerton when they were measuring to see if this flight deck is the longest one in the world. He said they came out about six feet longer than the Constellation, who claimed to be the longest. Apparently, they had a big ceremony with steel tapes and garden hose and strings and a lot of different ways of measuring it. I don't know if it is the longest or not, but it's sure got the most steps to get up and down anywhere. We've had meetings here and briefings there and drills everywhere. I'll be glad to start back flying so I can sit in the airplane and relax for a while.

...There's not much new news out here, since we are just steaming. Hope you are all doing okay back there. At least you can get out and shuffle around the block. Give a kiss around all three for me.

I love you very much.

My love always, Jimmie

USS Kitty Hawk
24 October '65

Hi Honey,

Looks like I'll have to wait a couple more days to get a look at Hawaii. Jack and I got airborne today but couldn't get our gear up, so didn't get to go in to the islands after all. Had a good system and what we thought was a good airplane and the weather was beautiful, but we still couldn't go. Can't get that far with the landing gear down, so we just sat here and orbited the ship till time to land. We did get some good pictures of the ship while we were at it, though.

This blue Pacific is just as blue as they all say it is. A real bright mellow blue that contrasts well with the white wake of the ship. Tell Jamey we also went by a large group of whales today.

...The Skipper has been real pleasant here lately, and I don't know if that's because he's decided we're going to war or if he's finally decided we aren't doing so badly after all. In fact, we're almost the fair-haired boys here on this boat. While most of the others are getting reamed apart, RVAH-13 gets plaudits and atta-

boys. So, actually, the last few days have been rather enjoyable, as far as possible that is, this far at sea...

Just heard mail call so will put this one in the box and go get some sweet love notes from you to give me pleasant dreams tonight. I dream of you often, Darling. Like all the time! And love you all the more every day.

Good night, my darling,
Your loving husband, Jimmie

USS Kitty Hawk
Monday, 25 October '65

Hi Darling,

...I'm sitting here with my stomach growling, waiting for the late sitting of dinner. I've been eating too much lately and decided today to cut down some. Didn't eat breakfast and ate early lunch, so this long wait for dinner is about as much as I can stand. Of course, all this isn't going to do me any good if I keep eating that big bag of popcorn in the Ready Room every night. We have our popcorn mess running on a limited scale, and it's sorta like the TV advertisement on potato chips. Someone comes and offers you one handful, then you knock the whole door down getting out to get a fist full. You can't eat just one handful!

...We're due in Pearl Harbor early tomorrow morning so it looks like my first sights of the island will come from the ship. Not scheduled for any liberty, but mainly just to pick up the observers who will start on our ORI inspection. We will probably come back out and fly tomorrow night.

...As for news out here, Jim Bell and Duffy Hutton (whose plane went down in Vietnam on October 16th) are still listed as "missing" as far as we know. Not much to hear from any source.

Poor Holly was about at the end of her rope when I saw her in Sanford, and now I guess all we can do is pray for her and Jim, too. If you can see her, please send my regards also.

I guess the war gets close to home whether we like it or not. But I know this isn't the first one, and it won't be the last one if we want to keep the happiness that the U S of A affords. Maybe that's where we all should be. Just thankful.

And I'm especially thankful for you, Darling.

I love you, Jimmie

USS Kitty Hawk
Ashore in Hawaii
27 October 1965

Aloha,

We're here, but we had a rough time making it. It really looks pretty from the ship and right now that's about all I can tell you. We got in late yesterday afternoon, and I had the duty section last night so haven't been ashore. Oh, I did walk off on the base for a minute, but that's just like staying on the ship.

We were about a half day behind schedule because one of our radiomen fell off the elevator night before last, and we had to turn around to pick him up. Luckily, he could swim quite well, and the ship did a beautiful job of spinning around to come back to him. He was from our squadron, and we had him back aboard in about 20 minutes. That may not be a record, but on a black night, it's better than average.

Then came the unfortunate part. When one of the enlisted helicopter crew was running to the plane and the ship made the hard turn to go back to the first man, the helo crewman fell over the side, and we searched all night and part of yesterday morning and never found any trace of him. We tell these guys over and over how dangerous it is on the flight deck, and they just won't believe it. You can bet that yesterday morning we didn't have any difficulty in getting these people to wear their life jackets. Luckily, our radioman that fell in could swim, but I doubt that half the men we have could last that long without a life jacket.

I talked to him this morning and asked if he wore his life jacket ashore last night and he said no. But he said he did think about wearing it when he went to the shower....I've got to go debrief my ORI mission folder, so I will have to finish this later. We had some of our ORI tests this morning and they only pick a few folders to look at, but Jack and I always seem to be the lucky ones...Well, it's time to get this bucket back out to sea, so I'll mail this and try to get another started later on tonight.

I love you very, very much,
Always, Jimmie

USS Kitty Hawk
Off Hawaii
28 October 1965

Hi Darlings,

...It sounds like you all had a nice weekend. The carnival must have been a lot of fun, and with all the new people, they must have made a mint for the school fund.

Tell Glyn I'm proud of her riding the pony, and she can surely be a cowgirl if she wants to. And if their tails ever fall off, it sounds like she's just the girl to pin them back on, too.

James is starting to feel some of the suffering of age now—when they tell him he is too old for little kids' things! Pretty soon, he will have to pay the high rate for movies, and then he will really think he is over the hump. I'm sure he still had more fun than any three there, though.

...I finally got to fly over the islands in daylight today and got to look at some beautiful scenery. I had color film in my camera and got some nice color shots of all the scenic areas. Only trouble was, it was camouflage detection film, and all the green trees turn out red. It made a pretty color against the deep blue water, though. The water is just as blue as they say it is, and the trees are just as green. The volcanic ash varies from an orange-red to a deep black, so, depending on which island you look at, the colors can be different.

We won't get into port until tomorrow and that is my duty day again, so I don't know when I'll be able to tell you what Honolulu looks like. Nite for now.

I love you, Jimmie

USS Kitty Hawk
7 November 1965

My Dearest Darling,

Sure nice to hear your voice the other night. Didn't feel much like talking too long, so hope you'll forgive me for not having much to say. As usual, though, we kind of run out of telephone talk so maybe the letter-writing plan is better after all. There are a lot of things that I can't tell you over the phone anyway that I don't mind putting down in the mail. They are still rather touchy about schedule and all that, but I do think you need to know something of where we will be. And I like you to know exactly how much I love you without a lot of operators having to interpret it.

Hope Glyn and Jamey didn't feel like I was cutting them off before they had a chance to tell me what they wanted to. They're sure a sweet pair of kids, and I miss them almost as much as missing you.

Had three letters from you today, so guess the mail train is catching up out here. There was a short note from Mother which reminded me that I hadn't written home since I've been out here. I'll try to get them off about one a week, but I'm not sure I'll be able to keep up with that, so hope you'll keep them on your regular list.

Mother says they do plan to go out to California for Christmas. I guess Gene and Christine plan to drive them out. Seems Gene expects to get called up next summer and wants to go ahead and make the trip now while he has the time. I don't know if he will get called or not, since Tennessee was not on the married call-up list for January.

We'll be leaving here tomorrow morning, so I doubt if any mail will go off for a few days. We may be able to COD some over to Wake Island as we go by there and then again around Okinawa. It will take us about two weeks to get across, and then I expect we will stay in Subic Bay a few days before we go on station. Hope to fly a couple of days going across, but it won't be much more than that.

...I didn't exactly get to play tourist in Hawaii. I did get down to the beach one day, but it was cloudy and even rained a little. Tell Jamey I got to see some hula girls with grass skirts, and I'll write to him about it. Most of the Tahitian dancers are young girls and most of them get kind of plump and chubby as they get older. If they stay with it very long, they look like the four we saw down at a club last night. They could have worn the stockings off the legs of the four horsemen from Notre Dame. Their calves were bigger than their thighs, and they had muscles like weight lifters.

...I have the CAG duty today, so I haven't even been able to catch up on my sleep. Have to get up early tomorrow, so had better write more then. I sure miss you a lot, Sweetheart. Seems almost a waste to let these days go by, but I'm sure we will more than make up for it when we're back together again. Nice thoughts to dream on, anyway.

I love you, Darling, more than ever,

Jimmie

USS Kitty Hawk
Sailing West
9 November 1965

My Dearest Darling,

We finally got underway sometime after supper last night. We were supposed to leave at noon, but we had some problems getting everything aboard. So, here we are now, chugging our way across the Pacific, and at a pretty fast pace right now, since they have to make this annual high-speed run to check out the engineering crew. I expect that to slow down tomorrow, though.

We weren't really too concerned whether we got out last night or not. None of us would have been able to go ashore anyway, since we were mostly laid up with shot reactions. Some of it could have been hangovers, but I had the duty Sunday, so I'm fairly sure it was the shots. I got six shots yesterday morning (three in each arm) and by mid-afternoon I had to hit the pad. Most of them never bother me, so it must have been the plague shot that was so bad. I got it in my right arm, and I can still hardly lift my elbow to eat. Everyone was having fevers and flashes, and the lectures this morning didn't have a very attentive audience. We still have a second plague shot to go, too, plus a hepatitis shot from a needle so big it is a hip shot only.

We've got some worse shot cowards around this squadron than Tom Quillin ever was. The XO kept putting his off, and by the time he got around to the stragglers line last night, he was really dreading it from having watched us ache and moan all day. Only problem I have today is getting in and out of that top rack, plus a little fever. We should be loosened back up in time to fly by Thursday.

I heard them announce that they will take mail into Midway as we go by, but they won't pick up any. So, maybe this will get to you before Christmas after all. It sure cuts down on my paperwork in the office when we don't receive any mail aboard, but it makes it Hell those first few days in port. Like a snowstorm of paper.

...I guess when they say that love is boundless, it means just that. And I can't think of a sweeter way to face the life ahead. With the kids we have and all that God has given us, we must be the most fortunate two people in the world...Give a kiss to the kids for me...

Your loving husband, Jimmie

USS Kitty Hawk
10 November 1965

Dear James and Glyn,

Sounds like you both had a fun Halloween. I got the picture Mother sent of your costumes, and they really look good. That's a fine scarecrow and a Bozo, too. Wish I had been there to take you around the block, but I expect the scout party was more fun anyway.

Mom says you are getting to be the Super Scout anyway, James, what with leading the singing and writing your own poems and all. Looks like I missed out on your best monthly scout meeting.

The hula dancers here in Hawaii were a lot of fun to watch, but I think I could have had a lot more fun at home with you all watching a football game. How is the Seminole team doing now? With Mr. Fraser in the hospital, I guess you haven't gotten to go to anymore games. They play football in Hawaii, but I didn't see any of the games.

I'll put in a map of the islands in with this letter so you can tell what the names are. The way to pronounce them is to sound all the vowels. The only island we went to was Oahu where Honolulu and Pearl Harbor are. But I did fly over all the rest, and I took pictures of them.

I am also enclosing a picture of the ship that I took today. It is making a turn to get in line with the wind to start landing airplanes. The destroyer follows along behind to pick up anyone who might fall in the water.

Hope you and Glyn are taking good care of Mother and having lots of fun.

I will have something real interesting to tell you about when we cross the International Date Line tomorrow. We are 12 hours behind you in time right now, and tomorrow night, we will skip a whole day and become 12 hours ahead of you. You look it up, and I'll write and tell you about it later.

I love you, James.

I love you, Glyn.

Good night and sleep tight, Dad

USS Kitty Hawk
10 Nov.1965

Hi Honey,

I've been on alert duty all day in a flight suit and then the shower tonight had cold water only, so I'm not as clean and comfortable as I would like to be. Guess that's their way of avoiding water hours.

They figure you won't stand under the shower long with cold water. Actually, I waste more waiting to see if it's going to get warm than I would taking the shower in the first place.

Had a last laugh on Jack tonight when I was bugging Air Ops to secure us so I could go change into a uniform for evening meal in the senior wardroom. I thought it was steak night so told the junior officers that I didn't want to eat with them wearing flight gear in Wardroom No. 1 because we have better steaks than they do. I've had them convinced for sometime that we get better food than they do—--which is false of course—but they fall for it anyway. Well, when I got to chow we had pork chops, and I could see them laughing at the way I had hurried around to get a good steak, and it wasn't even steak night. As it turned out, they ran out of chops, and the three of us that got missed wound up with steaks as a substitute. You can imagine how they were laughing when I walked into the Ready Room with "How did I like my steak?" and all that. I let them go on for awhile and then finally told them I really did have steak, and they were really mad.

Well, Darling, I'd better mail this and get to bed. Just wanted mostly to say I love you and wish you pleasant dreams.

Nite, Sweetheart, I love you, Jimmie

Aboard USS Kitty Hawk
Sailing West
11 Nov 1965

Hi Darling,

Today I got to see a thing of real beauty, and I forgot my hand camera to get color pictures of it. Flew over Midway Island to take some pictures with the airplane cameras and wished I had my Argus with me instead. It's really a small island, and there is nothing much there except the runways, but the color contrast is something altogether different. The island is about one mile by two miles in size, and the whole ring reef is only about seven miles in diameter. The water outside is all deep blue and inside the reef is the brightest milky kelly green you have ever seen. The housetops are red and the trees are dark green, and there are white sand and runways to make a nice contrast.

...Of course, the place is not nearly pretty enough that I would ever ask for duty there. There a few other rocky volcano tops about 60 miles away, but nobody lives there. For the most part, we left the nearest basic civilization over 1,000 miles away at Hawaii.

It was nice to get off the ship and fly around to see a spot of land for a change. There is an awful lot of blue Pacific out here, and I seldom go topside because that is all there is to see. It will be almost a week before we fly again, so should be a lot of paper shuffling between here and there. We still have to stand by for the overflights, though, so we still get plenty of flight suit time.

...I think I forgot to tell you I got an answer back from BuPers about the Astronaut Program. There was an X in the block by the word "overheight," and that was all it said plus "appreciation of your interest" and all that mishmash. Max's said he was screened by board action, and Al Perrella hasn't heard anything yet. He's the same height I am, so he will probably get the same treatment, but maybe he will luck through awhile before finding out.

Tomorrow will be a void since we won't have a Friday 12 Nov this year. So I will write you again Saturday night 13 Nov which is just 24 hours away. Wish I could be with you, Sweetheart...I love you so very, very much.

Always, Jimmie

Aboard USS Kitty Hawk
At Sea
13 Nov 1965

Dear James,

Yesterday was Thursday 11 Nov, and now, today it's Saturday already. What do you think about that? Well, last night we crossed the International Date Line, and everything moved up a whole day. This is the big step in the system that the world uses to keep sunrise and sunset at about the same hour on the clock as the earth rotates around.

From the rough map I've drawn, you can see how we are going. I'll give you the rest of the route after we have been there. The pencil line is where Mr. Walters and I flew yesterday, and you can see where we took off on Friday 11 November and flew over to look at Midway and Kure Islands, then flew across the Date Line to see what Friday 12 November looked like (cause that is what day it was on the other side of the line) and then flew back across the line back into Thursday to land on the ship. How is that for a spaceman look at the future? Ha.

Then, right after midnight last night, the ship crossed the line, and instead of it being real early Friday morning, all of a sudden, it was Saturday. So I had Thursday night supper last night and woke up this morning to have Saturday morning breakfast. (Already, I am forgetting what day it is.) Maybe you had best look it up in the encyclopedia for me!

I hear all kinds of good reports on how you are doing in school. Keep up the good work. Have you received any report cards yet? I am very anxious to know how you do this time. I am very proud of the way you are taking care of Mom and Glyn for me. Give them a big hug and a kiss straight from me. And here is one for you.

I love you, Son,

Dad

USS Kitty Hawk

Tuesday, 16 Nov 1965

Hi Darling,

I don't think I'm cut out to be a "black shoe." The blue Pacific is beautiful, and the sea air is refreshing, but how do I get off this boat?! We've been finding enough things to keep us moderately busy, but this constant steaming I can do without.

...It's hard to realize that days are flipping by as fast as they are. We came under Seventh Fleet control yesterday, and that's when the cruise actually begins. I don't know what they call all this time since last July, but I call that cruise also. But what it means anyway is rather immaterial since we'll be here as long as they need us, regardless of what the calendar says...

Bet Jamey and Glyn are starting to get anxious for Thanksgiving now with Ernie coming from West Palm Beach. Do wish Agnes and Lester the best, though I feel a bit left out that she only comes to see you when I'm not there! Ha. And I do hope you can all have a happy Thanksgiving together.

...Miss you, Sweetheart, and this ole bed gets awful empty about this time of night.....A kiss for you all. My love always,

I love you, Jimmie

USS Kitty Hawk
17 Nov 1965

Hi Darling,

We crossed through the Bonin Islands today about 100 miles north of Iwo Jima and got our first glimpse of land in quite a few miles. For the people on the ship, it was the first time they have seen land since we left Hawaii. Not much to see but a couple of rocks really, but I suppose they are inhabited since we saw what looked like a few fishing boats around.

Can't imagine what it would be like to live out on an island like that. Can't be more than 100 people or so, and it's mostly rock with no airfield or harbor which would take any reasonable-sized ship. Don't really see how they can raise enough food to subsist on.

I've often wondered if it wouldn't be nice, though, just living on an island with you and no worries or cares. I'm sure it would be real wonderful for awhile, but pretty soon, the little things become the big worries and then it settles down to pure existence...In fact, if I had my way, we would volunteer for an experiment to see how many consecutive hours we could spend together in happiness.

...I just finished a big bag of popcorn, and I'm about to drown from over-indulgence in water. Our popcorn mess is a bone of contention these days anyway. The ship has two big machines, and they sell it for Special Services, and the ship's XO told us we had to close ours down because we were competing with their money. Not exactly what you would call free enterprise aboard this ship. Our popcorn is better than theirs, so he told us we can't sell any more, but we can run the mess for our own private needs. So, now we just give it away and leave a cup sitting out by the window. And we can't help it if a guy wants to be free-hearted and donate ten cents to the mess every time we give him a free bag of popcorn, can we?

If he closes us down again, I told our XO we would call it a closed mess for members only. Then if someone wants to pay a dime for instantaneous membership while we are popping corn, well that's his business. We're still making good money on it, but not as good as we were before they curtailed our sales.

I'm running short on news here lately, and I expect you are too with no mail flow back and forth. How about going out and driving around the block for me at least. I take an occasional tour around the flight deck, but somehow, it always looks the same.

...Wish I had something to tell you, but guess you'll have to do with a simple I love you. Miss you, Sweetheart, James and Glyn, too. I love you all so very much,

Always, your lover, Jimmie

USS Kitty Hawk
Subic Bay, Philippines
23 November 1965

Hi Sweetheart,

...We've been in meetings here for the past two days, so I got to the PX for about an hour and that's been about it. Of course, this was a business stop anyway, but most everyone at least wanted to get a little Christmas shopping done. I have some little trinkets here to mail you, but you will have to do the major shopping for the kids. After the three big boats came in here on their way home last week, most of the exchanges are almost stripped bare anyway.

...A tropical storm is apparently going around (this part of the Pacific) so we will leave here tomorrow. Mail should get back on a regular basis from here on. The planes run back and forth to the ships most every day, but I don't know how they will be handling packages.

We're catching up on the backlog of mail here now. And the three letters I got today look mighty sweet indeed. I love you so much, Darling, and those few words, whatever they say, can do wonders for me after a long hard day. You just can't believe how welcome letters are when you're out here with no contact with what's going on...Better go get some supper now...Will get with answering your letters when we're back out at sea. I love you so very much and miss you all the more. My love to James and Glyn, too.

I love you, Jimmie

Wednesday, 24 November
At Sea
USS Kitty Hawk

My Dearest Darling,

...We're having briefings up a storm now, and I'm starting this while I wait for supper 'cause we have more lectures after supper tonight. They are need-to-know type, though, so most people aren't complaining too loudly. Everything we hear from here on in we may need before tomorrow, so I guess it is about time to get serious about this flying game. Looks like we will be doing quite a bit of flying, too, so if we can keep these birds up, maybe we will get to shake the cobwebs loose for a change.

The stay in Subic Bay wasn't too bad, except that we could have used another day or so. The tropical storm blew around, so actually the breeze helped keep it cooled off, and the weather was beautiful...I'm sitting here soaking wet right now. Either the air conditioner filters are clogged up or it is hotter than I think because it's really close in here. This whole end of the second deck is stuffy hot for some reason. Can imagine how it is on the Essex class boats out here with no air conditioning. Guess that cool operating spell off

California got my blood thickened up, and it hasn't had a chance to thin out yet.

Supper time now, and I will try to finish this up before I go to bed....Long-winded lectures as usual so it's quite late now. We're almost on exactly opposite sides of the globe from you, so I expect you and Glyn are sitting down to lunch about now. We are 13 hours earlier than you are, and by the time we get over land, we will be exactly 12 hours opposite. So you can tell Jamey that when it is 8 o'clock in the morning in Sanford, I will already be around to 8 o'clock that night.

...Jack told me about Jamey's car-washing job with Pat and how embarrassed he got when she tried to pay him. I guess she has gone on up to North Carolina for Thanksgiving now. It sure is a shame that Jack is missing out on a lot of the fun part of his (baby) son. Of course, Stan will be at the really cute stage when we get back, and he will have even more fun with him then.

...Goodnight for now, Sweetheart,

Your loving husband, Jimmie

As the ship entered the combat zone in the South China Sea, mail back to the States was "free" for personnel on the ships. The notation "free" indicates the* Kitty Hawk *was in a combat zone.

USS Kitty Hawk
"Free"
Sunday, 25 Nov 1965

My Dearest Darling,

Well, it's almost the witching hour, and I still don't know what tomorrow will bring. I'm due to kick off our first Ops over here bright and early in the morning, and so far, we don't even have the targets. First-day-itis, I'm sure, and they will settle down later on, but it's rather frustrating to begin it right off this way.

We had a big Thanksgiving full of briefings and planning, etc. I also had Condition III alert for the photo plane and didn't get to go to church. We did take off for a big Thanksgiving dinner tonight with turkey and all the trimmings. It was very good, too, and in fact, I will probably be tasting it all night.

Hope you all had a nice Turkey Day. Did Ginger and Wayne come along (with your sister) or are they too busy with dating these days to make the trip anymore? Would dearly have loved to have been there with you.

The air conditioning is going to pot on here, and it's really been hot all day. With these heavier green flight suits we are wearing, I can imagine what it's going to be like in the airplane. Today, even Michigan weather would feel good. It think it's cooler up on deck than it is here in my room.

Admiral Reedy gave us a brief in the Wardroom today, and he was soaking wet by the time he was finished. He came aboard with his staff in Cuba, so now we have to play a little bit of showboat with an admiral aboard. He used to be in Heavy Attack at Whidby many years ago and doesn't seem to sweat that stuff too much, though.

This will be my first letter of the Free postage variety. We came into the combat zone this afternoon, so our air mail letters now go out postage free. Parcel post packages also get air lifted back as far as San Francisco. Some minor compensation, I guess. Income tax deductions also come into play to the tune of $200 per month. Of course, we could give all that back to them if they could put a stop to these Viet Cong over there.

I guess being Thanksgiving, we should look at all the things we have to be thankful for, though. And you and I have just about as big a list as anyone could hope for. I could start counting my blessings with you and the kids, and the list would get so long it would never stop. The Good Lord has been most bountiful to us, Sweetheart, and I have no doubts that he has long-range plans of continuing to do so. And it's awful comforting at night just to look back along the way and count up the wonder of it all. I guess the most precious possession I have is the complete love that you give to me. And I get the most fun out of my life just trying to pay back a portion in return. I look forward to the time when we can pay more attention to that on a full-time basis.

I know how early that early call will come tomorrow, so I'd better leave you with a heart full of pleasant dreams. A Happy Thanksgiving to all, and a hug and kiss for Jamey and for Glyn and two extras for you.

I love you,

Jimmie

USS Kitty Hawk

Free

Sunday 28 Nov 1965

My Dearest Darling,

...We had a little mishap today, and I'm telling you so in case you hear tales around that RVAH-13 had an accident, you'll know what it is. Nobody was hurt, and it was real minor, so don't you go telling anybody about it.

The Skipper had a landing gear collapse on landing, and the plane rocked down on one wingtip. It mashed up the side of the airplane a bit where the gear folded, so that made it an accident. It was a pretty smooth ride for them, though, and it appears to have been caused by one bolt that broke. It's after Taps now, and I've got to be up at 0530, so had better stop for now.

I love you, Sweetheart, with all my heart.

Nite, my love, Jimmie

USS Kitty Hawk
Free
Saturday, 27 Nov 1965

Hi Darling,

Well, we're here, like or not, and I assume we'll be in consecutive Ops for quite some time now. Looks like most of us will get to fly every day, and that plus playing ODO and briefings means the letter-writing time will be cut down somewhat. It will be nice to fly every day, though, and I'm sure it will sharpen up our operations considerably.

We're operating off South Vietnam now, and I got down over the Mekong Delta yesterday. That must be the muddiest river in existence. It is a soupy brown, and it muddies the ocean out about 20 miles where it runs into it. They call it a delta for good reason, as everything you see down there has to grow up out of the water first.

Still, all in all, the countryside is quite beautiful and calm "looking." Everything is a deep green and each little field neatly laid out. They just finished the rainy season, so all the vegetation is fully gown up and very colorful. Hasn't really quit raining, though, as the weather has been mostly cloudy and rainy these past two days.

One thing for sure, though—this is the hottest place we've worked in for a long time. Can imagine how it must have been out here during the summer months or on those carriers with no air conditioning. I have a heavier dark-colored flight suit, and I come back soaking wet every time. Lots of salt and water is the menu, but even then I can see where those other people lost weight.

...I've got to go to a briefing now, and I have a real early launch tomorrow, so I'll try to get back and at least mail this before bedtime. I love you.

...Back again, and it is close to sleepy time. Max just showed me an outstandingly cute picture of (daughter) Kathryn, the Olan Mills picture with the toothless grin right out front. Guess Mary Durant has been taking snapshots of the kids and giving them to Rozelle to send Max. At least he had a handful of black and white to go along.

I've got a 36-exposure roll of film almost finished, but I need to take two more exposures. I keep saying I'll put in a South China Sea sunset, but so far I haven't been available at that time of day. Maybe a sunrise will do just as well. At any rate, I'll get them done before too long. I guess I'll have to have them sent back out here and labeled before I mail them to you, though, or you will never know what they are. Of course, Jamey could probably figure it all out.

Glad to hear you got the TV back into function. Hope it's a good clear picture and back in proper order. If not, we may as well ditch it when it breaks again. The car sounds good, and I'm glad you remembered to get the tires rotated and balanced. I assume you meant you got all this done at the dealer's. At any rate, the price was okay.

...As I've said before, you do so well taking care of things at home that maybe I should get away more often. Ha...Have to turn these lights off and get to bed or I won't make it up for that early

launch tomorrow. Can make good use of the time dreaming of you, though.....How about a big kiss for the kids. I love them, too.

...Always my dearest, Jimmie

USS Kitty Hawk

Free

Monday 29 Nov 1965

Hi Sweetheart,

Getting to be a bad day at black rock around here...Jack and I just manned our fourth airplane in a row for the past two days and had something wrong with it that we couldn't get out on the flight. In fact, the only hops the squadron has missed due to maintenance are the four that Jack and I have missed. So, naturally, the maintenance gang is treating us like the plague.

The bad part is the 3 1/2 hours each that goes into briefing and suiting up and manning the aircraft, then climbing out and coming back down again just about wipes out my whole day for nothing.

Bob put us on for the early again tomorrow, and I wouldn't lay two cents to one whether we will even get to taxi or not. Would sure like to get in a few more hops down here, though, before we head north. The weather is still pretty bad, so can't see too much on the beach anyway.

...This free mail service makes it almost a sin not to write more letters. It's only good while we are in the combat zone, too, and that's when we have the least time to write. Maybe I'll just write "I love you" on several sheets of paper and mail one or two each day. It's good for postcards, too, but I don't have any of those.

I do have lots of love for you, though, and miss you all the more each day. But I can think of all the fun we are going to have when I do get home and that makes the time go fleeting past—at least the time I am dreaming. I guess if we both keep busy, it will be there before we know it....Tell Glyn and James I miss them, too, and send them lots of love.

Nite and pleasant dreams, Darling,

I love you, Jimmie

USS Kitty Hawk

Free

Wednesday 1 Dec 1965

Hi Darling,

Going to be kind of catch-as-catch-can here for a while it seems. I flew the early, early and late, late launches yesterday, so it kinda wiped out that day. And I've been playing ODO today so have been pretty much on the go.

We're headed up north now, so things will get a little more active for the next few weeks. It has gone fairly well down here in the south end (Dixie Station) except for the lousy weather we have been having. Their monsoon season was supposed to be over, but we've had 30 to 40 knots of wind continuously and light rains on and off all day every day. I hear it is no better up north, and I guess we will find out for sure tomorrow.

Jack and I got over our jinx of downing aircraft and got two whole fights off yesterday, so maybe we can keep it going for a while and catch back up on our flights. It's gotten so lately I'd even forgotten what day it was, let alone what flight I was briefing for. Had to look at the lunch menu and compare what I ate just to figure out what day today was. The date I can keep up pretty well, but the day of the week just gets out of hand.

We're running behind on mail here again, and I can't figure out the reason for that. The COD has been coming out regularly, but I think he has had so many news reporters and VIPs that there was no room to put the mail. Of course, these poor destroyers and support ships are worse off than we are. That plane guard destroyer behind us stays out of sight under the spray most of the time. One tanker alongside of us today was pitching around so that his screws would come up clear out of the water. Makes us look sort of fat to sit there hardly moving while the ship alongside is bobbing up and down 20 or 30 feet.

We've had a flux of 24-hour flu these last couple of days, and I'm sure it's not seasickness. Just hope it doesn't spread around anymore than it already has. That would be about all we would need right now. Especially with the way we need maintenance on our airplanes.

Tell Bob (Fraser) thanks for helping out Jamey with his scout projects...It's sure nice to have someone who is interested enough to help Jamey and Bobby with their scouting. Maybe I'll be home to take the duty for Bob's cruise.

...Charlie Putnam ought to be heading out this way before too long (to be our XO now that the present Skipper is leaving)...By the time he gets here we will probably be heading for port anyway. He's such a tiger, though, that I'm sure he will come the first day they let him...

I didn't get back the way I intended to after supper. I had to go plan some routes for tomorrow, so it's back past bedtime again as it usually is. Wanted to get a letter off to Mother and may just drop her a note to say hello anyway.

Will be thinking of you, Sweetheart. Even if I don't always get a chance to write, I do always think of you. There is a sureness in our love that makes it all the sweeter. I guess that's why I can always have a certain comfort in the thoughts that you can take better care of things at home than I can. Maybe I don't tell you enough the pride I have as well as the love because you are my wife. I wish everyone could be so fortunate.

I love you, Darling,

Your loving husband, Jimmie

USS Kitty Hawk

Free

Friday, 3 December

Hi Darling,

Things are starting to pick up now, and I'm afraid the pace is about up to the stage of cutting short the letter writing, but I will try to get off a short note when I can. We just need about three more people right now or at least three more hours per day.

Mail has been about as extinct as the dodo bird for the past week. I hear that none has been going out either, so I'm afraid your Xmas packages may be Valentine's happy hearties. So many reporters and VIPs are out here, there is no room for mail.

Did get a nice long letter from you late last night, and it sure was a welcome sight. I got to enjoy your Thanksgiving with you even if it was a little late. Sounds like one I could really have enjoyed, and I'm so glad (your sister and family) got there as planned. Wish I had known Wayne was so interested in Hawaii. I imagine that comes from surfboards and the Beach Boys. Gotta go brief a hop now, so I'll try to write more tonight.

Much, much later: Got a big one tomorrow so will have to keep this short. Just got a mighty sweet card from you and that should make for pleasant dreams. You're my kind of people, too!

Only big news is that the lieutenants' list is out. AND Jack Walters made the list. So did Paul Stokes and Al Foster, but they were both pretty senior anyway. Jack was in that last bunch that they added on as an extra zone. It means he will be next summer getting it, but at least he is on the list. It made him quite happy anyway.

Well, Darling, it's nite for now with a hug and kiss and batches of I-love-you's. I just want you to know how much you mean to me and how wonderful it is to have you for my wife. Before we know it, the day will come when we can get back to more wifely and husbandly activities. Hooray for that day. 'Till then, I love you.

Nite, My Darling, Jimmie

"Free"
USS Kitty Hawk
4 Dec '65
Sat. nite

My Darling,

I L O V E Y O U
O
V
E
Y
O
U
Jimmie

USS Kitty Hawk
Mon. Nite
6 Dec '65

My Dearest Darling,

Little hard to write here in my room tonight, and will probably be even worse trying to sleep. Haven't even been able to get to the room since early this morning. They had a big fire in the main machinery room this morning, and it is right across the passageway from my room. I had to man aircraft to fly off, so don't know how bad the smoke got, but it must have been pretty bad. They lost two men, and sick bay is full with burns, etc. It wasn't as bad as the boiler explosion on the Bennington when I was a midshipman, but it must have been pretty rough for a while. I looked down in the hole a while ago, and it will take them several days to clean the mess up. Meanwhile, they have cross coupled the engine, and we are back to normal flight operations.

The smell in this room is terrible, though, and my clothes are saturated with smoke and foam smell. If I sleep here tonight I'll probably wake up in the morning feeling like I have a hangover. Of course, there is soot and black all over the room, also.

Luckily, most of the men were out of the engine room being paid or casualties would have been a lot worse than they were. Anytime you lose anybody, it is bad enough. They, apparently, have it well under control now, though, and I just hope it stays that way. So, contrary to any rumors you hear, we weren't put out of commission, and we actually got in our full schedule of flights today in spite of it all.

I haven't filled you in too much on what went on since we got up here on Yankee Station because I've been flying every day. With all the briefing and debriefing that goes on, it takes a full eight-hour day just to fly one hop. And there are so many rules about every little thing you would never believe it. In fact, if all this data ever gets back to those computers in Washington, they will probably give up and blow a fuse. I get tomorrow off to catch up on some of the regular paperwork around here, and I will probably have the ODO or something and won't be able to get a thing done.

We've been flying pretty well the past couple of days. We started getting a lot of mechanical gripes on airplanes that we haven't been plagued with for the last six months or so. It seemed to come all at once, but that's just normal for these airplanes, and we've been lucky to go this long without them. Bob Renner and Bill Johnson had to take one over to Da Nang when he lost oil pressure, and you should hear their tales about that place. They stayed two nights and got back yesterday. That was one liberty port that they didn't want to stay in any longer than necessary. Seems those guys over there just shoot it up all night long. The VCs are all out around the field there, and sometimes the planes take off, pick up their gear, and then roll right into their bombing run just across the fence. I guess the marines took real good care of them and told them so many tales that they won't want to go back for a while.

That's why you were right when you said it's much nicer to (fight the war) this way and come back to a warm meal and a nice clean bed every night, even if it doesn't quite have all the comforts of home. Of course, tonight it will also smell like smoke.

...Better pack up some laundry now and get to bed. Will dream of you, my darling.

I love you, Jimmie

USS Kitty Hawk
8 Dec 1965

My Dearest Darling,

I L O V E Y O U
O
V
E
Y
O
U

Your loving husband,
Jimmie

USS Kitty Hawk
Thurs Nite
9 Dec '65

Hi Darling,

...I've noticed that I only get about half as much done when I'm away from you as I do when you are around. I guess my mind doesn't stay oriented as well, and I don't get that good peaceful rest that I find when I have you snuggled up with me. What it says is that I need you, and every day I find you more and more a necessary part of my life. I guess we have to get away once in a while to make the obvious become evident, but this is surely a hard way to do it!

I didn't fly today for the first time in a long while. But I am getting a little ahead of the others—except for the Skipper, of course—and I will probably miss a few more days come next week.

We are still operating in North Vietnam, and the weather is holding us out of the areas we really want to get into. I hear the Enterprise is getting all the publicity down south, though, just like they are really in the thick of the battle. They will be up here one of these days and see what it really feels like to get their pants scared off.

The fire damage is about repaired, but my clothes still smell to high heaven as the dry-cleaning plant is also broken down. Had an influx of telegrams the other day from worried mothers to their sons on the ship. Seems some fink reporter out here got off the ship the day it happened and released the whole shebang, including the names of the dead, before the navy could get out a notification to the next of kin. The People's Press scores again. It's birds like him that give a bad name to hundreds of good reporters.

Anyway, the captain had an A-3D fly off a special mail package last night with letters from the crew to tell their folks at home that they were okay. I haven't had any sleep for a couple of nights, though, from the lights and the work going on outside our door.

People are starting to pick up a little Christmas spirit now with packages arriving from home. Max got a nice fruitcake from Rozelle the other day, and it was really good. People are starting to plan for liberty in Japan, and the leave chits are starting to filter thorough, so I expect to see things perk up in another week or so.

I'm sorry to hear your Dad is back in the hospital, and I'm really not sure he has enough lungs left in him to support pneumonia. I know you're aware of what a thread he is hanging onto anyway. I sure feel for your Mother and wish we could do something to help her. Of course, he and she are both better off if they will keep him in the hospital for a few days....

Love, Jimmie

PS: My love to your Mom and Dad

USS Kitty Hawk
10 Dec '65

My Darling Sanfordite,

How does Albany, Georgia look to you? I guess there is panic in the streets in Sanford tonight. We saw the news release this morning about closing all the SAC bases and turning Turner Air Force Base over to the navy. At that time, I jokingly said, "Well, guys, how does it feel to be a Georgia cracker?"

Tonight the bomb came, and everyone has been laughing all over the place, but in reality it isn't funny—especially not to those people who own houses in Sanford. And nobody else wants to move either as far as that goes.

What (the directive) said, though, was to set up a program for turnover of Turner to the navy, make up a schedule for deactivation of NAS Sanford, and prepare Turner for RVAH support by FY '68. And it will probably slip several months or even a year as they always do. It probably won't affect us, since my time in the squadron will be up in September of '67, and we will probably leave then anyway.

I really feel sorry for those people (civilians) in Sanford, though. They are as nice as any town where you might live. The ones over around Orlando won't even feel the effect, but I expect real estate in Sanford just went flat about 8 a.m. this morning...I can see it now—in about June of '67 a lot of old timers at Sanford will be retiring from the navy just to avoid making the move. Some of our chiefs even tonight were already making the decision.

...Hard to realize it's been two whole months since I last saw you. And I still love you.

A hug and kiss to Glyn and James, too,

Love, Jimmie

USS Kitty Hawk
Sat nite
10 Dec '65

My Dearest,

I

L

I L O V E Y O U

V

E

Y

O

U !!

Always,
Jim

USS Kitty Hawk
Sunday nite
12 Dec '65

Hi Honey,

We are changing to the alternate schedule tonight and will now fly from midnight to noon. Of course today we are just flying straight through from noon to noon to effect the changeover. It wasn't too bad on the noon-to-midnight shift, but I expect it's going to get hard to sleep on this new one. Most of the off time is spent planning anyway.

I've got a box stacked full of paperwork and haven't even gotten around to addressing any Christmas cards yet. It's going to be too late if I don't get with it pretty soon...Mail coming this way is running about 10 days on air mail letters, too, so I hope it isn't that bad your way.

In fact, the last letter I got from you was dated 1 Dec. I guess it must be the heavy Christmas traffic that is bogging everything down. I'm sure it will open up soon after that, because RVAH-1 didn't seem to have that much of a problem with mail.

Of course the VIPs are still riding around, and that takes up a lot of room that would normally be mail. In fact, I met a senator in the tower today while he was observing landings during his short tour to see how the troops are doing.

...Haven't answered James' letter yet, but I love him for sending it, and I will eventually get him an answer written. I love you and Glyn, too, and I miss you all so very much. They were playing Christmas music over the intercom at lunch today, and it just seemed off and out of place. This working straight through every day makes tomorrow just about as far ahead as you can ever see. But I can see you in my dreams—and awful plainly at times. It comes from...memories that never will grow old.

I love you, Darling,
With all my heart,
Jim

RECONNAISSANCE ATTACK SQUADRON THIRTEEN
FLEET POST OFFICE
SAN FRANCISCO, CALIFORNIA

Greetings from the Western Pacific. I'm happy to have this opportunity to once again pass to you information concerning our Squadron and your loved ones. I do hope you will pardon my mass-producing this letter, but it is the most rapid means of getting news to you.

First, let me review what has occurred since departing the States. In Hawaii, the "Bats" were inspected for Operational Readiness. I'm delighted to say that we were rated excellent. Every aspect of our operational posture was carefully examined and no area was found lacking. Our aircraft and crews performed extremely well—our maintenance was particularly pleasing—thanks to very long, hard hours by your men. We departed Hawaii knowing we were very well prepared to carry out our most demanding mission.

While sailing across the huge, blue Pacific, we conducted flight operations in the vicinity of Midway Island and Okinawa. Once again, your men produced excellent results. After the lengthy voyage, during which much training was conducted, we entered Subic Bay in the Philippines for two days. Our brief stay there was enjoyable even though training and briefings had to continue—all hands enjoyed getting ashore and good recreational facilities were available—golf course, beach, and pools, club, etc.

Departing Subic, we enjoyed an at-sea Thanksgiving, which included special Divine Services. Thanksgiving dinner was delicious—the cooks and bakers outdid themselves. But, of course, it was not quite the same without our families.

The following day, the "Bats" launched our first flights into South Vietnam in support of the government and U.S. forces there. We conducted our operations there for several days and then began moving north. Here, on the line, so to speak, there is no such thing as holiday routine. We are flying daily. All "Bats" are working hard and well—doing their job to enable us to execute our mission.

Although the hours are long, the work hard, and the living conditions crowded, the spirit and morale of your men are high. I have seen many, many examples of the impossible or near impossible task being accomplished in record-breaking time. It's truly amazing, and I'm sure that a great portion of their zeal comes from continued correspondence from and devotion to you.

We intend to remain here in the combat area for a few more weeks and then head north to Japan. We should be there for several days. All hands are looking forward to a break in the routine and an opportunity to do some shopping.

During our in-port period in Japan, I expect to be relieved as the "Bats'" Skipper. Since I have orders to RVAH-3, I will see those of you at Sanford to personally tell you of our experiences. I will get in touch with the Wives' Club and try to schedule it sometime in January or early February.

Until then, may each of you and your families have a Merry Christmas and a Happy New Year.

Dean Webster

DEAN E. WEBSTER

Commanding Officer

USS Kitty Hawk
At Sea
15 Dec '65

My Darling,

I
L
O
I L O V E Y O U
E
Y
O
U

Always,
Jim

USS Kitty Hawk
Thursday nite
16 Dec '65

Hi Honey,

...This is the first chance I've had to get a full night's sleep since we went on this new schedule. I've either been flying or had the ODO every day so far. I'm not kicking about the flying, though, but this one day off tomorrow without the ODO would be a welcome relief. I can sleep all the way to breakfast and maybe even catch up on some paperwork for a change.

I even sat down and watched two reels of a movie tonight. It was Jack Lemmon in "Under the Yum Yum Tree"-—the type you can come in on any reel and see through the story enough to get most of the laughs out of it.

...Our spare airplane is on the way, and, since Cdr. Putnam is bringing it, I expect he will bring it right aboard. I don't know if we will have time for a proper welcome of him right now, but I'm sure we will work something out by the time we get to Japan.

These weird sleeping hours have me so confused I can't remember what I've written you and what I haven't...I hate to talk about the weather all the time, especially those little black clouds that have the chunks of metal in them called flak. The mountains over here are really rugged, like California, so the saying is "The white clouds have rocks in them and the black ones have steel." Of course there are a lot of other sayings, too, such as the calendar on one of the fighter Ready Room doors: "Only five more bombing days 'til Christmas."

By the time you get this letter, it will probably be after Christmas, so I wish you a Merry Christmas, My Darling, and send you all my love. We will have our happy holidays about next July.

I love you,

Jimmie

USS Kitty Hawk
Fri Nite
17 Dec '65

Hi Honey,

...We had a Christmas show tonight with Martha Raye as the feature attraction. She had dinner with us in the wardroom tonight and then put on a show in the hangar bay for the troops afterward. They got some Christmas trees over from the supply ship yesterday and had the place all decorated up, Christmas-like. She was by herself, so the Kitty Hawk sailors brought out enough talent to fill in and make it a full show...The sailors thought she was great, and it was a welcome break from the routine.

We've got a Christmas tree in each end of the Ready Room now—ours is a silver aluminum one. Not much for decorations except ticker tape and colored paper and plastic rings that we can round up out of office supplies, but the thought was there.

Hope you all have a tree up by now. Wish I was there to set it up for you, but I'm sure you can manage with Jamey's help. Glyn should be big enough to really enjoy helping decorate this year. That's one of the good reasons to try to be at home there for Christmas Day. The kids must get half their anticipation out of fixing everything up their very own way.

I know I'll miss it more as the day draws nearer, but right now there just isn't time to realize what time of year it is. I'm sure we will have several worship services on the way up, though, and then we all can realize the true value of Christmas, whatever the season.

A white New Year's in Japan seems to be the real order of the day as their temperatures are running 15 to 30 degrees right now. And with all the snow on Mount Fuji, I'm sure all the squadrons will have an order out for us to go up and photograph a flight of their planes in formation over Fuji for PIO work...

Fly time comes early tomorrow, Darling. Just wish I had you here tonight. I could even do without the sleep just to be able to spend the whole time telling you how much I love you...Give the kids each a hug and kiss for me. I miss them so very much, too.

Good night to all,

I love you, Jimmie

USS Kitty Hawk
Sunday Nite
19 Dec '65

My Dearest Darling,

Guess you're on your way to church about now or at least to Sunday school. Know you have a special program for Advent Sunday with special music. Ours was a fairly normal Sunday, although the church service did have an Advent theme. It's really hard to realize that this was the last Sunday before Christmas. We're starting to get a little of the feel around here, but there is still so much lacking—mainly you. We do have several trees around and lots of trimmings, though.

Like the chaplain explained, we can't exactly call the bombing "out of context" since without the bombs communism would take over, and then there would be no Christmas for anyone. So maybe the Christmas present of freedom to the South Vietnamese is the most important one after all. Of course, I'm sure there are many believers in both countries, and it's just the hardcore communists who are in such total opposition...

We've been trimming our Ready Room tree with bits and pieces, but still none of the trimming you said the girls were going to mail to us from home. Ron got the..."old bats" picture (of you all at a wives' party) and has it posted in the Ready Room. You look real good there, Sweetie, and I sometimes just sit there in the Ready Room and stare. I'll be glad when we can take that down, and I can bring the picture here to my desk to look at while I write letters to you.

There is no way to explain the pleasure I get and the warmth of heart I feel just to look at a photograph and dream of you. Maybe that's the best part to true love...Maybe that's what Christmas means to me—the thanks for the bountiful love that we have always enjoyed and the knowledge that we will enjoy it all the more fully when we are together again.

...We have two more lieutenant commanders among us now, and notice of the third must be in the mail somewhere. Al Perrella and Ron Queen's letters came in a couple of nights ago, and no one knew but the Skipper and I. No one expected their promotion until at least April or so...Dick Daum's must be on the way. And they had dates of rank of 1 October, which meant they must have promoted over half of the group in the first three months. That's very unusual.

Well, at the AOM (all officer's meeting) they always ask if any of the department heads have anything to put out, and I told the CO, "It looks like we have two people out of uniform." Most of the time people know who it is, and as happened with Jim Brittain they already have the new insignias in their pockets, but not this time. The Skipper really played the part, and he hemmed and hawed around and thumbed through the papers and oversized shoulder boards I handed him. He makes them wear these for 24 hours.

...Ron Queen nearly fell out of his chair, and then he started bubbling about a photographer and PIO pictures and all that—which of course I had already arranged for him. Then the ship's store wasn't open, and they had to borrow insignia to wear for dinner. They had expected April, so now they are in a real panic to get uniforms striped before we get to Japan.

Naturally, since Dick Daum's promotion hasn't reached us yet, he is catching the brunt of humor, since Ron flies with him and numbers-wise he is really senior to Ron. They immediately changed the roster board and put Lcdr. Queen above Lt. Daum and started running Dick about getting up to IOIC and getting those flights planned for the Lcdr. The Skipper told Dick he is supposed to request permission to land from the senior officer in the back seat now before he comes aboard.

Of course Dick was a little disappointed, but he is happy to know that when his letter does get here it will be for 1 October also, which is about six months earlier than expected.

Another event here of note is an explanation of the cannon. I wasn't sure whether to tell you yet or not, but since Max has squealed to Rozelle I guess you can talk to her about it. I've never told you before because it was one of the best kept secrets in Sanford. Only three of us officers knew, and about seven or eight enlisted guys. And, in fact, very few people in Sanford know even today, so be careful whom you talk to and maybe you and Rozelle are enough until we decide to let it become general knowledge.

It all started over a year ago—last November a year ago to be exact. RVAH-3 had these two polished brass cannons sitting out in front of Building Three that had been their pride and joy for many years. Well, one cool morning one of them turned up missing and never will it be said by whose hand it was taken. George Kimmons was the CO at the time, and he blew his stack with both barrels. They locked up the other one in the spook shack (where it still remains) and had the base searched high and low. They accused RVAH-9 of taking it with them, since they left shortly after that, and then RVAH-1 and then they accused everybody.

The missing cannon was kept locked up in a cruise box and hauled around everywhere we went for well over a year. The damn thing weighs about 250 pounds! Even in the squadron, only about the ten people mentioned knew we had it until we got out on cruise. Then we started the debate as to when to break it out and show it, and the word got out to several of the chiefs and officers.

Well, the morning we left Pearl Harbor we decided was "the day" since the Skipper was flying on over here for all those conferences, and we wanted him to get to see it first. Of course (the unveiling) had to be after all the Sanford people who came out for our inspection had left.

We had the pictures made on the way to Okinawa with all the insignia blanked out, so they couldn't tell whose airplane it was or what ship it was on. We had some pictures with it strapped to a pylon on the wing with an ordnance man from another squadron pushing a rod down the barrel and calling it a new secret weapon. These photos were sent to Navy Air News, Navy Times, Orlando Sentinel, and Sanford Herald and plastered all over the bulletin boards on the base.

One of our men who had been transferred carried them back and put them in the mail in the States so no one would know where they came from. At the time (squadrons) 1, 7, 9, and 13 were all in the Pacific, so I'm sure there is still debate as to who has it. But, most important of all, we sent a special copy of the picture to Cdr. Kimmons.

Spies on the base tell us they have the wildest rumors on the base you ever heard about where the cannon is. Some of them at the Chief's Club are swearing up and down that Commander de Ganal had it in his stateroom for the whole cruise with RVAH-9. As you can see, we are going to rib them a little more before letting the cat out of the bag, so you have to be selective of what you say about this!

What we would like most is to find some way to get it back there to Sanford and unveil it at Cdr. Webster's change of command when he takes over RVAH-3. It's just too big to do that, so I don't know. Its longevity out here is in jeopardy, though, as several squadrons on here now have their eye on it, and we have to keep it chained to a stanchion in the Ready Room. I expect that during this in-port period in Japan, someone will make the big play to cut that chain and make off with it.

Enough of the history lesson—I've got an early up tomorrow... Give a big kiss to Glyn and James. I love them very, very much.

All my love to you, My Darling, and pleasant Christmas dreams,

I love you, Jimmie

USS Kitty Hawk
Tuesday nite
21 Dec '65

My Darling,

This one is a hard one to start, but I will go ahead with the bad news first. You may have heard that Dave (Johnson) and Lee (Nordahl) are missing in action. They went on a mission and never came out. I haven't heard anything and couldn't tell you if I did. No conversation is to be made of any of it, though.

Please offer my condolences, along with yours, and how sad we all feel about it. The families should have been notified yesterday. I sometimes have difficulty understanding God's ways, but His will is more infinite than the wisdom of any of us. We also are going to be a few more days (delayed) before heading north (to Japan). I may have to celebrate my birthday on board the way it looks now. Things are still quite busy here, though, and the past two days have been minus sleep...

I miss you very much, My Darling,
And I love you forever and always.
All my love, Jimmie

On 23 December the squadron lost a second plane. This time, Jimmie's roommate on the* Kitty Hawk *and his navigator were shot down over Haiphong Harbor. No letters to families were allowed to mention this for several days.

USS Kitty Hawk
December 25, 1965

(Two days after Max and Glen went down)

My Dearest Darlings, all three,

Wishing you a Joyous Noel and a wonderful Christmas to you all. We started our holiday yesterday morning when we left the line, and it is still going strong today as we head north for Japan. I guess the celebration started with a smoker and talent show we had last night in the hangar bay, with lots of fun Christmas songs and goodies to hand out for the crew.

Saint Nick got by here just about sundown last night, and we had a tough time getting him aboard. He got three bolters before we finally rigged the barricade and trapped him aboard. We thought at first he was getting the red nose of the lead reindeer, Rudolph, mixed up with the meatball on the mirror and that was the reason he was having trouble staying on the glide slope. As it turned out, though, it was just that his sleigh didn't come equipped with a tail hook, and he was boltering across the waves.

Well, after we got his goodie bag out and distributed to the group in the Ready Room, we decided to deck launch him so he could beat the sun around the world to the good ole USA.

The first one we got opened was a color film-family-gram, straight from some mighty sweet folks back there in Florida. After much duress and "proper" comments from the audience, our photographic officer finally got the show rolling. We all settled back with much fruitcake and bourbon balls and the afterglow of some earlier private cheer to witness the world's greatest show by our own world's greatest actors.

And Glyn, my little "sweetie pie," you stole the whole show. I thought the Skipper was going to break apart. He had them run that about three times and, though Carol and Carolyn's closing acts were great as they were, I'm afraid they had to take second seat to a little "going-on 5-year-old." Of course your ole dad got a bit of ribbing about strong-willed children and possibilities of where they inherited it from. But, Little Sweetheart, I love you the most, cause you were just naturally you.

And, James, my handsome young man with the nice big smile, I love you the most, too. Especially with your sign of "Hi, Dad" which, as always, shows you're thinking ahead. Here's a "Hi!" back for you, too. Hope you are taking good care of that beautiful doll who was standing behind you. The film was rather dark there, and I couldn't get too good a look, but I would swear she was more beautiful than ever.

I found out for sure a few minutes later when they brought down some mail just delivered from Santa's sleigh. The timing was perfect, because there was a big envelope for me marked "Photographs." And inside was the sweetest bunch of pictures I ever saw. I have the big one sitting here before me right now, and I must have the most beautiful family in the world. If I didn't feel like Christmas before, I took one look at that picture, and it was Christmas all over the world. I thank you all three so very, very much. It couldn't have come at a better time. I needed that lift so badly.

Well, the proofs (of your family portrait) made their rounds naturally, and...Glyn, you have a new ardent admirer, whether you want one or not. Dean Webster spent more time looking at the proofs than I did, and he thinks you are the greatest. It's the first time most any of us have laughed in over a week. I have them all pinned up here now, right over my desk, and it's impossible to look at a couple of them without at least a grin. The proofs will fade, but I'm sure that the love will remain.

...Our Christmas Eve church service came very late, but it was a well done story of the Christ child with music and scripture intertwined. We have a few sailors on here who can sing very well, and so the program was a joy to listen to. I could almost hear the Grace Church junior choir, though, while they were singing "What Child is This"! I hope your Christmas choir program there in Sanford went along as well. If Ophelia taped the music from it, I will anxiously await its arrival and love her all the more for thinking of me.

This morning, I almost didn't make it up for Communion, but I just skipped the shave and caught that and brunch after church was over. Had church and Communion in the hangar bay this morning, but I hope they move it back up to the forecastle tomorrow where there is less noise and a more reverent atmosphere.

Then I got back here in time to open Santa's box from Santa's Workshop back in Sanford! Found all kinds of little goodies that were all kinds of fun to open up. From sweets from my Sweetie to "bat" bow ties (bats are the squadron insignia) to billfolds, all filled with love and chock full of kisses that I will enjoy collecting all summer. In fact, I'll send along a few right now that you can pass around between you and then have an extra kiss apiece just because you love each other. And I thank you all, Dora, James, and Glyn Carol, for a specially nice Christmas.

It's just about time for two sleepy-headed youngsters I know to be shaking out the sugar plums and climbing out of bed to see what Santa has brought. I can see you now just as well as if I were there, and I hope you are enjoying every minute of it. So, while you open your toys, I'll go in and see what's on the Christmas menu.

Later...I'm stuffed! And your "too much Christmas" box is exactly what I need right now. We had a nice slab of rare roast beef, turkey, ham, potatoes and gravy, candied yams, salad, shrimp cocktail, pumpkin pie, etc., etc. I've been kind of off my feed for the past few days, and this was really a catcher upper. I tried to keep it down to a normal consumption, but just had to try a little of everything there.

James and Glyn, I hope the two of you did half so well with your Santa Claus. And, Glyn, I hope you get some of that turkey which you love. Jack told me about the blessing you said at Mrs. Walters' one night. I'll be waiting for a list of all the things you kids got for Christmas. Of course, I expect you to enjoy playing with them first and then write about them later when you have the time. For now, I will just say God bless and a Merry Christmas to you all.

I love you,

Jim

USS Kitty Hawk
Monday Nite
27 Dec 1965

Happy Birthday to Me!

Hi Darling,

This is a heck of a way to spend a birthday, but I guess that's the way it goes. I tried to convince them that I just had to get ashore today, but no one seemed to want to listen. We're still at sea, and we're due in (to port) tomorrow sometime. Maybe it's just as well, since I would have had the duty today anyway, and tomorrow is one of my liberty days. It just seems a crime not to have one wee bit of a celebration. Of course, if I get over soon enough tomorrow, it will still be the 27th of December where you are, and I can pretend we are celebrating together.

If I don't get through this stack of paper in front of me, there won't be any liberty tomorrow, though. As you can probably imagine, my fingers are sore and my back aches from the letter and message writing this past week. (Jimmie is Admin. Officer for the squadron.) I'm going to make good use of one of those hotsi baths as soon as we get there. If I thought it was involved last Christmas, these were four times the amount and as hard if not harder to write, also.

I don't know if you were at Sanford or at Memphis, and if you were at Memphis, I sure hope you found out (about our missing crews) in short order. It was a pretty rough week over all out here and especially so for us. Max and Glenn are missing, and we don't have anything else we can tell you. Naturally, the reason for no talk is for their own possible protection.

We haven't made any squadron shuffles yet, as we don't know who or when we will get as replacements. I do hope they get them on the way soon, though, because (with Max gone) this room is something else again to live with. I know I have to write Rozelle a letter, though, and I just can't work up the nerve. I can't tell her any facts anyway, but I could describe a really great guy.

Please try to give her all the help you can, as I know already you will. And convey my love, too, in case I do turn out to be a complete coward about writing. I have a feeling Anne (Johnson) may need the most help, though. Dave's mother came down to stay with Anne, and I don't know if Rozelle will come right back or stay in Superior....Irene (Daigle) is in Louisiana.

The squadron is holding on pretty well, but you can feel the effect. Most try to see the movies, play cards, work hard at some project or just squadron work to avoid sitting around and talking to each other. I would like very much just to sit and talk to you, even if right here on paper, but right now there are other people with worse problems than mine so that's where the efforts must go.

I do love you so very much, My Darling, and miss you all the more each day. I feel so badly that I can't be there to comfort you and help you when you need me. I hope you can forgive me for being away at a time when your father is ill and you need me to help. Please know, though, that you have all of my love and prayers to lend you whatever strength it can.

Good night, My Darling.

I love you,

Jim

USS Kitty Hawk
Japanese port
Tuesday nite
28 December '65

Hi Honey,

You're just the most beautiful thing in the world. We got into Yokusuka this morning, and I've been opening mail practically ever since. Bunches of letters from you and pictures and snapshots of a living doll. The ones of the kids are beautiful, too.

I also had over 25 cards from well wishers all over, even one from Rev. Oscar Cooper (our pastor when we lived in Ypsilanti) in Manchester, Michigan, lots from home and lots from Sanford and the nicest homemade one from Jamey. I also received a rather intriguing card from Glyn. Wish I had the time to write answers to all of them, but I know that will never be. I put them all on the wall, though, and they do help to cheer up the place.

I need something to warm this place right now, though. The temperature outside is in the low 30s, and it's rather dreary and drizzly. The heat they are pumping through the ventilation system leaves something to be desired; in fact, it feels like the air conditioning is still on. I found the electric space heater over behind my bed this morning, and when I got it out and dusted it off, I thought my knee chattering would be over. But it has a screw type 220 volt plug and guess what? Yep, there isn't a 220 screw-in type outlet anywhere in this room...So, here I am, all wrapped up in robes and teeth chattering trying to send warm thoughts to you.

...I found the goodie place of all goodie places today. Finally got loose for a couple of hours this afternoon and got over to the foreign merchandise building on the base here. I could go broke in there without even pulling out my wallet. So many nice things, you want to buy them all—crystal, china, tape recorders, silk, pearls, paintings, screens, clothes, toys, jewelry, golf and hunting equipment, silverware and silver coffee service. So I just looked today and didn't buy anything. I may go back tomorrow for some little trinkets to send home for the kids. I'm debating whether to save the purchases for later or not.

The Captain said today that we would come back by here on the way home, and he was encouraging everyone to leave things in storage here or wait until we come back to buy large items. He's mainly concerned with fire and theft....

...I doubt if I will try to call you on the phone (while we are in port) because the phones aren't very secure. I'm afraid I might say something about Max or Dave that would get picked up. Let me think about it for a few days. Don't know for sure whether you're in Sanford right now anyway...

I love you, My Darling, so very, very much.

Jim

USS Kitty Hawk
Wednesday nite
29 Dec '65

My Dearest Darling,

I just received your Christmas Eve letter, and the pictures of the kids with their smiling faces fills me with some of the tonic I need. I'm so glad that Santa was able to fill part of their desires and to do so right in the comfort of their own home. The knowledge that they can run and play freely and enjoy the day to their fullest makes up in a large part for the fact that I am not there to enjoy it, too.

...I got tied up here with an ONI man today on an investigation of a homosexual we have—like we don't have enough problems right now. And two other guys whose wives have decided they have found another true love back in Sanford and want a divorce. I'm trying to get them orders back to Sanford so they can straighten out their family mess. The other one I'll take care of here. You know, sometimes when we think we have problems, all we have to do is take five minutes to look around at some other poor soul.

...I had my eyes opened today...We were working on (one of the cases) here in my room and (...one of the men) looked at your picture and made the comment, "You have a beautiful wife." I smiled a thank you and then had to chuckle a bit, because all too infrequently, I fail to notice your physical beauty. You are so beautiful inside as a person that I see right past your face and my heart warms to the beauty of the wonderful person behind it. So, I will tell you now, you are beautiful of face...and it is very much a part of the love I have for you.

But, over the 14 years we've known each other, I've grown to love the personality that makes up you, even more than the appearance that others see. So a photograph to me is beautiful, also, but in a four-dimensional beauty which beams all the brighter. I guess I'm so enchanted by you myself that I fail to notice that other people find you beautiful, also. It thrills me that they do, and it sorrows me, too, that everyone can't be as fortunate as I. I wish that I had the literary talent for poems or such so I could describe all the millions of things you mean to me.

I read the poem Terri (Swenson) sent you, and I can think of the 14 years of light that God has sent us. And if something should happen to one of us, I know that the other must march on in the faith that those fourteen years have brought. We can't ask for better blessings than we have already had.

And if something did happen to me, I can only pray that someday later on, you can find another to share the love that you have in such bounty. It has done so much for me that it should never be shut off and bottled up. And I mean that, Darling, because life is meant to be shared—and shared in God's light.

I wish that I could tell you what you ask about Max, but I cannot. I'm still responsible to him and to his safety and, therefore, I can tell you nothing. I'm still writing the detail of circumstances—on all of them—and believe me, it's the hardest thing I ever did. There is hope in prayer, and how hard I pray. But "missing" is all I can tell you, and please just hold on to that.

I love you, My Darling. You can place all your faith in that.

Your loving husband, Jim

Yokusuka, Japan
Friday nite
31 Dec 1965

Hi Sweetheart,

This is a heck of a way to end the year, but if I can't be with you, I guess I can at least communicate by the best means available. Don't know if you are in Memphis right now or winging your way back to Sanford. Either way, I wish you a Happy New Year.

I've got two big juicy fruit cakes here that I haven't even opened—one from Lois and one from Mary McIntosh. So I could probably have a pretty good celebration on what I could squeeze out of them. Had even thought of staying here and getting some sleep for a change, but that is impossible. So guess I'll amble over to the club around 10 p.m. or so to catch the floor show and raise a couple. Really, I'm forced into it. Ha!

Actually, that's the truth. It's so cold in here right now that I have to blow on my hands to keep them warm enough to write. They have half the Japanese shipyard down here rebuilding that burned-out machinery room. All the hatches are open to bring in the pipes and materials, and my heater doesn't work, and it's below freezing outside.

But the funny part that really is bad is the location of my stateroom door. To get the pipes down into the hatch to the machinery room, they have to open my door, run in about six feet of pipe which extends up over my bed, and then start the other end down the hatch. So at all ungodly hours of the night, Bang, Bang on my door, "Excuse please." The door flies open with light right in my eyes and in comes a little Jap pipe fitter with one end of a pipe that flies around over my head and then vanishes out the door again. These guys are real little charmers that you would have to see to believe, but this same routine five or six times every night between midnight and 4 a.m. is getting old. In fact, after about one more night I'm going to find a bed elsewhere. War is hell!

I think there will be some peace tonight, though. The Japanese New Year lasts about three days, and everybody takes off work. Even the gyp joints in town close up, so I may not see those little elves again for the weekend.

Paul Stokes and I went out playing tourist today, cameras and all. It's such a crowded hustle bustle that I don't think I would want to stay very long. The people are exceptionally clean and polite, so I can see where some folks like this better than Europe.

...We went down to look at the old restored Japanese battleship Misaka, and it's quite an attraction. Then we walked through thieves' alley with all the bars and gyp joints and junk peddlers selling the sailors everything you can think of. It's funny just to go along and read the signs on the front doors of the bars. I don't know if they have any morals or laws, but sometimes, the words get pretty explicit. No wonder these lads come back broke every night.

The rest of the town is more or less like Chinatown in San Francisco or any place with little shops and small one-owner businesses packed as tightly together as you can make them. Everything is built small and to about 3/4 the normal size that I or Paul would need.

We had our going away party for the Skipper last night with the usual digs and skits. They nudged him a little bit, but not too hard, and he took it well. I hate to see him go as I've gotten to the point I can work through him without too much of a problem... The almost 4.0 fitness report he wrote on me the other day won't hurt any, I'm sure. And, actually, he wrote real good reports on all the others, too.

...Oh, nice surprise for Paul Stokes last night. I got his lieutenant's papers in yesterday, so the CO presented them to him last night, dated all the way back to July. That's a nice raise when you have in as many years as he has. We're getting to be a top-heavy squadron here without even trying.

We do have another crew on the way in, Gerry Coffee, but he is already selected for lieutenant commander. I don't know who his B/N is. I'm going to publish a whole new social roster anyway as soon as we get the new people and new jobs assigned. They were supposed to go to RVAH-9 and Bea (Coffee) has been socializing with them, so you might wait until Gerry checks in before you all welcome her into the 13-group. I don't think it makes much difference to Gerry, but I'll bet Jack Youngblade is raising noise because he didn't get him in 9.

...Hope your Dad has pulled though (his illness) okay, and he was able to enjoy your stay at home during the holidays. I know they had enough Christmas to keep you all filled for the next week or so. Maybe (your sister) Charlotte and Larry got there to see you, also.

I do wish you and Jamey and Glyn a Happy, Happy New Year, and maybe we can do enough in the last half of the year to make up for what we will miss during this first six months.

Nite, my darling. Kiss them all another round for me.

I love you,

Jimmie

→ 5 ←

1966 First Vietnam Cruise Continues

Yokusuka, Japan
Sun nite
2 Jan '66

Hi Darling,

Even duty days won't save you around here. I thought that at least I would get half the work done today, but somehow the day is all gone, and I'm right where I started. The chiefs had a going away party for the Skipper this afternoon, and they invited the XO and me over to join them. So here we are, and I would never have known but what it was the first day in port. And me with a change of command to get arranged for tomorrow! An early reveille is the only answer, and if the pipe fitters are back running through my room like they were this morning that won't be hard. I think I will go somewhere else and sleep, though, just for one decent night's rest. It's not that late yet, and if I get an early start, I can catch up on some of it.

We went out to the Komatsu Restaurant last night and dined real Japanese style. The place catered to mostly Japanese, so we had some difficulty with menu translation. Eventually, we got what we wanted, and it was outstanding. It was an interesting place with all the partitioned walls and individual little rooms for dining. The room was cold, but they had a charcoal burner under the table, and the table was warm. They have a quilted edge around the table that wraps around your lap to keep the heat down around your legs. No shoes, of course, so your feet cook while your head freezes. Even the hot saki got cold before we could drink it. We had tempura and sukiyaki, and it was great. We went chopsticks all the way—except for the Skipper—and it was fun. This Kobe beef is really good, so I can't complain about the food, though I like French better.

Of course, in France they don't have the hotsi bath, and that's another story all its own. I got your news clipping about the hotsi baths, so I had to try one out. They actually walk up and down your spine with their foot, and that loosens up spots you didn't even know were supposed to be loose. And bones popped that I didn't know I had.

It turns out, a steam bath comes before the massage. And the little girls walking on your back may be the Japanese way of getting back at "ugly Americans." The parlors cater to men and women alike, but mostly to Japanese businessmen. They take you right around, stripped bare, to a steam cabinet and leave you until you are lobster red, then to a pool bath of boiling hot water, followed by a rubdown with hot towels, and finally an oil bath massage that leaves you so unwound that any illicit thoughts you might have had are long gone!

...Pleasant dreams. Nite, my sweet.

I love you,

Jimmie

Yokusuka, Japan
Thursday nite
6 Jan '66

My Dearest Darlings, All three,

It was so nice to talk to you this morning...It was really a fine connection. I called the Tokyo operator and gave her the number, and by the time she had said, "Wait one..." you were answering right up. You must have only let the phone ring once.

...Glyn, I'm sorry to hear about your chicken pox, but I'm real glad you waited until you got back home to break out with it. You sounded really chipper about the whole thing, though. You're my number one sweet gal. I hear you are the best little doll dresser around there.

James, I'm glad you liked that weapons plaque, and that long tie (you got for Christmas) sounds like the real thing. I'll see if I can find you one of those Japanese pearl tie clasps to go with it. Maybe they will have some boys' size hand-painted ties here, too, but I haven't seen any.

Wish I could have talked longer to you, but I seemed to be reverting to mostly er's and ah's at that point.

...Our change of command went off really well on Monday. I think our new XO found out that if you don't sweat things too hard, they will work themselves out. It was simple and fast and got the job done. Cdr. Webster was sorry to leave in one way, but glad in another. He must have set a record getting home because (with another baby on the way) Mary Lois needs him now as much as she ever will.

The new CO was so sick with a cold he almost wasn't able to talk. Roy (McLain) can't get used to being called Skipper. We think he will do well, though, and the new XO is one little bundle of energy. Charlie (Putnam) and I had to leave the reception early Monday to ride on out to Atsugi to fly on Tuesday. It's a 12 1/2 hour trip that winds through the little side roads and narrow streets. This side of Japan seems to be just one big city, and no one knows what it means to drive over 40 miles an hour. Usually, you average 15 to 25 miles per hour.

We didn't get to fly on Tuesday because it rained and snowed so bad. Then yesterday it was absolutely beautiful with freezing cold temperatures, but the sky was clear and the sun was bright. So we flew over and took pictures of Fuji. Then we flew around the main island to look at Tokyo from the air. The city is so large, you just can't believe it. The white blanket of snow up in the mountains hovering over little villages in the valley was beautiful.

We spent some time getting an airplane fixed then went out again late last night. It was another calm, cold winter night. The moon was almost full, and the scenery was like something you'd see in a movie. Tokyo is the prettiest city at night I have ever seen. They have so many colored lights over here, the whole place just twinkles.

I flew right over the top of Mt. Fuji, and with the white snow at night, it is magnificent. The moon just lit up the whole scene. I'd give anything to have a color picture just the way it looked last night, but I don't think anyone has ever been able to make one like that. You would have to hang in a blimp at about 15,000 feet for a very long time exposure. The secret of all this Japan beauty is that "distance lends beauty." Up close, it's not so hot at all.

So I'm glad you don't have that Japanese charm. Because the closer I get to you, the more beautiful you become—and that's the way I want it—close to you...I'm sure when I am there I will remember Japan as more beautiful, too. Here's to that day.

I love you,

Jimmie

USS Kitty Hawk

7 Jan '66

Dear James,

I don't know if you are still keeping your scrapbook of planes or not, but this should fill up a page or two. I haven't seen this before, but it has just about all the airplanes the navy uses and some that aren't even out yet.

I'll have to send this regular mail, so it may be quite a while getting there.

Love, Dad

USS Kitty Hawk

Saturday nite,

Off Japan

8 Jan '66

Hi Darling,

...We're still in port, waiting for repairs to the engine room, but we expect to leave here tomorrow afternoon...

Our replacement planes got here today, and I got advance copies of Gerry Coffee's and Ltjg. Bob Hanson's orders, so I guess they are officially ours. You probably already have the word and have invited Bea to join your group. When I talked to C.C. Smith the other day, he said all of Gerry's gear was on the Ranger. Apparently, he already had orders to RVAH-9 before they left, so they carried all his gear back out to the ship with them when they were home in December.

Today I moved over into the single room across the hall, so the new crew can have my double room. It's a lot smaller than what I had, but without a roommate, I will have a lot more storage space, and I won't have to battle for the sink. I guess we will start trading jobs around, too, in a couple of weeks; then maybe everyone can get back on an even keel. We will still be a couple of officers short for quite a while I expect.

...I don't know if it's the change in room or if it's just cooled down outside, but it's COLD in here. This room has the same problem as the other one, too—no plug for a heater. We won't have much to do tomorrow anyway, since most everyone is at Atsugi, waiting to fly the planes back to the ship. I'm ahead of everyone on carrier landings now, so I don't get to fly a plane out.

I wanted to tell you more about Japan. The people are very polite and clean, and the insides of their houses are clean, but the outside and the cities are filthy. There is no grass to speak of, and everything is rocks and dirt and dust. Even their tiny backyards are dirt and rocks with dwarfed trees and very few flowers. The benjo is the bathroom, and you've heard of the benjo ditches. They are open slots that run alongside every street and down to large canal-type benjo ditches. The whole sewer system is one big open ditch, so you can understand why some people say Japan smells like one big sewer.

There is no countryside. Every place that is flat enough has a house on it or is farmed in some sort of a little truck patch. I've never seen so many people in my life. They drive on the left side of the road, like they do in England, and even with the little cars, the traffic is something to compare with Los Angeles.

Prices are low, and service is service—everywhere. Jamey might find it interesting that they have almost all lady barbers. Even the street sweepers are old women. And, actually, many of the laborers are women—coal miners as well as pearl divers. As you can tell, I didn't exactly flip over this quaint little country. I can see where a lot of people would like it, but I don't think I will place it at the top of my choices for duty.

The way this war is going, I'm not too sure how far ahead to plan on duty anyway. I say I'm not pessimistic, but we are going right back in the same thing we left behind in December. They have stopped bombing for who knows how long, but our reconnaissance work goes on. I know I catch myself not planning ahead more than one day at a time, and it's sure a miserable way to live. I'll tell you that. But letters just aren't the place for that type of discussion, so we'll just have faith. We'll talk it over when I get home.

...I'll just climb in bed now and hope a night of pleasant dreams will float via Telstar to give you the message:

I love you so very, very much,

Always, your loving husband, Jim

USS Kitty Hawk
Sunday nite
9 Jan '66

Hi Honey,

We're back on the road again—about time, too. From the looks of some of these troops, I don't know if they would have lasted another day in port. Of course, most of our crews are on the beach ready to fly the planes out, so we don't have a very representative showing yet anyway.

I haven't seen Gerry (Coffee) or the new JG yet. The new B/N is Ltjg Bob Hanson, and he does have a wife living in Winter Park. I'll put out a new social roster with everyone on it as soon as I can collect all the information.

...I'm sitting here munching on some of those Christmas goodies, and it makes it almost like home. Almost, I said! Mother says she sent me a prune cake, but so far, there is no sign of it. Lois sent some bourbon balls, and I've passed around some of the things you sent, but I still have batches left here.

I got the picture frame, too, but the glass was in itsy bitsy pieces. It was too tall to fit in my desk, but in this room I have a spot to put the picture right beside the head of the bed. Now I can see all three of you first thing each morning. I put in some plastic in place of the glass, so that solved that problem....I have to send thank you notes to Mary (McIntosh) and Lois, so I will write more tomorrow. Here are a couple of Japanese coins for Jamey. I will send him more later. These are 100 yen and 1 yen. It takes 360 yen to make a dollar.

Nite, My Darling,

I love you,

Jimmie

10 Jan 1966

Dear James,

It was nice to talk to you and to Glyn the other day. Wish we could have talked longer, but that costs a lot when calling all the way from Japan to Sanford. Did you know that was more than half the way around the world since the call went by way of the other side! It was nice and clear, though, and sounds like you are doing fine.

Seems like a mighty big boy if you have your own tie and can tie it yourself. I sent a couple of Japanese coins to you in a letter to

Mother yesterday, and I will put a few more in here. The Japanese money is called yen and it takes 360 yen to make one dollar. So one yen is worth about one third of a penny, and the 10 yen equals about three pennies.

Don't know if I spoke to you about it, but your report card looked ok to me. Mom says you are doing well and that your Cub Scout den won the Christmas window decorations contest. I'm real proud of that, and I guess you got Bobby Fraser into the best den there, didn't you? Hear you all have had some pretty good football games over there, too, while I have been gone.

We had a good stay in Japan, and I ate some of their raw octopus and things like that. Had a hard time with the little houses, though—bumping my head all the time; and their little cars don't leave anywhere to put my knees. Don't think I could stay here very long. A funny thing about their doors. They all slide sort of like our closet doors, and they don't have hinges like we do. Even on the old battleship I went to visit, they had sliding doors, too.

Well, have fun at school and write me a note when you can. Won't be long till swimming time and that will be real fun.

Give Mom and Glyn a big kiss.

Love,

Dad

USS Kitty Hawk
At Sea
10 Jan '66

Hi Darling,

...We have Gerry Coffee moved in across the way in my old room, and Jim Morgan is with him. We had some flying today, and we're supposed to have more tomorrow.

Just want to send you this (Christmas card with the Griffin house in Forked Deer on it) and a pack of love and kisses, too.

I
L
O
I L O V E Y O U
E
Y
O
U

Nite, Sweetheart,
Jimmie

USS Kitty Hawk
"Free"
Thursday nite
13 Jan '66

My Dearest Darling,

...We're back on the line again (in combat zone) tonight, as you will note by the "free" air mail. I don't know if that will speed things up or slow things down. We had a mild flail this week about mail delivery when we got a message from CNO about a congressional inquiry into a mail complaint from the wife of one of our enlisted men. It seems he had written comments back like I've made to you about the VIPs taking up all the COD space, leaving no room for mail delivery while at Yankee Station. She wrote her congressman, and he must have been one of those that got turned down on a junket out here, because he has been raising a big stink in Washington about the VIPs delaying mail delivery.

The poor enlisted man was scared to death until we told him it was all right, and maybe it would get us faster mail delivery.

Of course I had to write the letter to answer CNO, so we just took a survey and gave them the facts. It is taking an unusually long time to get mail. In fact, the COD came out today full of VIPs and no mail. I think the last letter I got from you was dated 2 January—but it's nothing the congressman can help.

As long as your letters keep saying "I love you," I don't quibble too much over the date. You never have been fickle enough to run out on me with only two weeks notice, have you?!

I wrote Mom, John, and Barbara tonight, so with most of the backlog out of the way I can concentrate on you for the near future. I have an early, early up tomorrow morning, so I don't know but what I might as well stay up. We're on the midnight-to-noon schedule this time, and I can see that this is going to be a sleepless week. We won't be down here quite as long this time before we go back into port, though. I wish I could say you were meeting me there, but that long, long trip is too much to ask of anybody. And with the price of that we can have a real honest-to-goodness honeymoon when I do get home.

...I would like to slip off into dreamland right now with thoughts of eiderdown and you and me.

Pleasant dreams, my love,

I love you, Jimmie

USS Kitty Hawk
"Free"
Friday nite
14 Jan '66

My Dearest Darling,

Forgive me for always cutting you short on letters, but the day always seems to end that way. I was up at 4 a.m. this morning, and I have to make an early flight tomorrow, so this witching hour should find me sound asleep.

The busyness these days comes from working at two jobs while I try to shift over to Operations and keep Admin going at the same time. I hope to have the swaps done by the time I hit port, and then I can settle down to one job again. The new troops we have seem real fine, so even though we will be short-handed, things should smooth out soon.

It was worth staying up tonight just to get two very sweet letters from you. I won't have time to answer them tonight, but I will get to them tomorrow. Of course there is no Saturday or Sunday (time off) out here, so I will have to fit things in as they come.

..I had one other piece of interesting correspondence tonight. It came down from Main Communications in a sealed envelope marked "For Cdr. Griffin's eyes only." My first thought was, "What the hell did I do now?" Especially since I made a supersonic boom across the bows of a group of Russian destroyers up off Formosa last week and had a batch of admirals up in arms. Ha!

Well, it turned out to be a message from the Enterprise, marked CO to Cdr. Jim Griffin and signed by Jim Holloway. He just wanted to say hello and glad to see us down here and hopes to see me soon. Now PacFleet has instructions out to send only operational messages out here, but J.L. never did sweat those things too much. I would like to see him, but they are due to leave tomorrow to head for their stint in a liberty port. I don't know where they are going right now since the nuclear boat is limited somewhat in who will let them come into port.

I hope the kids are all well by now and Glyn can get back out to play. Tell Jamey not to sweat those glasses. He doesn't know how proud we are of the way he takes care of them. Most kids would have broken or lost three or four pairs in the time he has had those. And I have bent and straightened those frames three or four times myself, expecting them to snap every time. So he shouldn't worry about something that he is already doing better than everybody else. I'm glad to see he takes an interest in taking care of things, though.

I wish I could be there to take care of some things myself. Mainly you. With lots of tender loving care. And you know how much I care, and care, and care. Nite for now, My Darling.

I love you,

Jimmie

USS Kitty Hawk
Saturday nite
15 Jan '66

Hi Darling,

Time kinda marches on by here...After all that early up and briefing this morning, I still didn't get out on my flight. I had a hydraulic leak, so I only got as far as the catapult. We're starting to have our aircraft problems again now, but that's mostly because they sat on the ground while we were in port, I suspect. It was a beautiful day today, too, with some of the first clear blue sky we have seen down here on Yankee Station.

Before I get too far along here, I had better remember to get you up-to-date on my checkbook. I had one check for January mess bill, naturally: #875 on 1/8/66 to Wardroom Mess, USS Kitty Hawk $40.00. The bill went up to 40 dollars because we had about 50 days running there with everyone eating on the ship. It should come back down next month after the two weeks we spent in Japan.

I got paid today also, so I am mailing the check to the bank. Deposit on 1/16/66 $361.00 which should help balance the cost of your trip to Memphis and my mess bill. I think that included my combat pay for November, after taxes, that is. I still don't have the combat pay for December since they are always a couple of months behind on that.

The fact is that trying to keep track of all this special pay for this and that, it has been the biggest headache in the squadron so far. I can't see why they don't just come through with a blanket pay raise, and then just rotate everyone through a tour over here if they are worried about some earning it more than others.

Tell James I'll start practicing up at Yahtze, so I can give him a go at it when I get home. It's an old Japanese bar game that is still the most popular around the country. But they play it very seriously, and anyone caught cheating or being a poor loser would be an outcast for life. The rules vary a little from place to place, but once the rules are established, you can lose a good friend by just breaking one of those rules. It is a lot of fun, though, and the Japanese people thoroughly enjoy it. It's one of the favorite games of the geishas.

...Do you know when Rozelle will be back in Sanford and what her address is in Madison? I have some money and registered items to send her, but we don't have an address, so she can sign a receipt for them. I need that info as soon as you can get it.

...I know it's hard to live on letters, Darling. But I dearly love you all.

Nite, Sweetheart.

I love you,

Jim

USS Kitty Hawk
Monday nite
17 Jan '66

My Darling,

Wish I had you with me these last few hours. I haven't laughed so much in years as at the movie we just saw, "Good Neighbor Sam" with Jack Lemmon. When it started off, I thought I had already seen the movie, but then as it went on, I remembered that I had only read the book and not seen the movie...Everyone laughed all the way through it.

The squadron has been loose as a goose the past two weeks, and the movie every night routine is just a part of it. I think it's going to have to tighten up in a few days, but no one is in any hurry to jump into it. Things seem to move along anyway, and I expect the pace will be set by what work we have to do.

Ray Vehorn...sent me a letter that I got today saying he got a thumbs-up on his ear (surgery recovery). Now just has a physical and a medical review board to go. If those are okay, he should re-carrier qual with RVAH-3 on the 24th and then head on out here to join us. I sure hope it all turns out for him, because we need him out here.

With the usual horny comments during the movie tonight, the XO said later, "Gee, you guys haven't been gone that long, you know." Then he thought about it for a second and added, "Well, I guess you have if I count all the way back to July." I asked him just where the hell else did he expect to count back to. Actually, that time does seem to have gone fast, Darling...I just hope the remainder of the time can pass as rapidly. I'm not going to start counting days or even months, but it can't be as long as it has been.

I just look forward to the day when I can settle back down to the comfort of your arms, and if the kids want to climb all over me, that will be all right, too. I can sit here and look at a picture of a mighty pretty family group and imagine how it will feel to envelop all three in one big hug with lots and lots of kisses. And I've got a signed certificate for an IOU of quite a few—among your Christmas presents!

I get some fine dreams, just thinking back over some mighty fond memories of the sweet times we have had together. Maybe that's what makes the time go fast. Just the multitude of sweet memories that is so great I can't possibly recall them all. Here's to the day when we can bank up a whole year's supply in just a short time together.

Sweet dreams, Sweetheart.

I love you,

Jimmie

USS Kitty Hawk
"Free"
Tuesday nite
18 Jan '66

My Dearest Wife,

```
      I
      L
      O
I L O V E   Y O U
      E
      Y
      O
      U
```

Your loving husband,

Jimmie

USS Kitty Hawk
"Free"
Wednesday Nite
19 Jan '66

Hi Darling,

I have to get a little shuteye early here tonight, as I have the wee hours 0200 launch. It's too early to sleep, but at least I can lie here and slumber. We're getting all kinds of weird hours' flights now, so I'll be glad when we shift to the other schedule so we can work on a reasonably regular basis. It may not change this time out, so I guess it's best just to relax and get used to it.

Bill Westerman finally got here to the ship yesterday. He asked how you and the kids were doing. He looks the same as ever and acts likewise....I don't remember if I ever told you that the reason one of the squadrons out here is getting a lot of new people is that they had some guys turn their wings in....I guess a lot of people have wanted to, but they were the only ones that did. We all get scared, and sometimes, it's even hard to eat or sleep or just sit around and think about it, but I don't think this is the time to quit. I guess all of us have thought about it many times over, but right now, we are obligated to ourselves and to the folks at home. I'll tell you one thing, there is not much of the old fun to flying here; most of it is deadly serious. But every once in a while, we get a regular fun hop and then remember about (our love of) flying.

...Sounds like the Cub Scout soapbox derby will be a true labor of love—and blisters. Wish I could be there to help you and Jamey, but it sounds like you have things well under control. I hope he understands that building it is supposed to be the big thing, and the race is just an added attraction. I wish him lots of luck in the

race, though. Maybe Glyn will be over her chicken pox in time to cheer him on.

I'm missing you all a bunch, and when things go slow I miss you even more. Seems I have time then to think of all the things we could do to make better use of that spare time. We always did manage to use it up pretty well.

...I love you.

And Jamey, too, and Glyn, too, Jim

USS Kitty Hawk
"Free"
Saturday nite
22 Jan '66

Hi Darling,

...We had a little additional ceremony tonight to commemorate a 500th landing. The CO got his 500th arrested landing yesterday, so we took the hook point off the aircraft and had the galley bake and decorate a cake for presentation ceremonies tonight. Most of the West Coast sailors on the ship out here never heard of doing that, so we told them we would indoctrinate them with a little East Coast tradition. We still have to get the thing plated and engraved, but that should be easily done in Hong Kong. The damn thing must weigh 20 pounds, though. I told them we should have swiped one off an A-4, so you could at least mount it on a plaque.

...We've got Gerry Coffee and the new XO well broken in now, so I guess they are pure bat shit like all the rest of us! I'm not sure Gerry feels on solid ground yet, but the XO (Charlie Putnam) sure does. This bunch can rattle your cage before you know it if you don't know who you are talking to. I think the XO finally figured out

that there was a lot of talk but not much bite, and if you let them alone, they get the job done.

I see where the gals have already welcomed their wives into the group. It's not exactly the circumstances they would like to have come in under, I'm sure, but they should make happy additions.

...Hard to believe this cruise has been as long as it has. But worse yet is the length of time we still have to go. We'll make it, though, Sweetheart, and if prayers and hope can make it, the time will pass as quickly as before.

I'm anxiously awaiting the soap box derby results. I had the wrong picture of what was going on until Frank Branson gave me all the details, since his son has been an annual entry. Now, it sounds even more fun, and I do miss not being there to help. Get James to send me a picture and tell me all about it—particularly Mom's mashed fingers.

I have to get back with the flying program tomorrow, and with luck, we will return to the day-to-night schedule to get our metabolism back in place. I guess we shouldn't complain too much, since there are people who don't ever get a hot meal or a good night's sleep in this war!

My sleep would be better, though, if I had you here to snuggle up beside me. And you do snuggle so nicely. Maybe that's the pleasure that I never can explain, just holding you closely wrapped in my arms. That's a feeling I can almost dream my way into. So I think I'll try it right now. Give Glyn and Jamey a kiss for me.

I love you all so very, very much,

Jimmie

USS Kitty Hawk
"Free"
Sunday nite
23 Jan '66

My Darling,

I
L
O
V
E
Y
I L O V E Y O U
U

Always,
Jimmie

USS Kitty Hawk
"Free"
Tuesday Nite
25 Jan '66

Hi Darling,

This month is easing along more rapidly each day. I guess that's because we are flying more now than we ever have, and with less people, everyone has enough extra jobs to keep them busy. The weather is getting lousy again, but it was at least a nice night out there for night flying tonight.

I had a letter from Mother today with all her exclamations about flying. It seems she took to it well enough; now she has questions to ask about this and that. I believe she left the West Coast all in good repair, so now she has nothing to do at home but sit and worry about Gene and the draft. And, actually, for their sakes, I do hope now that he doesn't have to go.

There was a sweet letter from you today, also. You know, maybe that letter written by one of our enlisted wives to her congressman may have done some good after all. We've really had good mail service this time out, and the one I got today only took about five days. And we've had mail call about every other day!

Hope ole Ray Vehorn can get on one of those fast planes out. Maybe we can get him in four or five days, too, then we can get him here before we leave the line. He should be carrier qual'd by now, and who knows, he may even be in Hawaii tonight. The XO and I were talking last night, or rather this morning early, and he was concerned about our not having a "court jester" for the squadron. He thinks that he and the new CO are too serious. So I told him not to sweat it, because the best (jester) in the business is on the way, and he will find that out as soon as he meets Ray.

...I'm glad to know you got the slides of pictures I took in Japan...I can't remember all that was on that roll, but I do recall finishing up the last one or two shots at the Japanese battleship. I'll be sending more later. Tell Jamey not to worry too much about counting the bullet holes on my plane in those pictures. I have some more on the back that he can't even see. And tell him Mr. Walters probably has a few more on the back as well.

...Honey, I miss you so much. Nite for now.

I love you, Jimmie

USS Kitty Hawk
"Free"
Friday Nite, 28 Jan

Hi Darling,

The squadron has settled down to normal, and we are getting more flying than ever before. In fact, I fly every day now, and the planes are doing better now that we fly them more often. It's really good for the men in the squadron to get the planes airborne regularly.

Today the big rub was trying to get the new job assignments all laid out. The XO and I have worked on it every night for a week now, and I'm sure the Skipper redid everything we set up, but that's his prerogative. I knew there were some changes he wouldn't go along with anyway, but I decided to let Charlie go ahead and get his feet wet. He probably thinks I led him down the primrose path, but it was worth a try anyway. He's sure fine to get along with, and he's a real charger right from the start.

...I hope Rozelle is back in Sanford now. I haven't written her because I didn't have her address at her mother's in Madison, and, though I wish I had some information about Max that would reassure her, I don't have any more news than Cdr. Webster had....

Dora, we haven't changed our job here. Even with "no bombing" in North Vietnam, we still fly our regular photo missions. The others don't go there anymore, but we do. I think some of the guys have let their wives believe that all of us were out of there, and I don't want you telling them any different. But I don't want you to think that I have ever told you anything to the contrary. It's a little better, since they (the Vietcong) are not stirred up, but not an awful lot...

Honey, I guess I appreciate you more each day. All I have to do is look around me, and you become a star...It is personal integrity and self-respect, I guess, and in both, you're straight A! I really can't explain, but I do hope you understand how I feel. I can be completely in the dumps, and just start naming things about you that I like, and the whole world becomes a new day.

....I love you, I love you, I love you, Jim

P.S. A hug and a kiss for Jamey and Glyn. Tell them I miss them, too.

USS Kitty Hawk
"Free"
Monday Nite
31 Jan '66

My Darling,

I got your letter and cards, all from the trip to West Palm Beach, today. Thanks so much for the pictures. Glyn is growing so fast, I won't even have a baby anymore when I get home. And tell her thanks so much for the valentine. She can be my little bunny girl anytime!

Sounds like you all had a pleasant trip, and I'm sure the kids had a ball. Did Jamey learn to ride that skateboard while he was down there? I'm sure (his cousin) Wayne has put it to good use, so I wonder whether he taught Jamey what to do with one.

...(As for the news about moving the Sanford base up to Georgia), I guess we can be thankful again that George Kimmons convinced us we should rent (rather than buy). I saw some information in a copy of the Sanfly (base newsletter) about the things homeowners will have to do to get the FHA to take a house back, and it isn't an easy process...I understand the plan at Turner Field is to make

it into a master reconnaissance base with VFP, VAP, and RVAH there, so there may be a lot more people than just Sanfordites up there. And those plans make the move seem more certain.

I hate for us to have to move, Honey, but sooner or later, we have to move somewhere, and so far we've always made out pretty well. I guess when we are together, it makes up for a lot of things. Right now it seems like the all-important part is to get back together again, regardless of where it is.

I sure miss you all a lot...I appreciate and love my family more than anything there could ever be. It seems everything is all right when we are together and all wrong when we're apart. I miss some cute kids climbing over me that I love an awful lot and some loving arms around me that I've grown so accustomed to for years. I'm glad we've got such pleasant memories, Darling. It makes the time go a lot faster out here. Give everyone an extra big hug for me.

I love you all so very much. Nite, Darling, I love you, Jimmie

USS Kitty Hawk
"Free"
Wednesday
2 Feb. 1966

Hi Darling,

...One more day and we get away from this place for a couple of weeks of liberty. Cubi isn't much liberty, of course, but we can at least have a party or two there, and they do have tennis courts and a swimming pool. We are also going to try and work in our one-day jungle survival school this time in. I hear these headhunter instructors are really something worth seeing anyway, and I'm not sure they allow cameras.

I hate to rub it in, but I don't think you will begrudge me a couple of afternoons at the pool soaking up a little sun. Actually, I really need it as the only time I've seen the sun in the past couple of months is through a Plexiglass canopy with a hardhat on. I'm so bleached white now that I will probably get burned the first day in Cubi. The temperature has been running around 80 degrees, so maybe it won't be too bad.

Of course we have to avoid getting our tails shot off tomorrow to get a chance to find out. And here lately that hasn't been the easiest task we ever ran into. I read in the paper today that the war in the north is back on again. That just gets them all stirred up again and doesn't help our job any. Actually, they seem to be better shots now than they were before, and recent hits seem to prove it. Not our squadron—as you know, you would have seen that by message by now if it were us. But we were getting by pretty well up there as long as we (recon planes) were the only ones going in. It sure leaves you time to wonder about a lot of this mess, though.

I expect I will fly off early to Cubi on Friday, just to get a little head start. There are some advantages to this new job of Operations Officer. We have most of the job shuffle done now, except for having Ray take over Maintenance. And we'd still like to know where he is. Al Perrella is taking Admin, and Gerry Coffee will have Safety, and Dick Daum will be Assistant Maintenance. There is some turnover in the junior jobs, but not a lot.

I did fight for Jack to get Line Officer, so he could have a big division officer job in his record. Jack is going to extend and apply for regular (he is now in the Reserves), so he needs that in his record...We're probably the most junior squadron in the Wing now, including the relative rank of the new CO and XO, and the Skipper wants to make a good showing.

(Later)...We had very good teriyaki steak tonight. In fact, it was so good I decided to have two. I may as well, since our mess bill this month is back up to $40 after we were promised a drop to $35...I dream of the day when we are together again.

Nite, My Love.

I love you always, Jimmie

(The next letter is written just after Jimmie learns of Dora's father's death.)

USS Kitty Hawk
"Free"
Thurs nite
3 Feb '66

My Darling,

I regret so much that I can't be there to help comfort you tonight. I got the message this morning from the Wing, notifying me that your father had died and that you were driving to Memphis. Of course, I will worry until you get there and back, but I intend to fly into Subic tomorrow and see if I can call and talk with you in Memphis.

Darling, I know you can't expect or be prepared for things like this, but Mr. Smith has been on the verge of this for quite some time. I'm just so thankful that you flew up there for Christmas and that (your sister) Charlotte came, too.

I know how much you loved him, and I thought a lot of him, also. In fact, I've admired him since I was a little kid. I only hope that my daughter can love me the way you loved him, and I hope you always understood the way that man loved you. I never was able to understand or feel it until I had a daughter of my own, and then I could recognize what he really felt for you. Then, once I did realize it, it explained a lot of things, even back as far as the days when we were still in the dating stage. I doubt he ever told you how he felt, and probably you didn't tell him, but he knew anyway.

I'm just thankful for him that he has been commended to God, and I'm sure he has found a happy rest. He was too helpful and generous to others to be any other way. My dad will have to tell you someday about some of the sacrifices your father had made for you to really appreciate him.

I'm worried about Mother Smith more than anything else. We must do everything we can to be of help to her. I hope she will keep on working just to keep herself busy, but I know it will be hard on her for a while.

...Darling, it bothers me so much when I can't be with you at a time like this. It's times like these when I wonder so much about this job which keeps me away for long periods at a time.

I so hate to put this in this letter, Sweetheart, but it did happen today, and you will know anyway by the time you get the letter. We lost our newest flight crew today, and so I've spent most of the night writing messages and letters on casualty reports. I feel so sorry for those girls (Bea and Pat) since they have only been gone such a short time, and the girls never really got to be a part of the squadron. Gerry and Bob were fine additions to 13, and we were all so glad to get them. I feel so bleached dry from all of this, and I can only tell you that they are missing. There have been so many now, though, that I must tell you at least that I think their chances of being alive are fairly good. But in reality, that is just my opinion.

Anyone who isn't convinced that this is a real war now—well, I don't know what it takes. Honey, I'm almost running out of guts, tears, prayers, and whatever else it takes to go with it. But right now your problems at home are more important, so forgive me for transgressing to mine for a moment. It doesn't take anything from the love and care that I have for you. Please know that my love and prayers are with you and with (your mother) Mrs. Aletha. Help her know that I feel for her, also.

I wish I could help you explain to the children, but I think Jamey understands and maybe it's better if he explains to Glyn. God bless our son. I love him more than I can ever say.

I'll try to write your mother tonight, also. I don't know what I will say, but I will try.

I love you, Darling
And pray for you,
Your husband, Jimmie

USS Kitty Hawk
The Philippines
Sunday Nite
6 Feb '66

Hi Darling,

It was nice to talk to you on the phone, even though I could only hear part of what you had to say. At the time when I should have done the most talking to you, I couldn't find the right words. You sounded in reasonably good spirits, and that's what I most wanted to hear.

The Skipper and I flew in Friday in the only two airplanes we had left that weren't broken in some way. I primarily came in so I could call you while you were still in Memphis (for the funeral). We got here too late to phone that night, so I waited until Saturday morning, so I wasn't intentionally trying to wake you up at midnight. It's just that it took me five hours to get the call through.

...Please give the kids a hug and a kiss for me. I love you all,

Always, your lover,

Jimmie

USS Kitty Hawk
The Philippines
Tuesday nite
8 Feb '66

Hi Darling,

I have become a lousy letter writer...and a lazy one, too. I don't mean to be, I assure you of that. I love you more than ever and want to remind you of it every day. I won't give excuses or promises since with the shuffle these next few days with planes to be flown out to the ship, I doubt if I will be near my desk very often.

We had a rip snorter of a day yesterday with a squadron all hands party over on Grande Island here in the bay. They have a very nice recreation facility out there, except it's about a two-mile boat ride to get there. Of course we took the slow but more fun way to get there. We checked out two L-14 sailing boats from the facility. With the XO and me in one and Frank (Bransom) and Paul (Stokes) in the other, we sailed out of there. It was fine going because the wind was mostly to our backs, but coming back we had to tack back and forth into the wind and it was really rough.

They had the small boat warnings out due to high winds, but we had to get them home anyway. The XO was signed out for the boats, so we told him it could only cost him his command if he lost one. The Skipper came back with the XO and me, and there wasn't a dry stitch on a one of us by the time we got back to the ship. It seemed we had more green water coming into the boat than there was outside of it. It really was a lot of fun, though, but I have rope-burned hands, and I can hardly hold this pencil. Not to mention my sunburned head.

When we got back, after fighting the headwind all the way, it was long past chow time on the ship, so we had to go to the club for dinner. I'm not sure what happened there, but we didn't get away until quite late, and we somehow missed out on the survival school class this morning. They wanted us to spend overnight in the woods, though, and I couldn't see that when I needed to be here writing a letter to you.

I would like to send you a nice, sexy valentine, but the only ones they had left on this base were "To my husband" or "To a wonderful guy," etc. So you may have to be satisfied with a homemade, old-fashioned "I love you."

Give the kids a huggy, lovey valentine kiss for me, too.

I love you all so very much.

Nite, My Darling,

Jimmie

USS Kitty Hawk
Philippines
Thursday morning
10 Feb '66

Hi Darling,

Just a quick note here in the breeze before we head back out to the boat. The ship pulled out this morning, and the Skipper and I will fly out this afternoon. I've got to get the last couple of hours of sun around the pool to try to even out the light spots. This hard life around here is really difficult to take. Ha!

Actually, we've been conducting business since Jim Olson just got back from seeing RVAH-7 and 9, so we're getting feedback on how they are doing and answers to some questions we sent out to them. It would be a nice way to do business if we had a permanent traveling ambassador to relay between us. I think I will try to set something up so we can visit back and forth about once a month. Right now, there is a lot of stuff we would like to pass around, but we don't dare put it all in print.

...The lack of a (store-bought) valentine doesn't mean that I don't think of you. With you and me, every day is Valentine's Day anyway. I just hope the little box of presents reached you in time.

Your arms, your lips, they are the best,
But most of all, I love the rest.
Happy Valentine's, Darling,
I love you,
Jimmie

USS Kitty Hawk
Hong Kong
Sunday afternoon
13 Feb '66

Hi Honey,

....Just had a priority message from Ray Vehorn at Cubi asking what to do. There is nobody on board except for a few of us who have duty, so it took a while to get him an answer underway. I started to put him a "Sorry 'bout that" for missing Hong Kong, but I didn't think the Command Duty Officer would release it that way. At any rate, we will pick him up about the end of the week, and it won't hurt him to get a little sunshine and pool time

at Cubi. He probably needs to thaw out from that winter carrier qual period anyway.

...This is really a bustling place, and most buildings are vertical with 25 to 30 floors. I can't see the top of Victoria Peak because of the clouds. We've had weather like they have in England for the past two days, so it makes all the limeys around here feel really at home. For that reason, I haven't taken any pictures. Tomorrow, I will try, regardless of the weather.

This place is clean, though, and you don't have to fight beggars off along the streets. I don't know how they cured them of that, but you can actually walk along and window shop with perfect peace of mind. It wasn't that way a few years ago from what most people tell me.

Well, it's about ferryboat time, and that's a cold 45-minute ride, so I'd better get my coat on. I may not feel much like writing tomorrow, but you know I love you all the same.

A kiss for Jamey and Glyn,

I love you,

Jimmie

USS Kitty Hawk
"Free"
Wednesday morning
16 Feb '66

Hi Darling,

...We had the usual shipboard panic as we pulled out of Hong Kong yesterday, and it carried well into the night. There were some new reporting procedures, etc. that no one was aware of...Actually, we were mostly in a fog after the three parties in a row. Naturally, the wetting down party last night was the most (debilitating) of all.

We need about two days recuperation for everyone, but there is no chance since we fly today and are on station tomorrow.

...(Late night) Seems I never get very far anymore when I start something. I have most of the targeting done for the next few days now, so maybe I can write the rest of this in peace.

...Just brought your valentine picture down to the room today... I'm sure missing you a bunch, Darling. Maybe this being at war while at sea does have some retributions over the old Med in port periods. Of course, then you could be there, and I wouldn't have that problem.

It really was hard on some of the guys in port this time. A few got their wives stopped before they left the States (to come to Hong Kong), but several others were already on the way and only got to stay for three days. Then there was the wife who didn't get her cholera shot until she reached Subic, so when she flew up here, the Hong Kong authorities placed her in quarantine for five days. So there are some frustrations that were almost insurmountable.

Well, about Hong Kong, we had a ball. The admin (hotel suite) ashore like we used to have in the Med really worked out fine. We had our own booze then, and it was a nice place to leave packages or to change from a sweater to a coat for dinner or to just plain relax after walking up and down those hills all day. It was a 45-minute ferry ride from the ship back to the pier, so (the admin) really was an advantage (for things like that). And, since that was probably the only time we would get one, we went first class and got rooms in the Hilton.

I think Hong Kong is really nice, and actually, it was very clean. Even Kowloon on the mainland side was cleaner than I had expected. The people are very nice, and I didn't hear one bad comment or witness one communist protest the entire three days.

And we had a pretty ideal group of sailors, so no one was put on report. First time I ever heard of that! Wonder if they are really sailors?

I guess that after the Enterprise was here, it was such a contrast that no one could really believe it. Of course, you have to take into account who the ringleader of the Enterprise is. Ha.

Speaking of Enterprise, it looks like we are going to get one of the crews from RVAH-7 transferred over to us...The message didn't give a date, but it said Lcdr. Larry Cox and Lt. Jim Currie are to transfer over to RVAH-13. Nobody had any forewarning on that, and I doubt if they did either. We'll be glad to have them, though, as they made a cruise in A5As when Cdr. McLain was in RVAH-7, and they are real fine people. It sure helps us fill our gaps in squadron organization.

And if the wind holds right, we'll get Ray Vehorn back with us tomorrow. The new B/N that is coming with him is Herb Nowlin, but John H. (Hurlburt) will go back to flying with Ray.

...Well, we start back (to flying) tomorrow, and I do need a good night's sleep. I do love you very much, My Darling. Wish you the pleasantest of dreams. I know mine will be.

Nite to Glyn and
Nite to James
I love you, Jimmie

USS Kitty Hawk
"Free"
16 Feb '66

Dear James,

Hong Kong was a big fun town with so many ships and boats in the harbor you couldn't count them.

I found a store just full of train parts, and I got these so you can fix your little engine and track. When you put these on and try them out, let me know if the transformer is working right. (I mean will it make the train back up and go forward the way it should?) If the transformer is bad, I will get a new one when we go back. Also, count the number of pieces of track you have.

How many pieces of curved track?

How many pieces of straight track?

I hear you are a real good schoolboy.

Take care of Mom and Glyn for me.

Love, Dad

USS Kitty Hawk
"Free"
Thurs nite
17 Feb '66

My Darling,

...This schedule we are on gets me here to my desk about one hour after bedtime each night, and it doesn't look like it intends to change...

Things will improve, I'm sure, as soon as we get all our drivers here. Ray got aboard today, and he is the same as ever. He brought us a beautiful new bird (airplane), too. It will be a few days before we get him checked out enough to fly, though. We sent Dick to Cubi to get back one of our birds that was being repaired, and with the CO in a conference, it only leaves four of us to fly. Thus, yesterday, today, tonight, and again tomorrow gets to be pretty regular on the schedule. You don't hear me complaining about the flying! Now if I could just get some of this other stuff knocked it would be great.

The weather is clearing up some out here now, but the heat is coming along with it. And if my perspiration today is any indicator, I hate to think how it will be in about two months. We went into the canned soda pop racket in our coffee mess, and in just three days we have sold out the whole 33 cases we brought out here with us. That was a sort of substitute for the popcorn racket that got sidelined by the ship's XO. This squadron is the best bunch of rabble-rousers ever gathered under one roof. It keeps the whole ship run ragged all the time.

Ensign Nowlin didn't come to us after all. He flew out with Ray, but he was assigned to go to RVAH-9, so we are still back as short as we were before. Everyone is about used to fast job shuffles now anyway, so I guess we can make a few more. As you may have noticed, I left the jobs off the last squadron roster anyway.

Hope things have come back to normal with you now. I know how much has been weighed on you lately, and I do love you so much the more for bearing it. You know if I had the choice, I would be there with you. If we keep our love, Darling, I'm sure we can manage anything. As strong as it is now, I see no chance of loss... I'll dream of you sweetly tonight.

I love you,
Always your loving husband,
Jimmie

USS Kitty Hawk
"Free"
Sunday nite
20 Feb '66

My Darling

...We had the afternoon off today and sat through a movie. That made for a rather nice Sunday afternoon, especially since we

are headed down south for operations for a few days. It's far from blissful there, but even so, the saying around here is "Happiness is Dixie Station."

Of course the young ones have changed the words to our favorite song "Dixie" to such as "No sampans and no damn SAM's, away, away, away down south in Dixie." Of course, they have changed the full chorus, and I can't remember all the words....We hope to get lots of flying if the planes stay up, and maybe we can get Ray worked well into the picture.

Of all the best parts of today, the best was a mail call that had two letters from you. And I got one from Mother. I had been concerned about Rozelle, and I'm sure the full impact (about Max) hit her when she got back to Sanford. Has Irene come back to Sanford yet? The group out here is as solid as ever, and I hope they are passing what strength they have on back to the home front... Sometimes they fail to understand the need of support at home as well as what they need out here...

...I sincerely hope you never have to face the same situation (as some of these gals whose husbands are missing), for my sake as well as yours, but if you do, I can only pray that you will face it with gratitude for the happiness we have had rather than (being destroyed by) the loss of the future. I know your capabilities, and I am sure you can have a bright future whether I am there or not. That in itself is one major factor that allows me to sleep well even on a night such as this.

I love you, Darling, and I will always love you. Have faith and hope and pray.

Good night, My Love.

I love you,

Jim

USS Kitty Hawk
"Free"
21 Feb '66

Hi Honey,

...Glad to hear that things are smoothing out somewhat back there. I know they will never be quite the same, but neither has anything else in the world...Your theories sound good to me, and right now I don't even know if I have any theories of my own.

I can almost appreciate why Dave (Johnson) didn't do much letter writing or movie watching (because this Ops job keeps me too busy to think about much else). What I need most right now is a sweet little angel to clean up this rat's nest I have for a room. Every day I say, "tomorrow, I'll get organized" and tomorrow never seems to come. But I guess as long as we stick with the important things, the rest will fall into place.

We had a very nice day today, and everything went along fine. About the most beautiful day we have had in several months. As one of the guys said tonight, it sure is a shame that this country is at war, because as pretty as these beaches are, they could make it into another Riviera.

It made me feel good to hear about Jamey's and Glyn's homemade valentine (for you). They are the best kind, and it's knowing that it comes from the heart that really counts. It's always good to find your children have the feelings you would want them to have. I just hope they can keep them all through their lives. Maybe if they are as lucky at finding a mate as I was, they won't have any problems at it.

And I do love you so very much. Maybe the part of you I love most is that part that is reflected directly through our children.

Sometimes, they are outstandingly sweet, and that is the time they are most like you.

Give them each a big kiss for me and then a couple extra for you.

I love you, Jimmie

USS Kitty Hawk
"Free"
Wednesday
23 Feb '66

Hi Darling,

I just had to get out the Raid to go after a roach. One thing that keeps me close to a feeling of Florida, I guess, is all the little creatures that share my room.

Well (the roaches) can have it tomorrow for a couple of days while I go to Saigon to do a little liaison work with the air force. They have some target work they want us to do, so I'm going in to talk to them about it. I also intend to see a little of the town while I am there...I hope. I had a few names jotted down here, and there are people who have brothers, cousins, etc. for me to look up if I ever got in there, and, as you can imagine, I can't find a one of those names now.

I don't expect to have time for any of that anyway, and, if I can get to see the people I want to talk with, I expect sightseeing will go by the wayside, too. If the targets our people have been bombing are any indication, I don't think I will care to venture out too far anyway. Apparently, the VC are everywhere, including the center of town. I'll tell you more of that when I get back here.

I saw Gig Conaughton last night—(remember him?) from PG School—and he is the Recco officer on the 7th Fleet Staff.

He spoiled my meal with the sad rumor that we may not go back to Hong Kong, but thus far, it's just a rumor, and I hope it stays one.

A rumor that you are probably hearing back there, that is not a rumor, is that we crunched another airplane. And it was my airplane again—603—but I wasn't flying it. Bob Renner was, and it wasn't his fault. Just one of those freak things where he blew a tire on landing, and it was rolling out okay and should have been nothing but a tire change. As luck would have it, the angle deck crosses the waist catapult track just at the end of the roll out, and a rim of the wheel got caught in the groove of the cat track.

Well, it twisted the gear and broke the strut and dropped that side down on the wing and broke that, too, all in the last ten feet of roll. We can't fix it now, so we are out another airplane. As Frank Bransom wrote in the logbook, "No injuries—except to the pilot's pride."

Maybe we ought to change our squadron number from 13 to 69 or something like that. I always thought 13 was my lucky number, but that (incident) was just pure rotten luck. One of our new airplanes, too—wouldn't have felt so bad if it was an old one. This sure (cuts) into our good maximum operating schedule here down south...

I had a letter from Lois also yesterday, and it was mostly chatter about the kids, but I was glad to get it. Leigh Ann is starting to string out now and with a mind of her own. It seems we've heard that somewhere before. She mentioned that Barbara may come up to Salinas for Easter and that was a day I had almost forgotten until the Catholics came in to dinner tonight, making it pretty obvious that today is Ash Wednesday. I find it almost impossible to keep up with the day of the week out here, and any special dates are just too much.

...My life now is just living for the day when we can be back together again. And my love grows stronger with each new day...

All my love, always,

Jimmie

USS Kitty Hawk
"Free"
26 Feb '66

Hi Darling,

I got back from Saigon last night, and I haven't caught up enough to get my breath since I got back. It was really a worthwhile trip, and I packed about as much into the two days as possible. I got a good fill-in on the air force recco work and sold a few ideas of our own, as well as picking up a pretty good piece of work for our stay here on the line.

Saigon is something of its own. There is no way to describe it except that you have to see it to believe it. Maybe I'd better go chronologically, or this may get too mixed up. Tan Son Nuit is the big airport there, and it is servicing civilian liners, civilian light plane traffic, air force fighters, recco and transports, army planes, Vietnam Air Force planes, navy diverts, and so many helicopters that you can't count them.

The poor tower operator must be a maniac. They handle about three times the traffic that Chicago Midway used to when it was the most active airfield in the world. There is no beauty to the field anymore. It is all dust, dirt, foxholes, barbed wire, and guns everywhere. The place is a real madhouse, and every little paper shack is somebody's office. It took me most of the first day just to locate the people I wanted to talk to.

The officers' billeting is downtown, where they have taken over three hotels and have leased parts of six others. I stayed in the Majestic, which is one of the nicest and is still open to normal trade as well. It is typically French, with the weak little yellow light bulbs, the tile floors, large mirrors, tall wooden boudoir closets, and bathrooms that have the chain pull flush and the ever-present bidet.

It's easy to see why the place was once called the Paris of the Orient. The basic structure and pattern is still here, and it must have been a beautiful town a few years ago. Now, it is filthy and sorely in need of paint and repair everywhere you go. It is truly a city on the move. You have never seen so many people on the streets in all your life, cars, scooters, bicycles, pedicabs, anything that will move. The streets are packed to capacity at all hours of day or night up to midnight. They have a midnight curfew, and no one dares violate it.

The smell is terrible, though. Dust and dirt are everywhere, and garbage is piled up along the sidewalks. There is virtually no unemployment in the city if you want to work. All the garbage truck drivers found they could make more money driving for the government, so they quit and went to work for higher pay. Thus, the garbage hasn't been picked up in months.

Children are everywhere—all over the streets. I saw many on the streets at midnight and others lay sleeping in doorways when I went to work the next morning. These are mostly refugees who have come into town by the thousands from their farms in the country. They at least have some protection in the city. Most of the beggars are cripples or children with no clothes or parents. It's hard to tell for sure, because they don't seem to use diapers around there.

All the babies and small children are carried around wearing only a shirt and a bare bottom. I guess when they have to "go" the mamas just hold them out over the sidewalk. A lot of them look extremely pitiful, though, with no place at all to go. Half the town is military, of course, but this doesn't seem to bother the populace. The civilians go right along just like it was an everyday business, and a lot of them are making fat profits, too.

The women of Saigon are as beautiful as advertised, and they have refused to become westernized. In fact, I don't think I saw more than three regular skirt-type dresses in the whole place. They wear these pajama-type long pants that look like nylon or thin silk but may be some type of thin poplin. Then, over the top, they wear the cheony dress, which is high-neck, long-sleeved, tight-fitting, and split from the waist down the sides, so a long flap hangs front and back down to the ankles.

Some wear thongs on their feet, but the native shoe appears to be the open toe—a sole with a wide band across the toe, but similar to a thong. They do wear the little round pointed (conical) straw hats, and some are bleached and lacquered for dress-up occasions. It looks a little out of place to see a girl in brightly colored almost formal-looking dress with white gloves and fancy hairdo out riding the garbage-laden streets on a bicycle. They have a sort of jacket-type blouse top that they wear over the pajama pants for working clothes. Even little kids wear the same type attire.

Men are quite the opposite, with the scroungiest looking clothes you can imagine. Some wear nothing but a tee shirt and short shorts that look like a pair of striped skivvies. Business suits are quite common in the downtown district, but short-sleeved shirt with tie is accepted formal attire for evenings. It was about 95 to 97 degrees both days I was there.

I had an interesting evening Thursday night with Mr. On Vi Wan, who is a friend of Ron Rydel. He is Chinese, so naturally, he took us to a Chinese club for dinner. It was very filling, as they usually are, and the scotch flowed like water—we can't drink the water because of the germs, naturally.

All in all, it was quite a trip, and I thoroughly enjoyed it. I don't want to get back anytime soon as the living there is rather uncomfortable. It makes the clean ship and cool air conditioning something to appreciate. I will try to get some stationery before I write tomorrow, Sweetheart, but regardless of the paper, it says I love you just the same.

...My love and kisses to Jamey and Glyn...

Nite, Sweetheart,

Jimmie

USS Kitty Hawk
"Free"
27 Feb '66

Hi Darling,

Got the snapshots today of my sweetest pair of girls and number one son. Looks like a rather good group—or at least one I would like to be more closely associated with—like about 12,000 miles closer to be exact.

...Glyn is growing up so it's almost too much. You probably don't notice the difference, but I might require introductions by the time we get back. She looks mighty pretty, though, as does her beautiful Mom and handsome brother.

...About the A-6 incident, I thought that would be in all the papers, and of course, it was. You didn't know the crew as they were fairly new. It was the last day we were up north before coming down

here, and it looked like he just pulled low and hit a hill. The bombs on the plane exploded, so it didn't leave much. I think sometimes the newspapers put out too much of what is going on over here.

USS Kitty Hawk
"Free"
2 March 1966

Dear James,

I hope you have your train fixed and running by now. If not, let me know what is wrong, and I will see if I can get the parts. We may not go back to Hong Kong, but I'm sure we will stop somewhere where I can find what we need. Also, please count the straight pieces and the curved pieces of track that you have so I can figure out how many more we need.

I'm sorry to hear that Bobby may move to Whidbey Island, but I guess we should be happy that we got to have fun with (the Frasers) as long as we did. I hear that there are some new people moving in on the street already. You will have to write and tell me about them.

Here are some real different kinds of money that you may not see any other like. The blue one is a five cents piece of MPC that they use on all the military bases out here in the Pacific. No, we still use American green dollars on the ship, but when we go ashore, we have to change it into this "funny" money. It looks like it came out of a Monopoly game, doesn't it?

The green paper money is from Saigon in Vietnam, and it is 20 dong or piastres and is about equal to 20 cents in U.D. money. They use mostly paper and don't have many coins, but I did find the 10 dong and the 1 dong coins. Also, I don't think I sent you a Hong Kong five cents piece before.

I hope school is going well for you. I know you are anxious to get back to the pool as soon as the weather warms. You and Mom teach Glyn how to swim good by the time I get home, okay?

I love you,

Dad

USS Kitty Hawk
"Free"
Thursday
3 March '66

My Darling,

Time flies by like it never has before, and somehow, I don't seem to control the schedule. I do love you so very, very much and think of you constantly. Please hold my love more important than my letters, and I will find time for the words soon. Must have sleep now and pleasant dreams of you.

My love and kisses for Jamey and Glyn.

I love you, Jim

USS Kitty Hawk
"Free"
Friday, March 4, '66

My Darling,

Don't know if it's Friday or not, and I am too lazy to get up to look and see, but I do know the date is right.

We've had airplane problems for the past few days, but now that we have the birds going again, we don't have any bird men. Al, Dick Daum, and I are it for tomorrow, and we were it for today, also. It's nice to fly regularly, but this turning right around for every cycle is too much. It seems the flu bug finally worked its way up to

Ready Room 4, and right after we had sent the XO to the beach to pick up our repaired airplane, too. I hope they live it up at Cubi, because they will have to fly their tails off when they get back.

It isn't flying that is wearing me out as bad as trying to set up the Ops for when we go back north this time. I think these long periods at sea with no breaks just tend to wear everyone down. Maybe I spent too much time in the Med, but, when we pass ten days to two weeks at sea, I get the feeling we ought to be headed to port. I guess they just don't intend to run wars that way.

Jack has been complaining about his flight time, so I guess he will catch up on it this week. He has been swapping for rides in the F4 fighters, and I have carried their RIO along with me. It seems they can see more out of the F4, but the RA5C has more knobs to twist and is a lot cooler. Our air conditioner is a big point down here in this hot South China Sea.

It's been looking like the South China Sea is supposed to look here lately. No wind, with almost a mirror glaze on the water, scattered cumulus clouds around, and a beaming hot sun. It's really taking the old boat to get enough wind to bring us aboard. Of course, we are only nine degrees above the equator here, so that makes the sun even hotter...

Please drop the folks a note since I haven't had a chance to write them. I miss you a bunch, and Glyn and Jamey, too. Have a big three-way hug for me, too, and I'll be there for a fourth before we know it.

...I do love you so extra special much. And I say thank you every night in my prayers for the wonderful marriage we have had and still have.

Nite, My Darling.

I love you,

Jim

USS Kitty Hawk
"Free"
Saturday night
5 March '66

My Darling,

...I did get two very sweet letters from you today and enjoyed them to the fullest—right after I landed for the fourth time in the past 24 hours and politely collapsed on this bed.

...I've got a rattling pipe or piece of tin or something over my room that sounds just like rain falling on a tin roof, and it is the most comforting sound you ever heard on a tired weary night. It sounds almost as good as the wind rustling through the palm trees outside our bedroom window (there in Sanford).

...You know I can sit here and think of that green grassy yard, those palm trees, and almost convince myself that we would like to stay on in Sanford forever. But I can remember several places we lived before that gave me that feeling, so it must be because you are there.

...We wound up (our flights in the) south today, and are headed back north. I sure hate that place, but guess that's where the action is. We got Ray (Vehorn) back in an "up" status today, but that gives us only four (pilots). Hope the rest will recover (from the flu) in a couple more days. Apparently, Larry Cox and Jim Currie will be coming over from RVAH-7 sometime next week, too, so it will get us back up to strength.

By the time you get this I expect it will be time to invite their wives over to your group, but they have been in 7 so long they may just decide not to leave the other group...Al Perrella has taken over all the Admin stuff now, so I don't have an old roster here that I can pull out and check anymore. This Ops job doesn't give me nearly the conversation pieces I used to get in Admin.

Kitty Hawk didn't quite get by unscathed this time down south, since my friend, Mal Guess, got his F4 shot down today. Both he and his RIO got out okay with sprains and minor injuries. So if you hear about a Kitty Hawk plane downed in South Vietnam that's what it was.

Looks like it will be Cubi for liberty the next time, and Hong Kong has kind of gone by the boards.

...For now, my darling, it's pleasant dreams.

I love you so very, very much.

Your loving husband, Jimmie

USS Kitty Hawk
Tuesday nite
March 5, '66

My Darling,

I
L
O
V
E
Y
I L O V E Y O U
U

Always,
Your loving husband,
Jimmie

USS Kitty Hawk
"Free"
Sunday nite
6 March '66

Hi Honey,

We're back on Yankee Station today, and with a clear day, we raised all kinds of hell with them. The haze is almost as bad as around the Norfolk area, but it's more of the country than I have seen at one time ever before. I did get to church this morning, but I climbed into an airplane right afterward.

I sure miss some of John's sermons and Ophie's singing, too, though. They tried a new song in our service today, and it dragged along like a dirge...This was the day for communion, so there wasn't too much of a sermon anyway. I could sure stand a Sunday or two with John (Hires), just to listen to a sermon I could pay attention to.

Let me know what rumors you hear bout John staying or leaving our church next year, because I would hate for them to get away before I get back to Sanford. We will miss that congregation as much as anything if we do have to move to Albany.

...Is Glyn still going to the nursery or does she sit in church with you and Jamey? Since you're not singing in the choir, I expect it is peaceful just to sit in quiet (contemplation) through a service for a change. But little girls can be trained to sit quietly a lot easier than boys if you're in the mood for trying. Granted, Glyn isn't exactly in the category of the average little girl in that respect.

Well, it's my turn to double up (flying duties) again tomorrow, so I had better get a good night's sleep. Maybe we can get some of these flu patients up and some wandering souls back from the beach (to join us on the flight schedule) soon. Actually, it's more fun to fly regularly, if I didn't have anything else to do.

I'll put in a special coin for Jamey with this letter. Here's love to you all, Glyn, James, and you.

I love you, Jimmie

USS Kitty Hawk
"Free"
Friday night
11 March '66

My Dearest,

It's after the witching hour, but his ole pad sure feels good. I got a test hop on our new bird today—or "my new bird," I guess I could say, since it is No. 603,—and it sure flies good. I looked back in my log book and saw that I had once had five flights in it back when it was an A-5, before it got converted to an RA5C...

Things are going reasonably well now, since we have all our crews up and flying. In fact, tomorrow, for the first time, I can take a day off the flight schedule and just play ODO. I'm not exactly taking a day off, but more or less being forced into it since I am several flights ahead of everyone.

It looks kind of pointed when you're Ops officer at the same time (that you're flying more than the rest). I only took hops from sick people, though, and I can't help it if I didn't get sick. So, I told them, no complaints. The Skipper is the farthest behind, so if he doesn't complain, nobody else can. In only a few more days, we get to port anyway, and then nobody will complain.

We'll be split up this time ashore with several people taking planes to Atsugi, Japan for painting, but I'm sure the rest will find some means of amusement. I think I will stay in Cubi myself; I can't recall losing a single thing in Japan. We will probably get back there for a few days on the way here anyway.

Of course the big attraction in the meantime is our own Big Star visit tomorrow night—Ann Margaret and Johnny Rivers will be aboard for a USO show. Flight Ops will continue as scheduled, I might add.

We have a group of comics on this ship in Air Ops, the Air Boss, and the new XO. They have a running contest to see who can come up with the wittiest of witticisms in their respective Plans of the Day (official publications, I might add.) It's nice to see a sense of humor around here, and it does make you read the things each day. You have to know the people and the circumstances to understand the things, so I'm afraid there are only about 100 people on the ship who really get the full benefit of this. And, as can be expected, about 90 percent of it is wisecracks directed at the Air Group...It must be that we have been at sea too long.

The Air Boss even had a combo from the ship's band up in Pri-Fly playing music over the flight deck public address system the other day. Appropriately, since it was the first launch of the day and the day was Sunday, they were playing "Never on a Sunday."

...We lost an A1 over the side today in an operational accident, but the pilot got out fine except for a scratch on his forehead. So Lady Luck is smiling on us thus far. We can pray for a continuance of that.

The guys who come out here from Sanford seem to think the Wing is a cinch to stay at Sanford (rather than relocate to Georgia). We haven't seen anything about it for over a month, so we assume the committee work is as furious as ever (to try to keep the base there). I would hate to think we might have to make the move during the short turnaround we will have at home between cruises.

For now, it's getting through tomorrow, and that only comes after I dream through tonight. Those dreams, I'm sure, will be filled with pleasant thoughts of you. Loving you always as I do right now. Sleep with me tonight in dreamland.

I love you, Jimmie

USS Kitty Hawk
"Free"
Sunday nite
13 March '66

Hi Darling,

...We had an early start today with the Ann-Margaret show just before the start of Air Ops, and these young sailors had a ball.

Then we somehow got in a full schedule of flying, and, in fact, we still have one plane out tonight. That's why I am still up, and as soon as he gets aboard I'll be fading fast since I have an early up and first launch tomorrow. We sent Bob Renner off to the beach with a plane today, so we will be short on drivers again for our last few days (on line). We won't need many while we are in Cubi, though—just R&R.

Larry Cox is turning out to be...steady as a rock as a pilot. It's nice to have someone new that we don't have to sweat about getting aboard. I don't know whether you have met his wife yet.

We were real glad to hear the news about Gerry (Coffee) and Bob (Hanson) (both now believed alive and captives). We don't get that much news out here, and then today we did get a copy of the news release from Captain Fowler about them. It sounds promising to say the least, and it does help confirm what we had surmised. I just wish we could hear something similar on the others....Time for the recovery (of a plane now landing), so I've got to go to CCA.

Nite, My Sweet

I love you,

Jimmie

USS Kitty Hawk
Cubi
17 March '66

My Darling,

I'm lying here in a semi-stupor, but I know I'd better write this now rather than depend on finding time to write tonight. I'm sorry to have missed writing the past few days, but as usual those last few days on the line get rather hectic and time slips right by.

We're safely planted on terra firma right now, and we finally made it through a full sea period intact. The Kitty Hawk has lost several planes, but no crews this time out, and 13's only crunch was the one Bob Renner had.

The Skipper and I flew in to Cubi last night, and I'm here in the BOQ now recuperating. After a couple more hours of naptime here, I think I'll make it to the club for a steak tonight.

The ship got in this morning, and I expect the rest of the troops will be ashore in short order. This Sunday afternoon the senior officers on the ship have challenged the senior officers in the Air Wing to a duel on the softball field. So it's lieutenant commanders and above in a beer bust bout with a few softball gloves as scenery. I hear they had quite a comedy presentation of gimmicks from the ship to the air group last night in the wardroom, so this wild pattern between the aviators and the blackshoes will just increase for the remainder of the cruise. Half the ship operates by nicknames now, and you can never tell when someone is serious.

If we weren't fighting this blamed war, we might even be able to enjoy the cruise. Of course the hideous environment of sweating out living until the next day might be what it is that relaxes people enough to laugh at their own mistakes. Quite often the comment is, "So I screwed up, so what are you going to do, fire me?" And they both laugh and go back to work.

A psychologist could have a ball out here, just studying the reaction of the personalities (in wartime situations). He couldn't predict anything, because even the individuals themselves can't know what they will do just prior to going out to get their ass shot off, but the psychologist could collect a lot of data.

Like yesterday we were laughing at John Caldwell, who flies F-4s. I don't know how much of this will get in the news, so don't say anything about it, but I just want to pass on the lighter side of the situation. Anyway our F-4s were out on a practice missile shoot and hit John in our own F-4. He already had one bad engine, and the missile knocked out the other one, so he had to start the bad one back up and bring it back aboard the ship. Luckily, the missile had an inert head with no explosive, but it still knocked most of the front end of the airplane off, and so when John landed and got out of the airplane, he looked back at the shambles he was flying for an airplane, and he fainted right there on the flight deck.

So last night the ship's CO got up at dinner and announced that he would issue a sparrow missile to each member of the Air Group, so they could knock each other off before Sunday afternoon, and the ship would win the softball game by default.

....Enough of the gossip now. Best I get down some facts before I head over for dinner. The most positive fact I know is that I love

you. Next, I miss you, need you, want you, and will be clawing the walls if I don't get home before too long...Best I go get with the troops now before happy hour closes.

I love you, Darling.

Always, Jimmie

USS Kitty Hawk
Subic Bay, Philippines
20 March '66

Hi Darling,

You'd never guess what I'm doing right now. Staying home on a liberty night in port is weird enough, but I missed dinner tonight, so...I'm sitting here fishing baby clams out of a can. It's a can you sent me that didn't have a can opener. I had to butcher it up pretty badly with my survival knife, but to avoid starvation, all obstacles were overcome, and they are ummm, juicy good. This hardly suffices for dinner, but maybe that will give me reason to get up early enough tomorrow for breakfast.

...Friday night we saw one of the funniest floor shows I've seen all year. Some 62-year-old hefty, platinum blonde Sophie Tucker type who played a violin. She came out in long flowing robes and played a Franz Liszt concerto as nicely as you could ever hear. Wow, you didn't know for sure if she was serious or not. Then she grabbed the mike and said, "G.D. good for an old bag like me, wasn't it?" Well, from then on with a lot of Sophie's old jokes, the place kinda came apart. Of course the audience was rather primed for that type of show, and it relaxed the group to say the least...We just saw a set of orders for our next XO—Len Higgenbotham, I believe. He and Al Perrella were in the squadron at one time, and I think his wife and Ann made a trip to the Med together. Maybe she is eager to go

back there again and will get him to do some advance legwork to get us a Med cruise!

Nite for now, My Sweet. Give my love to Glyn and James and a special comment on his good-looking car.

I love you,

Jimmie

26 March 1966
Saturday Afternoon
Yokusuka, Japan

Hi Darling,

...Just ate wardroom dinner and picked up a letter from you on the way back. I had heard about Gerry (Coffee) this morning, and Jack had a clipping from the paper. At least we know for sure he is alive, and they will most likely keep him that way. This BS they are putting out (about him) is all BS, and I hope you know that as well as I do. This talk of writing a 10-page letter with his left hand is idiotic. The broken arm makes him the logical choice for a propaganda stunt like this, since they can write whatever they like and just say he did it with his left hand. Bea is a fine gal, and I hope she is standing up under this with full faith in Gerry.

...Honey, I don't know how you girls are taking it back there. My hat's off to the whole bunch of you for the greatest group of gals in one bunch I've seen. And especially to you, Sweetheart, who seem to have had more than your ordinary share of sadness. Darling, I wish so much I could be there to assist, but our not being there is the root of the whole thing anyway. I do want you to know how much I appreciate and admire you though for standing up to it the way you do. I knew you were something special when I married you, but I wish I had never had to find out in any such way as this.

I guess we can look ahead to better days, cause there certainly have to be better ones somewhere. I do love you and will always love you. I've gotten so stirred up thinking about Bea that I've forgotten half the things I wanted to tell you. Maybe I'd better go have a drink and save them till tomorrow.

I miss you so much, Sweetheart.

I love you, Jim

USS Kitty Hawk
Cubi
Monday
28 March '66

Hi, Darling,

...We pull out (of Cubi) in the morning and run through the deck for a little landing practice before we head back over to "never land." It's going to be a long at-sea period this time, but I guess that's why they keep pulling us back in here to Cubi—it makes it seem almost a blessing to go back to sea.

...Give James and Glyn some big hugs and kisses for me. I love them, too.

I love you,
Very, very much,
Nite, Darling,
Jimmie

USS Kitty Hawk
"Free"
30 March '66

Hi Sweetheart,

...Your letter about (the birth of) Gerry (Coffee) Jr. was really good news. I'm so glad to hear they (Bea and the baby) are both

doing fine. Please convey my congratulations to Bea and young Gerry.

...I keep squirming around here, trying to get a comfortable position. We had our gamma globulin shots again today, and that big needle in each side of the rear end makes the old sitter pucker a bit. Nine cc's makes quite a lump! I don't know but whether I'd rather risk hepatitis.

We still don't have our other two birds back from Atsugi, so flying will be rather light these first few days (on line). We have an awards ceremony tomorrow anyway to catch up on the back awards of Air Medals. Just about everyone is on the list for the one tomorrow, so the ceremony will probably take half the morning.

...Good night for now...I love you, Jim

Love James and Glyn, too.

Give a big kiss to them both.

Nite, Jim

USS Kitty Hawk
"Free"
Thursday night
31 March '66

Hi Darling,

Ole sleepy eyes here again, but now I can put on some jazzy music to wake me up again. Of course the steam lines for the waist catapults run right up one wall to my room, and I'm not too sure whether that sound can be classed in the bass or the melody. One thing for sure, though, I can turn the sound up as loud as I like, and it won't disturb any of the neighbors.

...We started back in business today, and I guess that's as good a way as any to finish out the month. But it will be a long month in

April, with most of it spent on the line. That will make the time go fast, but the days only go one at a time, and we have to sweat out each and every one. We are still short two crews with the CO and Larry Cox both still in Japan. Mostly, we need those airplanes.

...We had an awards ceremony today, and Admiral Reedy passed out a batch of medals. I got an Air Medal and a gold star in lieu of the second Air Medal....Maybe they will send us pictures later so I can send you one.

Nitey time again, Sweetheart.

I love you very much.

Your loving husband, Jim

Hi, Kids, I love you, too, Dad

USS Kitty Hawk
"Free"
Friday nite
1 April '66

Hi Honey,

I don't feel much like practical jokes tonight myself, but I'm sure Jamey had his hands full of April fool jollies today. Things stayed in a rather serious vein here as you can suspect, and a fake air plan issued last night with more commitments than anyone could possibly meet was about as far as (the joking) went. It does signify the start of another big month, and, before you know it, we will have them all counted off.

...Your comments about (all the losses of) the A-4s out here are almost funny, but I guess that is the way it looks from your vantage point. Actually, the A-4 has the lowest knockdown rate of any of the aircraft out here because there are so many of them flying. So you

read about a lot of them down, but percentage-wise they are better off than any of the rest of us. Still, it's no good deal for anybody, as you well know.

...The swimming pool must be opening soon, so enjoy the sunshine. I'm delighted to hear that you and the kids are becoming almost professional gardeners. Tell James to keep up the good work.

My love to you all—with bundles of hugs and kisses.

Nite, My Darlings,

Jimmie

USS Kitty Hawk
"Free"
Sunday night
3 April '66

Hi Sweetheart,

Here it is Palm Sunday, and the days roll right along. Wish I could have been there in Sanford today and seen all the folks at Grace (Methodist Church).

...Things are going so great for us right now, flying-wise, I can hardly believe it. Larry and the Skipper are still in Japan, and even with two planes short we are flying more hops than we usually do. I'd better not say too much or it will all come in on us. It's too good a deal to keep going this way.

I just wish all we had to worry about was flying around whenever we wish. It might even make this part of the cruise enjoyable. I just can't say I care much for this part of always dodging bullets and being unable to shoot back. In peacetime this photo business is more fun than bombing, but I can't say much for it in wartime...I don't guess there is anything in this mess that falls under the fun classification, though.

.....It's about "Taps" time, and I need it tonight, Darling. I love you all very, very much. There are no cards out here to send you, but I do want to wish you, James, and Glyn a happy Easter. Also pass along a "happy Easter" to all my Sanford friends, including the folks at church.

I love you.

Your loving husband,

Jimmie

USS Kitty Hawk

"Free"

Monday nite

4 April '66

Hi Honey,

I may keep this short tonight, since I have another conference on the RA5C to work up for tomorrow night. It seems all we do lately is defend our machine instead of getting out to make it work. It seems that ought to be the job of somebody further up the (chain of command), but these DOD people who come out here want to hear it straight from the fleet and nobody else.

I sure wish the Skipper were here for this one. And, from the way he was asking about him tonight, I think Captain Carmody does too. But with one (conference) night before last, one last night, and one again tonight, I can't remember if I told them all the same thing or not. It's not the type thing you can write down, and, when you're speaking off the cuff, it's easy to contradict yourself. You thought we were out here to fight wars, didn't you?

Well, a message just came in saying our last bird will leave Atsugi tomorrow. Now, if we can just find the other one and get them both back out here, we will have something to work with.

...Got work to do now, Sweetheart. I love you all the same—Glyn and Jamey, too. A kiss for you all.

I love you,

Jim

USS Kitty Hawk
"Free"
Friday nite
8 April '66

Hi Darling,

Good Friday—and a good Friday it is! Time is sure clipping by out here, but at least this time out things have been going well for us. We flew over 100 hours this week, and I know we have never done that before, and I doubt that anyone else has either. It feels nice to fly every day and sometimes twice a day like I've done the past couple of days. It makes my paperwork about a month behind, but for right now we've got a good excuse to forget all of that.

The Skipper got back to the ship yesterday, and everyone has been about to run him ragged about hotsi baths, leave, change of command, etc. They even put a big blurb about his famous return on the back of the Air Plan tonight. It's a mark of distinction when you make the Air Plan!

He brought all the pictures from the (wives' recent) party with the "Rather Fight Than Switch" scene (in which everyone was sporting a "black eye"). It was quite a gathering, huh? You're looking great, Sweetheart, black eye and all. (The photos were to indicate our feelings about closing the Sanford base and moving it to Albany, Georgia)...

There was a sweet letter waiting tonight when I got back from landing in that big black void with no moon. Seems they always schedule night flying either just before the moon comes up or after it goes down...From your latest reports, I can hardly wait to see my daughter—and you and Jamey, too, of course.

Love and kisses to you all.

I love you, Jimmie

USS Kitty Hawk
"Free"
Saturday nite
9 April '66

Hi Darling,

I had a nice note from (my brother) John today with his latest appraisal of the younger generation. He included a picture of Leigh Ann with her own personal autograph, "x." She has become a very beautiful young lady....

We finally got the Danny Kaye show tonight (that was canceled last week for some reason), and he was as good as ever. We had them down for dinner in the wardroom and for a cake-cutting ceremony honoring Cliff Johns who got the 49,000th landing today. So we had two shows for the price of none.

Bill Westerman was in the groove today in an A-6 for that landing, but he didn't have his hood down so they waved him off, and Cliff was behind him and got the landing. Naturally, Bill has been taking quite a ribbing all afternoon.

Danny Kaye brought Vickie Carr, a singer, with him, and, though I'd never heard of her, she is very good. They baked her a special cake tonight, too, since it was her first month's wedding anniversary. Her husband of 30 days is back in the States. She cried, of course, but the cake was good. I guess it's not such a big deal for her to come over here so soon after the wedding, since we've got sailors who married with less time than that before we left, and they will be gone eight or nine months.

It was the best show we've had since we came out here, and everything was on time. Apparently, Danny Kaye is a stickler for time, because he started and stopped everything he was scheduled for right on the minute. And nobody on this ship has ever done that before, including the Air Boss.

Now I'm afraid the predawn launch tomorrow will go somewhere near on time, so I had better get a few hours of shuteye. Wish I could get it there with you—or anywhere with you.

I love you, Darling, so very, very much.

Nite, my love, Jim

USS Kitty Hawk
"Free"
Monday
11 April '66

Hi Darling,

Sorry, I didn't get to write you last night, but a big targeting conference came up and occupied all of the spare time. I did get three nice letters to make it a happy Easter, though, one each from you, Mother, and Barbara.

It didn't start off as the world's best day. I had a 4 a.m. reveille for a predawn launch, and you know how I hate to get up at those hours. But half the Air Group was up, too, and when we got to the wardroom for breakfast there was a sign that said Easter holiday routine: Brunch from 0700 to 1100. You know how that goes—holiday for the blackshoes and routine for the Air Group.

We started calling the mess treasurer, etc. and went on to our briefing. They did feed a few in Wardroom 1, but when the rest of us finished briefing and got there, they had closed that one again, and the grill wasn't hot in Wardroom 2 yet. So I just gave up and went ahead, and we manned airplanes. As Ray (Vehorn) said, I got to attend sunrise (Easter) services...because I reached the end of the catapult just about the time the first rays appeared over the horizon. I told Ray, "And I even fasted before the service!" At least it was a beautiful sunrise, and anytime you see that there must be some reverence.

Then the hop went well, and I got back aboard in time for brunch and the 1000 Easter services. The music for the service was really good. We have a Negro boy on the ship who has a very nice voice, particularly for spirituals, and he sang "Were You There When They Crucified My Lord?" I wish I could have attended the service at Grace Church, but I know you were all there for me. I'm sure that was one Sunday they had a good crowd anyway. I really miss being home on special days like that.

...I hope you got the flowers I ordered for you okay. They may not have suited what you were wearing, but it was worth taking a chance. Mostly, they were just to say I love you anyway....Much love to you all now. Tell the kids to have another chocolate Easter bunny for me, too.

I love you all.

Miss you, Honey,

Jim

USS Kitty Hawk
"Free"
Saturday nite
16 April '66

Hi Honey,

I'm lying here listening to some Andy Williams favorites now, and I can't recall for the life of me what I wrote you last. Or, for that matter, when I wrote you last. Listening to "The Twelfth of Never" reminds me that it's been too long.

...Whenever it was...things are relatively the same out here from day to day...Before I forget, I sent my paycheck to the bank today:

4/16 Deposit $347.00.

And I think I already wrote you about the two checks I wrote this month:

Wardroom mess $35.00
Mona's Flower Shop $15.00

Oh, I just got called out for a big change exercise for tomorrow, so I will have to stop for now.

I love you.

Your loving husband,

Jimmie

USS Kitty Hawk
"Free"
Monday
18 April '66

Hi Darlings,

It sounds like the kids are doing big things around there. I'm afraid they both are going to have a world of their own by the time

I get back home, and then it will be me who has to fit into their schedule.

...I do miss not being in on Glyn's nursery school days and listening to the evening reports (of her adventures). What do you do at dinnertime now that they both have a full day to report? Or has James got his reports down to nominal size?

I'm proud as peaches of our son as I always am. A few good shows like that now in the early years will pay big dividends in the later years. And when he can start on top, it doesn't take any more effort to stay there all the rest of the way. I'll try to write him in a few days and tell him myself.

We've had some worrisome days here lately. We have lost several planes, but, luckily, we got most of the people back. Our A-3 that got shot down over Hainan Island must have made big news back there. It seems likely that those guys lost pressurization and passed out, like some of the A-3s they lost in the States last year.

We're doing right well (in the squadron) so far, and I just hope the good Lord sees fit to stay with us. We did have a double wire engagement last week and cracked one plane, but it has been flown to Cubi to get fixed. The XO broke a nose wheel the very next flight, and we thought our black cloud was back again, but everyone smiled it off. We hope to keep it that way.

Honey, I sure wish I could snuggle up to you and spend a nice evening tonight. I must miss that tender warmth that seems to flow from you to me when we are close together. Just keep that something special...you are and always will be my one and only love.

I love you,

Jimmie

USS Kitty Hawk
"Free"
Wednesday nite
20 April '66

Hi Darling,

There were five letters here today. You get ahead of me fast, but, secretly, I like it that way. It sure is nice to see that letter in my routing box right after a mail call. You've been more than wonderful this cruise about sending me some cheery thoughts on paper to help me get through the evening when things haven't gone so good.

We had a good day today photo-wise, and we really cleaned up some tough areas, but there was a tragic note on the ship. We lost a good friend from the A-4 squadron—a good personal friend of mine as well...I'll give you the name at a later date. Kitty Hawk has lost several planes this time out.

The squadron had a pretty lousy day maintenance-wise yesterday, and Ray and I were the only ones who got airborne. And leave it to Ray to come back in and get the ship's 50,000th landing. He will get to cut the cake here in a day or so, I guess. It's just as well that he got that, since he probably won't get to be a centurion (100 combat hops) on this cruise.

Today we did much better and had airplanes flying all over the place. We reached 260 hours today, and that is more than any other squadron has ever flown in a month in the RA5C. And only 20 days of the month are gone, too. We have another week to go here, so we should pack up a bagful of flight hours before we are through. Of course, that's hoping we don't run into any problems.

We aren't really trying to set records out here, though. We're just trying to keep up with our commitments...The maintenance people are really working, as they want (to show a great performance record) more than anybody.

Frank Bransom got back from Japan today. He had gone up there to arrange for camouflage painting of our aircraft over five weeks ago. And Dick and Ron Queen also got back from a few days at Cubi. One of these days, I'm going to have to get one of those good beach deals!...I love you, My Darling,

So very, very much,

Always, Jimmie

USS Kitty Hawk
"Free"
Thursday
21 April '66

My Darling,

...Today isn't exactly the day for shouting...as we lost a couple of my good ole liberty buddies from VA-85 tonight. You don't know them, but I certainly pray for their chances. They are too fine to lose.

I guess the Kitty Hawk has accomplished more this time on the line than any other ship ever, but it sure hasn't been a soft ride by any means—and, regrettably, it's not over yet.

...I miss you very much...and dream...of the day I won't miss you much more because I won't let you out of my sight!

Nite, My Darling,

I love you,

Jimmie

USS Kitty Hawk
"Free"
Monday
25 April '66

Hi Darling,

...I had a rather "divine" Sunday. I did get to attend church for a change, and then during the movie I was deluged with an avalanche of divinity candy. Both packages arrived so I opened it there and routed it around the Ready Room.

...We passed our 300th hour (of flight time) for the month, and that really made the maintenance gang happy. I think the most any RA5C squadron has ever before flown in one month was about 250 hours. We still have a few days of flying left to do, but the planes are getting a little sick, so we don't want to overdo it. This was just the shot in the arm our maintenance troops needed after having worked so hard for so long this cruise.

I'm sure it's going to cost me a keg of beer for the chiefs when we get into port, but I guess I can afford that. It will give them something to crow about now that the cannon thing has all worn off. I got two letters from you this morning, and I'm glad to hear your postal drought has ended. We've had more regular mail here, too, this time out than ever before, and a lot fewer VIPs, too, I might add.

Time to run now, Sweetheart...I love you, Darling, so very, very much,

Jimmie

Cubi, The Philippines
28 April '66

Hi Darling,

I had just lain down to write this, and I got up to watch Ray bring plane No. 601 into the break. I can hardly miss that distinctive sound that makes you know it's an RA5C...Jack and I are here in Cubi BOQ. We flew in last night in a bird we need to get some repairs on. The ship doesn't come in until Saturday, but we had to bring the plane on in to get the repair work done before we go back out. Jack and I were long overdue for a good deal, so I didn't get too much argument on that one. We hadn't had more than one night off the ship during flight operations since we left Sanford in July, and...had to have the flight schedule all laid out before I left the ship yesterday.

We are ahead anyway on landings and on missions. Actually, I did my 100th landing on Tuesday and became the Kitty Hawk's first RA5C centurion. We've really had a great month, and Beef (Renner) and Al (Perrella) should have both made centurion yesterday. The CO and Dick Daum will pick up their 100th the next time out.

It sure has been nice just lazing about here in Cubi all day. I had to go over and confer with the maintenance people here most of the morning to set up repair of our airplanes, but after that, it was free and easy. I spent the afternoon just lying around the pool. The hot season arrived here since we were last in port. There are a few thunderstorms drifting around but there is no rain to cool this place off...and last night was kinda miserable with no air-conditioned room to sleep in...We have about 10 days off now with no flak traps, so let's relax and enjoy it, Sweetheart.

I love you so very, very much.

Have pleasant dreams, as I know I will.

My love always,

Jimmie

Cubi Point
The Philippines
Saturday nite
30 April '66

Hi Darling,

It's time to scratch another sheet off that calendar, but this is not as nice to rip off as the next month will be (when we are headed home)...Our XO was crowing this morning...Apparently, (the Wing sent) a plane each out to us and to Seven on the same day last December. And already the XO has 22 more landings in Thirteen than (their pilot) got in the same time. Of course, some of that can be attributed to the big month we just finished. We got 351 flight hours, and most all of it was on the line over Vietnam.

We don't want to come anywhere close to that this next time out, though, because the Air Group really took a beating this month. The only way RVAH-13 got through unscathed was just pure luck. Honey, we lost 11 people out of the Air Group this month and twice that many planes.

But the one I want to tell you about is Bill Westerman (who flew with me in VA-83 when we were on the Forrestal in 1960). He's alive and on the ship, so don't get the wrong impression. In fact, one of the VA-85 guys today said Bill was even up and walking around. He took a slug in the back that came out his chest, just missing his heart and lungs.

I haven't seen him yet, but his was the one that I told you happened just before we launched from the ship to fly in here. I had known it was Bill then, and the report at the time was bad, so you can imagine the couple of anxious days I spent here trying to find out his status. Apparently, his B/N saved his life about three times over. I'll try to see him tomorrow and find out for myself.

...I made a tour of the base today, searching for a Mother's Day card, and they just don't exist here. This place really makes me mad about things like that. I think if I were running the ship I would have the ship's print shop make up special cards and sell them on the boat.

You're my favorite mother of all, though, and I can wish you a Happy Mother's Day as well here as on a card. You're probably the prettiest and most loving mother my children could have ever hoped for, too. And I love you so very dearly for it all. I'd vote you as Number One Mom of the Year, every year, and I always want you to know how pleased and happy I am that I found you to be the mother of my kids. Of course, I'd want you, kids or no kids, but, additionally, it's always a great comfort to know that you are there guiding and directing their lives and bringing them up to be the kind of people we want them to be.

I am fully proud of them now, just the way they are, and I'm more proud of you for raising them that way. I mainly wish you didn't have to play both the mother and father roles quite so often. That is both for their sakes as well as mine, but I don't think they suffer from it so much as I do.

...I love you so very, very much,

Always, my love,

Jimmie

USS Kitty Hawk
"Free"
Sunday nite, 8 May

Hi Darling,

...Just read back though your letter about Glyn's outing to the zoo via a train ride from Longwood. I can understand her excitement, because I was about that same age when my granddad took John and me on our first train ride. It was from Gates to Halls, and I think it cost about a dime each. I can still remember that rickety old train car and the wooden bench seats—not much different from what you might see on a subway these days. It was a short ride, but I must have talked about it for a week.

...I know this is Mother's Day, and I hope the kids did well by you today. I know if I had been there James would have had me up to help make waffles. I just hope he managed on his own without too many difficulties—or too many anxious moments on his mother's part. I'm sure Glyn was a big help, though, and kept things going smoothly.

All it takes is love, and that we have—in abundance—and will always have. Please give a heaping share of it to Glyn and to Jamey for me, and then say a prayer of thanks for all the extra love we have left.

I love you, Darling.
With all my heart,
Jimmie

USS Kitty Hawk
"Free"Thursday nite
12 May '66

Hi Darling,

...I didn't get to write you last night. Things just whisked right by, but I know it was a big day for Glyn. (Her birthday!) You must

have had your share of the excitement, too. Five years is a little hard to realize in more ways than one. It seems only yesterday when I was just about the happiest father alive (the night she was born). I was flying high above Paso Robles when they passed me the word that it was a girl. I could almost have put that T-28 into orbit if it had had the power.

Darling, I would have given you the world that night if it were mine to possess. I hope you weren't too put out with me for going flying at a time like that. I will apologize now at his late date for such foolhardiness, and I can promise that I would never again do such a thing. I guess even more than the joy I felt that night is the beauty and love that that little daughter has brought me in the five years since then. Even more so, I believe, she has given me the inspiration so that I can love you even more fully than before. And I do love you more than I ever thought was possible.

It seems that love is so infinite that the more it is shared with others, the stronger it can become for the individual. I'm not proposing nor opposing a larger family, but it could certainly do nothing but increase the love that you and I have for each other.

I should say an extra prayer tonight for the happiness I have found in my family. And with God's blessing, we shall always keep it that way.

I do have to head to dreamville now. It's only a few hours until I have to be back on the flight deck for a new day.

My love and happiness to Glyn and Jamey,

I love you, Sweetheart,

Always,

Jim

USS Kitty Hawk
"Free"
19 May '66

Hi Darling,

Typhoon Irma has virtually cut off our mail supply, so I'm sure you are not getting much mail your way either. The storm is still hanging around over at the north side of the Philippines, but the CODs can't travel back and forth. We're not getting any weather effect from it here, but for a while it looked as if it would be coming our way.

We have had a lot of rain out here due to monsoons, and that has curtailed flying somewhat, but that is more of a seasonal thing. The Gulf of Tonkin must have the world's worst yearly average of weather.

There's not much to report in the way of news. We're healthy and happy, and I guess that's a lot to be thankful for. What I'm most thankful for, though, is this abundant love I have for you. I think that has carried me through these months more than anything else that could be called forth. I just want you to know how important it is to have a love that is so full and that is returned with such an equal abundance.

May it always be so for you, me, Jamey, and Glyn. I love you all so very much.

Good night, My Darling.
I love you,
Jimmie

USS Kitty Hawk
"Free"
Saturday nite
21 May '66

Hi Darling,

We finally had a mail call tonight after almost a week of (mail) drought. And the major cause of the drought was rather wet! In fact, in one 24-hour period, they had more than 17 inches of rain in Cubi. All our mail feeds out of Cubi, and their four-day tiedown for Typhoon Irma cut off the flow.

I don't think the winds were too bad, but they had a lot of rain. I'm sure we'll get a full report from Beef if we ever get him back. He and Bill have been in there since last Sunday and had to ride it out. Tough deal, huh? With a bar right there in the BOQ! We'll give them permanent duty if we ever get them back aboard.

...I know you are all basking in the sun there in Sanford now. It's noticeable on the smiling faces around that birthday cake (in the pictures I received today). It looks like a happy bunch of kids, and I'm sure Glyn got the full enjoyment of the party. I wished her a long distance "Happy Birthday." It is kind of hard to say "going on six," but facts are facts, and it will probably sound even worse to say "going on sixteen."

...Now, I have only about four hours to sleep before I get up to fly in the morning, so I'd better drop off to dreamland now.

Good night, my lover,

I love you, Jimmie

USS Kitty Hawk
Monday afternoon
23 May '66

My Darling,

E' fini. The glorious day has finally arrived. I flew the last combat sortie just a few hours ago, and we are all hale and hardy. The captain has this bucket steaming for Cubi now with just about all the knots she will make...These past few days really have been something to behold. How we all lived through them I'll never know. Just the good grace of God, I'm quite sure. I hear the captain is even shattered to the point he has Medical ordered to issue two-fifths of medicinal ration to each Ready Room right after supper. He says he will pay for it himself. And for "Dry-Ship" Carmody, that's quite a changeover.

They just passed the word that we are out of the free mail zone and that's a sweet sound all in itself. I went down to buy a book of airmail stamps a while ago before the post office closed. That was one of the most pleasing purchases I have made all cruise. "Happiness is licking a stamp to put on an outgoing letter." The main point is that we are headed toward "home." It may be about three weeks away, but that's of little or no consequence now.

We probably won't do any more flying except for a couple of test hops on the planes at Cubi before we hoist them aboard. Now, it would just be fun flying when we could just go out and flail around the sky without worry of being shot at. I don't know if I'm going to remember how to fly that way anymore. Ha!

...I love you, Darling, so cry a little happiness for me, too, and I'll be there to show you how much that love is about 13 June. We'll change the calendar that day and call it 11 June (our wedding anniversary) regardless, okay?

I love you,

Jimmie

→ 6 ←

After four months at home—which included returning to the ship for "shakedown"—RVAH-13 again flew west to join the USS* Kitty Hawk *for a second Vietnam combat cruise.

Second Cruise—1966

USS Kitty Hawk
Saturday nite
5 Nov '66

Hi Darling,

Whether we like it or not, I guess we're really on the way. I hate to get back to this letter-writing business, but it looks like it's our best substitute since we can't communicate in person...I tried to call you last night, but since it was the last night in port for both us and the Bennington, operators were an impossible acquisition. There was not much I could say anyway except I love you and miss you enough already to last for the entire cruise. It would have been nice to hear your voice, though.

...The flail here was the usual one, but things are starting to settle down now that we are out at sea. We will stop two days in Hawaii on the 10th and 11th and then get to Yoko on the 20th.

I just got four (immunization) shots, and I am starting to feel a little woozy, so I'd better go to bed for now. I will try to be more coherent tomorrow night. My love to James and Glyn, and a pat on the head for Samson.

I love you,

Jimmie

USS Kitty Hawk
Sailing west
8 Nov '66

Hi Darling,

....I got a little flying in today, and it sure felt nice to get off the boat for a while. We've only been here three days now, and already it's getting old. We didn't do too well with our airplanes—had to send Ray in to Barber's point to get some parts, but he should be back tomorrow morning. He thought it was a good deal (to get to go ashore) until he figured out that it was Election Day and all the bars would be closed. Then his usual comment came, "If it's such a good deal, why am I getting it?"

...I finally got some time tonight to get my room somewhat straightened up. I am still not fully unpacked, but it may be better to just get things out as I need them. I did get the record player hooked up, and Nat King Cole sounds mighty good right now. I have a rug on the floor and an extra chair to prop my feet up on—at least some of the comforts of home. I think most of the room shuffle is over now, and I have a little more room here than in the room I had last year with not quite so much noise.

I'm about to flake out here now, Honey, so let me wish you a good night before I close...

All my love,

Jimmie

USS Kitty Hawk
At Sea
Friday, 11 Nov '66

Hi Sweetheart,

I got your first letter (since we've been out here) today, and, glad as I was to receive it, it served as a reminder that that's all I will see of you for the next seven or eight months. We've managed well enough with letters before, though, so I'm sure we can make it through with this one, also.

As you said, the advantage of getting them started is that when I'm back this time, we can know it is over and that there is something definite to look forward to. I'm afraid that's the worst part of cruises—the month or two of dreading them before they start. I regret that we didn't get to do all the things we planned this summer, but maybe it was because we just planned too much. I enjoy so much just being at home with you and the kids that I sometimes overlook the fact that you all have to be there all the time.

(Later...the ship has arrived in Hawaii.) The best laid plans can go awry. We have two days here as I had planned, and I did get to shop for a few trinkets yesterday before the shops closed and after the briefings were over. But today is Armistice Day, and there isn't a post office open anywhere on the islands or on the ship, and we leave tomorrow before they open. So now I will have to mail the things in Japan and declare customs. Besides that, you won't get them until after Christmas. Well, it was a nice try anyway.

...I was busy all yesterday with meetings, and today I have enough to do to keep busy all day. I don't think I will even have a

chance to leave the ship today. Best I get busy now or I'll wind up tomorrow trying to do the things required today.

I miss you very much, My Darling, and I love you and James and Glyn more than I can ever say. I just want to thank you again for the beauty and love that is in my life.

I love you, Jimmie

USS Kitty Hawk
Friday night
11 Nov '66

Hi Darling,

...Got your letter today about the hospital-case puppy you have. Hope Samson is over (the illness) by now. It could have been some lawn spray or fertilizer he got into. He's sure a good little mutt, though, so I don't want anything to happen to him. I won't mind having him around even on our trips home or on vacations.

I think you made a good choice, and actually, a home just feels a little better in the first place when there is a dog around to rub against your foot when you come in. I guess as long as he's got his pep and vinegar back he must be back in shape, though. Give Samson a pat for me—I didn't get the word in time to send him a get well card!

You know we never did finish out his name and send those papers in to the American Kennel Club, along with a lot of other things that got neglected that last week. Whatever you and the kids pick out will be okay with me. Something else I didn't do was fertilize that back yard. They put solid fertilizer on the rest of the yard, but didn't put any inside the fence. We have plenty in that wooden box in the back utility room if you think the yard needs some. You won't need to use the spreader—Jamey can just sling it out there by hand if you pick a day when the wind isn't blowing.

I'm glad your mother is going to come down for Thanksgiving. It will give you all something to plan on, too.

Tell Glyn it was perfectly all right for her to laugh out at Rev. Temple's joke (during his sermon Sunday). And I expect he was right pleased about it, too. He must be proud that he can get a five-year-old to listen that attentively to what he is saying. And I'm proud that she showed enough interest to hear it. Oh, teach her all of the Lord's Prayer. She knows most of it now and says it along with everyone in the church fairly well. So I think she's ready to learn it all so she can say it with everyone.

I'd best put this in the mail now, Sweetheart. A hug and kiss for all of you.

I love you,

Jimmie

At Sea
USS Kitty Hawk
Monday night
14 Nov '66

My Darling,

This is the slow drag time now. We are steaming along with not too much to do except train and brief and keep a crew ready in case of Russian overflights. And get shots—I had my plague booster tonight, and it's already beginning to take effect. Maybe I should be passing all this along to Samson, since he is probably the one who can best sympathize with me. I assume you've gotten his boosters by now, or will soon. We've only got one more shot to go now, and we'll be glad to have that part over.

...We're just past Midway Island, and it was beautiful here last year, and we did some flying during these two days. We're trying to get across faster this year, so there will be no flying until just before we reach Japan. I think they did send some mail in to Midway today, though, or at least I hope so.

Tomorrow will be a rapid day, since it will only be a few minutes long. We cross the Date Line right after midnight tonight, so it will be Tuesday the 15th for only a few minutes and then we shift over to Wednesday the 16th.

We have our situation comedy almost every day now, and I guess it was my turn in the barrel. I've been bugging them so long to get an extension phone in the back of the Ready Room, so we don't have to climb over the crews in the front to answer the phone. Tonight we arrived in the Ready Room at movie time to find a small toy Princess phone attached to the arm of the Skipper's chair marked "Batman" and another on the arm of mine marked "Robin." It was Frank Bransom's coup for the day, I'm sure....

I love you,

Jimmie

USS Kitty Hawk
At Sea
Wednesday night
16 Nov '66

Hi Honey,

I didn't get to write yesterday. Sorry 'bout that, but that was the day that never was. I think it was Armistice Day we skipped last year, but this year was the 15th. Pay day, laundry day, and a few things like that, but the talker on the LSO platform had the saddest story. He was telling Beef, "Mr. Renner, the navy finally got to me."

His division gives everyone the day off on their birthday, and guess who was born on 15 November! Beef told him to stay in the navy long enough and maybe he would cross it the other way on 15 November some time and get to have two birthdays the same year. But he did seem heartbroken that he was going to have to go two whole years between birthdays. Most women would be overjoyed to have that happen!

...We finally got a little action out of all this Condition Watch standing today. It may make the newspapers back home, but it is becoming a common occurrence out here now. The Russkies joined us today with two of their big birds. We picked them up far out from the ship of course, and we gave them a good fighter escort all the way in. I don't see where they gain much from those long flights anymore except training. We probably get more from them by learning their capabilities. They have real pretty airplanes, though.

The seas have been pretty rough out here today. Not rough enough to be a bother, but it makes sleeping mighty good. In fact, that motion plus a slight reaction from my shots had me sleep through my alarm clock this morning.

...Miss you mighty much, Sweetheart.

I love you,

Jimmie

USS Kitty Hawk
At Sea
Monday afternoon
21 Nov '66

Hi Darling,

Don't know how much of this you will be able to read as my fingers are practically numb from the cold. The weather has been clear and nice thus far, but it's freezing on this boat. And to top it all off, guess which machinery room they have to take the tube down into this year!

Remember last year after the fire I told you how they had to carry the boiler pipes into my room and back out and down the hole into the boiler? Well, this year I'm in a different room up across the passageway from Boiler No. 2. As you have guessed by now, the pipes have to go down that hole this year, and this morning a rap-rap on the door and "Scuz please" and in come the pipes again. I give up. That's just too much to cope with, so I think I'll just go over to Atsugi and stay for the rest of the week. I have to be there to fly Wednesday anyway, and I want to stay one day or so to look up friends.

...Thanksgiving will probably be past by the time you get this. Hope your mother got down okay and a good time was enjoyed by all. I'm sure the kids were tickled to death with both grandparents visiting them so close together.

Miss you much, My Darling,

I love you,

Jimmie

Give James and Glyn a belated "Happy Thanksgiving" from me!

USS Kitty Hawk
At Sea
Thanksgiving Day
24 Nov 1966

My Darling,

As filled as I am with both food and love, I've got to spill a little of the love over to you to make room for more food later. We had our big Thanksgiving dinner a couple of hours ago, and I ate too much as usual. The Japanese had their Thanksgiving Day yesterday. I don't know the history on theirs or why it came out to be only one day difference. As someone said last night, they probably have a big celebration on December 7 also...

That was wonderful news in your letter today, Sweetheart. It must be real great to Holly Bell, too, to find out Jim is a captive after well over a year of no news at all. Maybe this will lend some comfort to the other girls who are so long without anything to hope for. And then there are the others who may be prisoner in some small camp back off in the hills and haven't been moved into the centers where any word can get out. But I'm sure glad to hear that news on Jim.

Maybe that should be our earnest Thanksgiving prayer this day—to do our best to get this thing over with so we can start action to get those people out of there and back home to their families. I'm sure that even when it is ended there will be long months of arbitration and dealing just to get the prisoners out. I'm sure our prayers can help on that, too.

I hope you were able to get your family together for Thanksgiving... I wish you a happy one and wish so much I were there to share it with you. I miss you, My Love, and love you so very, very much.

Hugs and kisses to Glyn and Jamey.

I love you,

Jimmie

USS Kitty Hawk
Sunday afternoon
27 Nov '66

My Darling,

My room is still on the frosty side here, so maybe it won't be so bad to get down south and just thaw out a bit. Even with coats and jackets, my teeth are chattering. It makes it hard to work and to write. I have a batch of fitness reports to do, too, so I have to get in the mood for that soon. It's difficult to write reports on the new people when I don't know how they are going to produce.

We pulled out of Yoko yesterday morning, and….today has been a solid round of briefings, and we are to reconvene after supper for more of the same. This group came up from Saigon, and I talked to Ron Oelbeck and a few others that I met there last year. We all have a tendency to talk about "last year," but we're just past the six months mark!

...Wish I could climb on one of these mail planes and come sailing back to you. But I guess we had better take it one day at a time and not start looking ahead too far or it will make the time even longer than it really is. Actually, we've been through longer stretches of time, but I can't say that I liked it a darn bit better. What I like is being with you...continuously...Togetherness is really the most important part of life, and for me to have togetherness, you are the really essential element...At any rate, Darling, always believe I miss you as much as you miss me, and my major aim is to keep us together as much as possible.

Until that happy reunion,
I love you,
Jimmie

USS Kitty Hawk
Tuesday morning
29 Nov '66

Hi Darling,

I got tied up with night flying and then trying to get our mission planning room rebuilt last night, so I never got a chance to write. I will try to get something scribbled out here before lunch.

...All I've been able to do these last few days is procrastinate and put off the multitude of jobs that need to be done. The big one for tonight will be to write ten fitness reports, and that is an all-night job. Most of them are fairly easy to write, but still time-consuming. That's why I guess I always put them off until the last minute. At sea we always say, "Let's wait and do it in port" and then in port we say "wait for the sea." Wish I could learn to do things when they are due instead of waiting. When I have more to do than I have time for, I seem to get them all done, but when there is time to spare, I don't accomplish a thing.

...I'm sitting here listening to a new tape I bought of Rachmaninoff concertos by the New York Philharmonic. A new young pianist, Philippe Entremont, is soloist, and he is really good. I think I will borrow George's recorder and start putting all this on long tapes tonight.

...Maybe we can save up money this year so we can take that long-awaited trip to Nassau or somewhere next summer. Since I'm not coming back here, we won't feel we have to spend much time at home...and we can find a quiet spot to enjoy on our own....I didn't mean to neglect your wishes this last time, but it's just that with the short turnaround, we never got back down off the step. That's hard to explain, but just is as it is. But I do love you all the more and long for you with each passing day.

Miss you much, My Darling,
and Glyn and Jamey, too.
I love you, Jimmie

USS Kitty Hawk
Subic Bay, Philippines
Thursday nite
1 Dec '66

Hi Sweetheart,

We're back in Cubi again, and this place looks like we never have left it. Seems like just another period in off the line, and, if we look back to last May, it really hasn't been much different than that. Can't say we didn't enjoy that little interlude in between, because we did! But I do wish it had been somewhat longer. At least we can look to a longer one next summer and maybe a whole new setting with a whole new outlook and not have to bother about feeling that I never left this place again come next fall.

...The "Free" mail will start for us in a couple more days, but I notice they say "air mail space available to the States" instead of "guaranteed air mail." I'm not sure that it didn't say the same thing last year and always went air mail anyway. I'll try it, and if you are really slow getting letter let me know, and I'll go back to using air mail stamps.

We'll be back on the line by the time you get this, so letter writing might be scarce for a few days here. No more South Station time, so our ops will start up north and stay there for the whole time this cruise. That kinda takes away our fun flying, but I guess it gets more results than the other way. It's kind of a rough way to go on extended line periods, and this first one will be a long one.

It gives the sailors lots of money to spend when they get back into port, though...

...Nite my lover, always,

I love you, Jimmie

USS Kitty Hawk
"Free"
Saturday nite
3 Dec 1966

Hi Darling,

As you can see, we entered the "Free" mail zone today, and we'll be here for a little more than the next month. As we used to say, "Happiness is putting an 8¢ stamp on an air mail letter." We won't see that again until next year now.

We start combat ops tomorrow, and as you can imagine all I can really worry about is, "Have I told these new guys all they need to know?" We've tried hard, but somehow you always feel like you've forgotten something. I've been so busy with them, I'm going to have to work all night to get my own flight gear in shape. I didn't have time to unrig very much of it from last summer, though, so it shouldn't be too big a problem.

...If you wonder what people do on the first night before combat, I might give you a hint what the skipper and I were doing. Drinking Booze! No, actually I carried my tape recorder up, and we have been recording tapes since the movie turned out to be so sad.

...We had a pretty rough crossing of the South China Sea, and a couple of reporters we had come aboard have been too sick to do any writing. That suits me well enough! The PIO types were aboard today to take pictures for press releases, and we told them we didn't care for any. Maybe that's the wrong attitude, but with the crank

calls back home, why bother to feed fuel to the fire? I don't see why they have to give a lot of publicity to individuals anyway. Make it a unit-type thing, and then nobody in particular gets hurt by it.

Right now I'd like your media with no news. Miss you lots and lots and find that just a little smile or touch of your hand would be all the world to me.

...I love you, I love you, I love you.

Nite, My Darling,

Always, Jimmie

USS Kitty Hawk
"Free"
Monday afternoon
5 Dec '66

Hi Darling,

The big flail is on and just as furious as it was when we left here last year. Thought they would learn something in six months, but not really. I'm chasing around as bad as I was that last period on the line. There must be a calmer way to run a war, and I'm sure it would be if there wasn't so much politics and PIO. It feels good to be back flying, and I guess that is some compensation. Everyone in the squadron has loosened a bit—as if we weren't loose enough already!

(Late night:) I got called out before I was able to get any further with this letter, and, as you can see, there are dirty water smudges right here where I am writing...A major catastrophe happened while I was out. Somehow, some drain pipes got stopped up along the line and a big chunk of air came backing through the pipe and chugged out the drain to my sink, bringing sludge and water and dirt all over my room. The sink is centrally located in my room,

so no spot was untouched. And the desk is straight across from the sink, and it got flooded with water. Plus, all of the fitness reports I had about finished and letters and reports that were signed in ink are smeared.

Ag'buya, my room steward, had just spent all morning cleaning my room and had the place really looking nice. He almost cried when he saw the mess tonight as we tried to clean it up. Even after partial cleaning, the place looks almost as bad now as when I moved into it. Wattuse (Al Wattay) and I have been under pressure by the ship to move into a double room and give some staff types our single rooms, and after the pipe routine and the banging door across the hall—and now this—they can have it any time.

I had some new power of attorney forms all signed and everything with a missing clause and a five-year term, but the signatures are somewhat run together on them now. I'll see what I can do with them tomorrow and get a long envelope to mail them to you...I'm out of paper! So until tomorrow, my sweet, think of our love, this abundance of love that God gave to us all,

I love you,
Jimmie

USS Kitty Hawk
"Free"
Wednesday nite
7 Dec '66

Hi Darling,

...Got your Christmas box today and everything was in good shape as far as I can tell. But tell James and Glyn I didn't open the packages to peek. I thank you all very much. I'll sit them around

the room to look nice and pretty until Santa's morning. Of course I will have mine a whole day ahead of you.

The package brought some smiling comments at the table tonight. Dickie Daum asked if I had opened it yet because Clare wrote him and said she had "sent his balls to him in Dora's package." I mean, this is one outfit in which you don't even breathe in or you'll hear about it for the next week. Someone said the other day that he was going to refuse to speak in the Ready Room anymore. So this morning he walks in with a "Good morning" greeting and right back comes, "If I'd wanted a weather report, I'd call Aerology!"

Poor Wattuse is starting to survive now, though. Everyone is letting him off for a couple of days until he gets to fly. Airplane troubles seem to always come to him, and he's only had one hop thus far. The weather has been bad anyway, but he would feel better if he got to fly more.

...We were just talking at lunch today about our obligations, and how 25 years ago the Japs broke loose at Pearl Harbor. Ray said, "And you know them silly Germans are at home tonight on top of the world, and the Japs are industrial giants and sitting at home with their families, and us silly American SOBs are out here in the middle of the puddle telling each other we won the war! Now where is the justice?"

The Christmas tree ball I got out of the package for me had to be rearranged. The picture had been moved around so far I could hardly see it. But now I have two smiling faces looking at me from the front and a pointed-eared watchdog I no longer recognize. That's quite a comparison—the picture of the floppy-eared mutt sitting in your lap with Jamey and Glyn on the couch compared with the one in the Christmas ball. No relation, I'm sure. It's hard to believe Samson could have grown that much. I'm sure he must be a pleasure to have around the house, and I'm glad I got to be with him as a pup so maybe he will let me in the house next summer!

I have an early hop tomorrow, my darling, so for now I'll send a hug and a kiss and long for the day when we can just enjoy some old-fashioned smooching and just laugh and love and be happy with each other. I do enjoy your company so very, very much. Nite, Sweetheart.

I love you,
Jimmie

USS Kitty Hawk
"Free"
Friday nite
9 December '66

My Darling,

...Well, the message (about the Skipper's orders) got here today, and he (Roy McLain) has been run something fierce ever since it arrived. Of course everyone feels sorry for him, but you can't help riding him a bit—especially since he came out here with a light load of clothes expecting only a short stay. He will relieve Cdr. Dick Case as Air Operations Officer on the ship, which is a good job but a long way from Florida. I think he was expecting a Mayport carrier, and this kind of knocked the blocks out. He's had about five consecutive cruises now, and he will surely see two more.

He was mostly worried about what June will say, but when I got your letter today, you indicated she already knows. He said his last letter was dated the 28th, so she must have found out since then.

...These nights are getting later and later my love, but, rest assured, you always know I love you. You and the kids mean all the

world to me, and I put nothing else before that. The time will soon pass, and we will be back together so we can fully show that love.

For now, I just have to say,

I love you

Jimmie

USS Kitty Hawk
"Free"
Monday night
12 Dec '66

Hi Darling,

Haven't written for a couple of days due to the big move. I have now lived in six rooms on this ship in the past 18 moths. Actually, this wasn't such a bad deal. That room I was in was so bad I was going to move one way or another. The staff commanders that came aboard in Yoko aren't on speaking terms, so when they found out some of us air wing lieutenant commanders were in single rooms, they reared their pointed little heads. So Al Wattay and I got kicked out yesterday, and we moved up to the 03 level just under the flight deck.

Al and I are roommates just next door to Ray Vehorn and Ron Queen. This is three times as good a room as the one I had down on the second deck, and last night was the first quiet night's rest I've had in a month. I think after a day or so those staff types are going to realize they stepped on their lizzy by squawking about these rooms.

...We've been planning all night on a big exercise for tomorrow, and that's why I'm late with this letter. Mail is starting to come through pretty good out here now, and the ones I got today only took five days. Have you had enough for any comparison of the "Free"

mail vs. those with an air mail stamp yet? I doubt that there is any notable difference.

I know that cool air is starting to be felt in Florida for the winter shopping, but right now I would surely like to shiver through it with you. Christmas shopping and all...

I love you,

Always, Jimmie

USS Kitty Hawk
"Free"
Thursday afternoon
15 Dec '66

Hi Darling,

Can't remember how far I am behind in writing, but I know it's quite a few days. You may have read in the papers about the Hanoi strikes the past few days, so that's what all the flail has been about and where my time has been devoted. Jack and I went up just south of there on a big one yesterday and had quite a jolly good ride of it. We got home in one piece with the pictures, and I guess that's what counts.

On the whole, it looks like things are going to be a little rougher this year than they were the last time out. I'm sure we'll manage our way through it. Maybe just one day at a time, but eventually that will get us there. Just wish someone would make up their mind to let us have at it and get the thing over with.

Jack and I had quite a hassle Tuesday when we were originally scheduled up toward the big city and the throttle linkage broke on the cat shot. I stuck full power on one engine so that was happiness. Had to go to Da Nang, though, and that's not my ideal as a divert field. That's the dirtiest rat hole of a place I ever saw, and bombs and guns going off all around the place. It was raining and muddy and the "BOQ" is a 20-man tent with cots.

I kinda figured my bed on the ship looked a lot better, and I was hungry besides, so we found the broken linkage and bolted it back together and headed back to the ship. It was already dark, and they had canceled night ops, so they sent me back to Da Nang again and said I could come back at 2200 if I wanted to. So we went back and refueled and then came out again and finally got aboard. I had my first meal since breakfast at midnight. I was so tired, but I had an early brief yesterday morning, so just went straight to bed and collapsed.

...There is all kind of action here now. There went CAG Williams off in the COD on his way back home. We had the change of command yesterday for the Air Wing, and Cdr. Hank Urban relieved Royce Williams as CAG. He is an ex-A-4 driver and seems to be a real nice gent. I've sort of got the day off today as far as flying goes. I've got a few hops ahead of everyone else this week, so I get to play ODO now. I need the time to catch up on paperwork, though. Reports are due and all kinds of regular routing stuff...it still feels more and more like we never left here in the first place.

I'm running through some of the tapes I copied, and they sound really nice. Ray Anthony, Jackie Gleason, and Billy Butterfield and the music is smooth and dreamy. Wish I had you here to enjoy it with me or rather me there to enjoy it with you. It's mostly nice old favorites for cuddling up close.

...I love you, Sweetheart so very, very much. I'll write you more tonight. Have to go to work now.

I love you,

Jimmie

USS Kitty Hawk
"Free"
Saturday nite
17 Dec '66

My Darling Wife,

Only six more shopping days until Christmas and not a thing I can do about that either...We had a little clearer weather today and finally got in for a look at some of the old familiar parts of the beach. Not that it brings any pangs of nostalgia, but it does seem rather familiar after the short respite. With luck, we will have another good day tomorrow and get something to look at other than clouds. I've had a few runs myself before this, but most of the others haven't been inland very far yet. It was the same way when we were here last December, so I don't know why we expected it to be any different this time.

Actually, there is one big advantage of having been through this mill once before. We just kinda shrug our shoulders and smile while the ship bigwigs are sweating out each day because we can't get in there and do all the good work. The weather has been this way every year from time immemorial, and it isn't apt to change this year, so why sweat it? But everyone figures we've been here two weeks and haven't set any records yet. Ha!

...Can't write any more tonight, Sweetheart, but I promise to do better tomorrow. Much as much...I love you,

Jimmie

USS Kitty Hawk
"Free"
Wednesday nite
21 Dec '66

My Darling Wife,

I was going to start this early tonight, but Al and I got off on a tangent, and I'm afraid I had to give him some of my voiced opinion of people who spend ten years getting to fly and fight a war and then turn their chits in as soon as the shooting starts. I don't include Al in the list, because he's out here being shot at, and any of those who have made one cruise out here and leave have their own out, too. But it's just some of those who are heading out for the first trip and bail out that I don't care to see anymore.

Got a little hopped on the subject when he said he didn't blame them because of the way the war is being run. Hell, if everyone quits just because they don't like the decision someone above them makes, it would be a helluva country to live in! For that matter, I guess it wouldn't be a country for very long.

Best I get off the subject and cool off a bit so I can get some sleep. Got much to do tomorrow and sweet dreams of you will make the whole day go much nicer. We still have rather bad weather and are only getting limited work done...

Did you know today was the first day of winter? I told that to my plane captain as he was strapping me in today with beads of sweat all over his face. He laughed and almost fell off the ladder. He's a southern-style colored boy, and this hot climate is about to do him in. When I told him it was only going to get hotter, I think he was ready to try some other line of work.

We put our Christmas cards up tonight, so the locker doors are fairly well covered. A nice sweet-tasting one from you with mistletoe

I put right in the middle. Have two trees down in the Ready Room. VAW-11 flew in and got a real live one from the beach and colored lights to go with it. And Jim Morgan brought his aluminum tree to hang all the squadron decorations on.

Sounds like you got a tree early enough this year to get a good one and get full enjoyment from it. Both of the kids are big enough now to really enjoy putting the decorations on—with Samson's help, I'm sure. I'll just have to plan on a big tree next year to make up for all of the last three I've missed...A cozy couch and a big thick rug in front of a warm fireplace sounds awfully nice...Until then, my love, I love you always.

Nite and sweet dreams,

I love you,

Jimmie

USS Kitty Hawk
"Free"
Tuesday nite
20 Dec '66

Hi Darling,

Seems I get less done on the days I don't fly than on the ones when I do. Either way, I'm here at the desk after midnight to start a letter. Maybe it's nice we are on the noon-to-midnight schedule now, because, whether or not I want it, I sure seem to be organized when we shift to some other cycle.

No need to get to bed too early, though, because Al just landed, and I'm sure it will be at least another hour before he gets to the room—with a big tale to tell. He gets full excitement out of every flight over here, and I'm sure we must have been the same way last year. I've got about twice as much night flying as anyone else now, so I don't feel one bit bad about letting them catch up.

...We just got our newest "Bat" aboard today from an oiler. Todd Crombie, who is Keith Nichols' relief, had been in Cubi a week. He finally caught one of the supply ships out to us. We didn't know he was there, so we couldn't get him a priority on a COD, and they wouldn't let him send a message to tell us. Too many senators to bring out, I suppose...

I'm getting groggy here now, Sweetheart, and I can see visions of very sweet dreams of you. I promise to meet you in dreamland and look forward to the day we can dream together in each other's arms...

I love you,

Jimmie

USS Kitty Hawk
"Free"
Saturday night
24 Dec '66

My Darling Wife,

...Just a few more minutes before midnight, and Christmas will be here...I've missed a couple of days writing here because of the mix-ups over who was supposed to work when and the constant chase to try and prepare a flight schedule. We actually got a day off today, but you'd never know it from the tired way my legs feel.

Some of the people got a rest, though, and we did have a chance for a Christmas service tonight. It was just over an hour ago, and the roar of the organ is still in my ears. The amplifier had a squeal in it, and I was sitting right under the speaker. They probably had a nice musical service, but I didn't hear too much of it. There was a good crowd in the hangar bay, though.

The other ships get tomorrow off, and we get a chance to work all day. I have the early one tomorrow morning, so I will get to have my Christmas morning sunrise service this year flying down the catapult on my way to North Vietnam. As usual, the time is a bombing truce, but that doesn't apply to the photos. Actually, it means increased work for us, because they want more and more pictures to see what is moving during the lull. This is only a two-day stand down, so it won't make much difference in the defenses the way that long one did last year. I don't particularly want any more of those unless, of course, it's one that stops it forever.

I've been opening Christmas presents now that it's Santa's Day. Of course, you and the kids have to wait because it's not even really Christmas Eve there yet. In fact, the stores aren't even closed, and I expect there is much last-minute shopping going on about now. Sorry I can't be there doing some for you!

...Right now I'm just so thankful to see the sun rise tomorrow with a Christmas that is so very different from the tasks I had before me in the past two years at this time. I guess it's a good reminder, and we can always say a special prayer for them (Max, Glenn, Dave, and Lee) each year at this time, and before another year maybe there will be some news on which to base our hope...

Now, while I chomp on this nice fruitcake from Glyn, I'll explain why I didn't get a letter written last night. Gordy's night hop was canceled, so we decided to throw him a wetting down party instead. The gold marks on his flight suit shoulder are Lcdr. stripes that we had the paraloft sew on for his night flight. Todd Crombie had a pair of king-sized shoulder boards, and thus we promoted two new "majors" last night...and at 3 a.m. we had a songfest going, accompanied by Al Wattay and his singing violin. Al actually can play the thing, and when he does it sounds more like a fiddle. He plays well enough that the songs are easily recognizable. The Skipper wasn't coming until the threat got strong toward going down to sing carols outside his door, so he decided the best tact would be to join the group. The Skipper kept looking up (at XO Charlie Putnam) and saying, "Soon, Charlie, they'll all be yours!"

...Billy Graham is coming on board tomorrow afternoon. I don't think he is going to have his service until 8 a.m. Monday morning, and I'm not sure I can get up that early! I may listen to him tomorrow night, though, if he gets here in time for the regular evening service.

...Sweetheart, I've got to get to bed, and I wish I could think of the million thoughts I would like to convey to you this Christmas Eve. But right now my brain is too dull to stay on the subject. Just know that I love you and James and Glyn, too. I miss you all very much this day and every day and I love you with all my heart.

Pray for me as I pray for you and place our hopes in things eternal. We can and shall overcome all things.

I love you,
Jimmie

USS Kitty Hawk
"Free"
Monday nite
26 Dec '66

Hi Darling,

...I guess you're battling the kids about now, trying to get some semblance of order after the shambles Christmas Day must have left their rooms in. I know they had a thoroughly enjoyable time, though, and I'm so glad for them. I wish I could have been there to

enjoy it with them and, most particularly, with you, too. It's just not fair for you to have to play Santa three years in a row. Maybe you didn't have too many assembly projects to contend with this year—and I'm sure Samson was more than willing to help out.

We opened all our packages here, and I thank you all very much. The leather toilet kit was just right and just in time, since the other one finally came apart. Your birthday package arrived today, and I will open it tomorrow morning. And I will write James and Glyn individual thank you's, but give them a kiss for me.

I didn't make it to the Billy Graham meeting because I had an early hop, but I never actually got airborne. It was raining cats and dogs, and I was soaking wet even before I got to the airplane. They finally canceled the rest of the launches for the day, and we got another day off whether we wanted it or not.

...The big COD got here today—in spite of the rain—and brought a goodly stack of mail. I got four letters dated from 12 to 20 December, so maybe they will catch up one day soon...The pictures are really good of the Christmas tree trimmings and of the door decorations. I'm sure you all must have had a lot of fun setting them up...I know I'm missing out by not being there to watch them, but just reading your description of things is a joy in itself...A kiss for all and my fullest Merry Christmas love.

I love you, Jimmie

USS Kitty Hawk
Wednesday night
28 Dec '66

Hi Honey,

...Tell Jamey and Glyn that (the guys) all sang Happy Birthday to me last night after the movie, so I got the equivalent of a birthday

party. Of course they used some slightly different words, but the song did have the same meaning. I got your package on the 26th, so I had present-opening time last night as well. The cards the children sent are great, and I enjoyed them very much. The handiest thing of all was the birthday Bat pillow you sent. I don't have a place to prop my pillow in this bed, so I'll get a lot of use out of that one. Thank you very much!

We have about six more days on the line here, and then we head for Cubi...I suppose a cease-fire will come again on the 31st and 1st, but, as usual, we will have full days of recco if the weather permits. It's hard to tell about weather prospects now with the typhoon that is south of Cubi. It looks like it is fading out now, so it might not affect us over here...Here is a kiss for each of you. I love you.

Always, Jimmie

USS Kitty Hawk
"Free"
Friday nite
30 December '66

Hi Darling,

...Would you believe that tomorrow is the last day of the year?... The only thing I really care about in '67 is that I get to spend a little more of it with you than I did in '66, and, one way or another, we will vow that to be true. I'm sure the cease-fire is all over the papers at home, but it means a double effort for us tomorrow...

I just stopped here for the chaplain's evening prayer, and I had to dwell a moment on his "Thanks for the fidelity of our mates." Did you ever stop to realize just how fantastic it is that out of the billions of people in the world that two could mate and be one as we have? We take our love and fidelity so much for granted when it is a thing that so few have or can ever hope to attain. Such a thing is so out of reach that it can only be made by God, and we should be ever so thankful that he has chosen us to share and be a part of it.

It never dawns on me that things could be any different until I look around at others that have parted or gone separate ways, and then I realize how truly fortunate we really are. We've had a fuss or two here or there but nothing to ever sway the trust that binds us. Someday, when we begin to worry about our children and the mates they will find, we will realize all the many things that should not be left for granted.

I give thanks now for all the blessings we have. I love you, my darling, so very, very much, and I thank you over and over for all the wonderful joys you brought me over these many years. But most of all I thank God for the gift of love that only He has the power to give.

Maybe if we teach our children properly, they too can find the happiness that we so want them to have. I guess I'm a big one to talk, since I'm the one who is never there to answer the questions. That bothers me too, Honey, quite a bit, and I never know really what to do about it....I guess they can be over-guided...and I'm not sure that those who spend the most time at home come out with a superior mode of guidance.

...Hope you have a Happy New Year! Give James and Glyn a big hug and kiss for me and give Samson a pat on the head...

I love you, My Darling.

Your loving husband, always,

Jimmie

→ 7 ←

Second Cruise Continues

USS Kitty Hawk
1 Jan '67

Hi Lover,

I guess it's really here now all the way for both you and me. It's just about one minute past midnight in Sanford right now, so pucker up sweet and catch this kiss from all around the world that I send to you. I sure wish we could ring this one in the way it should be done, but know for sure that the sentiment is there anyway. I'm looking forward to a whole new year to love you all the more, and that should be adequate in itself...

With love totally yours, my darling,
I love you,
Jimmie

USS Kitty Hawk
At Sea
Thursday afternoon
5 Jan '67

Hi Darling,

Don't know if we are going to get into port or not. We were slowed down at first by rough weather and seas, and then today we got turned back toward the Paracel Islands to help out a merchant ship in distress. Apparently, either they got off the reef okay, or they sank because the call for help was canceled about noon today.

We are headed back toward Cubi now, but it will be late tomorrow afternoon before we can get there. We flew four airplanes in today, but I'm still grounded because of my cold so I had to stay here on the ship. I never rode the ship in from this end before, and it sure is a drag just sitting here steaming. I haven't flown for about four days, so that makes it even worse. I don't think I would make a very good blackshoe...

My throat is almost cleared up now that I'm on these tetracycline tablets. The cold is still bad, though, and my head is all stopped up. I think some fresh air and sunshine are the necessary ingredients to cure that. We've been running about 50 knots of wind on the flight deck, so that's a little more than the medicinal variety.

I need you to nurse me back to health. We could have a lot of fun trying, I'm sure. We could just swap the cold back and forth... Such problems we would like to have! Maybe that will be our big worry next year—if we're lucky.

Nite, sweetheart,
I love you
Jimmie

USS Kitty Hawk
Subic Bay
Friday afternoon
6 January 1967

Hi Darling,

We finally made it into port, and it seemed everyone was waiting on the quarterdeck for the gangplank to drop. It's always a rush trying to get a car to get up the hill, so I'll just wait until later to go over...I can tell one difference right away. It feels like they turned the heaters on in here, and there is no doubt we're in Cubi. It must be at least 85 or 90 degrees, but at least there is a breeze to keep it from being unbearable. It might give me a worse cold rather than put a stop to this one, though...

I probably won't try to call you while we are in port until Saturday or Sunday. It's a rather lengthy process, and I have to have time available for waiting. I either have to call late at night or very early in the morning, and that's not always conducive to my habitual sleeping patterns. I might go to sleep while waiting for the call to go through. I hear that they have a new rule here now requiring that I go over to the Telephone Exchange building to make the call. I'll check that out tomorrow and give it a try.

...Bye for now, Sweetheart,

I love you,

Jim

USS Kitty Hawk
Subic Bay, Philippines
10 Jan '67

Hi Darling,

...I spent yesterday in jungle survival school, and...the jungle gig was not completely without reward. We had a 45-year-old Negrito guide who had been a guerrilla lieutenant in the Philippine forces in World War II, and just talking to him was an education in itself.

The Negritos in the Philippines are like the American Indians are in the U.S., and they have been treated about the same. They range from pygmy size to a little larger and have lived in tribes in the mountains, but they are not headhunters like the Huks. They are a very honest and hard-working people, and they don't like the "lazy Filipinos" at all.

They lived in the jungles during World War II until the U.S. forces gave them guns and organized them into guerrilla forces. Then after the war, the guide told us, the Philippine government put them on reservations and wouldn't let them have jobs or anything.

The U.S. Navy kind of adopted the tribe here in Zambales and gave them ground to build their village on, gave them a school, and guaranteed all of the men jobs. These people have nothing to do with Longapo or the Filipinos on the base. They all work on the base as guards, guides, instructors, or security police, and they do a real good job because they are honest and you can trust them.

I told this one guy he should be a recruiting officer for the U.S. Navy, because to hear him talk the U.S. Navy is the greatest thing that ever lived, and he really means it. Of course the navy has given him the opportunity to work and live like a human instead of cooped up on a reservation, so I guess it's easy to understand his feelings. We get our money's worth back from these guys, because they do twice the normal day's work and only get paid the equivalent of about $2 per day.

His view of the Japanese is really eye opening...I asked him what made his people willing to fight as guerrillas after the Japanese took over and had control of the Philippines. He talked about the bad treatment by the Japanese they experienced, and said MacArthur's statement, "I shall return," made them willing to risk fighting the Japs. He said they all knew about that man and knew what he had said. It was necessary for American soldiers to slip back and organize the guerrillas, though.

This little guy...actually was the one who made the knife, the Sally Moreno, I brought home last year. I thought when I got that knife that it bore a girl's name, but not quite so. In fact, he has seven kids, including one grown boy who works as a guard.

Jamey and Glyn are probably interested in what a real live jungle is like. First off, since it's tropical, it's hot and you have to wear long-sleeved shirts and keep the collar buttoned up to keep the bugs out—so you sweat even if it's not raining. And it rains most every day in the tropical jungle. That's what makes the vines grow so thick and the trees so tall.

The top of the trees are at around 200 feet, and you seldom see the sky. But, strangely enough, you don't see many snakes or animals, and I guess the biggest thing we ran into—or rather away from—was the wild boar hog. The animals are wild and curious, but they generally stay away from humans.

About the only things we could catch to eat were wild chickens, bats, fish, and crayfish. Those bats are really something to behold. They fly over by the thousands, mostly in late afternoon, and they are the biggest things I've ever seen. Some of the large ones had wingspans of three to four feet, and even the babies were bigger than any bats I'd seen. Of course we wanted a big one to bring back for the Ready Room, but the guide cooked and ate the two we caught. I ate some of it, and it wasn't bad.

There are all kinds of fruits and roots and shoots to eat, but they are not all that easy to find. There are water vines that give drinking water—you just chop off a three-foot length and hold it up and about a cup of water runs out. And there is a water tree that you tap at night like you would a maple tree, and it fills up a five-gallon can in just a few hours.

Two really interesting things were the simple vine from which you take a piece of wood, mash it up, and wet it with water to make as much soap suds as would a cup of laundry detergent and the breadfruit tree that gives off a sap that sticks better than epoxy. They cover a stick with the sap, warm it a little over a fire, and let it dry until it's tacky, then prop it up in a berry tree. When birds come along to sit on the limb, they stick like fly paper, and it's impossible for them to get loose.

They told us that last year a parrot got his feet stuck, and when he tried to pick the limb loose with his bill the bill got stuck, too. When they found him he was sitting with his head between his legs, and he couldn't move! They showed us the different types of snakes and the monitor lizard—and would you believe a lizard that grows as big as six feet long? That's the size of a small alligator. Then it was mostly walk, walk, walk and chop on bamboo to make a bed. They make beds out of three-inch diameter bamboo poles that are up on stilts, and the "mattress" is a row of about 12 eight-foot poles. It was the most miserable thing I've ever tried to sleep on because it's impossible to find poles that are even or straight. You can imagine how I feel today.

There isn't much noise in the jungle—it's nothing like what we've seen in the movies. In fact, it's even quieter than the woods in Tennessee, particularly at night. And the biggest fallacy is that the lion is king of the jungle. It's hard to decide whether that honor goes to the ants or the mosquitoes, but last night there was no doubt that the ant was the winner.

Missing you all very much, My Darling, even when I'm busy. I look forward to the time when Jamey, Glyn, and you and I can do our own fishing together. My love to you all,

I love you,

Jimmie

USS Kitty Hawk
Subic Bay, Philippines
10 January '67

My Darling Dora,

I have so many letters here to answer that it's difficult finding a place to start. I've just about run out of steam anyway after no sleep last night, and I want to ensure at least a full eight hours before I go to fly tomorrow.

...Well, there goes my letter and probably my sleep, too. I just got a call from the OOD, and they are having personnel trouble on Grande Island and need an Air Group Lcdr. down there as soon as possible. All their Lcdrs are on the beach, so guess that leaves the CAG duty officer—and that's me. Best I get going, so will finish this later.

Nite, Sweetheart, I love you.

Subic Bay, Philippines
Friday Night
13 January '67

...Man, when I say later, I really mean later. Well, it was a GREAT change of command, sweetheart. I'll go back and bring you up-to-date, though...The farewell party for Cdr. McLain last night was outstanding, even if I was the entertainment director. Beef, Ray, and I had worked for two weeks preparing the skit, and it went off as well if not better than we had expected. The Skipper took all the riding well, and most everyone caught on to all the digs the first time through. We gave him a nice silver punch bowl and cups, a plaque, one of the best scrapbooks I've seen (one advantage

of being in a photo squadron), and a big picture of himself in a Batman costume. The chiefs gave him even more stuff, and it seemed to get to him that he had to leave. I don't know of a CO who has ever been sent out in grander style.

This means I've got much work to do tomorrow to catch things up before the ship pulls out. I'm going to stay here in Cubi Saturday and Sunday to fly a plane out to the ship Monday. So for now, Sweet, I'd better get some much-needed sleep.

...Love you, my Darling,

A hug and kiss to Glyn and Jamey.

I love you, Jimmie

USS Kitty Hawk
Sunday night
16 January '67

My Darling,

I'm sitting here nodding asleep so I should take a short nap and then get up to write you a letter, but I know full well that if I ever reach the horizontal I won't wake up until at least noon tomorrow. The ship got underway this morning and, after closing down the base last night, we were all lying in the BOQ with visions of an afternoon in the sun and another night ashore before flying out to the ship tomorrow.

Well, it just wasn't meant to be, because here I sit on a reeling and rolling boat just about too pooped to pop. It seems they had a change of plans, and just in the middle of our naps, we were broken out to get some airplanes ready—and stand by to stand by.

They didn't finally call us out until late this afternoon, but they kept changing plans enough to effectively keep us out of bed... Actually, I'm just as glad we came on out. It will give us one day of rest tomorrow before we go back on the line. We are in rough seas right now, and it's expected to get worse tomorrow, so that's why they wanted to get us aboard today. The ship was bouncing around quite a bit when we came aboard as it was.

...Honey, I'll write you a long letter tomorrow, but now, I've got to get some sleep. I love you, Jimmie

USS Kitty Hawk
At Sea
Monday night
16 Jan '67

Hi Sweetheart,

...These rough seas are really something. They have slowed us down a day in getting back across the puddle. It was so rough last night we could hardly sleep.

Al put up the bed rail on his upper bunk to make sure he didn't fall out, but he forgot the wooden cruise box he had up on top of the lockers, so we got a rude reminder about 2 a.m. when the cruise box came crashing to the floor and splinters went flying! Luckily, it didn't break anything in the box, but we got a lot of inquiries from neighbors this morning about "who fell out of bed?"

I've been listening to a very long tape from Mother and Dad... I wish I had time to listen to the rest of it now, but I have to get cleaned up for supper. I've got targets to get laid out tonight and schedules to complete. We fly in the morning, so maybe I can get back to the tape by tomorrow afternoon. I'll finish this letter after supper. Love you, Jimmie

USS Kitty Hawk
"Free"
Thursday nite
19 Jan '67

Hi Darling,

The weather finally cleared up here for a couple of days, so you can imagine the flail we have been in. Getting a lot of work done for a change, so the bomber types are finding out what the photos are for. It's really a rat race for us, though, as far as getting any sleep or eats is concerned. Letters will be a little scarce until things settle down a bit.

We did have one highlight yesterday with distinguished visitors aboard. I got to meet "Mr." Barry Goldwater. He says that's what he is since he came out here as a taxpayer, and he is really out of office at the present. Charlie CO had dinner with him in the admiral's cabin and said he is a rather personable individual. He looks exactly like his pictures, and he is in good shape for his age. He is shorter than I imagined, though—a couple of inches shorter than I am. He only stayed aboard for a few hours, so I'm not sure whether there was a purpose to his visit. He did say that the only way to get along back in Washington was to act like a dove and think like a hawk. Ha!

...I'd better go now to see how tomorrow's pitch is going. My love to James and Glyn and a kiss for all.

I love you very, very much.

Your loving husband, Jimmie

USS Kitty Hawk
"Free"
Saturday nite
21 Jan '67

Hello Sweetheart,

...Just got out of Strike Ops, hassling out tomorrow's schedule. There's not time for a full letter now, because I have to get up early tomorrow—but I do want to tell you how much I love you.

...I called Charlie C.O. a little while ago to tell him about some schedule changes, and the answer on the phone was not quite repeatable. He did say "hello," and for a few seconds, I wondered if I had the right room. Then he explained. It seems he was asleep when the phone rang, and a vent pipe had overflowed, leaving about two inches of water in his room. So when he leaped out of bed in the dark to answer the phone, he was rather shocked to splash both bare feet into a pool of water! You can imagine the comment on the phone. I told him not to complain too heavily, because at least he had a few hours' sleep.

That's where I'm headed right now, Sweetheart. Into the land of sweet dreams, so I can dream only of you.

I love you.

Jimmie

USS Kitty Hawk
"Free"
Monday nite
23 Jan '67

Hi Darling,

This has really been a nice day. I had an early hop scheduled, but the weather socked in and the hop got canceled. So I just rolled over and slept in all the way to 9 a.m. I've felt about 900 percent better all day. We were getting to the point we needed a day off, and it came at just the right time. We even went further and had a movie in the Ready Room this afternoon, and it was just the right hilarious type, "Those Magnificent Men in Their Flying Machines. If you get a chance to see it, I'm sure even the kids would enjoy it. It's mostly slapstick comedy, but the type that would make Jamey laugh his head off. It may have been that we were really in need of a tension buster, but I thought the movie very funny.

The new XO (Len Higgenbotham) got here yesterday, and he's getting a real fast break-in...He seems like a welcome addition to the squadron thus far. He's no replacement for Roy McLain, as you can imagine, but we didn't expect one of those—I don't really expect that any exist. I think you thought as much of Roy and June as I did, so there's no need of a comment from me on their leaving.

We had a little "wetting down party" for Higgy last night, and I'm glad to find one that looks worse than I do the morning after. He's hot to get airborne, though, and he stayed at it all day to get checked out so I can start him flying tomorrow.

...I love you. Here's a kiss for Jamey and Glyn, too.

Nite, My Darling, Jimmie

USS Kitty Hawk
"Free"
Tuesday nite
24 Jan '67

Hi Sweetheart,

...It's really been raining here like hell today, and yesterday. It's just as well, since those couple of days' rest have felt awfully nice. That's enough now, though; we're ready to get back to flying—

especially the new XO, since I need to get him in the air before too long. He's really a charger (like you said).

We had a little ceremony tonight, primarily for the promotion of George Comstock to lieutenant and to razz him a little bit. Then we had a little award for Higgie commemorating his lengthy trip—14 days—to get here when most everyone else does it in four days.

It took an emergency meeting of the Bogus Award Committee (Ray, Beef, and I) to get the citation written. We didn't have as much to work on as we would like, but I don't think he feels like he slipped in unnoticed anymore now...I'm afraid Hig is now of the opinion that the squadron doesn't have a serious bone in its makeup, however. He doesn't strike me as the type who will look for any changes, though. George (Comstock) will be his b/n, so it was nice that he could make lieutenant before they start flying.

Once I get the new XO flying, I'll have to get him checked out on combat operations, and that will take up most of the spare hours for a few days. It will be a good review for me, too, so I don't mind doing it.

...Missing you very much, sweetheart. I miss Jamey and Glyn, too, and I hope school is going well for them. I will try to write them soon.

Nite, My Love, I love you,

Jimmie

USS Kitty Hawk
"Free"
Friday nite
27 Jan '67

Hi Darling,

...This line period seems to get longer by the day or maybe by the hour, since it seems like we've been here a month already, and

we are really only a third of the way through it. I just hope we can keep the rest of the guys from getting too frustrated over it.

One who is already getting the picture is our new XO. I can't seem to get him airborne yet. The first day the weather was too bad; the second day we ran out of airplanes; and then today they canceled his hop to get loaded for a big strike. So I scheduled him for a bright and early sunrise one tomorrow morning. Now watch the plane go down! I have to get up and brief him, too, so I had better remember to get to bed soon. He seems real fine, though, and we are glad to have him. He sidled over to me the other day and said, "You know, you just don't dare put out any big mouth in this outfit, do you?" And I said, "Man, you have learned more in three days than most people find out in a month." But I think he's pleased that it is that way...I will have to continue this tomorrow, Darling, 'cause I've got to get to bed tonight.

I love you,

Jimmie

USS Kitty Hawk
"Free"
Saturday nite
28 Jan '67

Hi Darling,

This day has really dragged for me because I had ODO, and those ten flights of steps to the tower get old after a while. Happiness was getting the XO airborne twice. I know it felt good to him to get back to flying, too. He hasn't complained, but it was obvious he was getting anxious. I told him I was probably more anxious than he was to get him flying since we were already essentially short one crew.

I heard some very sad news today via the rumor net. Someone says they heard a radio broadcast saying that Grissom, White, and Chaffee were lost on an attempted Apollo launch at Cape Kennedy. I didn't realize they were scheduled for any shots in January, but we get very little of the national news here anyway...Feel really sorry for their families, though, and all the beating they are going to have to take from the news people. They will be plagued to death with questions even before the funeral is over.

They just announced cancellation of the midnight launch tonight, so maybe we can get a full night's sleep before starting tomorrow morning. I have to fly through church hours tomorrow, and I really wanted to go to this service. We have a new chaplain aboard, Al Propst, and I wanted to hear him...

(Later) After dinner and three revisions of the flight schedule, I finally get back to you. Not that they won't change it again on us before I get to bed. At least I've got a head start. Actually, the only way to deal with it is to have patience. Last week, when things were really at their worst, I was laughing about how fouled up something was in the Ready Room, and Gary Long looked at me, shook his head, and said, "You must have the patience of Job. I would be stark raving mad by this time." It wouldn't have been so funny, except that Gary is the calmest, most easygoing guy in the squadron.

Everybody was all over him in the Ready Room one night about the movie, and he finally got mad and said "damn" once. The whole group cheered, because they finally found a spark of temper in him.

The tailor shop really got to him a couple of days ago. The dry-cleaning plant on ship is broken down, so he bought some wash khaki pants to wear, and they had to be hemmed up. He took them to the tailor shop, and they measured him for an inseam of 34 inches. You know how long-legged he is. Well, he got them back the next day and took them out of the package in the Ready Room and held them up to see how good a job they had done. You should have seen the expression on his face when they came to only about an inch below the knee. They looked like Bermuda shorts, and all three pairs were the same. The tailor had cut them 24 inches instead of 34. He swears somebody put them up to it, but no one did—I don't think! I could imagine a tailor making one mistake, but when he held them up to see if the bottoms were even, he should have noticed that we don't have any midgets on this ship. But then he went ahead and cut the other two pairs the same. Now that is rather stupid. They did replace the pants, though, so now he has three pairs the right size.

Come to think of it, I'd better check mine. I had one pair done the same day, plus I had those white trousers that were too long taken up an inch. 'Scuse me a minute while I check. Whew! Yep, they are all okay. Panic comes early in the tropics. They must have had a new man on the machine when mine came through.

I guess you girls had as good a change of command party as we did, but I do hope it was not quite as lively...It was nice of Bea (Coffee) to share her letter from Gerry with the group. We are sure glad to hear he is coming along okay.

I have been debating whether I should say anything or not, because I don't know what info has been passed out back there—particularly to Irene (Daigle). But I saw something that indicates that Glenn has been changed to a captured status. There is no reason given for the change, but he was on a list of status changes. Nothing new on the others. Maybe you should wait for Irene to say something before you repeat it.

I have to go brief some weather bureau experts now, so I will go ahead and mail this.

Give Glyn and James a kiss and Samson a pat for me.

I love you all very, very much,

and miss you so, My Darling,

Jimmie

USS Kitty Hawk

"Free"

Monday nite

30 Jan '67

Hi Darling,

...The chaplain's sermon yesterday was on the subject, "The Thrill of It All" and, of course, it was pointed at the thrill of finding Christ. But the sermon encompassed so much more, too. It came from a theme that Bishop Neil had written about how if he had his life to live over he would take more chances, do more unusual things, and venture farther from the comforts of the known.

He seemed to think it necessary that one experience all the emotions of life in order to have lived it to the fullest. I don't believe in sitting at home to the tune of an 8-to-5 job, but I can't agree with him that people go to war just for thrill of it!

Of course his major theme was one of contrasting the thrills from dope or narcotics to the kick you get from a cat shot or arrested landing or the thrill of a bordello to the true peak obtained in married love. I can't tell him much about his contrasts, but I guess there is something of a thrill from flying off carriers, or we wouldn't do it. But I can attest to the supreme thrill of married love with you, my darling.

I guess there is no feeling ever to compare, and I would never want to search for one to surpass it. Right now I just want to return to you, and then we will see what we can make of it.

To the love that warms my heart so deeply.

I love you, Jimmie

USS Kitty Hawk
"Free"
Friday nite
3 Feb '66

Hi Darling,

...We had one bit of interest today—a British news reporter named Bramby, who had conned his way into Haiphong on a Polish freighter about three months ago and spent over three weeks there while they unloaded the freighter, arrived. He was interesting to listen to, and of course he had many opinions on how everything was going. At least he agrees that our bombers are usually well on target and doing pinpoint bombing only.

He gave several examples to show that the Vietnamese believe this, too. He says the people who are away from the known target areas don't even stop working to run for cover anymore. He thinks the bombing is doing a lot of good and has surely slowed down their movement of supplies to a standstill. He doesn't see any hope for an end or even a conference any time soon, because the North Vietnamese are really banded together. To show how well propaganda is controlled, he says the average citizen still believes that North and South Vietnam are one country and that the Americans have invaded the north and intend to take over the whole country like the French did. And this even goes for some of the minor civic officials in the city.

The amazing part was how they (the North Vietnamese) treated him. He didn't have a visa or anything except an old one for South Vietnam that was three years out of date, and they didn't seem to mind. They kept an escort with him the first day or two and then let him come and go as he pleased. He said they have taught English as a primary language in school since 1954 and almost everyone speaks French, English, and Vietnamese. They all preferred to talk English with him so they could get in some practice.

He thinks the real way to get to them is to blockade the harbor, but you know LBJ isn't going to do that. So I guess things really sit at a status quo.

Somebody is going to have to make a play one way or the other before election time, just to ensure I get to cast my ballot. Ha! Of course I'd rather be there for other reasons...Until then,

I love you with all my heart,

Jimmie

USS Kitty Hawk
"Free"
Saturday nite
4 Feb '67

Hi Darling,

The last couple of days have been rather nice—the mail planes have been arriving in force, and I have about six or seven letters here in just two days. Including very sweet valentines from all three of you...Some of the letters brought jolly news, though, like the beam on the new Skipper's face when Mary said she had sold their old house. A lot of people in Sanford seem to be selling houses lately.

I don't know how Mary and Charlie hack it, but he sometimes goes two and three weeks without a letter. I don't think the new

XO is much different, but when you ask them how often they write it isn't much different. I can't quite understand people like that—they would bitch like hell if their marriage broke up because they couldn't understand what happened.

It's really true that you only get out of a marriage what you put into it, and I certainly like what I've got, and I feel sorry for anyone that has any less. I would also envy anyone who has any more than we have, but, thankfully, I don't know anybody like that.

...Sounds like Jamey and Glyn are managing pretty well, but I would like to be there to help him sail the kite. He's big enough to do it himself now, though, so he might not appreciate the help. You should have his school grades by now, and I will look forward to seeing them.

Mostly, though, I'm just looking forward to seeing you.

...Dream warmly, my love,

I love you,

Jimmie

USS Kitty Hawk
"Free"
Friday nite
10 February '67

Hi Sweetheart,

...I don't want to dampen your hopes, but I wish the peace feeler news out here looked as good as the news propaganda you get in the papers back there. And I do call it propaganda, because I think it is pure political hogwash. The info we get from people out here who have been in Vietnam and from the Hanoi News Agency looks pretty conclusive that they (the Vietnamese) aren't even interested (in an end to the war). Somebody appears to be selling

the public a bill of goods, and it's all from how the newspapers slant the articles.

It would be pure happiness if they were to work out a solution, but any backing off we do now without a full solution we will really have to earn later. I hoped they had learned that last year after the long stand down. I'm not convinced that we have any politicians capable of learning a darn thing, though. They need our prayers; that's for sure...

HAPPY VALENTINE'S DAY

Your loving husband

USS Kitty Hawk
"Free"
Saturday nite
12 February '67

My Dearest Darling,

If I can get Al to settle down from his slambamming around the space here, I'll concentrate long enough to write you a letter. He's on this "no smoking" kick again, except it really turns into a no-buying effort instead. He bums more per day than he could probably afford if he bought his own. Ha!

Al has had only six today, and he's bounding around like a nervous cat because he can't find anyone home to bum a cigarette from. I try to tell him it's just a lack of willpower, but as soon as he starts to talk about it he can't sit down again until he has one.

Last line period, he had a project that he would stop smoking in the room and that he would buy me a drink for every time he gave in to ole man nicotine. Well, after I had accumulated enough to make me an alcoholic for life, I decided just to cancel the deal, because I don't want to end life that way. Not that I have any objection to his smoking in the room—that was just his idea of an incentive to help him stop. He's like 97% of the other smokers, though, and no incentive would ever help him to stop.

Ted Wallace, on the other hand, decided to quit smoking, and I doubt that he's had a single cigarette in the past month. Guess Ted is the type who can make one flat decision, and that's the way it is. I don't know whether he plans to stop for good or not, though.

...Higgy (our new XO), so far, has turned out to be even better than we had anticipated. He really fell right into place and is a bigger boomer than I expect most of us will want to try to keep up with. He is real handy around the paperwork, too. You put it in one day, and he has it out the next...Even the other squadrons on the ship think we made out pretty good. One of the fighter outfits offered to swap us their XO plus two DFCs for our new XO. I told him we were holding out for at least a Silver Star as a bonus in the swap.

...We have a special event going on tomorrow that may just take a full day's effort from Higgy and me in order to get it to come off right. The Nancy Sinatra show is coming out to the ship, and we think we've got it wrangled so we will be the host squadron for Nancy herself...so now we have to work extra hard to make some kind of special deal out of it. If it was one of the A-4 or F-4 squadrons no one would expect anything unusual, but since it's us, they'll just be waiting to see what will come of it all. And we've got a few things planned. Ha! Sure hope she's got a good sense of humor.

If she has to put on two shows, though, there won't be much time to carry out the itinerary. And I don't think the admiral has approved it yet either. I'll let you know tomorrow night.

...Nite, my love,

I love you,

Jimmie

USS Kitty Hawk
"Free"
Monday nite
13 February '67

Hi Darling,

The show last night was a lot of fun...and we Bats pulled a full-scale coup of the whole thing. It was a full squadron effort that must have raised the morale of the men by at least 400 percent. The star of the show was Higgy, and he really went full bore for the whole effort. Our price just went up to at least a Medal of Honor in a swap for an exchange of our XO with the fighter squadrons now.

Maybe I should explain that nobody cares about all this escort duty and being host to these troops that come aboard for USO shows, but it's the principle of the thing. Usually, the PIO blackshoe types take the girl types and keep them under tow the entire time, except that they eat dinner with either the ship's captain or XO at the department heads' table.

Well, when the word came out that Nancy Sinatra was coming aboard in a mini-skirt, we made the comment that it's about time she sat at the Lcdr's table and that the No.1 table should get some of the beatniks. Everyone from other squadrons laughed, so we told them the Bats could hack it.

The night before they arrived it looked like things were going to be a bit difficult, so we decided to get the Skipper and XO involved. You know, honor, squadron pride, and all that were at stake. So we went whole hog and tried to take over the whole thing, hoping that if at least half of it came off, we would still be ahead. Well, we're still laughing, and nobody on the boat will even speak to us.

But if we didn't do anything for the rest of the cruise we would still be ahead of any group on this ship.

The troop that came aboard included Nancy Sinatra, Jimmy Boyd, and a band group from the University of Mississippi. Actually, the band included Ron Weatherly and four University of Mississippi boys who are pretty good. Weatherly was an All-American quarterback at Ole Miss a couple of years ago.

...We had regular flight ops the whole day, and the performers didn't even want to quit watching to go put on the show. They even got up before daybreak this morning to watch another launch and recovery before leaving. It was their first time ever on a carrier, and they all were totally fascinated. And I can see where it would be the first time you see it. Actually, it still is after 12 years, even when you do it every day!

Jimmy Boyd had been out here last year, but they weren't flying when he was aboard. I thought he looked familiar, and after I took a second look it was obvious—he was the sandy-haired, freckled-face, guitar-playing boyfriend of Kelly's on the Bachelor Father television show. He looks and sounds just the same, but he sings real good. Actually, he was the best performer of the entire tour. He also was the most interested in ship's spaces and wanted to go down to the ship's boiler rooms during his afternoon rest period. I talked to him for quite a while, and he talks more sense than the average youth of today. Of course he's a nut on the stage, just like he was on the TV show.

I took Nancy Sinatra around for a two-hour tour of the spaces and to observe flight ops—that is, I did until Charlie CO and Higg came panting along like a couple of pups in heat. Ha! The main thing was to get her down to the working spaces where our squadron personnel were working, and those white hats really ate it up.

Beef had a new LSO shirt, and one of our photo mates had painted her name in script on the front over the top of a big black bat. Actually, that was supposed to be the back of the shirt, but we had put "Property of RVAH-13" on the front, so she chose to wear the shirt backwards! She also wore the RVAH-13 ball cap so you know how our troops ran that all over the ship. She was fascinated by flight ops like all the rest, and she is really a good kid. She is a real tiny thing as you could imagine, and she looks a lot like her father.

...Higgy pretty well ran her afternoon while I went down to con the ship's XO into letting her sit at our table for dinner. We had a catch, of course: Dick Daum and Ron Queen got the 60,000th landing last week, so they were joint guests of honor. They had a big cake baked for the occasion. It didn't hurt any having my old friend from Mercer, Tennessee as the chief steward down there either. So they really set us up in full honors with ruffled napkins and hand-script place cards and all. We put Nancy between Ron and Dick and then Ray and I, and we invited Charlie CO and XO over to sit with us.

It's a very special occasion having a female sit at your table out here on the line as you can well imagine. The looks we got from some of those commanders on Tables No. 1 and No. 2 were indescribable. It was childish of us, I know, but out here, what the hell else do we have to do? And we did get one million laughs out of it.

Besides that, I thoroughly enjoyed talking to a female at dinner for a change. She's pretty darn intelligent and very interesting to talk to, especially explaining what they do over here and how the whole war impresses them. We made a few jokes about her old man, and she offered up a few of her own—such as his new wife who is younger than she that she calls "Mama-Mia." She says Dean

Martin doesn't really drink very much, but he can drink you under the table if you challenge him.

She presented Dick and Ron the lighters with a big kiss to boot. Can you imagine how red Dickie's ears got? One of the guys in the back said, "Let's go start flight ops and run through the deck to see if we can make 61,000 before she leaves!"

After dinner we got our senior first class to escort her down to the First Class Mess and cut a cake there. Funniest of them all was Chief Willford when we had him come up to escort her down to the Chief's Mess. I know you have met him so you know he is bashful around women. He was really grumbling about spending 26 years in the navy and some CO's order that got him into this situation. The rest of the chiefs will ride him unmercifully for at least the next month. So tonight, in our Plan of the Day, there is this line:

"Happiness is: Seeing Master Chief Willford holding hands with Nancy."

The comedy of the day was broken, though, when we learned RVAH-7 lost a plane. I know it must have been in the news back there, but their new XO, Don Jarvis, got shot down along the coast. Both he and his b/n were picked up okay, but Cdr. Jarvis has a broken arm. This happened during the stand down, but, as always, that doesn't mean (the Vietnamese) don't shoot back (at photo planes). I think Phil Ryan got his plane hit on the same day, but I doubt if that will appear in any news.

...Just got the schedule for tomorrow, and I have to be up just five hours from now to brief the flights, and then I will fly on in to Cubi in the afternoon...Happiness: Putting an 8-cent stamp on a letter!

Nite, My Love

I love you,

Jimmie

USS Kitty Hawk
Subic Bay
Wednesday afternoon
15 Feb '67

Dearest Dora,

It was really a joy to talk to you last night and to Glyn, too. I'm sorry it was at a time that Jamey wasn't home, but it couldn't be helped. It was totally unexpected anyway—for us as well as for you girls. But it sure made for a nice Happy Valentine's Day anyway. I slept with the sweetest dreams I have had for many a week. I didn't get up until noon today, in fact.

I guess you've talked to Mary and Pat and figured it out by now, but we were really calling Washington on the Autovon to get Chief Willford an extension in the squadron. We got the Bureau okay and got an approval to keep him another year, and, since we still had the Autovon operator in Hawaii, we decided to call Sanford and ask Capt. Fowler when he was sending us a new b/n.

The Sanford operator was real clear, and, since it sounded like Marge, we said, "Heck, we've just come in from the war, and since we can't talk to Capt. Fowler, how about hooking us up with our wives?" She laughed and said, "Okay. Give me some numbers." So that's why I didn't talk very long, and we had to keep getting you all to flash the operator back so we wouldn't lose the Autovon line. Almost lost it there once when you were clicking and the Hawaii operator came back on the line. She didn't quite buy that program anyway, because she kept wanting to know what our priority was. Of course, we had had just about enough by then that it was no sweat at all to tell her, "The highest you can get."

Pat kept wondering who was paying for it, and Jack couldn't shush her off the subject. So you shouldn't get any bill for that one. We may all wind up in court martial, but what can they do? Send us to war in Vietnam? Needless to say, you shouldn't spread the word around. If we say anything to anybody else, they all might want to try it and then we'd surely get into trouble. It was just one of those spur-of-the-moment ideas that worked. And, after all, it was Valentine's Day.

...We got in here about mid-afternoon yesterday, and the ship won't get here until tomorrow or the next day. We expect Bob Johnson and Beef in with two more airplanes any time now. I'm sitting by the pool in 88-degree clear warm sunshine. I moved over into the shade to write this because after only about an hour I could feel the red glow coming on my shoulders. It sure feels good to see the sun again, though. We have been flying around under the low overcast most of the past week, and I think yesterday was the first time in well over a week that I've seen blue sky.

...Sure love you a bunch, my darling. It just kind of made my whole day hearing your voice last night. Give James and Glyn a big hug and kiss for me. I have plenty of love to go around for all of you.

Nite, my wonderful, Darling Wife,

I love you,

Jimmie

USS Kitty Hawk
Subic Bay, Philippines
20 Feb '67

Hi Darling,

My arm is so stiff I can hardly hold this pen to write. We had a softball game/bar bust with the chiefs yesterday, and most of us old men had trouble climbing out of bed this morning. It was a lot of fun, though, and it wouldn't have been so bad except we had to accept their invite over to the Chief's Club afterward to encroach on a party that the VA-85 chiefs were throwing for their officers. It sort of killed the whole day after that.

A new ensign, Nick Carbone, checked in to the squadron yesterday. He is a maintenance type, straight from AMO school at Memphis, and has never seen anything of the navy before. We got him over to that beer bust yesterday, and he's probably looking for the nearest way out of here today. The chiefs were running him pretty fiercely, and that's really a hard way to break in a young tender ensign.

...The crew from RVAH-3 brought the new Vigilante for RVAH-7 in yesterday, and we talked to them last night. They went back today. I sure would have liked to climb in that TA3-B myself. Just for the ride home, of course. We leave here Wednesday for Hong Kong, though I may have to stay until Thursday to fly a plane back out to the boat.

...Got your letter today with my driver's license and income tax figures. The income tax data is okay, and it should be all I will need. As soon as I get that filled out, I'll send it back for your signature, but it will probably be after we pull out of Cubi.

...Glad to hear James, Glyn, and Samson are doing well. I know you must get irritated with them at times, but they are good company to have around. I'm really looking forward to being

back with all of you this summer, sharing in some of that love and affection. The kids are a lot of enjoyment to both of us.

I love you so very, very much,

Always, Jimmie

USS Kitty Hawk
At Sea
Wednesday Afternoon
22 Feb '67

Hi Darling,

We just pulled out of Cubi this morning and are en route to Hong Kong...George had his camera down to take some color Polaroids of the stuffed bat we now possess, so he took shots of everyone around the Ready Room. This a fruit bat, but that row of white teeth are sharp enough to take off a finger. We taped the one- foot ruler on the plaque so you could tell the relative size. This one has a four-foot wingspan, and his body, not counting the legs, is over one foot long. This was the one they had mounted up at the survival school—and we didn't steal this one either!

St. Amour, who is a First Class in the squadron, was once a Survival School instructor, so he went out in the woods and caught a six-foot bat to get stuffed for the school exhibit; he then swapped them his live one for this stuffed one. We wouldn't have room for a bigger one anyway. We have the bat bolted to the Ready Room wall right now, but I'm sure that as soon as the rest of the ship sees it, we will have to lock it up some place. When we get back to Sanford, we'll have to be particularly careful of it...I will put this in the mail this afternoon and write more tonight.

I love you, Sweetheart, so very much.

All my love, Jimmie

USS Kitty Hawk
At Sea
Thursday Afternoon
23 Feb '67

Hi Darling,

We're steaming on toward Hong Kong, and this is a sort of dead time, but the extra sleep does everyone good. We just got back from our first awards ceremony this year, and it was tiresome like all the rest. Mostly Air Medals were awarded, and only Dickie, Jack, and I were involved from our squadron.

Everyone had to dress up in whites and stand there for an hour, but at least it was shorter than the ceremonies we had last year. And there were a couple of laughs. Sid Banks is the admiral's aide and an old Heavy Attacker from Whidby, so when he was reading out my citation he said Heavy Attack Squadron Thirteen (instead of RVAH-13 which indicates a reconnaissance squadron). I gave him a big frown, and the admiral laughed, so Sid apologized over the microphone and then continued reading the citation. He also called VF-114 as Attack Squadron 114, so the captain got up after the ceremony and apologized on his behalf for that and said, "But they can drop bombs, you know." It all helped to keep it from being a complete bore anyway...

...I would like to mail myself along with the pictures for a little close contact communication, but I guess there will be a few months' delay on that. I sure miss you a lot, Sweetheart, and I miss the kids, too...Just a recall of the happiness I found the day I married you and the dividends and compound interest that has accumulated since that time.

I love you, My Darling,
Ever and always,
Jimmie

USS Kitty Hawk
Hong Kong
Monday morning
27 Feb '67

Hi Darling,

I guess you can tell by the mail, or rather the lack of it, that we are in Hong Kong...So, for once, we're spending some time touring and seeing a few of the things people are supposed to see in Hong Kong...Can you believe another month marked off? This one has really flown by, and I just wish the rest would do so well. Of course, shuffling between ports here has had a lot to do with it. We leave here tomorrow, though, and all of March will be spent at sea...

Guess we're going to still be short one b/n for a large part of the trip. Our new one checked aboard yesterday, but I just signed a leave extension for Jim Morgan this morning. We have heard that Fran's operation turned out not to be too serious, and she is doing well—I'm sure glad to hear that. Apparently, she is confined to the bed for a while, and he feels he should stay through part of that.

We had a worse event here a couple of days ago when our personnel man had a heart attack. They have him over in the Hong Kong Hospital now, but he is still in critical condition. The doctors feel he will make it, but he is only 40 years old, and the chances are not good for a person under 40 recovering from a heart attack. I guess we never know when we are well off.

...Hate to cut this letter short again, but Hong Kong comes only once a year...I love you, My Darling, and I miss you all so very, very much. Give many kisses for Jamey, Glyn, and for you—and even for Samson, too.

Gotta run to catch the 1300 boat ashore.

I love you!

Jimmie

USS Kitty Hawk
At Sea
Wednesday nite
1 March '67

Hi Darling,

...Yesterday was a day to remember in RVAH-13, and I don't think half of Hong Kong will forget it either. We went toy crazy, and I do mean completely out of it. I wanted to buy a few more track parts for Jamey's train and a couple of extra cars. Well, I had to carry along a few other fathers just to show them what the trains looked like. It started with Dick, then Jack and Beef, and finally Ray. Before the morning was over, they had completely depleted this little shop of its Marklin train stock.

All the guys were convinced that they had to get the trains now before the kids were big enough to take them away from the fathers! Naturally, this included all kinds of electrical switching circuits and things that it would take a high school kid to operate.

Well, that was just the start of it, and we wound up in a Japanese department store that had half the floor filled with mechanical toys. You know...things like the barking dogs and remote control tanks and all sorts of "adult" toys. We had that store going wild for over an hour, demonstrating everything in the place. Then, when the first group got back to the Admin in the Hilton, half of the rest of the squadron went down and did the same thing all over again. George Comstock, who doesn't have any kids yet, bought more than anyone.

We had a suite of rooms at the Hilton to use as a staging base in port, and, when everyone got back there, it looked like a three-ring circus. Naturally, everyone had to try out all the toys, and there were battery-powered battles going on in every direction. I guess word spread all over the hotel, because CAG, the ship's captain, and the XO of the ship came by. I think they thought we were all idiots before, and this event just confirmed it. But I'm sure everyone in the squadron had more fun than we'd had in a year.

Jack spent the afternoon in his room, trying to set up his track and train. He had plenty of help, and I only spent a few minutes there, but he already gave Dick and Beef the idea to set theirs up tomorrow. They all got such big tracks, though, that I'm sure there can't be room in any house to put them out very often. That's why I prefer to stick with the simple things so Jamey can run his own any way he wants. If he wants to go more complicated when he gets bigger, it will be well worth the price to keep him occupied.

We developed our own methods of shopping that would probably drive you girls nuts. We must stop for a beer at every corner, and we only shop in stores that serve free beer while we wait. Once we find a store that has the product we want, we must average a total of $10 per minute of purchases or we're taking too much time to make a decision. It sure drives the storekeepers nuts, but it takes all the pain out of shopping and gets rapid results. And none of us really went broke in the long run. The prices have gone up so since last year that there are really very few good buys here anymore...But, let's face it, I just plain hate to shop no matter how hard I try...

I love you, darling.

Always, Jimmie

USS Kitty Hawk
"Free"
2 March '67

Hi Darling,

...It was cold as hell when we left Hong Kong, but it's plenty warm here. The sun has been shining on the flight deck all day, and

it's almost a smelter here in the room. I'm going down to the Ready Room a little later to see the last reel of the movie, and it will be much cooler there. They are showing The Great Race tonight, and I never did get to see the last reel of that last year.

...I'm glad to hear that Dave Fall is trying to keep you girls informed (about what's going on out here). He always has been quite a nice guy, and I don't know how he works on the Wing, but I notice he is already starting to look out for RAVH-13's interests.

...James and Glyn's valentines sound quite interesting, but with James as her teacher, I couldn't expect much else. Tell Glyn I am proud that she has learned to read, and I will look forward to having her read me a story when I get home. I don't remember all the Dick and Jane books, but I'm sure we will all be well acquainted with them within the next year...I've got an early flight tomorrow, and so that's what I'd better be preparing for now. I'll try to get some shuteye now, so pleasant dreams.

I love you, darling,

Jimmie

USS Kitty Hawk

"Free"

9 March 1967

My Darling,

I wasn't going to say that this letter is rather difficult to write, but it is. Guess we never get used to the situation regardless of how much practice we have had. It always hurts, but at least there are some comforting tones to this one that we didn't have before.

We lost the Skipper (Commander Charles Putnam) today, and the search is still going. Frank Prendergast was with him, and a miraculous save rescued Frank. He is back with us and he is doing fine—no injuries. Both of them got out of the aircraft okay, and chutes were good, so we can hope and pray that Charlie is in good shape, also. He is probably on his way to the Hanoi Hilton. For you, personally, I believe that is the case.

I can't mail this, of course, until we hear that Mary has been notified, and obviously, I can't give you any details either. But please give her my love and comfort and help her all that you can. The other young girls in the squadron are going to require some help also when this news gets out—and so will you, I know.

Wish I could come and help you, My Darling, but you know that can't be. We can only pray and strive to do our best with what God gave us.

The cruise is a long way from being over, and this should be a very grim reminder of just how quickly the complexion of things can change. It wasn't a difficult flight at all, so there just can't be any prediction of the patterns established for us. I don't believe in predestination, and I don't believe in fate, but...I do believe that there is a pattern and purpose for every human being, and somewhere, there is an end good to everything.

I think Mary will find it very difficult to accept the situation. I just hope she will consider her own physical well-being and accept what help others may give. I don't know who they will assign to her assistance, but please ask Dave (Fall) to monitor the information she gets. And if he has questions about the facts or what is presented tell him to write me, and we will do what we can. I think he knows, though, that we get cut out of the pattern and receive little or nothing after the initial inputs.

The people in the squadron are fine, and it hasn't broken up the world. Some of the young b/n's had questions, but I think I was able to give them proper guidance. Let's hope so anyway, and the next few days should certainly tell. We have a good group, and there is strength all the way through. It makes me real proud of them.

I guess that for a while here, I'll be playing XO and Ops, too, so bear with me on the mail call.

I love you very, very much and cherish your love for me more than anything else in the world. I pray for God's help in the troubled days that I know you will have ahead. Keep your faith high and your love strong, and I know we can rise to all the tasks before us.

May God bless all of you wives and children who have the hardest job of this entire war.

I love you,

Jimmie

USS Kitty Hawk
"Free"
12 March 1967

Hi Darling,

It's hard to know what to say, and really I guess there isn't more to add to what I told you in the letter before. I hope Mary is pulling back together by now and the rest of you girls are over the initial shock. My love and prayers really go out to all of our families.

The squadron bounced back strong, and we've really done good work these past two days. I think our stock went up at least eleven points with the Staff as well as the Air Wing. It just helps wonderfully when an outfit can respond so well after receiving such a jolt.

I think Higgy sent a message to Joni, so the newspapers wouldn't give out bum dope to our group and shake everyone up more than necessary.

...They told us when we left not to expect another crew if we lost one, so I guess we will stick with what we've got for the rest of the cruise. Higgy sent them a message saying he didn't need another one anyway. We do need another airplane, though, and we need Jim Morgan back. Maybe they can work it so he can fly out in our replacement aircraft. I think it was nice of Dave Fall to offer to fly Jim to Travis—and if a new plane isn't available yet, he may still head Jim on this way. Ron's replacement b/n isn't here yet either, but he should already be on the way. We hope to see him soon.

...Jack and I got our 100th missions the other day—and the 101st since then...I've got an early hop tomorrow, so I'd better wait until then to answer your letters...Don't worry about us out here, Darling. Everything is under good control, and we will make it. Just take care of yourself and of things back there. I sure wish I could do more to help.

I love you very, very much, and my heart really goes out to you at times like these. Nite, My Love.

I love you,

Jimmie

USS Kitty Hawk
"Free"
13 March '67

Hi Darling,

...Had some very sweet letters tonight. From you, a nice note from Nancy Rape, and a special from Glyn. I will write her, her own private reply. I had to fill out a form today on housing requirements, and it was rather shocking to realize that in only two months, Glyn will be six years old. I shouldn't be so surprised that

she is writing letters when we realize the age, but I am still very pleased that she shows so much interest in learning.

...Tell her the postman read the address real fine, and the letter came straight to me. I need to write her and Jamey both, and maybe tomorrow I'll get the chance. This day got by before I realized it was gone.

I can't let it get away before I send a few words of love to you, though, and I do love you so very, very much. It makes cold nights warm and sad days bright, and I dislike very much even the thought of having to fend my way without it. I'm so glad that thought never has to cross my mind. If there ever was one happiness, happiness is: the love of you.

I love you, my darling.

Always, Jimmie

USS Kitty Hawk
"Free"
Thursday afternoon
16 March '67

Hi Darling,

I have night flying late tonight, so I'd better get a letter written this afternoon. It's been rather pleasant these past three days with a break in the weather, and we have been able to do some pretty good work for a change. It's been good for everyone to fly regularly and see some results.

I had a message today indicating that Jim Morgan is on his way back in the back seat of our replacement aircraft. I guess Charlie James is flying it, and Mike Durant is flying the TA3B... It looks like they are going to send us a new XO also, Ed Foy. The captain had sent a message saying we didn't need one, and he was naming Higg as CO and me as XO, but, apparently, the Wing was already working one through from that end. Suits me fine. I don't particularly like the demotion from Ops to XO, and out here that's certainly what it is. I would still have to spend a year as XO sometime when we come back to sea duty anyway, and I don't relish any more time at paper pushing than is necessary. I think the guys in the squadron will be happier if I keep Ops anyway.

Ed is real fine people, and I think Higgy is going to be a real fine CO. He's a wild one on the beach, but he sure is all business on the boat. He's very easy to get along with and smart enough to pick things up the first time through. So the squadron should stay pretty much the same as it always has been.

...Time to go brief for the next hop now and then get a bit to eat before we fly. Wish I was sitting down to dinner there with you... I'll keep that warm thought to comfort me until that day.

I love you, my darling, so very, very much,

Jimmie

USS Kitty Hawk
"Free"
Saturday nite
18 March '67

Hi Darling,

Got your letters today for the "after the 9th," and, needless to say, we have all been anxiously awaiting the news of how things were going back there. In reality, you are closer to that situation than we are out here. Agreed, we know more about what happened, but once the messages are sent and we are back to daily operations, there is much less time to think about what has gone before.

You see the continuation on a daily basis with very little new news to base things on. Maybe that is the fallacy in the system, and there should be some way we could pass along all that we know directly to the wives. But BuPers says no letters to the next of kin and no word to anybody except BuPers. They will pass it on to those who need to know. In certain cases that is right, and I know they are primarily trying to protect the wives and families.

We don't really know any more now than the news that has already been sent. It looks fairly probable that Charlie was captured. I'm sorry about the confusion about the identity of the b/n. Frank's rescue was a little touchy, so the admiral said no mention of it at all, and that's why his name was not included to begin with. It was on the aircraft accident report, and the Wing should have had that the day after the first message was received.

I can't figure out how the initial word got through unless somebody heard it on the radio on the way back to Cubi and told one of the people from (another squadron). Then they must have called home that night. That's the only way the word could have leaked through. We hope that doesn't happen again.

...As I have said, this is no time to get complacent about things. Granted, the cruise is over half gone, but the weather will clear soon, and the hard flying still lies ahead of us. I feel confident we can finish the year without further losses, but the wives must be prepared—as best you can—in case we do lose someone. I don't really suppose there is a way to prepare except to expect to get information in small bits and pieces—and never as much info as you want.

They have changed the rules on communicating with families while a prisoner. We now are allowed to write in free hand letters directly to the wives. We can only discuss weather, places, past happenings, or things not of a personal nature, but at least it will give them something to analyze so they can prove the letter's authenticity.

Please tell Pat and the other wives that we will never leave them in the dark...when and if ever they are involved in a situation (like the Skipper's shoot-down)...It's not always easy here to anticipate what questions will be most pressing (for the families) at the time. I hope by now most of them have been answered, though, so you gals are back on an even keel.

With prayers and hope, I'm sure we can weather out the days remaining on this cruise. With an increased effort, maybe this war can be brought to some final solution.

My love to James and Glyn.

I love you,

Jimmie

USS Kitty Hawk
"Free"
Wednesday nite
22 March 1967

Dear James,

I'm sending you a picture here, sort of like the one I sent earlier to Glyn. My fighter escort who flies along behind me took this with his hand camera. That's Mr. Walters in the back seat and a lot of the ship's island and superstructure in the background. The upside-down ice cream cone is a radio antenna.

Mother says you have started back to the Boy Scouts down at the church. I'm sure glad they have the den organized again. Please write and tell me all about it. Maybe you can be a Bear by the time you get this, and you can have most of the Lion achievements done too by the time I get home.

When does your school get out this summer? It seems like I've been gone the whole school year...When does the pool open at the base? You and Mom should have Glyn swimming like a fish by the time I get home.

Also, tell me how you are doing with teaching Samson his tricks. Glyn says he can dance, but I'm sure you've taught him more than that. And I need to learn all the signals so I will know how to talk to him this summer. He sounds like a very smart dog, and I don't want him to think I'm just some old dumb bunny.

You are taking good care of things for me while I'm gone, so keep up the good work. I love you very much, and it makes me proud.

Hope you all have a very Happy Easter!

Love, Dad

P.S. I saw Mr. Fraser out here, and he said to tell you Hi!

USS Kitty Hawk
"Free"
Wednesday nite
22 March 1967

Hi Darling,

...Jim Morgan arrived on the ship and brought me the divinity you sent. It arrived in good shape. Thank you very much. I left it in the Ready Room so all could share...along with Diane's special cake. That was absolutely great, particularly the poem that came along with it. Even after all the traveling, it was still fresh and so much better than the cake the wardroom had for supper. Everyone turned down dessert at dinner and came back to the Ready Room

for another piece of cake. We could definitely see that it was torso-shaped with the poem appropriately inscribed.

Our new ensign seems like a real charger...The officers of VAW-11 challenged us to a basketball game this time in port, so when we asked Jay Nevins if he had played (he's a good 6 foot five inches tall), he said, "Yeah, a little." Well, he played center on the Temple University team two years ago when they were runners up in the NIT!

We made him a Ltjg. last night and he almost broke up when the CO put the big, oversized shoulder boards on him. They had six-pointed stars instead of the normal five-pointed ones. The Skipper was a little hesitant to go that far so soon, but I said we may as well find out now if he's going to hack it in the squadron or not. Well, he took it beautifully, so, immediately, he became one of the squadron...It's way past bedtime now, and tomorrow is a new day. I look forward to sweet dreams of you tonight, my love.

I love you,

Jimmie

Kitty Hawk
"Free"
Easter Sunday
26 March '67

My Darling Dora,

And a Happy Easter to you, to James, to Glyn, and to Samson. It didn't look like much of one out here, but we did have baskets of colored eggs on the table for supper. I had to fly during the morning service, so I didn't get a chance to make it to church, but my thoughts were there just the same...The sun did shine, and the weather broke over the beach, so we got to work for a change, and that in itself made a lot of people feel better.

Today was mail day, and I got your letter with the pictures of the kids plus another of Glyn's masterpieces. She may not write the prettiest address in the world, but I think that postman gets the message that he dare not let that letter delay in reaching its desired objective. I'll be more than glad to write her a personal answer.

Nite my love,
I love you,
Jimmie

USS Kitty Hawk
"Free"
Monday nite
27 March '67

Hi Darling,

...We took Ron Queen off the flight schedule yesterday so he could have time to get all packed up to come home...I had to laugh at him today when he thought he had an early hop this morning that Dickie was scheduled for. Then he realized that someone else was flying with Dick now. We joked with him of course and asked him if he hadn't realized that now he has to start sweating dying of lung cancer—not to mention battling the nation's highway traffic!

...Your letter indicated you are concerned over us having both a new CO and a new XO out here. I thought you knew me better than that. Anyway, I haven't lost control yet, and I don't really expect to as I see it right now. That was one of the things I told Higgy about my being XO—I didn't want to take that demotion right now. The XO job is all tied up with paperwork out here,

and my job as Ops is really more of an assistant CO when it comes around to the flying part. So don't worry about that. We are working hard to try and get enough of the ones who are coming back next year checked out so there will be a sufficient carryover of experience. I haven't forgotten how to say "no," and once in a while, it comes out, "Hell, NO!"

...I know he doesn't show it, but the CO is only 37 years old. And I think Joni must be pretty close to my age. Gads, we're getting ancient when I can say someone is "only 37." Remember when Jim Holloway was CO at 34?...My, how times change. Thought I was going to get over to the Enterprise to see him tomorrow, but I hear they have all the helos filled up with people who are getting awards. They have a big Vietnamese Awards ceremony on the big "E" tomorrow for people with over 150 missions.

...For now, my love, just remember how much I love you and need you. And to Glyn and James, I send hugs and kisses and bundles of love. Looking forward to the day when we can all be together.

I love you,
Jimmie

USS Kitty Hawk
Subic Bay
Friday afternoon
31 March '67

Hi Darling,

...It made me really proud to learn of Jamey's church confirmation on Palm Sunday. I'll write him a letter about it. I owe one to Glyn, too.

...Well, lover, I'll go try to get my errands run. Missing you mighty much. A kiss to James and Glyn.

I love you,

Jimmie

Kitty Hawk
Subic Bay, Philippines
Tuesday nite
4 April '67

Hi Sweetheart,

I'm sitting in the BOQ to write this letter, because you wouldn't believe the temperatures in this place. The air conditioning on the ship split a pipe or something, and it's just been unbearable for the past three days...This old bucket (Kitty Hawk) is having so many breakdowns they will have to have a yard period on it before coming back out next year.

...It sounds like you had a nice Easter, and I'm glad the flowers arrived on time. I just wish I could have been there to join in with you. The picture of some mighty pretty kids helped me to share a lot in it, though...I notice Glyn has her front teeth back, so I'll have to write her a personal note on that. The kids both look quite a bit taller to me, but it's hard to tell, just comparing them with each other.

I won't mind spending the whole summer getting reacquainted, though. Especially with you, darling...Sure do love you, and miss you more each and every day.

It's going to be fun trying to see if we can wear out that love by seeing too much of each other. Bet it won't happen.

Nite my love,

I love you,

Jimmie

USS Kitty Hawk
4 April 1967

Dear James,

I was very glad to hear of your confirmation on Palm Sunday. You didn't tell me you were attending classes with Reverend Temple again, so I was very surprised. I am very proud of you. Mom says you went to the Maundy Thursday service at the church with her and that Rev. Temple had a special service.

She says you learned a lot from it, and I am very glad. Maybe I can help you with some of your questions this summer.

You must have about the smartest dog in all of Sanford. Samson must have learned all the tricks you taught him really well to be called "best in the show." I saw the picture of the statue they gave you, but the picture of Samson was kind of blurred. Please send me another of him when you get a good one. You and Glyn must be taking extra good care of him for him to be so handsome. How about that "handsome Samson." Bet you can't say that real fast!

...How is your bank account growing? I think that's a good idea to start putting it where you can save some. If spring has really sprung back there, the grass should grow fast enough to help you fatten the account pretty well now. A few car washes and waxes should help, too.

Might even help work off some of your Cub Scout achievements. How is the new den doing? Mom says one of the leaders lives down the street toward the Wallace's.

We had a basketball game with the officers from the other squadron in our Ready Room yesterday, and we really beat them good. They had about twice as many players as we had, so we beat them two games in a row so all their people could get to play.

I guess it's almost baseball season back there now, so maybe we can get to watch the Little Leagues play some this summer.

Well, take good care of Mom and Glyn for me. Try to do good work in school and have fun, too.

I love you,

Dad

USS Kitty Hawk
At Sea
Monday nite
10 April 1967

Hi Sweetheart,

It's kinda late tonight, and we have to be up early tomorrow for a practice G.Q. (General Quarters) and then an awards ceremony in the afternoon. But I'll write on here until I start nodding asleep. I would have started on this earlier, but we've been busy with a little accident report and just got finished—MY accident report to be more exact.

I had a nose gear collapse on landing aboard ship today, and kinda slid it out on the nose. It's a lot like the experience Al Wattay had out at San Diego on our fly out to the ship last fall, but this time, the whole strut exploded, and it will be a full-fledged accident.

We've had some of these struts split before, so it was really no big thing. I set us down on the deck fairly gently, and in the back seat, Jack didn't realize what was happening until it was all over. There was no damage to Jack or me, of course, and we'll probably have the airplane repaired in a few days. It was our best airplane, of course, and everything had been working really well on it. The breaks of Naval Air, I guess. As I told the LSO, I can't land them much better than that one, so we'll have to give credit for that event to North American Aviation.

The ship pulled out of port this morning, and we brought the planes out at noon. We won't be on the line until day after tomorrow, and then we stay there for three weeks. This month is starting to flow along now, so maybe it will keep going along at a fast pace.

Today I had letters from you and one from John Chaney...Next item in the mail was a letter to the C.O. from C.T. Butler, and it looks like you had better fix those leaky faucets, so they will last at least another good year. He said Renner and Griffin would receive orders to RVAH-3 for transfer in July and that Daum and Vehorn were not definite yet. Well, Beef got his orders today, and guess what? "When detached in July, proceed and report to RVAH-3." I had figured all along that would happen to him anyway.

He's not too overjoyed about it, and neither am I, but at least, as the saying goes, "It's not long and gray." And there are four other F-4 and A-4 types out here who wound up getting orders to boats after serving two combat cruises.

I'll see you in dreamland. I love you and long for you so very much.

My love always,

Jimmie

USS Kitty Hawk
"Free"
13 April 1967
Thursday nite

Hi Darling,
Fridays come early in the tropics.
See enclosed orders. Ha!
Need I say more?
I love you,
Jim

BUPERS ORDER 042491
LCDR JAMES L. GRIFFIN, USN
RECONATRON THIRTEEN
When directed in Jul detached DIFOT; proceed NAS, Sanford, Fla., report CO, RECONATKRON THREE, DIFOT.

B. J. SEMMES, JR.

USS Kitty Hawk
"Free"
Monday nite
17 April 1967

Hi Darling,

...I meant to start writing this earlier, but I wound up in a talk with Capt. Moorer, the Chief of Staff for Com Seventh Fleet. He came over to discuss the RA5C as well as other things, a friendly-type talk this time. He likes us! Then I missed writing last night because Ed Foy just got here, so we had to give him a fit and proper welcome...The plague shots and gamma globulin got the point across to him quite well today, also. We spent most of today checking him

out, and we'll finish tomorrow so he can start flying. He seems the same as ever, so he should fit right in.

Got your letter of the 11th, and I'm sorry about the confusion on that garbled message about my accident. I know you have the straight word by now. I did have a little stiff neck for a couple of days, caused by the whiplash effect when the nose dropped, but I didn't even notice it at the time. We didn't miss any flights because of it, though, and I guess it just hadn't entered my mind that there was any thought of getting hurt. So I am additionally sorry if the message caused you any worry...I will wrap this up now and get on to bed. I want to write a family gram to the West Coast contingent as soon as I get a chance to tell them the results of my orders. Maybe tomorrow that time will come, but I doubt it.

I will write Glyn and James again soon, too. I sent a package to Glyn a few days ago that is for her birthday only. I sent another one today for all of you that can be opened on arrival. I love you so very much, my darling, and miss you all the more each day.

Wish you a night of pleasant dreams,

I love you,

Jimmie

USS Kitty Hawk
"Free"
Thursday nite
20 April 1967

Hi Darling,

Today was a big day at Haiphong. I'm going up tonight to see if they have any electricity left for lights. Not enough time for a letter today.

I love you,

Jimmie

USS Kitty Hawk
"Free"
Monday nite
24 April '67

Hi Darling,

I guess you've been reading the papers, so it's fairly obvious why I haven't been up to my usual on letter writing. We're having one big one after another out here, and it seems that Kitty Hawk is in on all of them this year. That means that we are, too, and even though we aren't getting a lot of flying, no one can complain that we aren't in on the action.

We have four more days on this line period, and I expect them all to be big ones. But the hopeful part is that maybe that's what it will take to get a few people around to the conference table (to talk peace). We can pray that all of it will come to some good end. Certainly hope so for the sake of the great number of friends who are no longer with us out here this year. We're getting a lot more of them as hopeful Hanoi Hilton residents, though, and that's some consolation.

...Missing you very much and looking forward to some personal communication soon. I'm glad to hear you are as anxious as I am. A kiss to Glyn and James and my love to you all. I just guess I couldn't ever hope for a better family.

I love you,
Jimmie

USS Kitty Hawk
Subic Bay, Philippines
Saturday afternoon
29 April '67

Hi Darling,

I'm sitting here in the Cubi Point BOQ room to write this one. We flew two planes in last night to get some work done on them, and the ship won't come in until tomorrow. I couldn't ask for a better setting than I have right now. This is the closest thing I have seen to being a reminder of Florida. There's a great big thunderstorm raining down on the mountains across the bay with rumbles of thunder and lightening in the distance. We really needed it, too, since the temperature here is almost unbearable.

When I opened the canopy yesterday at the end of the runway, it was as if a blowtorch had enveloped the whole airplane. That was quite a shock after having ridden the whole way in air-conditioned comfort.

The only place air conditioned here is the club, and we stayed there last night until after midnight, hoping this BOQ room would cool off. No such luck—this place was like a sweatbox, even with the fan blowing directly on us. Don't think I got three hours sleep in all. I hope the air conditioning doesn't go out on the boat this time in port so we can spend the nights there.

...We go back on the line on the 8th for seventeen days and then come back here, but I doubt that we will have any time for sitting by the pool then. Those two days will be for turnover with the Connie (USS Constellation), and I'm sure most every hour will find us fully occupied. It does seem that time is moving right along now. It's hard to believe that just one month from today we

will be right back here in Cubi for the very last time. From the tempo of things, when we left the line, I'm sure that's going to be one helluva active month. And it may start to seem very, very long before it's over.

This activity we have going now will probably continue to build. I don't know if it will accomplish anything, but at least we're making a good try at it. But this is a rest period for the ship now, so let's just enjoy it.

...I don't know whether you can read this—Gordy and Jack are asleep, and the sun just went down, so in the dim light, I can hardly see what I am writing. I have to wake them up soon, though, to head out for dinner. This is the first time it's been cool enough to get any sleep, so I won't rush waking them for a little thing like food.

Just know for sure that if you can't read this letter, it's filled with thoughts of love for you. I guess I realize more each day just how much you really mean to me. I feel sorry each day for those who don't have the love that we have to bind them together. And soon I'll be there to make that even closer.

I love you, my darling, so very, very much,

Jimmie

USS Kitty Hawk
Subic Bay
Thursday nite
4 May '67

Hi Darling,

I guess it's high time for the delinquent child to return to the writing desk. Monday was a big softball game with our Ready Room mates and a big wetting down party that night for VAW-114 to celebrate their commissioning and change from a detachment to full-fledged squadron.

Tuesday was recovery and tennis and report time, and then yesterday we spent the entire day on a deep-sea fishing expedition. The chiefs organized it, and obviously, some of us were obligated to go. So Beef, Jack, and I were elected. Actually, it could have been a lot of fun, and it really was fun once I had recovered from the 0530 reveille that was part of the trip.

I slept most of the way out to the reef and got quite a ribbing about that, but the sleeping was nice and peaceful. It took about three hours to get out there, and we didn't get back to port until late last night. There weren't a lot of fish out there—we only caught a few triggerfish from bottom fishing on the reef. Then, on the way back in, Beef got to reel in a tuna and Chief Dove got a beautiful wahoo.

It sure was a long day for about 15 minutes worth of excitement, but we got a lot of sun, and it was really a beautiful day. That didn't sell me on all-day fishing trips, though. If we had caught more fish, I might have become convinced.

...I thought I had whipped out all my obligations for this in-port period, but I just heard VAS-114 wants a return softball match tomorrow. Maybe it will rain or something. I don't think my arm has limbered up sufficiently to pitch another game, and tomorrow is our last day in port. We pull out Saturday morning, and I guess I will fly one of the planes out. We go back on the line Monday, and then I expect 18 days of havoc before we finally turn around and start heading the way we have wanted to head for so long.

Still, time is moving right along now, and it's hard to believe that May date is really for real. After that comes June and that will be happiness indeed. I don't know exactly how the scheduled fly-back will be, and I'm sure we won't be anywhere as lucky with the deal as we were last year...At most, the early return will only be a week ahead of the rest of the squadron, and then some will have to make the trip back out to pick up the planes. Heck, Honey, anything that happens after we leave the line is just gravy from then on. I won't sweat a bit running back out to the West Coast for a day to pick up an airplane. That would get my June flight time out of the way anyway.

Got your letter of 28 April today, so mail is coming along fairly well now. I got quite a charge out of Glyn's school paper. I guess she really does like school, and I'm so glad that she enjoys learning. Most kids that age do anyway so long as we don't stifle them...I guess we are more fortunate with our children than we will ever realize. Maybe if we can keep enough love and warmth in our hearts, they will always wear that happy smile.

I suppose maybe I want more for them than I want for ourselves, but I'm sure that's the way God intends it. I just don't want the world to come too easily for them. I'm sure we won't have to put in any added effort to reach that goal, though.

I was sorry to hear about the death of Lamar Wiggins...His little son sure needs a father around. I see even more each day that we can't always choose what is in store for us. We just have to learn to manage with the days as they come and not build too narrow a world to live in...I guess it's nice to lay your life out in a book but that requires a lot of revised editions.

...Well, Darling, I've just got to get some shuteye. I can spend the time well dreaming of you, but I can't ask you to meet me there in dreamland with our 13-hour time difference.

I love you, sweetheart, with all my heart. It makes me so happy each day just to know I married you. It must have been the wisest thing I've ever done in my life. Nite, my love,

I love you,

Jimmie

USS Kitty Hawk
Subic Bay
Sunday afternoon
7 May '67

Hi Darling,

Looks like I was born to Cubi. We have been left here with three sick airplanes, and I'll bet Ray and the Skipper are going wild. I flew out yesterday, but my landing gear wouldn't come up...so they sent us back to Cubi. One of the others didn't even get airborne, and now all three of us are waiting for the ship to COD in some maintenance people so we can fly the planes out.

It should only take a day or two to fix two of them, but the other plane may take even longer. Meanwhile, I guess we get an overdose of sun. I got a little red yesterday afternoon, but this morning was something else. You just can't believe what 30 minutes in this tropical sun will do. I just looked at my nose when I came in, and it looks like a flashing red beacon. It's going to peel good, and I guess there is nothing now I can do about that. Just hope I can wear my oxygen mask with some comfort when I do get airborne.

And I have to stay in swim trunks so I can save my one set of slacks and shirt for dinner each night. We just didn't plan on any extended stay so clothes and money are going to soon become a priority item. Maybe some of us can get out of here tomorrow.

...I've got to get cleaned up now as I have been invited over to Larry Lavely's house for dinner. Larry is a classmate of Beef's and a supply officer here on the base. We have carried him and Diane out to the club for dinner a couple of times, so when they saw that we were still stuck here today, he called to see if I was busy. And, boy, the last thing I am here is busy. I'm so tired of the greasy food here at the club that it will sure be nice to eat in a real live house for a change. It will also be nice to talk about something besides war and airplanes.

Better get a shower and start on over there. Bye for now.

I love you,

Jimmie

USS Kitty Hawk
Subic Bay, Philippines
Tuesday afternoon
9 May '67

Hi Darling,

Guess who is still at Cubi? We got the XO in one plane yesterday and sent Gordy along with the second one today. But I still need one more part for my plane before I can go anywhere. I think if anything else goes wrong with it, I'll just take a COD back to the ship and send someone else back to get the plane. I can just imagine all the mouthing we are going to get now, so any longer and they will chase us off the ship. At least we sent them two planes out to work with, so that should pacify everyone for a day or so.

I did have a very enjoyable dinner over at the Lavelys' the other night. It was really different to sit and talk and eat like a human for a change even with the little ones screeching around the house. They have four girls and the oldest one turned six last month. It gave me an opportunity to talk with a young lady Glyn's age, so now I have some idea of what to expect next month. They are good kids, but I don't see how Larry manages with a houseful of six females. (That includes a maid.) But right now, I would gladly put up with ten of them just so long as you were one.

...What have you heard from Rozelle? We never found any more reason for the change in status on Max or Glenn (Daigle), so I don't really expect any new news. I sure wish we could get this thing over so we could track down some of those guys.

Well, I'd better get this in the mail. Jack is ready to go to lunch, and the mail pickup is at 1300. If I hustle, I may get this in on time.

With all the warmth of Cubi,
I love you, darling,
Jimmie

USS Kitty Hawk
Subic Bay
Tuesday nite
9 May '67

Hi Honey,

Would you believe one more day? At least I hope we can get out of here tomorrow morning. We hear the weather hasn't been too good out in the Gulf, but this continuous sunshine here is also a little more than I can take.

...We turned the airplane up tonight, and all the repair work checked out okay, so now all I need is one little valve from the ship so I can get the wheels up and we're on our way. It sure is a problem here with so many special parts when the only way we can get them is by hauling them all the way in from the ship. Oh, for those days

of the simple A-4. But it was just as bad back in the days when we had them as you can well remember. As Bob Fraser says, get yourself a nice old worn-out bird like the A-3 and then everybody has the parts. Then you only have to worry about how long they will hold together.

I don't think they have been flying much on the line so far, so Jack and I will probably wind up only one flight behind, the way Beef was last year. If we go into big strikes again, what few there are will be humdingers, but the frequency will be sparse. Our last flight should be the 25th, so by the time you get this, you can probably start counting the days. After that, it will only be a few days until we get home!

...For now, nite, My Love,

I love you, Jimmie

USS Kitty Hawk
"Free"
Thursday nite
11 May '67

Hi Darling,

Believe it or not, I'm finally back on the boat...I haven't missed too much as far as operations out here go, and I won't be behind at all it appears. I'm now due up early in the morning for a big "alpha" strike. Guess they are going to continue with these big ones as long as the weather will last.

I saw the biggest thunderstorms I've seen in ages on the way out here this afternoon. It was nice just to see some dark sky after all that sun, sun, sun in Cubi. We were out on the ramp all day today working on the airplane, and the temperature on that concrete must have been 120 degrees. I finally found the part that was sent to us two days ago over in the post office with a bunch of bags loaded for shipment back to the States!

I won't gripe about the postal service any more tonight, because I found three letters from you waiting in my box here on the ship. I can't remember what the time difference is with daylight-savings time, but I'm sure our daughter is six years old by now, and preparations for her birthday party must be well underway. I would like to be there for the fun of it, but I can't say I envy you mothers at times like these. There is some fun, but the parties are a lot of work and take a lot of patience. Maybe I'll have time to learn how to do all that when I get some shore duty.

Now, since I'm already short on hours to sleep, I'll just say I love you and let myself dream of all the millions of things that make me so happy I married you. It sure is nice that we met since we were meant for each other in so many, many ways. One of us could have been born in Kansas or someplace, and then it would have been difficult getting together!

Tell Jamey I'm proud of his earning efforts. Maybe he will have a big bankroll by the end of the summer.

Nite, My Lover,

I love you, Jimmie

USS Kitty Hawk
"Free"
Friday nite
12 May '67

My Darling Dora,

There was a group of pictures of some very striking young models posted in the Ready Room today. I must say I wanted to reach right out and grab you right there ...Don't know who sent all the pics, but I saw a couple of duplicates at least that Diane Wattay sent Al.

Everyone enjoys being wanted, I suppose. Today, I must have been the most popular guy on the ship—or at least the most greeted. I think every pilot on the ship has stopped by to personally greet me back aboard. Even half the blackshoes, too. I couldn't go anywhere without creating an uproar—at briefings and all. I expect a special note in the Air Plan any day now.

The Air Boss, of course, had to be the first last night when I trapped. Before I even picked up the hook, he passed over the radio, "Welcome back, Mr. Griffin." Then came the Captain with his two bits worth. Of course the big joke has been my suntan, and I didn't realize how much tan I had until today at the brief when I looked like an Indian among a group of pale faces. My tan will disappear like theirs, though, after two or three days of operations. It was a real sweatbox up on the roof today, and if the sun stays out I can see how hot it will become.

...Sorry to have to stop writing so early, but I have an early exercise scheduled for tomorrow, so I have to get some sleep. These 5 a.m. wakeups for weather holds are no fun, especially since I never got a chance to get back in the pad today. If I go now, though, I can get almost a full night of dreams of you. And very pleasant dreams they will be. Missing you much, my darling, and love you more than all the world.

A kiss for James and Glyn,

I love you,

Jimmie

USS Kitty Hawk
"Free"
Sunday nite
14 May '67

Hi Darling,

Happy Mother's Day, Mother! I do hope it's a pleasant day for you and hope it doesn't take too long to clean up all the mess I'm sure Jamey and Glyn are bound to make as they prepare your breakfast in bed. I know how industrious they can get over things like that.

I hope you can at least have a cooler day than we are having here. The sun is out full blast now, and it really is a corker. I wish we could at least take advantage of it for a little sunbathing on the flight deck, but we can't do that with flight operations going.

...Got your colored pictures today, and they are beautiful. Glyn is so tall I can't believe it, and Sam is much larger than I expected he would be. You can tell James the yard looks in outstandingly good shape, though I wondered if you were responsible for the clean edging beneath the fence. I especially like the picture of you, Darling. It's been a long cruise, but it's comforting to know I really haven't forgotten how beautiful you really are.

You asked about the early fly-back, and there isn't much definite on it yet. But I am scheduled to fly back early, so rest assured, we will get the right word to you gals this time. As you suggested, I'll try to make a phone call from Japan and then another at the last stop, so people won't have to be there so early waiting this time. Of course, last time, it was all such a big secret, and I don't think it will have to be that way anymore. Still, it's all a long way off when you look at some of the missions we have left to fly.

I know prayers and faith have brought us this far, so I surely have the faith that we can finish out what is left. Sometimes it makes me wonder, though, when we lose good friends like we lost today. I guess wars weren't meant to be popular, and I don't know if they are supposed to teach us something or not, but somehow, there must be a better solution.

Maybe someday we will all get the message on how to live with other people. But I guess human nature is not to be happy with your lot and always to strive to improve your own condition. As crowded as the world is, that is bound to encroach on someone else, so there you have the makings of a war. Maybe pink pills are the real answer after all!

I was surprised to learn your pet fish Tinkerbell has lived this long. Most of the minnows you get out of a pond die in a week, so it's easy to see why the others didn't survive. But I guess it's something to keep the kids occupied. I just feel sorry for the little fellow, all cooped up there by his lonesome. Maybe James and Glyn are ready for a goldfish, but they can be a real pain when you want to go off on a trip or you have to move.

...Well, Honey, I've got a paperwork day tomorrow since it's our stand-down day, so I had better get some rest in preparation for that. I love you so very, very much, and I am really looking forward to next month.

Until then, My Lover, I love you.

Jimmie

USS Kitty Hawk
"Free"
Monday nite
15 May '67

Hi Darling,

We just finished our one big stand-down day, so I guess we're caught up for the cruise. Things will start to move slowly now as they try to think up big closing events to schedule. Then, come 25 May, the time will whisk right along. I have about a thousand things I want to get done, but I know I'll be lucky if even one-tenth of them are completed by the time we leave Japan. I know how it was last time, so I certainly don't expect anything different.

Things will be different this time, though, knowing we don't have to face a short turnaround and come right back out to sea. I hope we can remain civil and show some respect for the people who will be making the return trip. Last year, at least most all of us were in the same boat.

Well, Honey, do you think we can hack it—having a whole year together? Or maybe two. I won't count on three years, but at least two will be nice. I think you should go ahead and let our landlords know we will be staying in Sanford to make sure they will honor our lease for a renewal.

...Someone said Mary would still be there, but I hardly think centering our activities at her house would be appropriate. Maybe we could descend on her once in a while, but she wouldn't want us as a steady diet for sure.

Frank (Bransom) said tonight that Rose had mentioned that Mary might move this summer. I think, in a way, it might be better from her standpoint to get out of Sanford, but the kids might prefer to stay right there. Now that they are used to the water, it will be really hard to move them away. In fact, I think the next time we move, we should try to find something on a lake, too. I'm not sure there are that many lake properties in Albany, Georgia, though, so that might prove to be difficult. They have a pretty nice river, from what I have seen driving across it.

...It is nice, though, to be down to the day-counting stage. I haven't started marking them on the calendar yet, but I may start

that even before we reach Cubi. Right now, I'm just spending my spare hours with sweet dreams of you. Until that sweetest of all days, my darling,

I love you,

Jimmie

USS Kitty Hawk
"Free"
Friday morning
19 May '67

Hi Darling,

I

L

I L O V E Y O U

V

E

Y

O

U !!

With all my heart,

Jimmie

→ 8 ←

June, 1967

No more letters from Jimmie will come in the mail, and life goes on for me and the children in Sanford, Florida while waiting for the war to end.

Being a wife without a squadron in a navy community can be difficult, especially after years of participation in the many activities that serve to boost the spirits of families whose men are away on cruise...and in combat. Now that the men in the squadron have finished the cruise and returned to Sanford, I am concerned that our presence—that of Pat and me and the other wives of those missing and captured—is a downer for those who still face returning to Vietnam. We talk about forming our own social group, but in the end we are adopted by RVAH-3, the retraining air group—or as we call it: the RAG. If our husbands had returned home, Pat and I realize, they would be joining the RAG anyway. They had received orders assigning them there. We attend wives' club activities, we are invited to change-of-command events, and we spend more time traveling to be with our families in our home states.

For some reason, perhaps to avoid publicity about our missing men, when the squadron wives hold a farewell gathering for us, we are quietly given "going away" gifts, but the event is not mentioned in the navy wives' column in the Sanford newspaper. The men, some of whom are moving from RVAH-13 to the wing or the RAG or leaving on orders to other duty stations, continue to phone or stop by when they can.

Our spirits are lifted when our casualty officers inform us that we are to be allowed to send letters to our captured husbands. Even those whose men are in an MIA status are invited to write. We have no guarantee that the men will ever get the letters, but some prisoners, including Gerry Coffee, have written home to their families, so we make the effort and pray that these letters, however brief and vague, can be of some help if they are received by our men.

Bob Watson, my CACO (casualty officer), brings me the suggested guidelines for writing:

DIRECTIVE CONCERNING PROCEDURES FOR SENDING LETTERS TO CAPTURED SERVICEMEN IN VIETNAM:

FOR THE WIFE OR MOTHER OF CAPTURED OR MISSING PERSON:

LETTERS SHOULD BE BRIEF, CONTAIN ONLY PERSONAL INFORMATION, AND SHOULD NOT BE SENT TOO FREQUENTLY, POSSIBLY TWO OR THREE LETTERS EACH MONTH. EACH LETTER SHOULD BE ENCLOSED IN A SEALED ENVELOPE ADDRESSED TO YOUR HUSBAND. THIS ENVELOPE SHOULD BE ENCLOSED IN ANOTHER ENVELOPE ADDRESSED TO THE AMERICAN NATIONAL RED CROSS, MISSING AND PRISONER SECTION, 17TH AND D STREETS, WASHINGTON, D.C. 20006. THE AMERICAN NATIONAL RED CROSS WILL FORWARD THE LETTERS OR CARDS TO THE INTERNATIONAL COMMITTEE OF THE RED CROSS FOR ATTEMPTED DELIVERY.

IF YOU RECEIVE A LETTER FROM YOUR HUSBAND OR FROM SOMEONE WHO HAS WRITTEN IN HIS BEHALF, PLEASE NOTIFY YOUR CASUALTY ASSISTANCE OFFICER IMMEDIATELY.

THE FOLLOWING METHOD MAY BE USED IN LIEU OR IN CONJUNCTION WITH THE ABOVE:

1. ADDRESS LETTER TO:
LCDR JOHN J. DOE
CAMP OF DETENTION OF U.S. PILOTS CAPTURED IN THE D.R.V.,
C/O HANOI POST OFFICE

2. LETTERS MUST COME BY REGULAR OR AIR MAIL AND MAY BE POSTED AT ANY POST OFFICE.

3. EACH ENVELOPE MAY CONTAIN LETTERS, CARD, OR PHOTO, NOT EXCEEDING 20 GRAMS TOTAL WEIGHT INCLUDING ENVELOPE.

4. ONLY ONE ENVELOPE OF 20 GRAMS MAXIMUM WEIGHT PER MONTH. IN THE ENVELOPE MAY BE LETTERS FROM WIFE, CHILDREN, FATHER, MOTHER, BROTHER, AND SISTER (JUST IMMEDIATE FAMILY). NOTE: 20 GRAMS IS ABOUT 0.7 OZ.

And so I begin to write, making my letters a sort of diary for Jimmie, letting him know—if he is allowed to receive letters—generally what we are doing during his absence. And I keep copies myself, so that he can read them when he comes home if he is not allowed to receive them in while he is a prisoner.

Letter mailed June 11, 1967 to Jimmie in Hanoi:

We have received word that you are alive and safe, and we are so thankful. Our prayers are with you, and there are many, many friends praying for you, also.

End of school activities have kept us all busy here. We will save pictures for you.

Your family has been with us, and we will be visiting them for a few weeks before returning here for summer swimming.

We would like to send you a Bible if it is permitted.

Our spirits are good because of our faith in God and because we know of your own faith and strength. We are all well, and our thoughts are constantly with you,

Sending all our love,

Your Dora

Letter mailed July 24, 1967 to Jimmie in Hanoi:

We are back in Florida after a trip to Tennessee to visit the relatives. Everyone there is fine and thinking of you. It was good to get together with the Salinas cousins—they are all so grown up. Our newest nephew is so handsome and sweet. We plan to return for a short visit when Barbara comes.

John and Lois left their children with the grandparents to drive to Florida with us for a few days. He was surprised to find the state much more pleasant than he had expected, but he still prefers the west. They did enjoy the beach, despite a sunburn, and promised a return visit with the children next time.

We spent the July 4th holiday in West Palm Beach, and we have enjoyed frequent outings to the beach here since then. James is at Camp Moki this week, and they tell me he is a very good camper. He promised to take me out in a canoe next Sunday.

Glyn has been receiving special swim lessons this week at the McIntoshes'. She hopes to make the AAU Swim Team next spring. And with those two upper front teeth out now, she is precious.

Sam is being a "good boy," taking care of us while James is away.

We are all strong, healthy, and full of faith. Our prayers and love are with you every minute. The very special love we have shared so long will grow even stronger as it sustains us through this difficult separation. We all love you so very, very much.

Until the time when we can be together again, I send you all my love, always,

Your Dora

While we try to go on with our lives, the sleepless nights turn into weeks. My friends and family give me emotional support, and I do my best to comfort Jamey and Glyn Carol. Each night we continue to have prayers at bedtime, and each prayer ends with a plea for "Daddy to come home." We talk about the situation, and I try to instill in them the pride that I know Jimmie had in the mission he was on for his country in Vietnam.

"Why doesn't Daddy come home?" is a frequent question. "Because God needs him somewhere else," is the only answer I know to give them. Having reassurance from the navy that Jimmie is alive keeps us going. "Daddy is tough," I tell the children. "He'll survive and come home to us when he can."

When we get together, Pat and I fantasize about Jimmie and Jack arriving in our driveways in a taxi. While, on a conscious level, we know it can't happen, I think we both look out the window often, halfway expecting them to return home that way after having made a daring escape from the Vietnam prisons. We frequently spend evenings together, having a glass of wine and taking our children out to Shoney's for dinner.

August 1967

We return to Tennessee by train to spend time with Jimmie's sister Barbara and Bill and their girls, who are now visiting from San Diego. My sister Charlotte and her husband come to Memphis while we are there, and James and his Uncle Larry really hit it off. A college professor, Larry has brought some board games to share with the children. We return to Florida by plane, and we enjoy it much more than we did the train ride going up. The Daums are waiting dinner for us when we get home. Dick and Al Wattay have hooked up a turntable for our hi-fi cabinet. We realize that Al is leaving the navy this summer to be a pilot with American Airlines, and we are sad to see his family move away, but, obviously, life must go on for all of us...

I play bridge with the navy wives several times a week, but being with women who still have their husbands is not the distraction I need. So, as time approaches for Jamey and Glyn Carol to begin school in the fall, I decide to find a new focus for my life. I apply to become a student at the new community college that has just opened in Sanford. My plan is to take a few courses toward the bachelor's degree in journalism that I never completed after leaving college to get married in 1955.

Letter Mailed August 29, 1967 to Jimmie in Hanoi:

We have completed our summer travels and are glad to be home again. We were so glad to meet Bill, Beth, and Susan at last, and the girls got along famously with Glyn and Jamey. Barb is as young as ever, and she sends you much love.

We went up on the train, and Glyn loved the new experience, but we all were glad to be returning home by plane. Kinda cool for August up there, and of course, we had expected hot weather. Betty came to my rescue with slacks and a long-sleeved shirt that saved the day. There was no heat because of the transition to natural gas this fall. We spent some time at both Grandmas' and everyone is doing well.

Charlotte and Larry arrived for a short visit while we were there, and he made quite a hit with the children. He bought them some new games—very intellectual—that we are all enjoying, and he was quite taken with Jamey's vocabulary and intelligence.

Camp was a good experience for Jamey. He won top honors for canoeing, and also got ribbons in archery and riflery.

Glyn eagerly began first grade yesterday, with shiny new shoes, two top teeth missing, and a short, short, a la Twiggy, haircut. It figures—she came home disgusted because they didn't do any addition or subtraction, and it was not their day to play on the monkey bars! James brought home a stack of perfect papers so I guess he has decided to star in his last year at Pinecrest.

Hope I can do half as well in the two classes I have scheduled at the junior college this fall. Thought I would try for that long-postponed degree now that the little ones are in school. Perhaps you and I can both teach school someday. First, I must see if my learning ability is still there, and so I am beginning very modestly at Seminole Junior College.

Our lease has been extended again, so we are all settled here and plan to stay until your return.

Sam was glad to have us back again, and we had a birthday party for him last week. It is hard to believe he is about grown up. I had hoped to skip mine this year, but you know James would not let me get by without a cake and candles so guess I will have to count it. My prayer is that you can be home with us before my next one. And our thoughts, prayers, and love will be with you constantly until then.

Your Dora

Another Letter Opportunity

406 Satusma Drive
Sanford, Florida
September 6, 1967

Cmdr. H.L. Jenkins, Director
Personal Affairs Division
Department of the Navy
Bureau of Naval Personnel
Washington, D.C. 20370

Dear Commander Jenkins:

Enclosed is my letter to my husband to be included in the "bundle" you hope to get through to Hanoi via the Quaker hospital ship. I hope it arrives in time. Jim's mother also is mailing you a letter from Tennessee in case it is permissible for him to receive it, also.

I want to thank you for sending me the tape alleged to be Jim's voice as picked up on a monitored English-speaking Hanoi Radio broadcast. Lcdr. Barlow delivered the tape to me, and I have spent many hours playing it over. Eventually, I was able to make out some of the words, although it is impossible to say for certain that the voice is really that of my husband. Comparing it to the voice-pattern, i.e. the pauses and emphasis on certain words, of his voice on tapes he has sent home from time to time during the cruises, it seems possible that it is Jim speaking.

Included in the portions I have been able to decipher are:

ANNOUNCER:

"The High Command of the Vietnamese Peace Force Army held a press conference in Hanoi on the morning of May 20th on the great victory of Hanoi Armed Forces...(unintelligible)...shot down 10 U.S. planes and killed or captured a sizable number of pilots.

"...(unintelligible)...Peace Force Army High Command.... escalating step of utmost gravity, but the United States met with powerful rebuffs."

(Next followed a list with identifying numbers I was able to make out fairly clearly as identical to the list, etc. of the five captured that was carried in newspapers around the world.) After identifying my husband, RVAH-13, 11th Wing, from the Kitty Hawk, etc., etc., the announcer said:

"Here is the voice of James Griffin, one of the captured pilots..........talking."

"I am Lcdr. James L. Griffin, RVAH-13, 11th Wing, Kitty Hawk, Serial No. 595955. I was born 27 December 1932 in the state of Tennessee.

"On May 19 (or "When I was downed"), I was on an RA5C photo mission...Hanoi...(unintelligible for about a sentence

including a phrase that sounds like 'R-C-A')...Before I could complete my mission, I was brought (or shot) down by heavy ground fire and received serious injuries and heavy burns during ejection."...(more unintelligible for a sentence)..."and I am grateful for the treatment..."

This is what I have been able to understand from the tape. Perhaps your men have been able to decipher more. It hardly coincides with the so-called statement attributed to Jim in various newspapers, but I had been prepared for that sort of thing.

Thank you very much for all you have done. Lcdr. Barlow told me that appeals have been made though the Red Cross concerning Jim, Lt. Walters, and Lcdr. Stark, all of whom were captured May 19 and identified by Hanoi Radio as "injured" according to newspaper accounts. The tape certainly is proof of their own admission that Jim was "injured" (although I feel he is all well now) so the Red Cross could use that as basis for more appeals for inspection or even Jim's return under provisions of the Geneva Convention. I know, of course, that they are not honoring the Convention, so I do not really expect anything to come of it. We will keep hoping, though.

Again, let me thank you for all your efforts and pledge my continued cooperation...and patience.

Sincerely yours,
Dora Smith Griffin
(Mrs. James L. Griffin)

September 6, 1967 Letter to Jimmie in Hanoi:

The school year has begun—for all of us! James is doing outstanding work, at the top of his class so far. Glyn is a happy first-grader, anxious to show off her reading ability. She has resumed dancing classes, and her group may be in another program soon wearing the colorful tap costumes they had for recital.

I have attended my first two classes at SJC, and I find it is going to be a challenge—especially the science course. There is a wonderful enthusiasm for learning there, though, so I hope it will inspire me to apply myself, also.

Guess we saw everyone in the family during the summer, and everyone was well and sending you their love and prayers.

Everyone at Grace Church sends good wishes, and the choir, with special thoughts of you, has added a prayer song at the close of each worship service. You know Ophelia and how much she thinks of you!

We all are doing well and our spirits are high. We know God is with you, as He watches over us. I love you so very, very much, My Darling,

Your Dora

Letter from Jamey enclosed with above letter:

Dear Dad,

School started last week, and Glyn started first grade. So far, I have made all E's. I'm still in the top room at school.

I lost a tooth two weeks ago and another one this morning. I have two more loose, also.

I hope you'll be home soon.

With lots of love,

James

PS. We had a birthday party for Samson recently. He's full grown now.

LETTER FROM DEPARTMENT OF THE NAVY
DATED 8 SEPTEMBER 1967

Dear Mrs. Griffin,

As you are aware, your husband, Lieutenant Commander James Lloyd Griffin, United States Navy, was placed in a captured status following the loss of his aircraft on 19 May 1967 while on a combat mission over North Vietnam.

A full report of the circumstances surrounding this incident now has been received, and it confirms the information already furnished you by the Chief of Naval Personnel.

In accordance with the provisions of the Missing Persons Act, as amended, your husband's pay and allowances will accrue to his account so long as he remains in a captured status. Should a change in his status occur or should additional information be received concerning him, you will be promptly notified.

I join you in the hope for your husband's early release from his captors.

By direction of the Chief of Naval Personnel:

Sincerely yours,
H.L. JENKINS
Commander, USN
Director, Personal Affairs Division

I'm finding it difficult to fit in with these young people at the junior college. I don't feel comfortable having lunch in the campus cafeteria since I see very few people in my age range to talk with, so I take my bag lunch to my car. Then I find the kids eat in the parking lot, too, boom boxes booming and loud X-rated conversations ring out through the parking lot. I don't remember college being like this twelve years ago.

Participating in class is challenging, though. I actually enjoy exercising my brain again after all this time. The biggest problems are trying to use my rusty math skills to convert temperature from Fahrenheit to Celsius and being available to Glyn and James when they get home from school. It's difficult finding time to study, but I don't sit around moping as much as I did during the summer.

The news from Vietnam is not good. Newscasts seem to indicate the war may last much, much longer. And I had been counting on us being near the end of this horrible conflict!

I try to keep a diary for Jimmie, but there seems less and less to write, and I have less and less faith that he ever will read the words. I sit alone late in the evening, watching a television show and as performer Glenn Yarborough sings, "I remember the outline of you lying next to me, and I memorized the hills and gullies of your body, because I knew that someday, it would be good to recall..." and the long pent-up tears flow. *Will I ever lie next to him again?*

Letter sent to Jimmie in Hanoi October 6, 1967 (Jamey's Birthday)

Dearest Jim,

This special day finds us preparing for a trip to see a circus nearby. Wish you could join us; the children are so excited.

Aunt Rachel and Jan spent Sunday with us. They are all settled on Merritt Island, and Alice is in school in Tampa. Hope we can all get together Christmas since the folks plan to come down.

You will be very glad to know we are all doing very well in school. My initial feeling of being "too rusty" subsided, and I find it easier to learn with each class meeting. James is a big help since he is studying many of the same things in science. They are both doing fine work, too.

Glyn's tap class presented its "Mammy" number for a benefit dance to raise money for cerebral palsy Saturday. As before, it was a big hit! Those youngsters can really sing, and the ballet is coming along nicely, too.

The World Series is in full swing now. The Cards ran away with the National Pennant, but the Red Sox had to really work to pull off their championship from the Twins and Detroit. But the Series is on now, and after two games it is all tied up, and they are headed for St. Louis for the weekend. You know who will win of course (Ha), but I will include the official results in my letter next month.

You can be sure we are all well with constant thoughts of you…and constant prayers.

We all send all our love…and my very special love,

Your Dora

Letter Mailed to Jimmie November 15, 1967

My Darling Jim,

The holidays are just around the corner, and we are beginning to look forward to them. The folks will spend Christmas with us this year, so we will have all the outdoor lights up to greet them.

We sent you a small package of gifts in hopes that, somehow, it might get through. There is a tiny chess set in it because all our children are becoming expert chess players—even Glyn Carol. They have taught me to play it, also, but my game presents no real challenge to them. I am counting on you to give them some real chess competition when you return home, so practice up. Also sent a deck of cards in hopes you will learn to play bridge if you are allowed to have roommates.

You can be very proud of your family. All of us are doing well in school—even me! I have learned all about Coriolis force, magmatic differentiation, and thermals; and there are a few perfect scores to my credit! The little ones are good scholars, too. Perhaps my "good example" is a help.

Most recent house guests were the Davises; and Jack and Jackie flew down last week. He was purchasing a new plane in Kissimmee. There are frequent phone calls with good wishes from all our out-of-town friends—Bob and Donna, and of course, John.

Our Boy Scout has about completed his qualifying tests and hopes to get his uniform this week. They are all really growing up.

Much, much love from each of us,

Your loving wife.

December 8, 1967

Christmas Card sent with letter:

Across the Miles at Christmas...

How nice it would be to be with you today,

But since wishing won't make it come true

This little card's sent as an alternate way

Of sharing this Christmas with you!

Merry Christmas—Happy New Year

My Darling Jim,

We have been Christmas shopping, and tomorrow we will be putting up the outside lights and the lighted toy soldiers.

Santa landed by helicopter at the Plaza last Saturday, and we were there to meet him, getting a face full of sand from the 'copter wind. The children want new bicycles this year, along with dolls and camping equipment. James will be on his first Scout camperee soon.

Your mother and father will join us several days before Christmas. Hope to take them over to the Cape to see Rachel, where we spent Thanksgiving.

We will be selecting our tree on Monday. Think we will have a Scotch pine this year—I have enough of those little spruce cones to build a mountain!

Our thoughts will be with you every moment, from Christmas Eve Communion to hanging up stockings, and our prayer is that you can join us by Christmas, 1968.

All our love always, Your Dora

Our holiday season is marred by a telephone call bringing news of Mary Putnam's death. Mary has talked with me on the phone often during the past few months, and she called again just before leaving to drive to New Orleans with her five children to spend Christmas with relatives. She had decided to drive at night, and so she may have been a little less alert when a drunk driver came across the median and hit her car head-on. Some of the children were injured, but Mary was the only fatality in her car. We still don't know Putt's fate in Hanoi. God, this is too much for that family. What can be next?

⇢ 9 ⇠

1968

Letter mailed to Jimmie in Hanoi on January 15, 1968

My Darling Jim,

The holidays are over, and a new year filled with hope has arrived. James stayed up until midnight New Year's Eve, and our neighborhood rang with firecrackers and cheers. He said, "Now I know why everyone celebrates—so at midnight, they can finally go to bed!"

Mother and Dad Griffin came down by train and spent Christmas week with us. Now that your Dad is teaching, he has a longer holiday, and he enjoyed the rest. We all went to the Cape one day to visit Rachel and Whitey and met Alice's boyfriend. Whitey had broken out one gift early, so we all had a fine time playing "Skittles" on the patio. They spent Christmas Day with us in Sanford.

Your dad helped Mrs. Santa fill the stockings—had stored the shiny new bicycles down the street, so at 11 p.m. we hiked down and rolled them back. There was a baby doll for our daughter, and James got a Boy Scout model camera. He will send you a picture he took himself when the roll is complete.

We received many phone calls, messages of prayers and encouragement from friends during the holidays, including a phone call from Dan and Betty Peckham in Canada, and visits from the Leiberts and the Jack Adamses. I will save all the cards for you.

I am enclosing a letter from John Chaney. It arrived too late to be enclosed in our letter last month. We hope that eventually you will be allowed to write a letter to us.

All my love to you, Dear Heart,

Your own Dora

The semester ends at the community college, and, much as I have enjoyed getting the cobwebs out of my brain, I decide it is time to return to being a mommy and a navy wife. I have actually been missing those frequent afternoons of playing bridge with my friends, and it is time to start looking ahead to the relocation of Sanford Naval Air Station to Georgia. I withdraw from the college and, once again, interrupt my quest for a college degree.

Letter sent to Jimmie in Hanoi on March 1, 1968

My Darling Jim,

The winter chill is still hovering over Florida, but the children saw a robin this week, so we are all looking forward to spring. We pray that you will be home with us soon to enjoy the rest of the year.

Many of our friends have moved on to Georgia, and we are considering joining them there when school is out—unless you can return by then! We will go up to visit friends there soon and look over the area to see if we like it.

The schools provided the children with some unscheduled holidays last week during a statewide teachers' strike. Classes have resumed now, and they are glad to be back in school, though we played many games of chess and Monopoly last week! Tomorrow we will be going to the Central Florida Fair in Orlando, and I am wondering how many "fun houses" and mazes the children will insist on going through this year.

Aunt Rachel came over from the Cape to spend a weekend with us recently. Jamey was on a Boy Scout campout at the church, but we all went down to see their camping exhibits at "open house." They are planning another campout in a few weeks, so I'll have to get him some hiking boots.

Glyn's class has begun learning their dance recital pieces. She will be a graceful "Little Red Riding Hood" in a ballet number.

We all have had haircuts, but mine, I think, is most noticeable. It will grow fast, but is so neat and comfortably short for a few weeks.

Have been playing lots of bridge and doing some volunteer work for NRS (Navy Relief Society), and the change of pace is very refreshing. We now have some new dining furniture, and I managed it without disturbing our growing savings funds. How I long for the day when you can be home again with us to share all these things.

We all love you very, very much and trust that God will bring you home soon. He is with you, My love,

Your Dora

PS: Just talked with your mother, and they are all well there and send you their love as do Barbara and John.

LETTER FROM DEPT OF THE NAVY
NAVAL INTELLIGENCE COMMAND
Dated 18 April 1968

Dear Mrs. Griffin,

I am sure you have wondered why I haven't answered your April 6th letter. As so often happens in the Pentagon, your letter went astray. I got it only this morning, and it arrived from the Army Surgeons General Office.

Enclosed is a copy of the photograph of your husband's ID card. I am sure this is the same photograph that appeared in the *Vue* magazine. It is a typical propaganda release by the North Vietnamese, and I feel that it is unlikely any reporter from *Vue* was ever in Hanoi or had an opportunity to talk with your husband.

On the matter of your conversation with Captain Williams about the 21 May article in Hong Kong, the captain is out of town with LTJG Matheny. I'll mention it to him when he returns but don't think you will learn much. As you know, when we have a particularly bad day such as on May 19th, the North Vietnamese have a propaganda heyday. We have had occasion to check the 21 May Hong Kong papers on other incidents the same day and found that the 20 May press conference in Hanoi was the basis of that story as well as similar articles in other communist papers. We have not heard of any photos of your husband other than the ID photo enclosed.

Hope this answers some of your questions. Sorry about the letter taking so long to be delivered. We had a reorganization April 1st, and if you will address future letters to the new address on the envelope, maybe we'll have better luck on the next one.

Sincerely,

R. S. Boroughs, CDR USNR

Head, Special Warfare Division

Letter Mailed to Jimmie in Hanoi on April 25, 1968

My Darling Jim

Soon a year will have passed since you arrived in the "Hanoi Hilton," and again, spring is here.

We had Easter Week visitors from Wisconsin and you wouldn't believe how much Stevie and Kathryn have grown! Got to the beach with them twice and everyone got sunburned on the second outing. Hope to get a little tanner before WE leave Florida next month. Cooked out one night and the bottom of our grill fell out so will have to buy a new one after we move. Jamey insisted we make a freezer of homemade ice cream, but you can imagine who ended up turning the crank most.

Had lots of fun preparing extra Easter baskets—we had dyed eggs before our company arrived. They were convinced we had a very smart Easter Bunny. Their kiddies are early risers so had us all up at 6 a.m. to hunt eggs. We waited to attend 11 a.m. worship services, however, and had neighbors take our Max Snapper friends to noon mass.

Our swimming pool finally opened this week, and we have been taking advantage of it. We will be leaving here the day school is out, and after June 1, our address will be 315 Riverview, Albany. Hope you will like our house up there—it's right on the golf course, in sight of the chapel and the river. Neighbors include several friends, both for me and the children.

Meanwhile, end-of-school activities keep us busy. James is art editor of his class paper now. It features his original cartoon strip, Blob and Glob, a couple of lumpy-looking characters that spout his typical wisecracks. His terrific caricature of Samson was featured in a school art show.

Glyn is dancing hours every day preparing to be "Little Red Riding Hood" in a little red satin cape for her ballet program and a "Little Miss America" in a sequined outfit for tap. She is getting so long-legged, but retains her grace on the stage. We may purchase a movie camera to take pictures of the program for you.

I have been trying to learn to use your camera on the automatic setting, but the Christmas pictures didn't come out.

Aggie and family came up to visit last Sunday. Ginger is doing newspaper work (advertising), and Wayne will attend college there this fall. My mother will be here in May for the recital and Wayne's graduation.

We just learned that John Chaney got a fellowship to the University of Florida, so they will be nearby in Gainesville for a year starting in September. How great to finally get them all to Florida—and we hope they can be here when you return home. Know one reason he applied there was to be near us, and Albany will be just about as close to them!

I pray you can be home with us to complete our very wonderful family circle before the summer is over, or even by Christmas. The children do need their Dad. So until the day when we can be a united family again, we send all our love, growing stronger each day. God is with you, My Darling, as he is with us.

All my love always,

Your Dora

Letter mailed to Jimmie in Hanoi May 17, 1968

My Darling Jim,

With the school year nearing an end, we are preparing for our move to Georgia. John and family will be nearby in Gainesville for a year beginning this fall. The children keep me running with class picnics and recital practice. They have grown quite a bit this year.

Mother will be coming down in a few days on her vacation and to see the recital. Last month, we had house guests from Wisconsin.

Everyone in Tennessee is doing fine. We hope to get up there for more frequent visits after our move since the drive will not be so long.

It soon will be a year since your capture, and we have been sending a letter about every five or six weeks. We hope that before long, we will receive a letter from you.

I
I L O V E Y O U
O
V
E
Y
O
U

With all my heart,
Your Dora

For two years, we have known that the Sanford Naval Air Station is closing, moving operations to what had been Turner Air Force Base in Albany, Georgia. We do not want to be left behind, waiting for Jimmie's return. So, when the Command offers us quarters on the new Georgia base, I decide to drive up and look around. The children and I arrive early one evening a few days after Dr. Martin Luther King Jr.'s march through Albany. The NAACP has moved some former slave quarters alongside the highway on the east side of town. There have been picket lines outside the gate to the naval air station, too, war protesters expressing their disapproval of the military establishment. We are not moving to a quiet little town where nothing ever happens, but the prospect of moving and staying with our friends in the Wing gives me a good feeling.

The quarters assigned to me are not on a lake or the Flint River that runs through the town. Instead, we are to live in one of the older houses with a backyard adjacent to the base golf course. It isn't spacious, but I can imagine sitting at a picnic table in that backyard, watching the golfers go by and enjoying tranquil sunsets. I take measurements of the windows so I can adjust the curtains we have for their new home. Then we return to Sanford to plan our move. I paint bookcases for our new quarters and start looking forward to a change of pace. I feel better about things because we will still be part of the military community that already has begun its relocation to the new base.

Then, in the midst of our preparations for the move, I receive a phone call from the Wing Commander that shatters my excitement. He has given the quarters originally assigned to me to the commander of a squadron, one of his friends, who has chosen for his own family the very house where I made my measurements. I am to be assigned a similar house that does not adjoin the golf course. It's a small thing, but when the call comes, I lose my composure. I go into a crying jag that lasts for days. All my confident outlook for the future has crumbled. My comfort level has been destroyed, and I no longer want to go to Georgia. Packing boxes are everywhere, and my mother has come to help us prepare for the move. I know my reaction distresses her, but I am not able to stop crying.

Billie Kimmons, the Wing Commander's wife, arrives to try to calm me. She explains the importance of giving the squadron commander the house he wants because he is headed into combat. When I tell her I want to withdraw from the move, she convinces me it is important to stay with the Vigilante community. She feels the other wives whose husbands are headed into combat will feel better if they see that life will go on as usual for us. Reluctantly, I try to "buck up" and remember what Jimmie would expect of me. I dry my tears and resume packing.

We have not seen our new house prior to our arrival in Albany, so it is a surprise when we find it is located diagonally across the street from the base commander. It is late afternoon when we get there, and I am too confused to tell the movers where to put things. They unload our belongings and set up the beds once I have assigned bedrooms to Jamey and Glyn, then the men leave me to face piles and stacks of unlabeled boxes. A neighbor has brought over sandwiches, so we eat standing at the kitchen counter. Then I search for light bulbs and sheets so the children can find a place to sleep.

Because we are living on base, the utilities are already on, and I have managed to have the telephone connected before our arrival. Still, I am startled when late in the evening I receive a call from my mother. Among the sea of boxes, I have difficulty locating the ringing phone. After helping us pack for the move in Sanford, mother went on to West Palm Beach to visit my sister. Now, headed back to Tennessee, she has stopped in Albany at the Greyhound bus terminal, asking if I could come and get her. She wants to help me with the unpacking.

I am beside myself. I have no idea where the bus station is located in Albany. I also have not yet obtained a base sticker, and I have yet to find all the sheets for the beds. Not only am I completely exhausted, my nerves are shot. There is much anguish in my voice as I tell my mother it will be best if she continues on to her home in Memphis. She seems to understand, but, much as I need her, it nearly destroys me to have to refuse to drive into town to bring her out to our new place.

The first days in our new home are difficult, but eventually we get things unpacked and fitted into the small quarters...a four-bedroom houseful of furniture force-fitted into three bedrooms and a storage shed that adjoins the carport. We have moved nine times during Jimmie's career, but this is only the second time I have done it entirely on my own with no one to help me unpack and make arrangements. Somehow, though, it all comes together.

The neighbors, all navy families attached to the base or the air wing, are helpful. There is a special bond among military families, and they always seem closer than the families we were born with. It is to this community that I so want to stay attached. They have been my security blanket. Some wives of missing men have gone back to their hometowns and families, but Jimmie has always encouraged me to stay "on my own" if anything happened to him. He knew that the hometown folks would be full of sympathy, but the people there could not possibly understand how we in the military feel under these circumstances.

In the past two years, anti-war protesters have become more and more vocal across the country. Many of the wives who went home found themselves influenced by these well-meaning protesters. And some of the anti-war sentiment has become anti-military. Sometimes, the bond between these women and their missing husbands weakened. So, despite the difficulties I have had with the move, I still feel connected with Jimmie by being on the naval air station with his comrades and their families.

Some of the branches of service have a Big Brother program for the children of the missing men. There is no such program in the navy, but there is a team of casualty officers who call on the family frequently, keeping us abreast of any news regarding our husband's status and word of any policies that might affect us or give us encouragement. These men do their best to help us solve problems that arise, keeping us in touch with legal officers and with the Wing. However, they have families of their own, children of their own; they do not try to take the place of our husbands or of our children's fathers in any way. And the same has been true for Jim's squadron mates. In a way, those in the squadron must get lumps in their throats every time they look at us or at the children. We are constant reminders that, but for the luck of the draw, their own wives and children might have found themselves in our situation.

We are settled in now in the military quarters assigned to us, a Wherry housing structure with a master bedroom and two smaller ones. I have made a sort of den adjacent to the kitchen using a rust-colored carpet remnant as focal point for the slipcovered hide-a-bed, TV, and a rattan chair that has been in our home for thirteen years. I've bought and painted three stools to pull up to the counter for casual meals, where we face the kitchen. The washer and clothes dryer stare at us from their perch beside the ever-humming new refrigerator, and a kind neighbor has installed a disposal in the antiquated kitchen sink and somehow turned our portable dishwasher into a permanent fixture. I feel that we can live here until the war is over and Jimmie comes. I pray that will be only a matter of months!

As soon as we arrived in June, I dug a flowerbed outside the living room windows and planted nasturtiums, marigolds, and petunias. Now, while the children are asleep, I start each morning there, enjoying a cup of coffee and the morning paper. I sit with my feet pulled up in one of two new green barrel-shaped chairs that sit beside the windows looking out over the flowers. Then I waken the children and get them fed and dressed. We don't talk much about the war, and I try to limit the evening news coverage to times when they are out playing with the neighborhood children in the large open space behind our house.

Here on the navy base we are very close to air operations. The planes take off and land right above our quarters, but we are accustomed to the deafening sound. When we lived in Sanford, the sound of planes turning up their engines was expected every morning. On Sunday mornings, when they lifted off to take to the skies with a roar, even the minister at Grace Methodist Church continued his sermon without missing a beat, because he knew we had all become lip readers.

Now, as I see the Vigilantes, the jets my husband flew, streak through the clouds overhead, I shiver. Sometimes I envision his plane breaking apart, and tears overcome me as I imagine Jimmie ejecting and falling to earth amid a shower of bullets. Then I shake it off, remembering that he was captured alive in Hanoi. It has been more than a year now, and he must have recovered from whatever injuries he sustained in that ejection.

In an effort to keep my mind off our situation, I begin writing the navy social column for the city newspaper, *The Albany Herald*. Each squadron has a reporter who submits their social news to me, and I rewrite it as a Navy Wives' column each week. It seems pretty elementary for a former newspaper reporter, and I know the gals who bring their reports to me may be disappointed in my rewriting them, but I manage to turn out a fairly decent column each week. It helps to pass the time, brings in about five bucks or so a week, and helps me to keep in touch with the other women and what is going on at the base.

Letter sent to Jimmie in Hanoi on July 7, 1968

My Darling Jim,

We just had friends from Sanford drop by unexpectedly—Ophelia and Morgan. The gang back there is still praying for you and thinking of all of us.

The children love our new home in Georgia and are looking forward to fishing and picnicking with you along the Flint River one of these days. People here are so friendly, and many of our old friends are around us, too.

James has made several new friends, including one very close buddy, also named Jim. He is learning to bowl, and he has improved his average quite a bit in the few weeks we have been here.

Glyn Carol has joined the Brownies, and this month she is attending their summer day camp two days a week. She also is continuing her dancing in a weekly class at the Junior Museum. I hope we can get her an inexpensive piano this fall, since music seems to be her chief interest.

I am being very leisurely about settling in our new house in Albany, because we hope you can return home before the end of the year. Wherever we live, that king-sized bed we have wanted for so long is now a reality! We will wait until August furniture sales before purchasing new bedroom furniture, but the mattress and frame are here, and NO house guest will be allowed to sleep on it before you return. I may have to tie a red ribbon across your side when John and Lois come to visit this fall, but it will be kept new for you!

Your mother and dad were our first houseguests here last weekend, but Barbara Jane visited later in the week. We have a family room with breakfast bar and a dining room, too.

Hope you don't mind my indulging in a bit of journalism while you are away. I am writing a weekly navy social column for the local newspaper. It is my intention to keep its quality better than the Sanford column, and my readers tell me that it is. The activity is a very temporary diversion until you can come home to let me devote all my time and talents to loving you.

My faith is strong in the Lord and in you. Our great day will come soon, and we will make use of every moment the rest of our lives being happy together. Please write us if you can.

Remember always that we love you,

Your Dora

Letter No. 13, Mailed to Jimmie in Hanoi on August 10, 1968

My Darling Jim,

We are preparing for the annual trip to Tennessee. James went up on the train last week, and he tells us by phone he is having a great time with Johnny and Rodney up there. He really seemed to enjoy that train ride.

Glyn and I took Samson to the kennel today. She has been helping me cook and plant flowers this week.

We have all been enjoying our new home in Georgia, and we are looking forward to the colorful autumn, hoping you can share the beautiful scenery with us. The children will be taking piano lessons when school starts. We have rented a pretty spinet, and if they continue to show interest, we will buy it!

Can you believe our little son will be in junior high school this year?! He is not very tall, but he is really growing up to be like his dad in so many ways. Glyn IS growing taller and prettier every day. We all send our love and prayers and wishes for a wonderful Christmas together.

May the Lord watch between me and thee, while we are absent one from another.

Your Dora

Letter No. 14, Mailed to Jimmie in Hanoi on September 1, 1968

My Darling Jim,

A touch of autumn already has begun to cool the air and tint the leaves of the Georgia pecan trees. How we wish you could share this time with us!

The children are eager to begin school this week, and we are happy so many familiar faces will be with them as they ride buses for the first time. James has already found his homeroom at the junior high school and will have some old friends in his room.

Our daughter also has been placed in the top class at the nearby grammar school. Glyn will continue her dancing this year with new teachers we have found since moving here. All of us will be learning to play the piano—and we are enjoying that piano more than we ever dreamed possible.

We had a very nice trip to Tennessee, and everyone was fine. Your family was remodeling the kitchen to be convenient and attractive. We took movies of the children, along with Salinas and Tennessee cousins.

John's family stopped by here on their way south to the university this past week. We hope to get together often this year while they are so near. We all plan to be home for Christmas this year, and we pray that you can be with us, too.

All my love always,

Your Dora

Autumn 1968

James and Glyn Carol join other navy children on the curb each morning for the three-mile bus ride to elementary and junior high schools located off the base. I have volunteered to be a room mother in Glyn's school, so I am often called on to monitor a class while the teacher takes a break or to handle the entire day if she is sick. But I have fallen into a routine that helps to pass the days, if not the nights. At least two times a week, after the school bus has left, beds are made, and the breakfast dishes cleared, I drive over to the base golf course to join Pat and a few other "waiting" wives in what should be a competitive round of golf.

I have never been much of an athlete, so, though I take repeated lessons from the golf pro, my skill has not improved beyond "novice." But it keeps me busy through the morning, gets me walking, since we do not use the electric carts, and it costs very little. Golf club dues here on base are just $40 for a year, though in the beginning, I just paid a dollar to play nine holes since I felt certain I would never develop into a real golfer. The time together gives us, Pat and me, a chance to talk things over away from the children's ears. We commiserate about our situation, try to second guess the future, and in our own way we try to lift one another's spirits. Sometimes we succeed by injecting a little humor into the day. Then we hurry home, knowing the mail has arrived, because one or two of the other waiting wives have received a letter from her captured husband. Day after day, I rush to the mailbox and empty it of bills and junk mail, but I find no letter from Jimmie.

He is too strong to do whatever they want him to do to write a letter. He knows I have faith in him and that I can make it through this with no letters. But I would give anything to have a letter! Just one letter!

Pat and I take our children out to dinner every week or so. Little Stan, just a toddler who could not possibly remember his father because he was only a year old when Jack left on this last cruise, always wants a milkshake and a burger. He rarely eats more than a few morsels, but it makes us all feel good to see his little eyes light up when that tray of food is placed before him.

Having no brothers of his own, James likes to play "big brother" to Stan. I'm sure the waitresses and the diners around us wonder who we are, two women with our three children laughing and chatting over dinner, week after week. Albany has not long been a navy town, and when the air force, who previously occupied the space where our naval air station is located, assigns personnel to overseas duty, the families often accompany their men, rather than stay behind. Having navy families here is different.

From time to time, we are summoned to attend a briefing for MIA wives. We have seen some top brass from Washington who gave us words of encouragement, and once we heard a talk by a POW early returnee who confirmed only that Jimmie and Jack's names had been heard in the POW camp in Vietnam but nothing more. Today we saw films of a Vietnam prison camp. It showed some captives whose photos were published in *Life* magazine wearing what looked like pajamas with wide stripes. Since the movie we were shown was not in color, the pajamas looked gray, but in published photos, they appeared to be maroon and gray. Their faces are grim as they sweep a dirt courtyard or sit on what appears to be a hard, concrete bench in a cell. Occasionally, while "posing" for the camera, the prisoner manages to do a finger gesture that indicates that he is being forced to participate. When we see the finger sign, we all cheer. *I am glad Jimmie does not appear in the film....No, I'm not! I wish so much I could see him and know that he is still alive!*

Day after day, I check the mailbox for a letter, but there is no letter from Jimmie. Our family members write and come to Albany to visit, but what I need more than anything is a letter like two air force POW wives shared with me last year. *Even if he only was able to sign his name on a postcard, it would mean so much.*

The children have been asking for a piano. Pat has a piano and has been taking lessons. While I, myself, have no wish to learn to play, I know it would be a good diversion for James and Glyn Carol. They began taking lessons when we lived in Sanford, practicing on a piano at a neighbor's house or at the church. I arrange a rental from an Albany music store and have the piano delivered to our quarters. Both kids are excited at first, and James takes special lessons that allow him to accelerate by using chords and, thus, advance more quickly. Glyn takes regular piano lessons and makes progress, too.

At night, after the children are asleep, I pour a glass of wine and sit down at the piano. Although I took voice lessons as a child, I never learned to read music. Now, using some simple sheet music for a few popular songs, I manage to pick out the basic tunes of a few popular songs. The songs are sad, and it gives me a chance to shed tears in private.

Pat has been urging me to update my record collection, so I purchase some LP's of Bobbie Gentry and Helen Reddy. Playing sad songs and pecking at the piano helps me get through many quiet, lonely evenings.

At this point, families of those missing in action are given more specific instructions regarding the format to be used in letters to their loved ones. Most of the letters I have mailed up to now have been returned to me, so I try to adhere to this special format to increase the odds that the letters will be delivered. Each letter now has to be typewritten or printed and some Vietnamese words are to be included in the address.

Letter No. 15 mailed to Jimmie in Hanoi on October 25, 1968

My Darling Jimmie,

The children are really growing up. You will be proud to know our son made the honor roll for his first term in junior high school, and our daughter had almost straight A's on her report card from school. James is doing well with his piano lessons, too. We are all hale and hearty, enjoying the brisk autumn weather in Georgia, the colorful leaves, and the plentiful pecans. We will travel to Florida next week to see John and family at the university. Your parents will be down to see us soon, and we plan to spend Christmas in Tennessee with all the relatives.

God be with you until you can be home with us. I will not forget to keep the champagne warm.

Your loving wife,

DBSG Dora

Letter Mailed to Jimmie in Hanoi on December 11, 1968

Dearest Jimmie,

Merry Christmas and happy birthday, Darling. We will spend the holidays with our families in Tennessee, taking along Santa's bag of surprises, including a pogo stick for our daughter and a gas-powered airplane for our son.

We are all well, but missing you very, very much. I pray that 1969 will be the year we can all be together again. That will be HAPPINESS.

I love you much as much,

Your Dora B.

⇢ 10 ⇠

Letter mailed to Jimmie in Hanoi on February 14, 1969

Dearest Jim,

My Valentine, we hope you received the Christmas package. My knitting has now much improved—those foot warmers were my very first item. You were in our thoughts as we all gathered in Tennessee for the holidays. We kept your birthday gift here—a painting by D.J. Warren.

James made first-semester honor roll, and he has become a very good bowler. Glyn, our straight A's girl, is happy in her new dancing school. Both are preparing special piano numbers to play for you when you come home, and we pray that time will come soon.

Sending all the love and hope that spring can bring,

Your Dora

Letter Mailed to Jimmie in Hanoi on March 29, 1969

My Dearest Jim,

We have a new car. I know you will like it! It is an Olds Delta 88, beige with dark brown roof. Hope you can drive it before the "new" wears off.

To greet spring, we drove recently to beautiful Callaway Gardens, and the children think it a perfect spot for our "family honeymoon" when you return. This weekend we will drive down to the University of Florida to visit John Chaney and family. They will be returning to California this summer.

All are well, sprucing up the yard, thinking always of you, praying for your safety and for your return to us soon.

Until I can more appropriately express my love,

Your loving wife,

Dora

Typewritten letter mailed to Jimmie in Hanoi on May 1, 1969

Dearest Jim,

Since last you were with us, our daughter has grown taller and more beautiful and charming than we ever dreamed. As you can see from the photo enclosed, she helps me cook, and Samson thinks she makes the best doggie biscuits in the world!

James is growing up, too—in fact, he has had his first two pimples though his 13th birthday is months away. He loves to wash the new Oldsmobile with his jet-action suds-thrower.

Samson has matured, too, of course, but I haven't changed a bit. Ha! Oh, I have let my hair return to its natural color and grow to shoulder length, and in Georgia, my suntan has completely disappeared, but with thoughts of you, I am trying to watch my weight and stop those "laugh-lines" as much as possible.

We have planted roses and other flowers in the yard, and currently, we are painting and fixing up the front door and carport as our spring project. I pray that we really are getting things ready for your homecoming before too many more months.

Recently, we enjoyed a visit with John Chaney's family in Gainesville, and we will be seeing Barbara in June. The children want us to go to the Smoky Mountains this summer, and we would love to have you with us at the same spot we planned to visit 14 years ago. We love you so very much. God be with you.

Your Dora

Letter to Jimmie in Hanoi mailed July 3, 1969

My Dearest Jim,

We have just returned home from a long trip that included visits in Tennessee with parents and Barbara and John's families. Everyone is well and sends you love and prayers. Glyn and James enjoyed spending time with all their cousins.

Later, we went to the Smoky Mountains, accompanied by Mother, to visit my Uncle Louis. We all tried a little mountain climbing, and even Glyn enjoyed the ride! Also paid visits to the Tignors and other friends in Virginia, as well as Jack Adamses and Charlotte in North Carolina. It was quite a trip, but took the entire month of June, and the new car made driving so easy and pleasant.

The travel-vacation was fun, but we are glad to be home again. Samson was glad to see us, and so was our pet turtle. Glyn Carol is attending Brownie day camp two days a week, and she is excited because she is going fishing next week. James is proud of his first bowling trophy. He is helping with the yard work and tomato and flower beds this summer. In August we may go to the beach for a few days.

Always, our thoughts and prayers are with you, Darling, and we send you much, much love,

Your Dora

At some point I received a copy of a photo that had been published in a Hong Kong newspaper in May of 1967 showing a captured American pilot being presented at a press conference. Because it appeared with certainty to me that it was Jimmie, I called my Casualty Officer and asked him to have the photo analyzed. The Navy Photo Lab analyzed the picture and was of the opinion that it was of Charlie Plumb, also captured on May 19, 1967, but digging out old photos of Jimmie, I was convinced that it was he, and so I sent several old snapshots to the photo lab. This was their report:

> CDR. J.L. GRIFFIN:
>
> The individual appearing in the POW photos labeled as Plumb greatly resembles Cdr. Griffin. They are definitely similar types; however, there are a few differences noted between the two.
>
> Firstly, the area of temporal recession, which is evident in each, seems to differ. The POW's does not seem as pronounced and is more clearly defined than Griffin's. Secondly, the shapes of their ears differ. Griffin's ear appears larger and more oval shaped, while the POW's is rounded. The POW's upper helix appears to have an acute angle in the rear; Griffin's does not. The other visible features of the two individuals appear to be very similar (i.e., nose shapes and length, eyebrow placement, chin and mouth area). The head shape of the POW is not visible in the rear position; therefore, a comparison cannot be made on that feature. It is the opinion of the technicians of this office that they are very similar, but are probably not the same individual. Regarding the possibility of the photographs originating from the same film: It is not possible for the technicians of this office to make a definite statement regarding the origin of the photos. It would appear, however, since the angles of the photo are quite

similar, and because the individuals (POW and "local" type wearing glasses) are similar, they could well come from the same film sequence.

LETTER FROM CDR. BOROUGHS

DEPARTMENT OF THE NAVY
NAVAL INTELLIGENCE COMMAND
Washington, D.C.
Dated 10 July 1969

Dear Mrs. Griffin,

Please excuse the delay, but we have been quite busy ever since the North Vietnamese made their announcement about releasing three POWs. No names so far, but we must be ready just in case there are navy personnel among the three. I also wanted to hold off until we had received the enclosed photo comparison report. As you can see, the result of the analysis is not favorable.

Let me give you some background on what we have done while attempting to track down information on the New China News Agency photograph.

Soon after they were shot down on 19 May 1967, Lt. Plumb and Lt. Anderson were paraded in front of a rather large press conference. Many members of the communist news media were there and both still photographs and movies of the proceedings were made. Every report (newspaper clipping, etc.) we have available indicates that only Plumb and Anderson were shown at the conference, although a tape reportedly made by your husband was played at the same time.

We have reviewed all of the Plumb-Anderson films and have been unable to find the exact frame depicted in the New China

News Agency release. However, while going though our files on Plumb, we did find a similar photograph (a poor copy of which is enclosed) which appeared in an East German newspaper. I believe the Asian correspondent in the German paper is the same one circled on the New China photo. (Also see last paragraph in analysis report.) As you can see, there are many similarities between the pilot named and clearly identifiable as Plumb in the German paper and the pilot shown in the New China paper. We believe both photographs are of Lt. Plumb.

I hope that this has been of some help to you in clearing up any questions that you may have had.

Sincerely,

R.S. Boroughs
Cdr USNR

The analysis does not satisfy me. I still feel certain that the photo from the China News Agency is Jimmie!!! I'll keep pushing.

Letter sent via Quaker, Dr. Joseph Elder, "hand-carried" for Jimmie in Hanoi on 20 July 1969

Dearest Jim,

On this special day, when man has actually walked on the moon, I send much love from all of us.

We are having a beautiful summer in Albany, and with our trip to Tennessee and Norfolk completed, we are getting ready for the Chapel's Vacation Church School. After a week of teaching those youngsters, I plan to take James and Glyn Carol to the beach for a few days and to visit our Florida relatives and friends.

Wish we could send you a ton of sunshine, Darling, but we do send much, much love. Your loving wife, Dora

Letter No. 22 Mailed to Jimmie in Hanoi on 27 August 1969

My Dearest Jim,

This new electric typewriter is terrific—if I can learn where the new keys are located, my "penmanship" should improve. This even has some keys which can be replaced with engineering symbols.

After a terrific summer that included quite a bit of travel, we are settling down to routine again, preparing for another school year. James, in eighth grade now, will be allowed to take a high school algebra course. Yes, he is still a "whiz" at math! Glyn is getting her outside activities lined up—better known as Mother's Chauffeur Schedule. Ha. Both will have piano lessons, and she will have Brownie Scouts and two days of dancing each week, ballet and tap.

We just returned from visiting everyone in Florida. A few friends are left in Sanford, and we spent several days with Rachel and Whitey at the Cape and a weekend at Aggie's. Spent a day at the beach with Rachel, hunting shells, and the children discovered a huge turtle, about 14 inches across, in a field near the parking lot.

While in Orlando, the children and I took in some current movies—screen version of the play Oliver and a comedy about a crazy Volkswagen called The Love Bug. And with Jordan Marsh so handy, I even bought myself a wig. It's a short fall, not much longer than my own hair, but very pretty and handy. Had a lovely boat ride down the inter-coastal waterway with Lester, and the children enjoyed a Tarzan swing set up on an inlet near the ocean where we picnicked. It is still beautiful country down there, but we are looking forward to another colorful autumn in Georgia.

In addition to sewing school dresses for Glyn Carol, I have also resumed my knitting. I am knitting a dress for her. Hope to knit a sweater or vest of some sort to include in the package I send you for Christmas this year. My knitting has vastly improved since the humble beginnings I made last winter.

When the children are back in school, I hope to join one of the bowling teams this fall. Also, I want to get back out to the driving range to resume golf lessons. It will be quite a while before I become much of a golfer, though. I hope you will give me a few private lessons when you get home. My progress so far consists of just learning how to hit the ball. I still haven't really played around the course.

That birthday is coming up for me this week. James proudly informed me that I would be old enough for Serutan. But don't you believe it!

Until that happy day when we are together again,

I send all my love,

Your Dora

PS: Much love and prayers from Jamey and Glyn, also.

HANDWRITTEN NOTE FROM CASUALTY OFFICER, JAMES B. WOLFE

Dated 8-12-1969

Mrs. James L. Griffin:

Your husband's name appears on a list of POWs which was accumulated by recently released POWs from various sources. The releases had no personal contact with him or positive knowledge that he is in fact a POW. Your husband's name came into their possession through hearsay information only. If any additional information becomes available in future debriefings, you will be informed.

The above information was passed to me by telephone this afternoon. Mrs. Yaksich from Pers Casualty section passed it to me. Good news, as meager as it is.

Sincerely,
James B. Wolfe

Letter mailed to Jimmie in Hanoi September 19, 1969

My Darling Jim!

Georgia hay fever has us all sneezing this week, but we are almost too busy to notice with fall activities.

First, I must tell you that the Mets are leading the National League, though the Pirates took a doubleheader from them yesterday. They're still four games ahead.

I finally played around the golf course Monday and scored an 89! Well, that's only on nine holes, but that isn't bad for a first time, is it? Boy, were my muscles sore.

James starts bowling again, now in the junior league. He is up to a 12-pound ball. I still use a ten.

Both resumed piano this weekend, and Glyn wants to add acrobatic dancing to her schedule.

Just talked with Barb and Bill, and they have moved to a rental house while waiting to build a bigger home. John and Lois are in a new home, too, and I guess all is great on the western coast. Things are well in Tennessee, too. Your Dad is getting false teeth, and they will join us here for Thanksgiving—if he is able to chew by then!

All my love, Darling,
Your Dora

Handwritten Letter on Airmail Folder sent September 22, 1969

Dearest Jim,

Autumn finds us busy with school activities again. Can you believe that in just two weeks, we will be parents of a teenager? In eighth grade, James is almost as tall as I am and his feet are even bigger.

I will be teaching Glyn's third grade class next Friday while her teacher attends a meeting. It is a common practice in Georgia schools to ask parents to help out. She also has begun ballet and tap dancing lessons, which meant more new shoes. After a summer of travels, away from the piano, I didn't expect them to remember how to play, but they have picked right up where they left off.

Have I told you lately that I love you? Or that the Mets are in first place? Or that I am learning to play golf? Or that I miss you?

Much, much love,

Your Dora

Letter sent to Jimmie on October 31, 1969

My Darling Jim,

You can imagine the activity here on his Halloween Day. James, our new teenager, will sit at the door wearing a sheet and pass out cookies that Glyn helped me bake. Samson and I will take it easy for a change.

We expect to have your parents and Gene's family here for Thanksgiving. In the meantime, I hope our new bedroom furniture will be delivered. After years of shopping, I decided on a very simple, traditional suite that I am sure you will like. Last weekend, James and I repainted the bedroom a soft beige tone.

The Renners just became parents of their third son! It is great having good friends like them around.

I am still teaching fifth graders in Sunday school, and the New Year brought me an excellent group of children. I may be the most improved lady golfer in our current ringer tournament. Every week, my score has improved, and I do enjoy getting out in the fresh air and walking. Hope you can soon enjoy golfing with me, too, among other things!

I love you very much,

Your Dora

Letter mailed November 15, 1969

Dearest Jim,

On Thanksgiving Day, your mother and father, Gene's family, and Rachel's family all will be here with us. It should be quite a holiday. Your dad enjoys teaching shop at Carver High School. John and family have returned to Salinas after a year at University of Florida. We saw Barb and her bunch in Tennessee this summer.

Everyone is well and praying constantly for peace and your return home. We have saved enough for a good start on that new home with the long-dreamed-of fireplace and a wonderful life as a family again when you come home!

With thoughts of that day, I send

All my love,

Your Dora B.

Letter received from American Friends Service Committee of Philadelphia in early December 1969:

Dear Friend,

Following upon Joseph Elder's October 1969 visit to North Vietnam, it now appears that I will be able to make a two-week visit to North Vietnam beginning in late December.

I have been invited to come to the Democratic Republic of North Vietnam as part of an international delegation to discuss questions of reconstruction and humanitarian aid. In addition, I will make a delivery of a quantity of open-heart surgical equipment on behalf of the American Friends Service Committee for use in the civilian hospital in Hanoi.

I would be glad to take with me a letter from you to your family member who is a prisoner of war in North Vietnam, should you want to write at this time. I would plan to turn over all letters to authorities of the Democratic Republic of North Vietnam in Hanoi with my request that they be delivered to the individual prisoners.

If you wish to send mail to your family member in this way, the letter should be received here in Philadelphia by Monday, December 15, 1969 and addressed to:

Louis W. Schneider
International Service Division
American Friends Service Committee
160 North Fifteenth Street
Philadelphia, PA 19102

I welcome this opportunity to serve you in this way.

Most sincerely yours,

Louis Schneider
Associate Executive Secretary

Letter sent to Jimmie in Hanoi on December 12, 1969 via American Friends Service Committee:

My Dearest Jimmie,

We had a jolly Thanksgiving feast with your mother and dad, Gene, Christine, and Perry, Rachel, and Whitey all here.

We are preparing for Christmas, soaking the Scotch pine tree, hanging outdoor lights, mailing packages. James wants a telescope this year to study the stars, and Glyn Carol is excitedly awaiting arrival of a ballerina doll. She will be in a Christmas dance recital next week, and James will be a "wise man" in the Chapel Christmas pageant.

Before another year, we pray that you can be here to share the holidays with us.

We all send our love,

Your Dora

Letter Enclosed with Christmas card and letter from Mother Griffin, mailed December 1969:

Merry Christmas, Jim Darling,

This will be our second Christmas in Albany, and we have decided to spend the holiday with other families whose men are away. Your mother, dad, Gene, Chris, Perry, Rachel, and Whitey all were here to enjoy Thanksgiving with us.

Our house is decorated with bright lights, and we have been making and wrapping gifts. James plans to surprise me with something he made in "Shop" class at school. He will be portraying one of the three wise men in the church Christmas pageant Sunday.

Glyn Carol is still young enough to be excited about Christmas. She is helping bake cookies to take to her class party Friday.

You can imagine that we are planning to keep Christmas just as we always have, but we will be missing you and thinking ahead to the next Christmas that you can again share here with us. We pray that the New Year will bring your freedom.

All our love,

Dora, James, and Glyn Carol

Letter sent December 31, 1969:

My Dearest Jimmie

How I would like to share this evening with you in person. With visions of our reunion, a cup of cheer, that fireplace we have always wanted, and happy moments together—I look forward to the New Year with prayerful hope that it all may come true.

The children are enjoying the new toys they received for Christmas. James is becoming an amateur astronomer with his new telescope that goes to 225 power, and already he is more familiar with constellations and more landmarks than I. Glyn loves her new Dancerina doll that dances just like our own prima ballerina.

Agnes, Lester, and Ernie came to spend the holiday with us, and then they stopped in Jacksonville to see Florida upset Tennessee in the Gator Bowl. We talked on Christmas Day to your mother and father and to John and Lois. There had been snow in Tennessee so it was good that they had come down here for Thanksgiving.

Darling, all of us are well and full of hope that we may hear from you soon. May 1970 be the year we have been waiting for—when we can be a happy family again.

All of us send you much, much love,

Especially Your Dora

→ 11 ←

January 1970

Each day we see more and more MIA wives appearing in television news stories. They gather in Washington to get the attention of the media and Congress, trying to be sure that our men are not forgotten. Some of them fly to Paris and are photographed on television day after day outside the building where the Paris Peace Talks are underway. *I wonder, are these trips productive? I am sure the women making those trips think so, but I do not feel Jimmie would have wanted me to participate in these things. I think he would want me to keep a low profile, and "paddle like hell."*

Letter Mailed to Jimmie in Hanoi on February 3, 1970:

> *My Darling Jim,*
>
> *Warm greetings to my Valentine from chilly Albany, Georgia! We have begun the New Year with hopes that we will see you again soon.*
>
> *James has become quite a stargazer since receiving his new telescope for Christmas. He made an A in industrial arts last term, and, so far, having a teenage son is a breeze!*
>
> *Glyn Carol has new sidewalk skates and keeps busy skinning knees.*
>
> *All of us are fine and send all our love until we can be together again.*
>
> *Your Dora*

Letter sent to Jimmie in Hanoi on March 7, 1970:

My Dearest Jim,

Our amateur astronomer son is all set today to watch an eclipse of the sun—the safe way. He is quite a stargazer these days with his new telescope.

James and Glyn Carol are both doing well with piano lessons. All three of us, your parents, and all the family are well and send much, much love.

Praying for your health and safe return.

I love you very much,

Forever and always,

Your Dora

IN MARCH OF 1970 AN ARTICLE IN THE JACKSONVILLE, FLORIDA *TIMES-UNION* AND JOURNAL SAID THE FOLLOWING:

(Headline:) **Hanoi Seen Yielding on Naming Prisoners**

Editor's Note: The following dispatch is the first report from Associated Press staff member Daniel De Luce since completion of his escorted 18-day stay in North Vietnam, the most extensive visit permitted to a Western correspondent since the United States became involved in the war.

by DANIEL DE LUCE

Associated Press Writer

North Vietnamese officials have acknowledged that they are holding 320 American military prisoners in their country and say that the names of the men may be released soon.

But, obviously sensitive to the pressures on them concerning this issue, government officials say the Americans are "browbeating" them on the question and assert they will never bow to "coercion."

These statements were given to this correspondent during an 18-day visit to North Vietnam, in response to requests for details on the identity and welfare of the Americans.

ASKED HOW THE NAMES would be released, government officials in Hanoi said on March 3 that several means were being considered. One possibility mentioned by them is to make available post office records to a news agency correspondent from a friendly power.

The officials said that the 320 men, many of whom already have been identified by North Vietnam as prisoners, are exchanging mail with their families in the United States.

If 320 American prisoners are identified by the North Vietnamese post office, this will cover about three-fourths of the total which the U.S. Department of Defense gives for Americans "known or believed captured or interned" in North Vietnam.

THE PRISONER ISSUE CAME up at my first reception at the Foreign Ministry office in Hanoi.

I was told:

"We understand the concerns of mothers and wives. Perhaps Vietnamese mothers and wives should go to the United States and ask for their children and husbands killed by U.S. bombs. Once the war ends, the prisoner question will be easy to solve."

I told officials that many believe the policy of withholding details on prisoners was hurting North Vietnam's cause in the world and damaging the efforts of antiwar elements in the United States.

Can't details be given out by unofficial means?

The statement March 3 that release may be through post office records seemed to be the answer.

FOREIGN MINISTRY SPOKESMEN say prisoners have been treated humanely after capture. They indicated that the agitation in 1968 to try prisoners as "war criminals" is a closed chapter.

I was told that arrangements for me to see any prisoners would be very difficult to make.

Instead, I was taken to the People's Army exhibition at Hanoi, where information on a number of American prisoners was on view.

Some American identification cards were displayed.

I have compared my notes with a U.S. list of American military personnel missing in Southeast Asia, which was presented last Dec. 30 to the North Vietnamese and Viet Cong delegations at the Paris talks.

The names I noted with their official U.S. spelling and rank in parenthesis follows:

David George Rehmann (David George Rehmann, lieutenant jg)

Richard Eugene Smith (Richard Eugene Smith Jr., major)

Ratzen Eduyn Tempeli (Russell Edward Temperley, major)

Gareth Laverne Anderson (Gareth Laverne Anderson, lieutenant jg)

Eduyn Athey (Edwin Lee Atterberry, major)

Jim Kabler (James Helms Kasler, lieutenant colonel)

Edward B. Burdett (Edward Burke Burdett, colonel)

William R. Stark (William Robert Stark, lieutenant commander)

Thomas V. Parrott (Thomas Vance Parrott, captain)

Jack Walters Jr. (Jack Walters Jr., lieutenant)

James L. Griffin (James Lloyd Griffin, lieutenant commander)

Norman Gardis (Norman Carl Gaddis, colonel)

It is a painful experience for an American to see the wreckage of American planes and the personal effects of American airmen shot down in combat and to realize that some, like Lt. (jg) Everett N. Alvarez Jr., San Jose, Calif. have been prisoners since Aug. 5, 1964.

Letter mailed March 16, 1970

My Dearest Jim,

Wish you could have been with us yesterday for a special folk music service in the chapel. James is an usher, and Glyn Carol sings in the junior choir.

A lovely spring with Albany azaleas blooming finds us all well. Your mother is coming to visit next month. She, your dad, Gene, Chris, and Perry all spent Thanksgiving with us.

James is planning his ninth-grade curriculum to include French and geometry, and Glyn Carol is readying for another dance recital in May.

Golfing and teaching Sunday school keeps me occupied, but thinking always of you, Love, and the happiness we will all know when together again.

Much, much love always,

Your Dora

Letter Mailed to Jimmie on April 10, 1970

My Darling Jimmie,

Our "garden" is growing beautiful lettuce and tomatoes and bell peppers. I will mail some lettuce seed to you in my next package in case you are allowed to have a garden, too.

I have been playing a lot of golf since we live so near the course. James played golf with me during spring vacation and will be beating me in a few months. We have a new color television—with remote control—so that is the main recreation for us these days.

Longing to hear from you,

All my love,

Your Smitty

Letter sent from family farm in Tennessee on May 1, 1970:

Dearest Jim,

We are all well, living near friends in Albany. James is completing eighth-grade honors class. Glyn did fine in third grade. I am learning to play golf. Please write to tell where to put that fireplace.

Your mother and dad join us sending much love, Dora

During our 1970 summer vacation in Panama City, Florida, while having lunch at Holiday Inn, we see a news story that lists names of the POWs in Vietnam...the list has been released by Sen. Ted Kennedy. Jimmie's name is not on the list! We are shocked and confused. I know something is wrong, but I cannot abandon hope.

Letter Mailed July 15, 1970:

My Darling Jim,

The children and I had fun last week at Panama City beach. James is taller than I am and plays a good game of golf. Glyn Carol is looking forward to seeing Leigh Ann in Tennessee next week.

We love you very much and hope you can be home soon.

Always, your Dora

Contents of Package Mailed to Jimmie on August 14, 1970:

5 sticks of peppermint candy
15 small soaps
1 hand towel
2 chocolate bars
1 washcloth
1 bag of candy
6 packages of chewing gum
1 bottle of eye drops
1 tube of lip balm
1 container of aftershave lotion
1 deodorant stick
7 packages throat lozenges
2 medicinal soaps
1 bottle aspirin
1 bottle antacid medicine
1 bottle Tinactin
1 bottle Actifed
1 bottle multi-vitamins
1 bottle Lomotil
assorted bandages

spoon
coffee
lemonade mix
plastic container lemon juice
toothbrush and toothpaste
small bag of sugar
photograph

Letter from Former CO of RVAH-13, Capt. Dean Webster, dated

19 August 1970

Dear Mrs. Griffin,

The enclosed material consisting of photographs and the newspaper clippings which you provided for photo comparison purposes, are returned. Unfortunately, the photo comparison personnel were not able to help. The following is their statement:

"The poor quality of photograph number one (unidentified POW) does not provide sufficient feature definition to make the requested comparison."

With regard to the request made to the French for an inquiry into Commander Griffin's status, they have not yet made a second inquiry because..."There had as yet been no propitious opportunity to do so."

I regret being unable to pass something more constructive.

By direction of the Chief of Naval Personnel:

Sincerely yours,

DEAN E. WEBSTER

Captain, USN

Special Assistant for POW Matters

→ 12 ←

A Change in Direction

While Jane Fonda gained worldwide attention in Vietnam, causing (hopefully unintended) additional suffering for our prisoners in Hanoi, and while the anti-war groups marched on Washington and in other places around the country, there was a patriotic movement afoot as well. Jimmie's brother, John, in California became involved in a campaign to put up billboards appealing for release of our POWs.

I begin rethinking what I should do, and I decide I should at least gather letters to be sent to the Vietnamese government on behalf of our men. When material is made available through the League of Families, I rent billboards around South Georgia and arrange to have signs put up, intended to rouse sentiment for our missing in action. Ann Crain, an MIA wife living in Albany, and I join with the Albany mayor in appealing for letters to the North Vietnamese, demanding fair treatment for the POWs. When the public gets involved, the message takes on new meaning. The writers want more than fair treatment for our men. They want an end to the war! Most important of all, they want our men held prisoner returned to their families. To ask this of the Vietnamese is not the same as telling our government to end the war, I reason.

"This is Major Dick Beason," a confident voice greets me via telephone on a late autumn afternoon. I have just come in from trudging around nine holes on the golf course, and my guard is down, so I have answered the phone without my usual wariness.

The affable marine quickly makes his point, giving me little opportunity to cut the conversation short before hearing what he has to say. He wants me to appear with him on a local television talk show to promote the "Letters to Hanoi" campaign. He has heard that I may fly to Paris to deliver letters from Georgia children and other concerned citizens to Vietnamese delegates to the peace conference, asking for the release of American prisoners of war.

My knees buckle. My voice fails me. This is not what Jimmie would have wanted. It has been difficult to make the decision to back a letter-writing campaign. Now, someone wants me to appear in public to make an appeal. The major is still talking, apologizing for catching me off guard.

"My wife and I would like to get together with you, because her brother is also a prisoner of war. Would you come out and have lunch with us at our quarters on the marine base?"

I would feel more comfortable if his wife had phoned me, but after listening to his plea for several minutes, I agree to meet with them. Putting the phone down, I break into tears at the prospect of appearing on television to talk about Jimmie. He held a very bad opinion of the press, and this is the press!

But the day arrives, and I go to the Beasons' home on the nearby marine supply base where I do my commissary shopping. His wife is quiet but gracious as she tells me that she and Dick are Mormons. She proudly shows me a closet stockpiled with food that they keep as a matter of course to offer to people in need or to have on hand for an emergency. The conversation is relaxed, and she tells me about her brother. They appeal once again to me to do the TV interview with

Dick on *The Town and Country Show*, a daily noon talk show. In the end, I reluctantly agree.

"You were great on the show," a friend assures me. "You were just like a professional." This I know is not true, but as I look back on that brief TV appearance, I find the experience was not so unsettling as I had expected. The host and hostess of the program did not subject us to political criticism or question me about my feelings. They simply let us use the show as a forum to rally support for our military in Vietnam and to encourage the viewers to write letters to the Hanoi government asking for fair and humane treatment for our men who are held captive. Until now, I have avoided any sort of interviews or public statements about the war, but I find this experience was not such a bad thing.

The Paris Peace Talks continue in Paris, making little progress, but continuing to saturate the international news. I begin planning to join some of the POW wives in Paris, taking along letters from people in Southwest Georgia pleading for information or the release of Jimmie. While it is against my better judgment to make a public show of our plight, the idea seems to mushroom after my TV appearance. Albany citizens who have never met my husband, but who had been watching TV coverage of many other MIA wives in Paris outside the Paris Peace Talks, seem eager to get involved. After all, we had positive word from the beginning that Jimmie is alive, but now suddenly, he is not on lists of POWs that are being made public by the North Vietnamese. I arrange to rent a billboard in Paris, asking:

"What Have You Done With Jim Griffin?"

A special "Write to Hanoi Week" was proclaimed for November 30 to December 6th, 1970.

It is a cold November day when I load the children in the car to drive from Albany to Atlanta for a gathering of Georgia families of MIAs and POWs. We have been invited to the state capitol for a day that is to be informative for the adults and fun for the children. I have carefully prepared for the trip by studying an Atlanta map, but finding a parking place near the state government buildings is always difficult, and today, it is a near impossibility. After much driving around, I manage to find a long-term meter about six blocks away from our destination, and we pull on our coats and trudge toward the capitol.

Soon after we reach the building, James and Glyn Carol are spirited away with the other children to the governor's mansion where they are given lunch and treated to entertainment. We, the wives and parents of the missing men, are regaled with speeches by officials of the state government as well as a few military representatives who try to reassure us that all that can be done for our men is being done. I find myself seated next to Frank Wells, a reporter from *The Atlanta Constitution* during lunch, and he talks with me "off the record" about our missing men.

After lunch the children come back to join us, and Christmas gifts are distributed to them. Since Ann Hyatt, a POW wife who lives near us on the base, was not able to come with us to Atlanta, we pick up presents meant for her children as well as those for James and Glyn. This leaves us rather loaded down with packages. As we start to leave the building, we find that it has begun to drizzle with a few snowflakes mixed in. I groan, thinking of the six long blocks back to the car. It seems almost more than I can handle.

But suddenly appearing beside me is a polite young man who was on stage with other speakers during the program. "Excuse me, ma'am. I'm Sam Nunn. Maybe I can help you."

I recognize at once one of the Georgia state senators, and I take him up on his offer. I leave James and Glyn, clinging to their stash of presents, standing with him in the capitol foyer while I race back through a chilly rain to retrieve the car. The children seem to be having a good time when I return to pick them up.

The three-hour drive back to Albany leaves us all exhausted, but we stop by the Hyatts' quarters to deliver the gifts to Ann's youngsters. While I don't usually enjoy these large gatherings of families brought together by tragedy, I realize we have had an enjoyable day.

COMMITTEE OF LIAISON
with Families of Servicemen Detained in North Vietnam
365 West 42nd Street, New York, N.Y. 10036

(212) 549-4478

CABLE ADDRESS:
COLIAFAM

Co-chairmen:
Dave Dellinger
Cora Weiss

Treasurer:
Mrs. Anne Bennett

Committee
Richard J. Barnett
Rennie Davis
Madeline Duckles
Prof. Richard Falk
Rev. Richard Fernandez
Norman Fruchter
*Maggie Geddes
Steve Halliwell
Prof. Donald Kalish
Stewart Meacham
Prof. Bea Seitzman
Prof. Franz Schurmann
Ethel Taylor
*Barbara Webster
Trudi Young

*staff

November 16, 1970

Dear Mrs. Griffin:

We are enclosing a copy of the written confirmation from the North Vietnamese, which is all the information we have.

We are sorry to have to send this news to you and extend our deepest sympathy.

Sincerely,
Barbara Webster

Letter Received from Committee of Liaison in 1970

ỦY BAN VIỆT-NAM ĐOÀN KẾT VỚI NHÂN DÂN MỸ
VIETNAM COMMITTEE FOR SOLIDARITY WITH THE AMERICAN PEOPLE
Hanoi — D. R. Vietnam Cable Address: VIET-MY-Hanoi

Hanoi November 6, 1970

Dear Mrs. Cora Weiss,

On your July 2 and September 9 letters inquiring about the 17 missing US pilots, we would like to inform you of the following details that we get from the contact with the DRVN Defense Ministry :

1/ Atterberry Edwin Lee	3065474	dead
2/ Connell James J.	647438	present in DRV detention camps
3/ Burdett, Edward Burke	10138A	dead
4/ Ellison John Cooly	554918	never been captured in North-Vietnam
5/ Grubb Wilmer Newlin	FV 2211784	dead
6/ Hamm James E.	FV 3171400	never been captured in North-Vietnam
7/ Plowman James E.	693579	never been captured in North-Vietnam
8/ Cutter (or Cutler)		never been captured in North-Vietnam
9/ Walters Jack	666504	dead
10/ Griffin James L.	595955	dead
11/ Broms Edward J. Jr.		never been captured in North-Vietnam
12/ Ford Randolph		never been captured in North-Vietnam
13/ Hartman Richard D.	613595	dead
14/ Perricone Richard		never been captured in North-

List supplied with letter from Committee of Liaison, naming prisoners said by Hanoi government to have died in captivity.

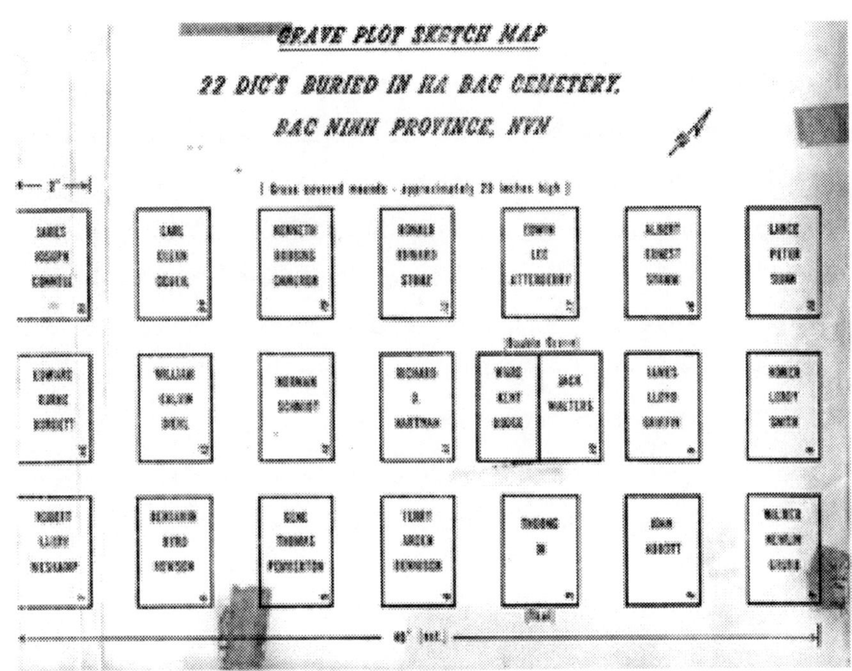

Chart of graves buried in Vietnamese cemetery near Hanoi, released by Vietnamese government in 1973.

Second burial site of James L. Griffin, photo released by Vietnamese government in 1973.

The knock on my door is unexpected as I rush to assemble dinner for the children. I push hair out of my eyes and straighten my skirt, calling to the kids to turn down the TV. There on my doorstep stand Capt. Ken Enney, commander of the air wing, and his wife Betsy, my neighbors. Their faces look serious as they might look when making a condolence call. *Good Lord, what are they going to tell me now?*

Betsy, always the affable wing commander's wife, seems a little shaky as I usher them into the living room. "Has there been some news?" I ask, not sure I want to hear Ken's reply.

He tells me he has received a telegram saying that Cora Weiss, a member of a dissident group that has been quite vocal about the war in Vietnam, has indicated that she plans to hold a press conference tomorrow to release names of seventeen men who have died while being held captive in Vietnam.

"Your husband's name is on the list," Ken mumbles. "And Jack Walters' name, too."

Here we go again! Just when I was so sure that the end of the war is in sight. Just when I was feeling so good about things.

"What do we do?" I ask.

Ken says there isn't much we can do. Mrs. Weiss will be releasing the list to the press tomorrow.

Suddenly, I remember the reporter who sat beside me at lunch in Atlanta just days ago. I ask Ken and Betsy what they think about my heading Cora Weiss off at the pass. After talking it over with them, I go to the phone and call Frank Wells at the *Atlanta Constitution.* My moment of weakness has passed, and I decide to take action. Mr. Wells listens calmly as I tell him about the expected news. I tell him that I do not believe Mrs. Weiss. I do not believe the North Vietnamese.

"They announced on May 19, 1967 that my husband is a prisoner. They would not have done that if he were not alive." And, if he is, I don't intend to let the Committee of Liaison release my husband's death to the press.

I am still fired up when I get off the phone. Betsy and Ken leave with astonished grins on their faces. The reporter has begun writing his story.

Next day, Nov. 13, 1970, the *Atlanta Constitution* carried this article:

Wife Questions Report of POW's Death

by Frank Wells

The young Albany, GA., wife of a North Vietnam prisoner of war, said Thursday night she had received word that her husband had died in captivity, but that she "doubts the authenticity of the report."

Mrs. Dora Griffin, wife of Navy Cmdr. James L. Griffin, said she had "been informed that Cora Weiss of the Committee of Liaison with Families of Prisoners of War claims to have received word that my husband has died in captivity in North Vietnam."

Mrs. Griffin said she understood the liaison committee had notified some other families of the death of their loved ones, too.

Mrs. Griffin said that she, her husband's family, and some of his hometown friends had identified him recently from a wire service photo released in Warsaw showing him playing basketball.

"It's a shame that this kind of announcement should come from a dissident group who has no standing whatsoever," Mrs. Griffin said in a statement.

Mrs. Griffin said she has ample proof through photographs and a recorded statement that her husband was alive when captured.

"I do not feel the communists would have announced my husband's capture at all if his injuries were so extensive as to possibly cause his death," Mrs. Griffin said. "If this were the case, under the Geneva Convention regarding treatment of prisoners of war, my husband should have been repatriated immediately after his capture."

Mrs. Griffin said that a similar announcement about the deaths of five men was made by the Liaison Committee just before Christmas holidays in 1969.

"The inhumanity of this announcement by a questionable source such as the Liaison Committee is that the information may or may not be true," Mrs. Griffin said. "Before I could accept my husband's death, after so much evidence that he was captured alive and the recent photograph, there would have to be proof of some sort and an explanation of the circumstances of his death."

Mrs. Griffin said that if the North Vietnamese government "wants to inform me that my husband has died in captivity, they can do the humane thing and make a responsible report through proper channels such as our representative at the Paris Peace Talks or the International Red Cross."

It should be noted that Cora Weiss' statement did not appear in the Atlanta newspaper the next day....but several days later, I received a letter from the Committee of the Liaison and Cora Weiss...

Meanwhile, Jimmie's brother, John, is busy in California with his own campaign to get Jimmie accounted for.

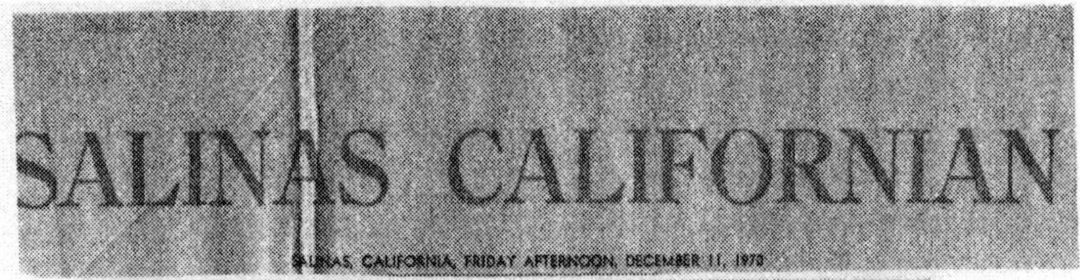

SALINAS CALIFORNIAN

SALINAS, CALIFORNIA, FRIDAY AFTERNOON, DECEMBER 11, 1970

Help Sought for POWs

Families of five Monterey County men who are prisoners of war in North Vietnam are sponsoring billboards, like this one for Jim Griffin, of Salinas, at Monterey and Market streets. Billboards with names of other prisoners are on the Monterey Peninsula. The families, using theme "Help Us Help Them," hope to raise funds to attend the Paris peace talks.

Our campaign for letters to Hanoi does not stop after Cora Weiss and her group try to steal the headlines. Their intention to release the names of men who had died in Hanoi prison camps only adds to my determination. But I am careful to avoid involvement or any display of dissatisfaction with the U.S. government or with the navy.

The Albany Herald
Sunday, December l6, 1970
Write to Hanoi
Youngsters Take Up POWs' Cause
by Suzanne Shingler
"Deer Government of Vietnam,

Please be good to our men and send them home for Christmas. We miss them..." read the misspelled words of a first-grader who had written a letter to Hanoi.

Response to a letter-writing campaign being promoted by Mayor Eugene Clark and the Albany Jaycees in hopes of obtaining information about, and obtaining the immediate release of, three men from the Albany area now being held prisoner in North Vietnam, Saturday seemed more than proof Americans feel for their fellow man. Especially in Albany.

More than 4,000 letters have flooded the mayor's office. They have come from more than 2,000 elementary and high school students, persons from surrounding counties, and more than a thousand Tennessee friends of Cmdr. James L. Griffin, one of the men who had been held prisoner since May 1967.

High school students wrote expressing their opinion of the North Vietnam government.

Wrote one Dougherty High School student: "We, the people of the United States, are ashamed at the treatment that you are giving our boys."

Stated a second student, "The least you can do is let them get in touch with their families. Do you know how it feels not to know whether your father or husband is dead or alive?"

And still another said, "They have families and loved ones that need them back home where they belong. Feel a little kindness for your fellow man. There must be an end to this war. Your releasing these prisoners may be the beginning to the end."

First and second graders, who still "print," colorfully decorated their scribbled notes to Hanoi.

One drew a man parachuting from a plane, while another brightly crayoned a Viet Cong looking at a prisoner behind bars.

In one letter, under the drawing of a Christmas tree, was printed in a seven-year-old's handwriting, "We send our love and best wishes for a Merry Christmas. Please be good to our prisoners. Let them come home to us soon."

On a torn piece of notebook paper was an awkwardly drawn peace symbol, and by it were the misspelled words, "Peece Sine," while another printed boldly, "We want peace for the world."

A group of Monroe High School students made a 15-foot scroll, signing more than 400 names to it. The scroll reads, "We, the undersigned students of Monroe High School, Doughtery County, Georgia, petition the Government of North Vietnam for the immediate release of Cmdr. James Griffin, Cmdr. Lee Hyatt, and Cmdr. C.O. Crain."

"Letters are still being collected by the Jaycees and Jaycettes and more are expected to be turned into the office Monday," Mayor Clark said. "You know how I feel about this campaign, and I am deeply grateful for the tremendous response. It makes you want to cry when you read some of the letters from kids. I just hope we do some good."

December 23, 1970

As I wrap Christmas gifts and prepare for the gathering of my family for the holidays, I feel optimistic about things once again. I am still making plans to fly to Paris to plead for Jimmie's release. We have amassed almost 20,000 letters, and I want to confront someone at the peace talks with them.

My mother, born in 1900 and now seventy years old, has made the trip from Tennessee to be with us for Christmas, and she is making coconut cake from scratch. Mother always starts with a fresh coconut, drains out the coconut milk, and uses it to saturate the cooled cake layers while adding the grated coconut to the icing. Glyn Carol is studiously watching this process when the phone rings, and James tells me there is "some lady" wanting to talk with me.

It is December 23rd, the anniversary of the day that Max Lukenbach and Glen Daigle were shot down in Vietnam, and, in fact, the date that our former commanding officer, Tony Nolta, died in a plane crash in DeBary, Florida a year before that. The date of December 23rd does not bode well for phone calls at my house, so I should not be surprised when the voice of Cora Weiss greets me.

It is not the first time I have spoken with Mrs. Weiss. A year or so earlier she phoned me to say her organization was delivering letters to POW camps in Vietnam and asked me if I wanted to send anything. At the time, I refused, not wanting to be associated with a group who had so openly opposed our government in its actions in Vietnam.

"I am so sorry to have to bring you this news, Mrs. Griffin, but it is a fact and the North Vietnamese government has confirmed that your husband, James Griffin, has died." Is it my imagination that she doesn't sound sorry? She almost sounds pleased to be able to deliver this word two days before Christmas.

"Thank you very much, Mrs. Weiss. Thank you for calling," I say. Then I ask her to have the North Vietnamese government confirm the information through proper channels—that would be the International Red Cross. Slowly, I hang up the phone.

Is it true then? Has he really died? Must I believe this woman? I'd like to think that she means well, but if she does, why is she making this call today of all days, ruining our Christmas?

However hard we try to celebrate the holidays in the usual way, a pall has fallen over our spirits. James and Glyn still enjoy their new toys, and my mother tries to cheer us by making waffles for Christmas morning breakfast. By mid-afternoon my sister Agnes and her family arrive from West Palm Beach—a long drive to spend just the one afternoon, but throughout the time since Jimmie was captured my family has gone the extra mile to be supportive. My nephew Ernie, just a year older than Glyn Carol, gets the kids busy playing games, and the feast Mother has prepared keeps us distracted for the day.

The day after Christmas, Mother goes to Florida with Aggie and Les. Somehow, despite the call from Mrs. Weiss, we have made it through Christmas without completely breaking down. Now I know I have to do something. I can no longer sit here and do nothing. I call my other sister in North Carolina. Car trouble prevented Charlotte and

Larry from being able to join us in Albany on Christmas day, so we decide to meet in Knoxville for the weekend.

I load up the children and we drive north, barely noticing Atlanta as we pass by, and hardly slowing down in Chattanooga. I am returning to the city where I went to college, where I studied journalism and worked for the Tennessee Press Association. I know that Professor Tucker is still on staff there. Professor Tucker who believed I could be a darn successful journalist. I am not sure what questions are in my mind, but I know there must be an answer for me in Knoxville.

It is snowing when we arrive at our motel on the west side of town. I call the university and learn that Professor Tucker is on Christmas vacation. *Of course, what could I have been thinking? The entire university closes down for the holidays.* We stop by a real-estate office and ask assistance in finding houses near the campus. For three hours, we drive around the city, covered in a blanket of snow. The children are patient as I check out half a dozen houses, but none of them appeals to me. I thank the real-estate agent for her time and head back to the Holiday Inn to meet my sister.

Charlotte and Larry live in Boone, North Carolina, just about an hour's drive through the mountains from Knoxville. Larry is a professor at Appalachian State University and a Methodist minister. They have no children, but they do have two cuddly black poodles, and the children are excited to see them. We visit for a while in our adjoining hotel rooms, and after the doggies are settled down we go down to the restaurant for dinner. We try to chat about Christmas and what new toys the kids got. I must be a basket case. My dinner seems all wrong. It isn't what I thought I ordered, and I make the first restaurant complaint of my life, sending my food back to the kitchen.

We return to our rooms, and Larry introduces the kids to a new board game he has brought along. James and Glyn are fully aware that

I am upset about things, but they are being very supportive. After the children go to sleep we grownups talk about my ill-timed phone call from Cora Weiss. I can't really explain my refusal to accept the report that Jimmie is dead. It just doesn't seem right, I say.

Next morning after breakfast we say our goodbyes, and I head back south. One thing has become apparent during the trip to East Tennessee: I am not going to move to Knoxville to continue work on a college degree. And as I drive back into Georgia the pecan trees, barren in winter, appear alongside the road, and that makes us smile. Georgia is now our home, and we all know it.

In January a letter comes from Sweden, repeating the information that Cora Weiss had given me two weeks earlier. Several months ago I wrote Olaf Palme, the Swedish foreign minister, asking for his help in getting information about Jimmie. This letter refers to my request and states, "It is my sad duty to convey to you the information given to the Swedish government by the government of the Democratic Republic of Vietnam, namely that your husband died in North Vietnam on May 21, 1967." My last hope seems destroyed. The letter is signed by Rune Nystrom, Head of Division, Royal Ministry for Foreign Affairs.

Now the time for tears has come. But my tears are private. When the children are in bed, I pour a glass of Chardonnay, pile sad songs on the record player, and reread the letter over and over. In private, I know. In public, my hope will continue until it is confirmed by the US government. And, just maybe, these reports are wrong.

⇾ 14 ⇽

1971

The sunshine is brilliant, dancing off the pink and white dogwood blossoms that almost meet in an arch above Slappy Boulevard as I drive my favorite route to my new job. After getting the children off to school and the breakfast dishes stowed in the dishwasher, I have made the fifteen-minute drive across Albany from our quarters on the naval air station to WALB-TV. I smile as I realize that I now actually look forward to sessions in front of the television cameras.

I have almost forgotten that terrible day, during my first week on the job, when the glaring lights failed to block my view of Vickie, the previous hostess of *The Town and Country Show*, as she angrily stalked across the studio toward me. Still new as a weather broadcaster for the station, I had given too much detail about the day's forecast in my report. And Vickie, who had chosen me out of the twelve or so women who auditioned for the position as talk show hostess and weather reporter, realized that I had a lot to learn. And she had only a few days left in which to train me. Her furious stare made me want to run away from the TV studio and never come back.

After, quivering with rage, Vickie had thoroughly read me the riot act during a commercial break, the show went on as scheduled. That was her last week as co-host of the program, and she had been horrified that I—her replacement—was not up to the task. At the end of the show I had raced out of the studio and driven to the nearest McDonald's for lunch. I did not realize how much the incident had upset me until I tried to eat. I suddenly choked and threw up my lunch in the front seat of my car.

It was not until the next day, when again I was giving the weather report as part of the noon-hour talk show, that I realized the verbal onslaught by Vickie had caused my upset stomach. Prior to that day's broadcast I was so nervous I thought my voice would fail me. Then, as I finished my much-abbreviated weather report, I quickly looked up, checking to see if Vickie was again storming across the studio. She was not. In fact, she was smiling across the way from her perch at the hosts' desk. At that moment, I realized that I was no longer an amateur. I was now a professional broadcaster.

Vickie left a few days later, and I assumed her position as co-host and co-producer of the hour-long daily talk show. My partner is Jack Reynolds, a tall, likable guy who has been in television broadcasting for several years. He took the lead, especially at the beginning, both on the air and in booking guests for the show, and he coached me in techniques for relaxing and being comfortable before the camera.

In addition to the noon broadcast, I am responsible for two additional weather reports each day. The most important of these is the 6 p.m. weather report, usually done live along with a news team that consists of the anchor and a sports commentator. The late-night weather report is generally videotaped prior to the 6 p.m. broadcast, so it means redoing my weather board, using magic markers and my imagination to advance weather conditions that existed in the late afternoon.

No one warned me that I would have to use poetic license in weather reporting, but, except for frequent reports off the news wire, I have no other source for weather information. And I am not a meteorologist! In fact, my only real training for this part of my new job was the course in physical science I took in 1967 at Seminole Community College in Sanford.

At the close of the live *Town and Country Show* broadcast each day, I drive back across town to my quarters at the naval air station. This gives me some time to put dinner in the oven and allows me to be home when the children return from school. Even though we are surrounded by friendly neighbors and their youngsters and though security is not an issue, I still don't feel comfortable having James and Glyn Carol come home to an empty house. Once they are settled in for the afternoon, doing homework or playing with their friends, I return to the TV studio to work on booking guests for future shows and to videotape my late-night weather before doing a live 6 p.m. broadcast. It is a bit complicated, but it doesn't require eight hours of office time like some jobs might—and it is something I can do!

Of course at first the station management had wanted me to bleach my hair and change my name to "Dorie" instead of Dora. I was told that I must learn to say "To-mah-row" instead of pronouncing the word in the southern way of "tuh-mah-rah." Ducky Wall, the sportscaster, always says tuh-mah-rah, however, with a Georgian's pronounced southern drawl. I agreed to some of the changes suggested, but I draw the line at changing my name. I am Dora, not Dorie. And as for bleaching my hair, that would be my decision. Maybe later. Maybe just highlights like I used to have.

Now, three months into the job, I am fairly comfortable with it. My years of journalism study in college have given me some preparation for this work. I was a fairly good interviewer even during auditions for this job, and as the weeks have passed I have been getting better. As Jack has come to be more comfortable having me as a co-host, he has allowed me to suggest changes to the show's format. It has taken time, but he now lets me do a few solo interviews. And now there is fan mail. Fan mail for me!

The drives across town beneath the dogwood blossoms give a new focus to my life. On returning to my quarters each day I still carefully examine every piece of mail, hoping that, somehow, there will magically appear a letter from Jimmie. I still want to believe he is alive in Hanoi. But I now have other things to think about. The driving has grown to be a chore, so I change my route each day while watching for a house to buy. That is the next step—moving off base and becoming a part of the community of Albany, Georgia. Once again I find myself attached to a naval air station that is scheduled to close and move its operations—this time the base will be relocated to Key West, Florida. The move will take place in about two years.

The house hunt ends when friends tell me about a navy wife who is selling her house located about a mile from the television station. I drive by it often, counting the spindly pine trees in the back yard—almost fifty—and admiring the pale rose brick construction and the soft green wrought-iron grillwork that adorns the front of the house on Green Valley Lane. Jimmie had fantasized about our moving to Albany and living on a lake. I would so like to have a house waiting for him when he returns. The house is not on a lake, but it is surrounded by dozens of blooming azaleas. And there is a fireplace.

I call my navy casualty officer to see what can be done to release funds from the navy savings account for a down payment on this property.

The children instantly fall in love with the house, and even Sam is excited when he sees the spacious fenced yard and the multitude of pine trees. James will be near Westover High School, and Glyn Carol will have several friends from her dancing class in the neighborhood. Pleased that I will no longer have the long drive to and from work every day, I purchase a gigantic side-by-side refrigerator and have it delivered to the new kitchen. Each day I go to the empty house to eat my lunch alone while waiting for the end of the school year when we will move our household belongings. There will still be dogwoods to see along the way as I make the drive on the spring mornings to come, but the drive will be much shorter.

Surprisingly, the TV station management seems not to capitalize on my situation as a POW wife. Little mention has been made on the air of my personal history since I began this job in January. Only a few viewers who remember my appearances last year mention this in the dozen or so fan letters that come each month. This is not a big TV station, and our viewing audience is comprised of only about 200,000 people, many of them farmers in southwest Georgia, southeastern Alabama, and the Florida panhandle. And many of those people depend on my weather report to tell them when to spray fungicide on their peanut crops and when to head out into the Gulf of Mexico for fishing. At least for these things, I have a reliable source of information.

I still see my navy friends, especially when I go back to the base to shop at the PX and on social occasions, but those social events become fewer and fewer as I immerse myself in a new life. Pat has moved back to Florida to continue her education, and now Ann Hyatt, whose husband was captured in the fall of 1967, is the only POW wife remaining in quarters aboard the naval air station.

The squadrons continue to come and go on deployments both in the Atlantic and Pacific, and the list of men from the Wing who are missing in action continues to grow. RVAH-13 returns to the war, and in 1972 the squadron again loses an airplane in combat. Veda Poulfer, who lives less than a mile from our new house on the west side of town, finds herself waiting for word of her husband Ron. During the Christmas season I join Veda and her family as they talk about the war, and Veda vows that she will not take down the Christmas tree until Ron comes home. I thought the same thing five years ago, and look how long it has been!

There is another MIA wife who lives near us, but her husband was not a part of our navy community. Ann Crain lives on a nearby lake, and I often pass her house on my way to the television station. Sometimes I stop to chat with her after work or I ride over there on my newly purchased bicycle after dinner. Ann has one small boy, and she has bravely moved to Albany although she has no family here and no ties to our military community.

I find myself making new civilian friends, especially women friends, who give me much-needed support as, anticipating their move to Key West, I begin to see less and less of our navy friends. There comes a time, I tell myself, when I must become a person, not just a navy wife.

The guests on our talk show vary. Sometimes we are content to feature a new Eagle Scout, and we let him tell about his achievements. Occasionally a celebrity passes through the area, and we get him or her to appear on the show. We interview Jimmy Carter when he is running for governor. There is Dean Rusk's brother who is headed to North Georgia to visit him at his North Carolina cabin. Edgar Bergen makes an appearance with a couple of his puppets. We have countless beauty queens, and county extension agents who tell us how to fertilize our trees or how to bake a pecan pie. And we have singers and dancers and songwriters who are convinced that an appearance on our program will help them along on their way to stardom.

Once, after Jack Reynolds has left the show to give full time to his other love—the ministry—I decide to set up an interview with two candidates who are running for the U.S. Senate. One of those candidates is Sam Nunn, the state senator who befriended me and my children last year when were at the state capitol. He now has ambitions for national office. Unable to get the two candidates to appear for a joint interview, I arrange to have the studio sealed off to videotape interviews with the two candidates, one at a time, asking them the same questions. Then I have the tapes locked up so they can be played back-to-back just prior to the election.

And, although I am the only on-air person at WALB-TV who studied journalism in college, I am not allowed to do news coverage. I am never included in election night coverage. After all, I am a woman, and this is 1971. And, while the station arranges for a local salon to do my hair almost every day and having the job has convinced me to splurge on some new clothes, the glamour ends there. I still have to set up my own weather boards, and at the end of each broadcast, I usually have to clean the marker off the weather boards, using a rag and a smelly solvent.

I do get some of the invasion of privacy that celebrities often endure, but it is on a small scale. Going to the supermarket means I can't go in shorts or dash in without combing my hair. And occasionally someone will walk up behind me, place their hand on my shoulder, and say, "Are you Dora Griffin?" But I don't mind it. At least no one is asking, "Are you the one whose husband is missing in Vietnam?" Even if they are thinking it.

The children's lives change, too. James is now a high school student, and he is involved first with school band, Later he takes an interest in the TV station and gets a job running the camera during the summer months. Glyn Carol is also growing up. When she sees a representative from the Albany Little Theater appear on my show, encouraging youngsters to take classes and try out for parts in a play about Helen Keller, she begs to go. Our daily routines suddenly revolve around play practice, and she gets the starring role in *The Miracle Worker*.

We have become members of Porterfield Methodist Church in Albany, rather than continue driving back to the base to attend services at the chapel. Now the Methodist church here is praying for Jimmie's return just as earnestly as the Grace Methodist congregation in Sanford where he was a dedicated member of the church board. What will he think when he returns to find me a working mother, not staying at home with the children, not following the navy when it moves away again? There have been a lot of changes since he went away—not just for me but for most women in the country.

I have stopped writing letters to be sent to Jimmie in Hanoi. Even if he should turn up alive at the end of the war, the North Vietnamese government would not accept letters intended for a man they now say is not alive.

→ 15 ←

Albany, Georgia — January 1973

As the news gets more and more encouraging about an end to the war, the children and I try not to let ourselves get too excited. I know that each of us, secretly, harbors some glimmer of hope that Jimmie will be among the returned POWs when they arrive, despite all the negative word we have had from Cora Weiss and her group.

Then, once again, our hopes are dashed when late in January another of the dreaded telegrams arrives. I receive it just as the nation is waiting expectantly for the return of POWs from Vietnam. But while we are waiting, the US government has been in negotiations with the North Vietnamese, and information has been exchanged.

TELEGRAM RECEIVED IN JANUARY 1973

DATED: 01/28/73

(REPORT DLY DO NOT PHONE DO NOT DELIVER BETWEEN 1000 P.M. AND 600 A.M.)

MRS. DORA SMITH GRIFFIN

817 GREEN VALLEY LANE

ALBANY, GEORGIA

ON BEHALF OF THE UNITED STATES NAVY I REGRET TO INFORM YOU THAT THE LIST OF CAPTURED PERSONNEL IN SOUTHEAST ASIA PROVIDED TO OUR GOVERNMENT IN PARIS ON 27 JANUARY 1973 BY THE NORTH VIETNAMESE

GOVERNMENT STATED THAT YOUR HUSBAND, CDR JAMES LLOYD GRIFFIN, USN, 410 64 3866 1310, DIED IN CAPTIVITY ON 21 MAY 1967. YOUR HUSBAND WILL HOWEVER BE CONTINUED IN HIS PRESENT STATUS UNTIL ALL INFORMATION PROVIDED OUR GOVERNMENT FROM DEBRIEFINGS AND OTHER SOURCES MAY BE ANALYZED. PLEASE BE ASSURED THAT THE NAVY SHARES YOUR CONCERN AND STANDS READY TO ASSIST YOU IN ANY WAY POSSIBLE. YOU MAY BE CERTAIN THAT YOU WILL BE PROMPTLY INFORMED OF ANY NEW INFORMATION. THIS TELEGRAM IS IN CONFIRMATION OF THE INFORMATION PASSED TO YOU EARLIER BY YOUR CASUALTY ASSISTANCE CALLS OFFICER.

VICE ADMIRAL DAVID H. BAGLEY, CHIEF OF NAVAL PERSONNEL

The bombing in Vietnam picks up again, then stops. But, for us, the war should have ended. Our situation has evolved just as Cora Weiss told us it would.

Finally one evening in February we sit, hearts in our throats, watching planes that are bringing home the repatriated POWs land in the Philippines, as the men, gaunt and wide-eyed, step off the planes. A short speech is made by the first to come down the ramp, then he is followed by dozens of others. The name of each man is called out as he deplanes. We watch and watch. Maybe there has been a mistake. Maybe he will be one of them. Do we dare hope? Must we give up now? But there is no Jimmie. But more are coming later; maybe he will be in the next group.

Days later more planes arrive at Clark Air Force Base. Jimmie is still not among the returned prisoners. James and Glyn Carol and I hug each other closely and cry together. All that we have hoped and prayed for is now lost. My casualty officer comes by the next day, and confirms my worst fears. As the returned prisoners are debriefed, they tell that Jimmie's name was passed through the prison network, but no one ever saw him. It is assumed that he died shortly after being captured.

I stumble through the motions of broadcasting at Channel Ten, trying to not look too despondent. There are many cards and letters from viewers, offering their sympathy. I realize that my fans have been hoping and praying right along with us. My talk show co-host, Jack Reynolds, helps to keep my spirits up, literally carrying the show for me, joking only when it seems appropriate. Flowers arrive from kind-hearted strangers. Neighbors bring over casseroles, just as though we are in the immediate aftermath of a family member's death in an ordinary situation.

We begin planning a memorial service at Porterfield Church, where we have become a part of the church family since moving from the naval base into the community. It seems only appropriate, now that we know with some certainty that Jimmie has died, to offer closure to the community, the church, and to ourselves if that is possible.

Eulogy delivered at memorial service, Albany, Georgia

An air force plane flying over his farm home in Tennessee first sparked Jim Griffin's interest in flying. But he chose the navy as his service, and after graduation with distinction from the U.S. Naval Academy in 1955 he entered flight training in Pensacola.

Upon receiving his wings (just before his first child was born), he proceeded to Oceana, Virginia, where he joined VA-83, flying F-7Us and A-4Ds. During a tour aboard the USS *Essex*, the squadron served during the 1958 Lebanon Crisis and traveled through the Suez Canal to join the Seventh Fleet off Formosa.

As a lieutenant, Jim proved as proficient in "books" as in the handling of aircraft, with an outstanding academic record both at the Naval Post Graduate School in Monterey and the University of Michigan. He was awarded a professional degree in aeronautic and astronautical engineering and—for his scientific research—honorary membership in Sigma Xi fraternity.

In 1963 Jim joined "Heavy Attack Squadron Three" to begin training in the Vigilante. He joined RVAH-13 in 1964, serving as Admin, then Operations Officer, and for a few weeks following the loss of the squadron commander, as Executive Officer. With RVAH-13, he served two combat tours to Southeast Asia, completing some 150 combat missions.

On May 19, 1967 Commander Griffin was piloting a Vigilante when it was shot down over the city of Hanoi on a reconnaissance mission. Within hours Hanoi Radio announced the capture of Commander Griffin and his navigator, Lieutenant Jack Walters, and broadcast a tape of Jim's voice. It was on this evidence—as well as subsequent publication of his ID card and other things—that his family based their long vigil of hope for his safe return. This past Saturday, the government of North Vietnam announced that both Jim and Jack died of injuries received in the crash within a matter of days.

Jim's leadership and courage are evident from the awards he received: Distinguished Flying Cross (2), Navy Commendation Medal (2), and nine Air Medals.

He also was in inspiration, both morally and spiritually, to the men who served with him. His family, his church, and his community all benefited from his dedication to duty, his devotion to his fellow man, and his unwavering faith in God.

While he carried out his orders without question, his last letters to his loved ones indicated he felt there "must be a better way to solve men's conflicts..." than war, and he expressed gratitude for the medical treatment he received at the hands of his captors.

Other memorial services are held in Sanford at Grace Methodist Church and in Tennessee at Eureka Methodist Church in Forked Deer. It was going to be a challenge to make it through three services, and though we make plans to attend all of them, nature intervenes. On the morning we are to drive to Florida for the Sanford service, there is a heavy snow in Albany—the first snow in one hundred years or more! I am sure that our car, an Olds 98, cannot make it through the snow because South Georgia is not equipped with snow removal equipment. In tears, I call our friends in Sanford and tell them we are unable to make it to the service. I know it would mean a great deal to the church members who have been so close to us and to Jimmie to have us there, but now that I am head of household I dare not take the chance of trying to drive 500 miles, starting out on a snow-covered highway.

Then, on April 19th, a service is held in the community where Jimmie grew up and where his parents live, and we are packing the car to go. But the weather report indicates there are dangerous storms in Mississippi along the route we are to drive to reach western Tennessee. The storms have been going on for several days. Again, we do not make it to the service. I wonder whether it would have been our undoing to sit through three memorial services. We have been brave through one, but to repeat the experience might have been too much for all of us.

Eventually, when and if the remains come home, we will have to do one more. We will save our strength for that day.

Article with photo from the *Albany Herald,* dated April 9, 1973

Mrs. Dora Griffin (left foreground), whose husband Lt. Cmdr. James Griffin died in a communist prisoner of war camp, is shown placing a wreath before the "Bell of Freedom" at Albany Junior College. The bell, donated to the school by the Etcetera Club, was dedicated to U.S. soldiers killed in action in Indochina "for the cause of democracy" in ceremonies on the campus yesterday.

NEWS ARTICLE (*ATLANTA CONSTITUTION*)
Dated 6 May 1973

REDS TO INVITE DEAD POW KIN TO GRAVES

SAIGON (UPI)—North Vietnam plans to invite relatives of some of the Americans who died in prison camps or plane crashes there to visit the servicemen's graves, a spokesman from Hanoi said Monday.

The spokesman, Maj. Phu Binh, is a North Vietnamese representative on the four-party Joint Military Team (JMT) that has been assigned to verify identification of servicemen's graves and to determine the fate of 1,328 Americans still listed as missing in Indochina.

He said the team will go to Hanoi "in the next few days" to begin its work. Other sources said the team will leave Saigon Friday for Hanoi.

It will be the second such trip by the JMT, which includes officers from North Vietnam, South Vietnam, the Viet Cong, and United States. The first one was made about three weeks ago.

Binh said relatives would not be along on the upcoming trip but would be invited to come later.

He said he did not know how long the team would stay in the north and observed that "There a large number of burial sites spread over a large area. It depends on the places they go to."

Team members also will try to get the ultimate information available about the deaths, he said.

Informed sources said the U.S. government has no official policy on visits to North Vietnam by relatives of Americans who died there.

Two hundred communist civilian war prisoners were taken to the Thac Ham riverbank near Quang Tri City by South Vietnam Monday in the resumption of prisoner exchanges after a 10-day suspension due to a dispute over the width of air corridors used by the four-power truce-keeping team.

In May 1973, I receive, via the Department of the Navy, a chart showing a sketch of twenty-two graves of American servicemen buried in Ha Bac Cemetery, BAC Ninh Province, NVN.

I also receive a photo of the cemetery and two very blurred photos said to be pictures of Ltjg Joseph C. Plumb, also captured on May 19, 1967. The photos were of Plumb being presented at the press conference, shortly after his capture.

ACCOMPANYING LETTER FROM
DEPARTMENT OF THE NAVY
Dated 5 June 1973:

FROM: Chief of Naval Personnel
To: Commanding Officer
Naval Air Station
Albany, Georgia 31703
ATTN: LCDR LAGASSEE
CACO FOR GRIFFIN

Subj: Gravesite Photos
encl: (1) Two photos in the case of CDR J.L. GRIFFIN

1. Enclosed are photographs of the graves of those POWs who reportedly died in captivity. These photographs, taken by the Four-Power Joint Military Team near Hanoi on 18 May 1973, may be retained by next of kin if desired. Please return those photos not retained to BUPERS.

T.F. RUSH
By direction

➛ 16 ➛

A Visitor

We finish dinner early on a May evening and, after loading the dishwasher, I decide Samson, our schnauzer, needs a haircut. Now six years old, Sam has always been such a little gentleman that he actually enjoys getting groomed. I drag out my box of grooming tools while he patiently waits atop the washing machine, my makeshift grooming table. Then there is an interruption—the phone rings, and the children seem to have vanished, busy with homework perhaps.

A hesitant, unfamiliar male voice on the phone puts me on guard, and my suspicious nature immediately kicks in. My phone number has been unlisted since I began working as a television broadcaster, and from time to time I get crank calls. Once a call had come to the television station summoning me to the local hospital, an anxious voice telling me that my daughter had been injured in school. I had been in the middle of the noon broadcast, and I was called off the set to take the call. Fortunately, I had the presence of mind to phone the school before racing across town to the hospital, and I learned that Glyn Carol was in her classroom, and there had been no incident, no injury.

"Who is this?!" I almost bellow into the phone.

The quiet voice tells me that he is looking for Dora Griffin, and that he is Jim Bell, formerly of Heavy Attack Squadron One. My throat constricts as I realize that, for the first time, I am speaking with one of the returning POWs who knew my husband. He tells me that he is passing through town and has stopped to meet some friends at the

Officers' Club. He seems very shy, and immediately my suspicions are transformed into compassion.

I put down the clippers, leaving Sam with half a haircut. I change my clothes and tell James and Glyn Carol that they will be on their own for a couple hours because I am going to meet with someone who was in Hanoi when their father was captured. James at age sixteen is very responsible, and I have no qualms leaving him in charge of things.

Remembering how a few months earlier we had sat tearfully watching the returning POWs step off airplanes, I am excited at the possibility of talking to one of them. Jim Bell might have more information about Jimmie than the navy has been able to give us.

As I drive through town to the naval air station where we had lived in quarters for three years before moving to Green Valley Lane, I am suddenly nervous. I realize that Jim Bell, whose wife got a divorce and remarried during his time in Hanoi, does not really know me. We met, of course, as couples at a party in Monterey, California when the men were students at the Naval Post Graduate School in 1961. He knew Jimmie because at the Naval Academy they were just a year apart and in the same battalion. And I knew his wife from our conversations while sitting around the base swimming pool, where we often talked while our children frolicked in the water.

The Bells' daughter Ann, just a newborn when her father left on the cruise from which he did not return, had been put in a cast from hip to toes to correct a malformation. My Glyn Carol also had worn a corrective leg cast for three months when she was a baby. The girls were several years apart in age, but it brought us two mothers together as we shared experiences. Now that mother has remarried, and she lives with her children and her "new" husband in another state. As I drive to the club, I fret over how I am going to begin a conversation with this man who has lost more than seven years of his life as well as his family.

Not being one to frequent the O Club except for squadron gatherings, I hesitate and almost turn back toward home. But the chance to personally meet with one of the POW returnees is too much for me to dismiss. I am feeling shy myself as I look around the club lobby for a familiar face, and soon I am joining friends who know both Jim Bell and me. Kay and Bob Recknor have been seeing him at Bethesda Naval Hospital in Washington, since their daughter is being treated there for leukemia, and they have been making frequent visits during her hospitalization. They take me in hand and introduce us, making an awkward situation into an almost festive occasion.

The conversation remains light, and the guest of honor seems more relaxed after a few stories are exchanged. I have to strain to hear him as he quietly describes the last evening the men spent in Hanoi, when an assortment of clothing was distributed to the POWs in preparation for their flight to the Philippines the next day. Apparently, the clothes were of a one-size-fits-all variety, and the men, still not confident they were on their way home, had a few laughs about the dilemma.

He then begins to retell a joke he had told in Hanoi that evening, and as he talks, we slowly realize that he is telling a shaggy-dog story—a very long one. To illustrate the end of the story, Jim Bell acts out the part of a man wearing an ill-fitting suit bought on sale that has been sold with the understanding that there are no alterations. He waddles around, penguin-style, with one lapel tucked under his chin, one sleeve held tightly in his hand, with his knees held together to disguise trousers that are too long. Our solemn evening gathering explodes in riotous laughter. It is wonderful to see that this man and his fellow prisoners were able to have a sense of humor during extremely difficult times.

We all chat together, and eventually the group wanders away, leaving me to talk with the reluctant celebrity. He looks very thin, not at all like the chubby-faced guy in the photos published shortly after he went missing in the war. He still is very handsome, but he seems hesitant as he talks, so I realize that he is even more nervous than I am. I find that he has very little new information about my husband. He tells me the men all knew, having passed the word through the camps by various means of communication, that Jim Griffin had been captured, but they never saw him there alive.

Eventually, I offer to drive Jim Bell back to the BOQ where he is staying. We sit in the car and talk for an hour or so after he begins the conversation with a frustrated, "I am SO tired of being a POW!" He says, "I wish people would just let me be myself again."

I am not sure what he means by this, having only talked with him a short time, but soon he tells me about the special treatment he has been receiving since returning to the States. Apparently, he has even more trouble going places without being recognized and pointed out than I, a local TV personality, have in going to the grocery store. While I am sure he doesn't want to be ignored, I think he would like to receive the same homecoming he would have had if he were coming home after an eight-month cruise.

On learning Jim will be in Albany for several days, I invite him to come to our house for dinner the next evening. The next morning I call the Recknors and make arrangements for a cookout—my first time to entertain guests what seems like years. I rummage in the freezer for some thick, juicy steaks that have been "on hold" through the recent beef boycott. Having the group for dinner gives me a chance to extend the conversation of last evening. The Recknors and their children plus my own two keep up lively chatter for several hours, and when the evening is over, I realize that in Jim Bell, we have found a new friend.

Our lives go on, tempered by the activities of my television job. James works after school as a cameraman at the television station. Glyn Carol, now a celebrated young actress in the Albany Little Theater, continues her activities there as she tries out for a part in *Fiddler on the Roof.* The air station closes, and we bid farewell to our navy friends as they move again; this time to Key West, Florida. During the summer we drive to the farm to be with the Griffins and my mother in Tennessee, and Glyn Carol has her first experience at a girls' camp in northern Georgia. Then in August we go to Washington, D.C. to play tourist, stopping on the way to visit my sister in Boone, North Carolina.

Washington, D.C., August 1973

Throughout the war we watched television coverage of our POW wives and other groups marching outside our nation's capitol, but we have waited until now, when the demonstrators have left, to come here. We look forward to seeing the places where so many decisions affecting our lives have been made.

We had hoped to arrive at our hotel in Rosslyn while it was still daylight, but the sun has disappeared when we approach the Washington Beltway. To someone who spent the previous six years in a small town in Georgia, the heavy traffic is overwhelming. I have driven through the Atlanta area several times on our travels to Tennessee, but I have never encountered this many cars and huge trucks at one time, and it is getting dark!

Eventually, we make our way to the Marriott Hotel in Rosslyn, after crossing the Potomac River by mistake during rush hour and having to find our way back amid what seems to be complete chaos. We have told Jim Bell, who lives in nearby Arlington, that we were coming, and when we arrive at the hotel, there he is, having sat in that lobby waiting for hours for our arrival! He struggles a bit helping us with our luggage, and I remember that this guy has been injured in the war! During the summer Jim has undergone surgery on his left shoulder to repair a break that occurred in 1965 when he ejected from his plane in the South China Sea. Now he stays to see us settled in for the night and gives us a few suggestions for sightseeing, but tomorrow he is headed out to join his parents and a girlfriend at his family's cottage in Stone Harbor, New Jersey.

We are the typical tourists in Washington. We purchase tickets on the Washington Tourmobile, and each day we go into the city to see exhibits at the Smithsonian, National Archives, and the art galleries. I had written our congressman to get passes to sit in on a session of Congress, and we are ushered into the gallery just in time to see the historic vote on the Alaska pipeline. The vice president has to vote to break the tie. It is an exciting day for us.

The Washington Tourmobile takes us to Arlington Cemetery where we watch the changing of the guard at the Tomb of the Unknown Soldier, and we all become very quiet as we look out across rows of thousands of graves of men killed in battle. There are graves of men who had died in Vietnam, but we see no graves of POWs from the war.

On the day we set out for our VIP tour of the White House I make sure the children dress "properly," which means I insist Glyn wear a dress and patent leather shoes. We stand in line for the tour for almost an hour, and the day grows quite warm by the time we emerge from the exit door. Glyn is nearly in tears, her feet hurt so much. We get in the car and return to the hotel to change clothes, then drive back to Maine Avenue to board a big paddle wheeler for a relaxing voyage down the Potomac to see Mount Vernon. It is just the right way to end our Washington tour.

Through all the emotional roller coaster our family experiences during the aftermath of the Vietnam War, I continue working at WALB-TV. The job has been a lifesaver for me, keeping me focused on the present while I deal privately with grief and keep a smile on my face in public. I have a new co-host on the talk show, Bob Baker, and though he has a lot of broadcast experience, most of it has been in radio. There is little doubt that I am now in charge of the show, but I know I could not make it through these months without Bob's help.

On one program I am given the opportunity to interview a former POW, Dale Doss, a handsome guy who spent five years in prison in Hanoi. Shot down in 1968 while flying an A6 Intruder off the USS *Enterprise* with Ned Shuman, Dale returned home during Operation Homecoming in February. During the broadcast, he tells the story of how one day, while a captive in Hanoi, he was communicating with the prisoner in the adjacent cell by knocking on the wall. The other prisoner told him, "I'm feeling so low I have to look up to see the soles of my shoes." Then Dale reveals that the other POW's name is Jim Bell. After we are off the air I tell Dale that I know Jim and that we have become good friends.

Orson Swindle, another POW, has returned to our area because his wife has lived through the war in her hometown of Camilla, about twenty miles from Albany. While we still lived in quarters on the naval air station, I had received a phone call from Orson's wife Gail. She was very worried about his problem with asthma, she said, and she wanted my opinion on how she might get some asthma medicine to him in Vietnam. Now Orson, a marine, has returned home to the delight of his family and, in fact, to all of Camilla! Although Orson does not appear as a guest on our talk show, he is in our viewing audience. Just a little over two years earlier I was sitting in the guest seat on the program, talking about our POWs. Now I am the interviewer, asking the prisoners about their experiences!

In September I get a call from Washington that takes me by surprise. Jim Bell is inviting me to join him for Homecoming at the Naval Academy. I have not been to Annapolis since 1955 when I attended Jimmie's graduation just a week before our wedding. I have not seen a navy football game since my trip to Philadelphia for the Army-Navy game in 1954. And, except for a few dinners with a male friend I met through my television job, I have not had a "date" since learning that I have been a single woman for six years. After a bit of stuttering, I manage to accept his invitation. On hanging up the phone I realize that this might not really be a date. He may just need a friend to accompany him to his class gathering. Or he may be taking pity on a gal who has not been out much for a long, long time.

I talk it over with James and Glyn Carol, who ask to stay with friends while I am away. Then I go shopping. I have nothing to wear! Excitedly, I make airplane reservations and realize that this will be the first big outing for me in many years.

On meeting me at the Dulles airport, Jim tells me that in Annapolis we will be staying with Cheron and Bill Hargrave in a large house on the Academy grounds since Bill is on staff there. Cheron, he says, is the cousin of his former wife, Holly. Suddenly, I feel nervous. Then I remember that Cheron Hargrave was in a group of navy wives with whom I played bridge when we lived in Norfolk where Jimmie served in VA-83 in 1957.

Though I am still a little uncomfortable, Cheron and Bill are gracious hosts as they show me to my room for the weekend, a room that normally is occupied by one of their four children. Jim is sleeping in the attic, and several other classmates are bunking around the house as well during the homecoming event. I find members of the Class of 1954 very hospitable, perhaps because they are so very glad to have their classmate, Jim Bell, back home again.

One difficult moment comes when a woman who was a friend of Jim and his wife before the war confronts me and expresses her wish for Jim's marriage to repair itself. She, apparently, does not realize that I am already a basket case on this my first date and in a group of people I don't know. She pulls him aside to talk—for the third time—as we are leaving Dahlgren Hall, leaving me to emerge in an alleyway alone, wondering where my escort has gone. I sit on a bench and wait for him, wondering what I am doing here. If I knew how to get to the airport by myself I would get the heck out of here! Then he emerges from the building, and we have a serious talk as we walk back to the Hargraves' quarters.

Back in Albany, I try to concentrate on the pleasant memories of my Annapolis outing. I have met John McCain, whose wife Carol sat beside me when I attended a briefing for POW wives in Jacksonville in 1968. A lot has occurred since then, and both John and Carol now walk with limps. John is undergoing physical therapy for injuries from ejecting from his aircraft over Hanoi in 1967, and Carol is still recuperating from severe injuries incurred in an automobile accident in 1969.

While I was in Annapolis Jim took me to Memorial Hall, where a special display lists graduates of the Naval Academy who were prisoners during the Vietnam War. My Jimmie's name was the only one I saw from the Class of 1955. There were several names from 1954, Jim Bell's class. I realize that now it is time to think of the former prisoners who are still living and what they suffered during the war.

Now back in Albany, I find that my job is becoming more and more interesting. I have changed the format of *The Town and Country Show* so we are able to have more theme shows, rather than programs made up of five- and ten-minute segments. We have programs in which the entire hour is devoted to camping, to gardening, to home improvements, or to music. Bob Baker, my new co-host, lets me take the lead in the planning, and my new producer seems to be pleased with the show's ratings. He asks me whether I would like the name changed to *The Dora Griffin Show*. The idea is overwhelming, and I realize that I like things just the way they are.

I receive several interesting job offers, but I am not ready to make any changes. I am invited to accompany a state senator to the governor's ball, but I decide too much would be involved in getting a ball gown and going to Atlanta. And a gubernatorial candidate's office calls to ask whether I would consider handling a series of ladies' teas to promote his candidacy. My fan mail increases, and so does some unwanted personal attention from viewers. It may be time to think about going back to a normal life.

Agnes and Lester again join us in Albany on Christmas afternoon, after having their own gift exchange in West Palm Beach the night before and rising early to drive up to Georgia on Christmas morning. Because we know Jim is unable to be with his children in Texas for the holidays, we had invited him to come down to share the holidays with us, but he has arranged to meet another POW friend in Bermuda.

He spends Christmas morning with his parents first and then takes a plane to the island, anticipating an outing that will distract him from missing his children, Tom, Matthew, and Ann, who live in Texas with their mother. When he phones to tell about his holiday a few days later, he sadly tells me that he spent the time in Bermuda alone; his friend backed out of the trip at the last minute.

17

Final Days

January 1974

THE GOVT PO WASHINGTON DC 18 JANUARY 1974

(REPORT ONLY DO NOT PHONE DO NOT DELIVER BETWEEN 1000 P.M. AND 600 A.M.)

MRS. DORA SMITH GRIFFIN
1817 GREEN VALLEY LANE
ALBANY, GA 32705

ON BEHALF OF THE DEPARTMENT OF THE NAVY IT IS MY SAD DUTY TO CONFIRM THAT YOUR HUSBAND, COMMANDER JAMES LLOYD GRIFFIN, UNITED STATES NAVY, IS DETERMINED TO HAVE BEEN KILLED IN ACTION HAVING DIED IN CAPTIVITY ON 21 MAY 1967. THIS DETERMINATION WAS MADE UNDER THE PROVISIONS OF THE MISSING PERSONS ACT ON 16 JANUARY 1974. I EXTEND TO YOU MY SINCERE SYMPATHY ON YOUR GREAT LOSS. YOUR HUSBAND DIED WHILE SERVING HIS COUNTRY. A LETTER SETTING FORTH THE CIRCUMSTANCES ON WHICH THIS DETERMINATION WAS MADE WILL FOLLOW. IF I CAN BE OF ASSISTANCE TO YOU PLEASE WRITE OR TELEGRAPH THE CHIEF OF NAVAL PERSONNEL, DEPARTMENT OF THE NAVY, WASHINGTON DC 20370.

MY PERSONAL REPRESENTATIVE MAY BE REACHED BY TELEPHONE AT (202) OXFORD 42746 DURING WORKING HOURS, OR (202) OXFORD 42768 AFTER WORKING HOURS. AGAIN ON BEHALF OF THE NAVY PLEASE BE ASSURED OF MY SINCERE SYMPATHY IN YOUR TRAGIC LOSS.

VICE ADMIRAL DAVID M. BAGLEY, CHIEF OF NAVAL PERSONNEL.

LETTER FROM
THE SECRETARY OF THE NAVY
WASHINGTON, D.C. 20350

January 22, 1974

Dear Mrs. Griffin:

It was with sincere regret that I noted that your husband, Commander James Lloyd Griffin, United States Navy, was determined to have died as a result of our conflict with North Vietnam.

After these more than six years of waiting and hoping, I pray that the strength which has sustained you through this long ordeal will continue, and that you will be able to draw further strength from your husband's faith in his country, and his willingness to fight for it and for the ideals for which it stands. Please know that my thoughts are with you and your family in your loss.

Sincerely yours,
JOHN W. WARNER

LETTER FROM CHIEF OF NAVAL OPERATIONS

24 JANUARY 1974

Dear Mrs. Griffin,

I realize that words of sympathy can do little to ease your grief, a grief compounded by these more than six long years of uncertainty.

The determination that your husband did not survive his captivity in North Vietnam in May 1967 was not easily done. Each of those involved in that decision was torn by the same mixed feelings which I am sure you are experiencing; the sorrow of death and the relief from the cruelty of the unknown.

Your husband was one of those heroic Americans who answered the call of liberty and freedom. He was truly one of our finest citizens, whose loss is keenly felt by each of us in uniform.

On behalf of Commander James Lloyd Griffin's fellow servicemen, I wish to express my deepest sympathy to you and your family and to assure you that we in the navy stand ready to do anything possible to assist you.

Sincerely,

E. R. Zumwalt, Jr.

Admiral, U.S. Navy

LETTER THAT WAS A FOLLOW-UP TO ADM. BAGLEY'S TELEGRAM OF 18 JAN

DEPARTMENT OF THE NAVY

BUREAU OF NAVAL PERSONNEL

WASHINGTON, D.C. 20370

Dear Mrs. Griffin,

Writing letters of this nature is never an easy thing to do, but it is my unhappy task to confirm that your husband, Commander James Lloyd Griffin, United States Navy, has been determined to have died while a prisoner in North Vietnam on 21 May 1967.

I know that you have been provided all of the information on which this action was based, but we have set forth a resume below for your review.

On 19 May 1967 Commander Griffin was the pilot of an RA-5C aircraft launched from the USS *KITTY HAWK* in the Gulf of Tonkin. The assigned mission was bomb damage assessment (photography of the Hanoi Thermal Power Plant, supply surface-to-air missile depot, and Van Dien Vehicle Depot as a weather alternative). He began his mission with an escort at two-thirty p.m. and proceeded over the Song Yen River. There was no ground fire or surface-to-air missiles noted during ingress, but upon reaching his turn point north of Hanoi he came under attack. Cloud conditions in the area were broken to scattered, bottoms 1500 feet variable to 3000 feet, tops 4000 to 6000 feet. Commander Griffin's aircraft was hit and fire engulfed it. The forward two-thirds of the aircraft initially pitched up and began to disintegrate rapidly. A fifteen- to twenty-foot portion of the aircraft appeared intact but burning together with many small, non-burning fragments. One fragment appeared to separate from the rest; this was thought to be his radar intercept officer's seat. A parachute blossomed several seconds later. Then a second parachute deployed rapidly. No beepers were heard. Due to the hostile location of the downed crew, the other aircraft could not stay in the area; search or rescue efforts could not be initiated. No radio contact was established.

Commander Griffin was subsequently placed in a prisoner-of-war status. He had been continued in that status until 16 January 1974.

The repatriated prisoners of war reported hearing the propaganda statement attributed to Commander Griffin shortly after his loss. Although his name was known by returnees, he was not seen in the prisoner-of-war system nor was any additional information regarding his fate provided. The North Vietnamese reported that Commander Griffin and his crew member had died in captivity. They said he died two days after being captured; this would be 21 May 1967.

An intelligence report of 15 October 1971 stated that a source reported seeing downing of an American aircraft over Hanoi on 19 May 1967 and that the two injured pilots were captured. The reliability of the source was uncertain.

In view of the list furnished by the North Vietnamese stating that Commander Griffin died in captivity and in the absence of further information, the determination of death was made on 17 January 1974. Notwithstanding this determination, our intent is to continue to pursue all available information from North Vietnam relating to the loss of his and all other aircraft and the return of remains of our unaccounted for men. We will, of course, keep you advised of any information developed in these efforts.

On behalf of the navy, I extend to you deepest sympathies for your long ordeal. If I may assist you, please do not hesitate to call.

David H. Bagley
Vice Admiral, USN
Chief of Naval Personnel

LETTER FROM DEPT. OF THE NAVY
BUREAU OF NAVAL PERSONNEL
WASHINGTON, D.C. 20370
31 JAN 1974

Dear Mrs. Griffin:

As Chief of Naval Personnel, it is a privilege to inform you that your husband, Commander James L. Griffin, United States Navy, has been posthumously awarded the following:

Distinguished Flying Cross with Gold Star

Air Medal with Bronze Star and numeral "8" in lieu of subsequent awards

Navy Commendation Medal with Gold Star and Combat Distinguishing Device

Navy Achievement Medal

Purple Heart

Combat Action Ribbon

Bronze Star in lieu of second Navy Unit Commendation awarded USS *Kitty Hawk* (CVA-63) during the period 4 December 1966 to 28 April 1967

Republic of Vietnam Meritorious Unit Citation (Gallantry Cross Medal Color with Palm)

In addition, the earned the National Defense Service Medal, Vietnam Service Medal with three bronze stars, and the Republic of Vietnam Campaign Medal during his naval service.

These awards have been forwarded to the Commandant, Sixth Naval District, Naval Base, Charleston, South Carolina 29408. He will communicate with you in the near future regarding your wishes for a presentation ceremony.

I realize that medals are small consolation for the loss of a loved one and they can do little to assuage the grief which you have experienced. However, I hope that they will serve as symbols of your husband's devotion to duty in the service of his country.

Sincerely yours,

DAVID H. BAGLEY,

Vice Admiral, USN

Chief of Naval Personnel

LETTER RECEIVED FROM
THE WHITE HOUSE
WASHINGTON, D.C.
January 28, 1974

Dear Mrs. Griffin,

It is with great sadness that I have learned of the official confirmation of the death of your husband, Commander James Lloyd Griffin, United States Navy. The hope you held out for so long and the immense ordeal you have suffered makes the news of his loss especially tragic.

I know there is little I can say to ease your sorrow. But I do want assure you that he has left a legacy which cannot die so long as men are willing to make the highest sacrifice for freedom so that others may live in a world at peace.

Mrs. Nixon joins me in extending our deepest sympathy and our hope that the profound respect your husband has earned will sustain and comfort you in this time of mourning. You and your family are in our thoughts and prayers.

Sincerely,
Richard Nixon

LETTER RECEIVED FROM
OFFICE OF THE GOVERNOR
ATLANTA 30334
February 4, 1974

Dear Mrs. Griffin:

I have been advised that the Department of Defense has now reported that your husband lost his life in the conflict in Southeast Asia. I know you have suffered a great loss, and words of sympathy, however sincere, cannot lighten the grief that has come to you.

Even so, as Governor and as a spokesman for the people of Georgia, I want to express to you my deep appreciation for what you and your family have given to us and to our country. Please know that my thoughts and prayers are with you. God bless you.

Sincerely,
Jimmy Carter

LETTER FROM: STATE OF GEORGIA
OFFICE OF THE ADJUTANT GENERAL
POST OFFICE BOX 4839
ATLANTA, GEORGIA 30302
4 February 1974

Dear Mrs. Griffin:

I have been advised that the Department of Defense has now reported that your husband lost his life in the conflict in Southeast Asia. I extend to you my deepest sympathy in your great loss. I know the grief that has come to you is great to bear and I hope you will find a measure of consolation in the realization that your husband gave his life in the service of his country.

To me the greatest service to the world is the service to one's country. Your husband gave his all in the line of duty.

My prayers and thoughts are with you in your sorrow. May God bless you.

Sincerely,
Joel B. Paris, III
Major General
The Adjutant General

All of the official pronouncements have been made now, and the children and I realize it is time to discuss burial sites. I know the Griffins would like Jimmie brought to Tennessee to the little churchyard near their home where many of his and my ancestors were laid to rest. But I have the instructions Jimmie left with me before he began the combat tour. He asked to be buried either in Arlington National Cemetery or in a national cemetery in Memphis. Uncertain about what to do, I ask my son what he thinks would be best.

As a family, we had toured Arlington Cemetery just a few months before, and now Jamey asks that he be allowed to go to Memphis to look at the cemetery there. I send him on the train, and he stays with my mother and sister and visits Memphis National Cemetery. When he returns, he tells me the cemetery there is not well kept up, and he thinks Dad should go to Arlington.

TELEGRAM DATED 4/19/1974

FROM NAVCMST WASH B

...ARRANGEMENTS ARE BEING MADE TO TRANSPORT THE REMAINS OF YOUR HUSBAND, CDR JAMES LLOYD GRIFFIN, USN, TO ARLINGTON NATIONAL CEMETERY, WITH MILITARY ESCORT CDR DANIEL E. PECKHAM, USN FOR INTERMENT AT 1300 HRS, MONDAY 22 APRIL 1974.

YOU WILL BE INFORMED BY THE NAVAL DISPENSARY, TREASURE ISLAND, SAN FRANCISCO, OF TRANSPORTATION SCHEDULE TO DESTINATION. IN ACCORDANCE WITH YOUR DESIRES THE HEADSTONE RECEIVED WILL BE

PLACED IN CASKET BENEATH THE REMAINS OF YOUR HUSBAND. SINCEREST SYMPATHY IS EXTENDED.

BUREAU OF MEDICINE AND SURGERY

NAVY DEPARTMENT DU MED WASHINGTON, D.C.

It seems the absolute end now, but not everything has been resolved. We still are waiting for the navy to bring Jimmie home from Vietnam. Finally, in April, his remains are brought back to America. Dan Peckham, a longtime friend and Naval Academy classmate of Jimmie's, flies to the West Coast to intercept the remains, identify them, and accompany them back to Washington for burial. Dan phones me from California to ask me some specifics about dental records, and after conferring with our family dentist, we conclude that there is no doubt that the remains Dan is bringing back east are those of Jimmie Griffin, the man I have loved for more than twenty years, the father of my children. We prepare to go to Arlington Cemetery.

Jim Dickenson, a friend from Jimmie's days at the Naval Academy, meets us at the airport when we arrive in Washington for the burial service. During his midshipman days, Jimmie had arranged for me to stay in Annapolis with Jim Dickenson's girlfriend, Pat, when I went up for drag weekends a couple of times. We had lost touch with Jim and Pat after graduation since he joined the air force, but he somehow has learned about the funeral and has come to do this favor for his old friend.

The *Washington Post*

April 22, 1974

CDR. J.L. GRIFFIN, DIED AS PRISONER IN VIETNAM

Funeral services for Cdr. James Lloyd Griffin, U.S. Navy pilot who died while a prisoner of war in North Vietnam, will be held today at Arlington National Cemetery at 1 p.m.

Cdr. Griffin was captured in Hanoi, North Vietnam on May 19, 1967 and died two days later from injuries received ejecting from his plane. He had previously been reported missing in action.

He served as squadron operations officer aboard the U.S.S. *Kitty Hawk*, flying 150 combat missions in Southeast Asia. News of his capture in May 1967 was announced by Hanoi Radio.

Commander Griffin was born in Gates, Tenn., and he attended the University of Tennessee before entering the Naval Academy. Upon graduation from the academy in 1955, he entered flight training at Pensacola, Fla., and got his wings in 1956.

He received an aeronautical engineering degree from the U.S. Naval Postgraduate School at Monterey, Calif., and continued his graduate study at the University of Michigan, earning a professional degree in aeronautical engineering in 1963.

Cdr. Griffin's awards include the Distinguished Flying Cross with gold star; the Air Medal with bronze star and Numeral 8, in lieu of subsequent awards; the Navy Commendation Medal with gold star and combat distinguishing device; the

Navy Achievement Medal; the Purple Heart; Combat Action Ribbon; Navy Unit Commendation Medal with bronze star; Republic of Vietnam Meritorious Unit Citation (Gallantry Cross Medal Color with Palm); Vietnam Service Medal with three bronze stars; and the Republic of Vietnam Campaign Medal.

He was considered missing in action until January 1973, when his death was revealed by the North Vietnamese. On Jan. 16, 1974, the Secretary of the Navy verified that Cdr. Griffin had died while a prisoner of war.

He is survived by his widow, Dora, and two children, James and Glyn Carol, of Albany, Ga., his parents, two brothers, and a sister.

On a sunny April day we assemble for a graveside service amid the blooming dogwoods and cherry trees that make Arlington Cemetery one of the most beautiful burial sites in the United States. Not many family members are able to make the journey, but Gene Griffin, Jimmie's younger brother, has come from Tennessee and many Washington-area friends are present with us.

The casket is transported from the chapel by horse-drawn caisson, the chaplain says some nice words, the cannons are fired, "Taps" is played. Two flags, folded after being draped on Jimmie's casket, are presented, one to me and one to Gene to take home to his parents. The service that is repeated several times a day in this most honored of cemeteries is very special to us. It is, indeed, a fitting place for our nation's heroes.

After the graveside service we all go to the chapel visitor center for a reception. Friends have brought cakes and cookies and other food for the gathering of what must have been dozens and dozens of people, but we are unable to eat. Jim Bell accompanies us to the gravesite and returns us to the airport.

The two-hour plane ride back to Albany seems much longer than it is, and the children and I feel very empty when we get back to our home. That evening, as usual, I tuck James and Glyn Carol into bed, and we say prayers together, but we do not change the words—"God bless Mommy and Daddy and Glyn Carol and Jamey and Samson." The phrase continues as long as we continue to say prayers together.

LETTER FROM JAMES L. HOLLOWAY, Vice Chief of (Naval) Personnel and Former Skipper of VA-83
LETTER DATED 6 MAY 1974:

Dear Dora,

Captain Charlie Hunter called my office while I was on an extended trip out of the country to inform me about Jim's funeral on April twenty-second. I am truly sorry that I was unable to be present at the rites for such an outstanding naval officer and grand personal friend.

Both you and Jim were great favorites of ours back in VA-83. Those were wonderful days for all of us. I always expected great things from Jim and his courageous actions in Vietnam were in keeping with the high standards of loyalty, dedication, and patriotism which were characteristic of his service career.

It is always difficult to understand why some are touched by the tragedies of war while others are free to go on as before. We can only hope that we will all gain from the legacy of brave shipmates like Jim.

Dabney joins me in sending our warmest regards and highest hopes for your future happiness. If there is anything that I may be able to do for you, please feel free to call on me.

Sincerely,

Jim J.L. HOLLOWAY III

ADMIRAL, U. S. Navy

→ 18 ←

Throughout the spring Jim Bell phones frequently, telling me about his frustration in dealing with his family situation. He agonizes about not being with his children. While I realize he is overwhelmed by anger and a feeling of rejection, I also know that his wife had a difficult time during the war, and I try to encourage him not to judge her actions too harshly. But the more I try to calm troubled waters, the more I realize that I now have feelings for Jim that are much more than friendship.

He comes to Albany, staying with neighbors from the navy community, and each time we are together it is apparent that we are very much attracted to one another. We both have suffered great losses, and we each have stored up love that now has no recipient. Letters and phone calls become more frequent while he completes his graduate studies at the Industrial College of the Armed Forces in Washington. I go up to see him and meet his parents, and he manages another visit to Georgia during the late spring.

On a beautiful Saturday morning in May I drive to the Albany airport to pick up Jim. Now that there is a direct flight from Dulles Airport to Albany, it is an easy trip for him. After the months of grim events that led to the burial at Arlington Cemetery, I look forward to some fun activities.

Jim, looking a little more confident than he did when he came here a year ago, throws his overnight bag in the back seat and says he wants to introduce me to his Aunt Olive in Apalachicola, Florida. It sounds like a great plan. The children and I have not been to the Gulf Coast since the Pensacola vacation in 1970 when we first saw the list of POWs released by Ted Kennedy.

Today Jamey is busy with his friends, but Glyn Carol is excited about going to the beach again. We put on swimsuits and top them with loose-fitting shirts and shorts, and I pack a picnic lunch. Jim takes the wheel, and as we drive south, he tells us about Aunt Olive, who was married to Jim's mother's brother. Now in her eighties, Olive Ruge Rusmisel has been a widow since World War II and lives alone in a huge Victorian-style house built by her parents around the turn of the century.

When we reach the Rusmisel house, we are greeted by a black man who is polishing Olive's car, parked just outside the garage. Jim tells me Eddie has been Olive's driver and handyman for many years, and that Eddie cleans the house, shops for her groceries, and sees to it that Olive gets to the doctor when she needs to. Eddie makes it possible for Olive, now struggling with glaucoma, to live alone though she is at least eighty years old.

Olive's house smells of furniture polish but seems a bit musty, reminding me of childhood visits to my grandmother's home. She appears a little feeble but gives Jim a spirited hug, then crosses her arms and looks at me and Glyn Carol.

"I knew that when he found the right girl he'd bring her down for me to meet," Olive says with a wrinkled smile.

Whatever does she mean? Has he been telling her something about me?

Olive ushers us into a dark kitchen, and Jim helps her serve us Cokes and chips. It is too early for lunch, and I have a picnic in a cooler in the car. We only stay about an hour, but our visit is long enough to conclude that I have "passed inspection," though I had no idea I was even being considered a candidate that needed inspecting!

We drive on a causeway out to St. George's Island, where years earlier I had rented a cottage and brought the children for vacations several times when we first moved to Georgia. The island runs parallel to the mainland, and rental cottages range from the elaborate to tiny dwellings not much more substantial than shacks. The sand is blowing through our hair and teeth when we finally set up our picnic things on the beach, but all three of us are ravenously hungry. Glyn devours her tuna sandwich, hunching over her food to protect it from the sand and then races out to collect shells along the beach.

Sitting beside Jim, who lies face down on the towel, I note the deep scar on his left shoulder. It has been less than a year since he had surgery at Bethesda Hospital to graft bone from his hip into the shoulder joint—this to correct an injury he had incurred when ejecting from his plane in Vietnam in 1965. The broken bone had never been reset during his time in prison.

He tells me more about Aunt Olive, whose late husband, Jim's Uncle Paul, was a meteorologist. After Paul's death, Olive came back to her family home in Apalachicola and has lived here alone since then except the time during the war that she rented out a few rooms. When Jim was a young student at the navy flight school in Pensacola almost twenty years ago, he and some of his buddies often hitched rides across the Florida panhandle to visit Olive. She enjoyed the attention and provided plenty of beer for the boys, and they relished sleeping in the huge antique four-poster beds in her guest rooms.

The afternoon sun is warm, and the wind never lets up, so after two hours of wading in the surf, looking for seashells with Glyn Carol, we are ready to call it a day. We find a makeshift shower on the beach near the place where we are turn onto the causeway for our drive back to the mainland, so we stop and rinse off as much sand as we can, towel down, and pull on shirts and shorts over our swimsuits. Then we head for Maude's.

Years ago, when the children and I first came to St. George's Island on vacation, we discovered Maude's, a little café perched on the outskirts of Apalachicola. Of course, it is run by a woman named Maude. You can't get better fried oysters or fresher shrimp than the food sold at Maude's. We have an early supper of crispy fried seafood washed down with iced tea, and Jim and I realize that years earlier, we each "discovered" Maude's on our own, and it is now a mutual memory for us.

Back in Albany, I have allowed Jim to stay in our guest room on this visit since the friends who hosted him on previous trips are out of town. He shares a bathroom with James, whose room is just across the hall from his. Glyn Carol's room is next to mine.

When we get back from our beach outing, James is waiting for us, and we exchange stories about our day at the beach and James' adventures with his buddies. Soon the children bring out the board games, and Jim joins them in a lively game of Scrabble. As I am bringing in a tray of dessert and coffee, I overhear him having a very serious conversation with James and Glyn.

"What would you think about that? We could all be a family," he is saying.

Maybe I am misunderstanding him. Is he proposing to the children when he hasn't even talked about it with me? I try to pretend I haven't heard what was going on. After that, we all are ready to call it a night.

Jim, who may have gotten a bit more sun than he'd intended, retires first. I still go in to have prayers with the children, and each of them has a few comments to make about our house guest. Glyn, who has observed him all day, thinks, "He's very nice, Mom." James, my teenage son and self-proclaimed protector, is a little more reserved, and he has a few questions. "Is he talking about joining our family, Mom?"

"I'm not sure, honey. But I do think he likes us, and he doesn't have a family of his own anymore."

I have put bulky rollers in my hair, but after such a long day I have no trouble falling asleep. The house is silent when, hours later, I am awakened by the awareness that my bedroom door is open, and there seems to be a shadow of someone standing there.

"James? Is something wrong?" I whisper. There is no answer.

"Glyn Carol?" I try again, realizing that the shadow is too tall for a twelve-year-old.

Then the shadow moves toward the vacant side of my bed and lies down atop the covers and bedspread!

"NO!!" I whisper loudly and insistently. "You can't come in here! I'm sorry, Jim, but this just isn't right. Please, you have to leave. I can't let you come in my bedroom."

He lies very still and doesn't respond for a minute or so, while I tremble in terror that one of the children will find Jim Bell in my room.

"I just want to lie here for a few minutes...to see what it's like," he says.

Thank goodness it is dark, because if he could see the blush on my cheeks and the anxiety in my eyes, he would run. But I realize that he is trying to get a feeling as to whether he could fit into our family. I never should have let him stay here in the house!...It's going to be all right. He isn't "trying anything." He's just lying there, and I cannot imagine what is going through his mind. I don't dare to move a muscle, and I try to breathe quietly. After about fifteen minutes, he gets up and leaves, returning to the guest room.

Jim invites me to come back in June for his graduation from the Industrial College of the Armed Forces. In addition to the course at ICAF, he also has been taking a graduate course at George Washington University, but those classes will continue through the summer. By now we have moved from a friendly relationship to what surely must be called a romance. I have told my mother and my sisters that I may be in love. They assure me that it is not too soon, because I have been alone now for seven years even though I held out hope for my husband for much of that time.

The Griffins come to Albany to stay with the children while I attend Jim's graduation in Washington. By now they know a great deal about this handsome man with the shy smile, and they know something about his Vietnam experiences and his coming home to find he had lost his family. While I am away Mother G. will be making cookies with Glyn and preparing a few of the children's favorite meals. Mr. Billy, as my father-in-law is called, will be helping James get the lawn mower in shape for the summer season ahead.

During my visit to Arlington I stay with Jim's neighbor in an adjacent townhouse in Fairlington. He calls her "Marion the Librarian." She, whose real name is Nancy, has been very concerned about Jim since he moved into the condo next door last year. Nancy has been one of many people who took an interest in his return to normal life after he completed his surgery and rehab at Bethesda Naval Hospital, and so she has many stories to tell me about his "coming back."

Graduation takes place on a warm sunny day, and his parents join us for lunch after the ceremony at a seafood restaurant on Maine Avenue. "They have terrific rum buns," his mother tells me. Jim's parents are just a few years younger than my mother, and they live in Cumberland, Maryland, about two hours northwest of Washington.

Throughout the seven and a half his son was a POW, Ted Bell took an active role in the League of Families organization. Then his wife Miriam took a tumble down the stairs and learned that she had blacked out because she was diabetic, so Ted spends more time these days giving support to her health problems. And I think he may have a few health problems as well. They make a very cute couple, toddling along, arm in arm, giving support to one another.

The next morning, Jim and I drive across the Maryland countryside to the little town of Cumberland, where the Bells moved when Jim was a sophomore in high school. Nestled in the mountains, Cumberland was once the center of a number of industries, including Pittsburgh Plate Glass, Celanese, a couple of breweries, and Kelly Springfield Tire Company, where, before retirement, Jim's father was the personnel manager. Now, most of these businesses are moving out of the area, and no new manufacturers are moving in to replace them.

Jim has brought me here to see the area where his family was living when he graduated from high school. Last year the city of Cumberland gave a joyous homecoming for Jim, complete with a gigantic billboard welcoming him back to his hometown. Here, he is a celebrity.

Jim's parents' home is located in the small community of La Vale, just outside of Cumberland. The house resembles the Sears and Roebuck houses that were popular in the early part of the century, and they have lived here since around the end of World War II. The Bells enjoy playing bridge with their neighbors, and Ted spends a lot of time playing an electric organ that presides over the front entry hall. He received the organ as a gift when he retired from Kelly Springfield Tire Company.

The next morning when we leave, Jim drives us up to the top of Haystack Mountain that overlooks Cumberland, and we hike out through scrubby underbrush past several picnickers. As we look down on the valley, he surprises me by saying, "Shall we do it?" I am not sure whether he is suggesting we jump off the side of the mountain or just hit the road back to Washington, but he seems to be making a serious suggestion. Then he takes a small box out of his pocket and pulls out his grandmother's diamond ring, the real reason we have followed his parents to Cumberland. Fortunately, I have stopped wearing the wedding and engagement rings that had been on my fingers for almost twenty years, and so he slips the ring on my finger as tears roll down my cheeks. I think I say, yes, as a pair of picnickers look on with smiles and take our picture.

During the ride back to Dulles Airport we don't talk a great deal. Both of us know we have just made a commitment that will bring about enormous changes and adjustments in our lives. There is much to consider.

Back in Albany, the Griffins have been babysitting while I took this trip, and when I get home I sit down with them and tell them about our plans for the future. After hearing about the visit to Cumberland and the Bells, Dad Griffin ambles out to the carport and smokes his pipe for a while. When he returns, he takes my hand and says, "Well, Dora, I think it's going to be all right." He grins. "When you talk in your sleep, you won't ever get in trouble!" And I know that it really is going to be all right.

Cumberland, Maryland welcomes back its hero,
Commander Jim Bell, 1973.

Commander Jim Bell with wife Dora at awards ceremony in San Diego December 1975.

Dora and Jim Bell at 1975 reception at NAS Miramar, San Diego, CA.

"Mom, when you and Jim get married, are you going to change your name?" my daughter asks.

There so many things to think of, things other than just talking in my sleep, and this is one of them.

"Well, I guess I'll have to, honey. I know nowadays some women keep their name when they marry, but I'll be Dora Bell, or maybe I'll be Dora Griffin Bell. But I won't use a hyphen. Bell will be my last name."

Glyn sits quietly for a few minutes. "Could I change my name, too?" she asks. *My golly! I can't believe she has asked that. The Griffins have been very supportive in my decision up to now. What will they think if I change my children's name? I can't do it! Their father…Jimmie...would never, ever forgive me.*

"Are you sure you would want to do that? Why would you want to change your name?" I ask.

"Well, Mom," she squirms a bit, then smiles, "I never really liked being called Glyn. I'd like to be called Carrie!"

I breathe a huge sigh of relief, remembering how she suffered in third grade when her classmates had teased her about having a special friend named "Campbell." They would do the crossed fingers thing and chant, "Glyn Campbell, Glyn Campbell." I can't blame her for wanting to avoid that in the future, and in her young mind, although the little boy named Campbell is far across the country, they might meet up again, and she remembers the teasing. I also know she has spent some time watching a soap opera in which the character Carrie plays a major role.

"I think that would be just fine, honey. You can be Carrie if you want to!"

Talks with James are more serious. While he likes Jim Bell well enough, he has not forgotten his own role in my life. When Jimmie went away on his first cruise to Vietnam, he made the mistake that so many military men make. He said, "You're the man of the house now, Son. Take good care of your mother and sister while I am away." This admonition places a burden of responsibility on young boys that they ought not have to carry.

James, who was just a little kid called Jamey when his dad left for the war, is now seventeen years old. He has been accepted at Georgia Tech, and he has earned half the money to buy his own car. I matched his earnings to complete the deal, and he became the proud owner of a small white Opel. It is understandable that he is uncertain just what his role in my life is going to be when I marry Jim Bell.

Jim now has learned that in a few months, he will be leaving for San Diego where he will take command of a squadron. He wants me to be with him to handle the duties of "Skipper's wife." Jim still has to do a lot of adjusting to the changes in navy life since he went away. I've more or less been away, too, but together we can be a team. But we'll be two thousand miles away from James

If it is hard for me to let go of my son and let him grow up, it is going to be even harder for him to let me move forward in my life, with a new husband, not his father. And there will be stepbrothers and a stepsister. Although Jim's children will continue to live with their mother, they will be coming for visits, and my children will no longer be the only ones around. In our talks, James seems to feel very sorry for them, especially Jim's boys, who lost their father and now are not able to be with him even though he is home from the war. Perhaps James envisions himself in the "big brother" role.

Another major hurdle to beginning my life with Jim Bell is leaving my job at WALB-TV. Over the past year, the station management has given me more autonomy over the *Town and Country Show.* They like my ideas, and they want me to consider handling the program solo. Even if I were not leaving, I know I could never handle the host job alone, and so when I approach the production manager to tell him my plans, I am not only turning down a sort of promotion. I am actually resigning, with plans to leave the program toward the end of July.

We begin interviewing women to replace me as co-host of the talk show, but the management decides to hire a professional meteorologist to report the weather. They select a man who works for the airport and is familiar with weather for pilots if not for farmers. I choose a young woman who has often appeared as a guest on the show to handle my duties as hostess. My fans flood the station with farewell wishes. They don't want to see me go, but they like to see a happy ending, and they all seem to feel that I deserve one, so they wish me well. I feel a little like Cinderella!

→ 19 ←

Life with Jim

The sun is shining on the first day of August when we arrive at Jim's townhouse in Arlington, Virginia for the wedding. The children and I left Albany two days ago, stopping overnight in southwest Virginia and driving north in our Oldsmobile. Jim's children, Ann, Tom, and Matt, all arrive by plane on the same day.

It has been more than eight years since we last saw one another in Florida, and, of course, the children all were very young then. It was too long ago for them to remember those days when Jamey, Glyn Carol, and I often saw the Bell children at the base swimming pool in Sanford. I still have vivid memories, however, of the time that Tom, then about eight years old, did a fancy dive into the pool, clipping his head on the edge of the diving board. He had to be rushed to the base dispensary, leaving behind a large amount of blood in the pool.

We have a sort of bunking party at Jim's Arlington townhouse, the girls and I sleeping in the basement rec room—formerly occupied by Jim's POW friend, Admiral Bill Lawrence. The foldout bed that Bill slept on for more than a year barely meets my minimum comfort standards, so I wonder how he managed to sleep there. Of course, the bed must have seemed almost luxurious to Bill after the concrete slabs the men slept on in Vietnam.

Jim leaves us behind early today, driving into Washington for his final oral exams at George Washington University, where he has been working toward a graduate degree in business. When he first returned from Vietnam, he was a patient at the National Naval Medical Center in Bethesda for several months. When he left the hospital he looked around for a place to live that would be close enough to GW and to the Industrial College of the Armed Forces. Now he will be leaving this area, having found a tenant for the townhouse, and he will take command of an A-4 utility squadron in San Diego. Jim is really excited about the prospect of flying again, and no doubt he will feel more comfortable as CO of a squadron with a wife by his side.

The children and I find very little food in his refrigerator for our breakfast, so a trip to the neighborhood grocery store is necessary, and we get provisions for lunch as well. In Jim's absence, we spend the morning getting acquainted. While we are all a bit shy coming together for this important event, we have fun putting together our impromptu meals.

Finally, around two o'clock, Jim arrives, and we head for Annapolis in two cars. I drive James and Glyn Carol, and Jim ferries Tom, Matt, and Ann in his car across the Potomac River, around the Beltway, and out Route 50 to the Naval Academy. I have purchased yellow organdy dresses for our daughters, since my dress for the occasion is also yellow. Ann's mother also had bought her a dress for the wedding, but Ann graciously accepts the yellow dress and decides to wear it. We are like three yellow birds!

My mother, Charlotte and Larry, Jim's sisters, Mary and Peggy, and their families all have come to town for this joyous occasion. In addition to our families, we have invited a dozen or so other friends in the area to join us. We exchange vows in the small downstairs chapel adjacent to John Paul Jones' tomb at the Naval Academy. The children are all part of our little wedding party, and having no rehearsal beforehand, we get the giggles during the middle of the ceremony. But the navy chaplain manages to hold things together, and after about thirty minutes we are man and wife, and our group all moves next door to the Officer's Club for dinner.

I am so delighted that my mother met Jim a few weeks earlier when he drove down from Washington to join our July 4th celebration at my sister Charlotte's home in North Carolina. I worry that Mother might be concerned about my remarrying so soon after we have buried Jimmie at Arlington. Only a few months have passed since then. But his death took place seven years ago. When finally we have a chance to talk, Mother assures me that I am doing the right thing.

"He wouldn't want you to be alone any longer," she says.

That's right. This is what he told me to do.

The day goes smoothly, as I meet some of Jim's friends and introduce him to mine. The children all look a bit uncomfortable, but they manage to get through the day with no tears. No tears that I can see.

In the evening Jim and I head back to his townhouse for our wedding night, while all the children accompany his family to Stone Harbour, New Jersey where the Bells have a summer cottage. We have left Samson, our schnauzer, to stand guard over the townhouse, so he is there to greet us when we arrive. It is a strange feeling. I am married again, and Samson seems to understand that Jim Bell is now the master of the house.

Stone Harbour is a small town, situated between Ocean City and Avalon, and youngsters here can freely roam about the streets to go to the candy stores, movies, and soda shops without parents' worrying. The Bells' cottage is just a block away from the ocean, so there is plenty of activity to interest our kids here, and Jim and I enjoy walking Samson at the beach—when Pop doesn't beat us to it.

James, Tom, Glyn, Matt, and Ann occupy the two upstairs bedrooms in the cottage, boys in one room, girls in the other. Mom and Pop, as I have come to call them, are in the master bedroom, and Jim and I have the foldout couch in the family room. This is a honeymoon like no other!

In the evenings we play games, and little Annie stands guard on the stair landing, giving us tickets to pass between the living room and the family room. Jim's children have stayed with him at Stone Harbor a couple of times since he came home from Vietnam, and their older cousins worked at the village candy store during their last visit, so they know where to find the best ice cream cones.

During the week Jim and I make frequent trips to the grocery store. Three growing boys and two girls can consume an enormous amount of milk, bread, cold cuts, and peanut butter. The kids, for the most part, get along fairly well during this merging of families, but by week's end any idea we may have entertained about having more children is out the window. As much as we love the five we have, we agree that our family is already large enough, though only my two will be living with us most of the time.

Then we pack up and go back to Washington. We put Tom, Matt, and Ann on a plane to return to their home in Texas, and we let Glyn Carol fly to Jacksonville to spend a few days with her former playmate, Cindy Johns, and her family in Jacksonville. James leaves to drive Jim's car to Albany, where we will join him in about a week, and Jim and I head north in the Oldsmobile. We are actually having a honeymoon, and our trip includes Niagara Falls.

Back in Georgia, we hold a huge yard sale at my house which has sold while I was away. Knowing we are about to combine two households,

I make sweeping decisions about getting rid of things. Because my television audience has not forgotten me in the two weeks I've been off the air, a large crowd turns out for the sale. People are eagerly purchasing the children's discarded books and toys, tools, outgrown clothing, and even potted plants from the yard. Jim really gets into the spirit of things, scooping up armloads of things that he feels we will no longer need. I have to send him back to return a few things to their rightful place in the house, but we sell our hide-a-bed to a neighbor, and our "take" for the day is amazing.

It is a momentous week. The movers are coming to load up all my household belongings—the ones we don't sell in the yard sale—to move them to San Diego. Jim is slated to take command of a squadron there in a few weeks, and the children and I are preparing to return to life as a navy family. The school year starts in just a few days, and because it seems important to get Glyn Carol into the San Diego school system we put her on another plane to fly west ahead of us. She will stay with her aunt and uncle, Barbara and Bill Blount, and we will follow by car, hoping to find a place to live in the Blounts' school district. James is staying behind in Georgia, since he begins classes at Georgia Tech next week. *Am I making too many changes at once for the children? I have to assume that they are strong, because a change in our lives has long been needed, and this change seems to be what we all want.*

October 1975

We all are seated in rows of chairs on the tarmac at Miramar Naval Air Station, awaiting the beginning of the Change of Command ceremony that marks the end of our year in California. Jim, handsome in his naval uniform adorned with captain's stripes, is making his farewell speech, and I sit watching proudly as he reads his orders to the

Naval Air Systems Command in Washington, D.C. We're going back to where we started just a year ago.

Succeeding Jim as Skipper of VC-7 is Ed Wingerter, who had been in line for the command himself in 1974, but Ed, like many other commanders in the navy, stepped aside as the returning POWs were worked back into the command rotation. I'm sure Ed and his wife Sandy must have been disappointed to have to wait for that command when Jim and I arrived in San Diego last year, but we all became good friends. If they resented the postponement of Ed's turn at the helm, they never let it show.

Now I sit with Sandy, her eyes sparkling and her brown hair shining, as she grins at her husband from the front row. Their children are all seated with us, Wendy, Guy, and Ron, and Ed makes appropriate remarks about the devoted support of his family that have made this day possible for him. Jim and I are here without our children. His are in Texas with their mother, James is in Georgia, and Glyn Carol is in Virginia, having already begun the school year.

During this year, while we lived in Rancho Bernardo near the Wingerters, Jim has been the "flyingest captain in the navy." Eager to make up for all those years of sitting in a prison cell in Vietnam with no airplane, no Happy Hours, no family, he has flown that little A-4 as often as the schedule would allow. He had no trouble picking up where he left off as a pilot, and he has learned that his love of the navy has not all been for patriotic reasons. He just really loves flying!

The year has not been altogether a trip down Easy Street, however. Unlike the navy he left behind in 1965, there now are women officers in the squadron. And some of these women officers are pregnant, although no maternity uniforms have yet been made available in the uniform shops. Jim also has had to deal with officers with enough DUIs to send them to jail, and other discipline problems he had never envisioned. He also was the object of a couple of lawsuits—one because of his sending the men to survival school and another for joining other former POWs in signing a petition about a political candidate.

The most difficult day came when we had been with the squadron only a few months. One of the young pilots, a Naval Academy graduate with a promising aviation career ahead of him, was killed in an aircraft collision out over the Pacific. For me, it was a sobering experience, joining Jim in calling on the pilot's wife, a beautiful young woman who was expecting their first child. I shake even now to think about that day, having seen so many official navy cars arrive at my own house, always bringing bad news. I know now that the courage of those commanding officers and their wives is sorely challenged each time they must make a condolence call on a survivor. There really is no way to offer comfort. I still hurt for the young widow and for her unborn child and the rest of the family.

Jim has enjoyed this year, this return to navy flying, this opportunity to command and to share with others the wisdom he gained during his time in Vietnam. He has especially benefited from the camaraderie of the young men in his squadron. Almost a year ago, soon after we arrived in San Diego, Jim bought a Honda motorcycle to use for his commute to Miramar, some fifteen miles south of our home. It gave him the excuse to go out with the other biking guys and ride up and down the hills around San Diego.

A few times he talked me into getting on the back of the bike. "Just ride to the end of the block, Dora. You'll like it!" he'd say, knowing that I was terrified. He bought a helmet for me, and he would convince me that we would only go a short distance. Then, he would ease forward a few yards before taking off across the countryside. Meanwhile, I shuddered in fear behind him, clinging to his waist. He thought I was having fun, and I did enjoy seeing him have so much fun, but I prefer the Olds 98 and a solid steel frame of protection around me every time.

Now we look forward to another life change. Jim will be doing office work and very little flying in his new job in Washington. We have bought a house just a few miles south of Crystal City where he will be working, and the commute will be easy, but the motorcycle will have to go. There is no safe place to go joyriding on the Washington Beltway. And Jim will be hanging up his uniform again, at least for four days a week. Working around the Pentagon and in NavAir these days, military personnel wear civilian attire for all but one day a week. There may be a move afoot to make the military less visible in the aftermath of bad feelings about the Vietnam War.

→ 20 ←

Jim Bell's Story

Some twenty-three years after Jim had stepped off the plane in the Philippines to learn that the family he had left behind was no longer his as it had been when he left in 1965, I suggest that he write something about his experiences. Thinking of his grandchildren and questions they might ask about him someday, this is what he writes.

And What Did You Do During the War Granddad?

Why am I writing this? Because I've reached that stage in life where I frequently find myself reflecting on what I've done with my life, the good and the bad days, and how some of this history can be preserved for those family members who follow and might wonder one day and ask, "Who was Jim Bell and what did he do that was different and of interest to us in the twentieth century?"

As I write this in the winter of 1996, I'm shortly going to join the ranks of officially recognized senior citizens, turn sixty-five years old, get my Medicare card, and become more involved with enjoying my grandchildren. At this stage in life, I also spend a lot of time thinking how I got here, how my life has been affected by others, and what were those unique actions and events in my parents' and grandparents' lives that had a lasting effect on their lives and by trickle-down or osmosis somehow had an affect on my life or character.

Some of this I know. I know my Great-grandfather Bell brought his family with eight children from Canada to the plains of Kansas after the Civil War. I think of the daily challenges that trip across the plains in a covered wagon must have presented as they pushed on in search of a new and better life in this country. I think about how my grandfather walked from Kansas to Illinois to obtain the college degree he needed to pursue his chosen vocation as a high school principal and school superintendent. I think of my dad and his brother and sisters who somehow managed to achieve college educations when college was a dream achieved only by a chosen few.

And I think of my own life and what I've done with it, and how one day in 1965 has had such a lasting impact on me and those around me and how all of this might be of interest to you. There is an old adage that I truly believe—"People are like tea bags, you never know their true quality until they're in hot water." I'd like to relate to you my story of one day in 1965 when I ended up in hot water and how that one day led to another 2677 days that will forever be inscribed in my memory.

In June of 1962 I graduated from the Naval Postgraduate School in Monterey, California with a graduate degree in aeronautical engineering and headed for Sanford, Florida with orders to an A-5A Vigilante squadron. At that time the A-5 was the latest and greatest in naval aviation with a top speed exceeding Mach II, and holding a series of international records for high-altitude flight and speed. Within a year, the plane was converted to a reconnaissance airplane and acquired a lot of sophisticated equipment for photography and electronic information gathering.

By early 1965, I had been promoted to Lieutenant Commander and was the maintenance officer of my squadron, VAH-1, and the squadron was scheduled to deploy aboard the USS *Independence* in May for a seven-month cruise to the Mediterranean. In February of 1965, however, things began to change in response to a changing world situation that would dominate and affect so many Americans for years to come. We were informed that we could forget the summer cruise to the Med that most of us were looking forward to, for the *Independence* and its air wing was being reassigned to the Pacific fleet to assist with the rapidly escalating hostilities in Vietnam. In February of 1965 there were probably less than 50,000 Americans in Vietnam; by the end of the year, there were over 200,000.

We departed Norfolk the first Sunday in May. I believe it was Mother's Day. I had been fortunate to hitch a ride home to Sanford a few days earlier in a helicopter to see my new daughter Ann who had been born just a few days prior while I was in Norfolk preparing to go to sea. We had originally been scheduled to stop in Cape Town for a few days, but those plans were scrapped when there was no resolution to the question of our black sailors taking shore leave in then racially divided South Africa. As a result, our first stop after Norfolk was Singapore, and we made the most of five or six days of shore leave in that intriguing city. Our squadron rented a suite at the famous Raffles Hotel which served as our "headquarters ashore" while we enjoyed the sights and pleasures of this wonderful city. That quickly came to an end, though, and by early June we were in the Gulf of Tonkin as a key component of Task Force 77 charged with carrying the naval air war to North Vietnam in support of our forces and the South Vietnamese government in the south.

By October of 1965 I had flown about thirty-five missions over North Vietnam, and was looking forward with great anticipation to our return home and my new duty station. I had just received orders to the English Test Pilot School at Farnborough, and as soon as we returned I was to pack up my family and head off to England. We'd go for the next test pilot class convening in January. For two or three weeks I was the happiest aviator in the navy. The navy only sends one aviator a year to this renowned school, and I was overjoyed to be chosen for this very coveted honor.

Then came 16 October 1965. I was scheduled for a low-level reconnaissance mission along the coast east of Haiphong and near the town of Hon Gay. The commander of the air wing (CAG) escorted me up the Gulf until I accelerated for my run in over the coast.

CAG stayed out to sea to monitor the radio and assist if I ran into trouble. I made the east-to-west run all right, reversing my direction when I got within twenty miles or so of Haiphong. I was flying at 1200 to 1500 feet at a speed of 620 knots. The thinking at that time was there was no way a gunner could track such a fast-moving target at a low altitude. I remember seeing a lot of truck traffic on the coast highway, but not much else, and no one was firing at me. When I got within fifteen miles of Hon Gay on my way out, my electronic warning gear suddenly lit up indicating that I was being "painted" by anti-aircraft search radar. A few seconds later, I had indications they were "locked on." I put my gear in the jamming mode, but why I didn't make a radical course change at this point, I don't really know. Like most carrier pilots, I'm sure I harbored some illusions of invincibility, and I was within a few miles of completing my mission as planned. Whatever my thinking process was, it was faulty because a few seconds later I was in trouble.

As I approached Hon Gay, I felt a couple of "thumps" from the aft end of the aircraft and a few yellow CAUTION lights lit up on the instrument panel. Shortly afterward there was a small explosion from somewhere in the aircraft, almost all the CAUTION and WARNING lights lit up, and the stick became immobile as I lost all hydraulic pressure. The plane was still flying but not under my control, and I still thought I could get it out to sea where I could be picked up. I tried to contact CAG, but there was no background noise on the radio. I was pretty sure it was dead. I succeeded in raising the nose a little in preparation for an ejection, and shortly after that the plane began a rapid roll to the left, and it was all over. I pulled the ejection handle ejecting both myself and Duffy Hutton, my navigator, into the wind stream at 600 kts (about 700 mph) at an altitude of about 3,000 feet.

The next thing I knew, I was hanging in my chute, and I couldn't see anything. I was really concerned about this until I realized the high-speed ejection had torn my oxygen mask through the plastic fitting that holds the mask tight to my face, and the broken plastic cup was cutting into my face. Once I unhooked the cup fitting, I could see again just in time to go into the water with my parachute and seat harness still attached. (In a "perfect ejection sequence," if there ever is such a thing, one should release the seat pack while still in the air which will deploy and inflate a small life raft. You should also try and release the parachute fittings as you go into the water to avoid becoming entangled in all the shroud lines in the water. I did none of that.)

Almost immediately, I was dragged underwater due to the weight of the wet parachute and seat pack. I released the seat pack which again could have been a disastrous mistake, since it contained the life raft and other survival equipment. My concern at the moment, though, was short-term survival, and I had to do what was necessary to get my nose above water. I also released my parachute fittings and concentrated on not becoming enmeshed in the shroud lines. I anticipated a problem with this, the shroud lines and parachute were everywhere, but miraculously, the chute seemed to just fall away from me and sink.

Somewhere in this process I also discovered I had a problem with my left arm. It was hanging at an odd angle, and I couldn't control it—it was just hanging free. I somehow got my boots off using my one good hand and then started looking around for my mae west. I was still having trouble staying afloat, and I needed some flotation assistance. The mae wests which we wore were like a doughnut that snapped on to your flight harness around your belly and could be inflated with CO2 cartridges. My mae west had been all but torn away during the ejection. It was still attached with one or two snaps but was lying stretched out straight on the surface of the water. It was attached to my torso harness with only one snap. I managed to pull it around me and get it under my right arm and actuate one of the CO2 cartridges.

I was now floating safely on the surface and could look around at the surroundings. I was in the midst of what we called "the Northern Islands," a group of small islands a few miles off the mainland and probably twenty miles from the Chinese border. Everything was very quiet and peaceful, and there was no sign of my escort.

After I had been in the water for fifteen or twenty minutes I heard a noise behind me and turned to see a fishing junk bearing down on me. They soon pulled up alongside, and a couple of the men tied me up with wire while I was still in the water. They then hauled me up on deck and tied me to the mainmast. I had been captured by fishermen, and my new life as a POW was just beginning.

They gave me a cigarette and lit it for me. I was not a smoker, but I thought it best to go through the motions. As I sat there puffing on the cigarette and wondering at the sudden change in fortune my life had just taken, I was reminded of the movie I had watched in the wardroom the night before, *Two Years Before the Mast,* with Dana Andrews. The irony of it all made me laugh, and with that the fishermen decided maybe I wasn't all that bad. They loosened one of my arms and brought me up a beer from below. They also brought up all the women and children from below decks to view the new addition. We soon put in at one of the islands to spend the afternoon. I guess they were worried about air attacks and wanted to avoid any aircraft that might be looking for me. I saw my back-seater, Duffy Hutton, at the other end of the beach. He gave me a thumbs-up that he was okay, but it would be several years before I saw him again.

That evening we were blindfolded and then taken to the mainland, where we were greeted by an angry crowd of North Vietnamese. As we stepped from the boat, they beat on us with sticks and made a big ruckus, but we were soon put in the back of a car and set out on a circuitous route to our final destination of Hanoi. Somewhere along the way we stopped for our initial interrogation at an army facility and were photographed with the local gentry. A NVN army officer asked a lot of questions, and I stuck to name, rank, and serial number, but it became obvious this was not going to be easy. He kept reaching across the table to hit me in the head, and a few times he directed a guard standing behind me to hit me with the rifle butt. I took a pretty good pounding before they put us back in the car to continue our journey.

It was early in the morning when we finally arrived at what came to be known as the Hanoi Hilton. The prison, called Hoa Loa by the Vietnamese, was built by the French and served as the main city jail in Hanoi. I ended up in a cell in a section we called Heartbreak Hotel. It had seven small two-man cells and a washroom, and it was where almost all new arrivals spent their first days or weeks. I was taken out for interrogation every day, but there wasn't any rough treatment. After a couple of days, I heard someone calling me during the quiet time in the afternoon when most of the camp took a siesta. I got up on a bed and peered over the transom to see Ray Merritt, an air force major, in the cell directly across the hall from me. I gave Ray my specifics, and he, in turn, oriented me on what was going on and what I could expect. He told me I was the thirty-ninth American captured alive in North Vietnam.

I think I spent about ten days in Heartbreak before, one night, I was blindfolded and loaded on a truck for transfer to another camp on the south side of Hanoi. "The Zoo," as it was called, had been a movie or filming studio during its better days, and now it was being converted to a POW camp. The buildings were all brick, and small rooms or cells were being built in each of the seven major buildings. I was the first resident of room three of "The Stable." Other buildings had names like "The Pool House," "The Barracks," and "The Gate House." We called it the Zoo because it seemed to be the only place in the world where the people were behind bars, and the animals were running loose.

My broken arm caused me a lot of concern. It didn't hurt that much, but there was a huge, dark red swelling that had started at my shoulder and slowly worked itself down my arm. I assume it was pooled blood from internal bleeding, but it sure looked weird. With time, it slowly dissipated and went away.

The discipline in camp was not too bad as yet. The windows in the rooms had been either bricked in or covered with straw screens, but up to a point, we could talk between rooms. One day I was looking through a peephole in my window screen and saw my neighbor, Tom Barrett, coming back from an interrogation, or quiz as we called them. His arms were tied tightly behind his back, and he'd obviously been knocked around some. This was my first indication that maybe this incarceration was going to be a challenge.

At about this time one of the air force guys, anticipating that communications might become a problem, introduced us to the "prisoners' code." This code, which could be tapped on walls or water lines or whatever, was to become a literal lifesaver in the years to come. Supposedly, it had been around for hundreds of years and used by prisoners in jails whenever communications were restricted. It could be visualized as a simple five-by-five matrix with the letter A being tapped as 1-1, B as 1-2, E 1-5, F 2-1, etc. As the matrix limits us to twenty-five characters, we made C and K the same letter. Little did I realize that this simple code would soon become almost my sole method of communicating with my friends, and we would all become as proficient with its use as I am today with a computer.

On the first of December, twelve of us were blindfolded, bundled up, and put on a bus for a two-hour trip to a camp about thirty miles west of Hanoi. This camp had been built by the French and seemed to be remotely situated out in the middle of nowhere. There was no electrical power, no running water, no nothing. We were back to basics, kerosene lanterns and drawing water from a well. We called this camp Briar Patch. There were six buildings with four double rooms in each building. Leg irons were built into most of the beds. Each of the buildings was surrounded by a ten-foot high wall. Meals were brought to us twice a day, and we washed the dishes after each meal in stone basins outside each room. Baths were once or twice a week in a common bathing area next to the camp's only well. We soon had pretty good communications between the buildings by using a "mailbox" in the bath area. We would write notes to each other and leave them in a hidden spot at the bath.

I was the SRO (senior ranking officer) for most of my time at the Briar Patch, which meant I was responsible for dictating the resistance posture of all the POWs in response to the policies and dictates of the V. Not long after we got to Briar Patch, the V put the pressure on us to complete a "Blue Book Biography" on ourselves. It was an eight-to-ten page detailed questionnaire of who we were, where we came from, specifics on our family, etc. This was clearly far in excess of the name, rank, and serial number info permitted by the Geneva Convention, and I told everyone to resist filling it out.

Although most of the time the V chose to ignore the POW command structure, they knew it was there, and when they undertook a camp-wide program like the Blue Books, they'd usually start with the SRO. Their plan was obviously to start with the SRO, and once he had submitted, the rest of the camp would fall in line. As a result, I spent about two months in leg chains. My legs were tightly chained together at the ankles and to the bed. I was released once a week to take my toilet bucket outside for emptying and to take a walk up the hill for a quiz to see if I was ready to fill out the Blue Book yet. I finally did, but after two months my ankles were rubbed raw and bleeding, and I didn't seem to have another option. I was also developing what I think was impetigo on my lower body from not bathing.

I filled out the book, but most of the info I provided was bogus. This made it difficult in later years when they questioned me about my Aunt Mabel in Chicago, etc. Once you tell a lie, you've got to remember it and stick with it. All the other POWs were subjected to the same ordeal, and some of them went through the sitting-up endurance test. They sat on a stool twenty-four hours a day with a guard standing by. If they fell asleep or fell off the stool, the guard would jar them back to reality with his rifle butt. Some of them did this for three or four days.

After eating our evening meal we had to sit in the dark until the guard came to let us out to wash the dishes. Our dishes were enameled metal dishes that I'd place across the room on the other bunk after I'd finished eating. As soon as I'd put them down, the roaches would attack the crumbs, and the dishes would rattle like crazy as these monster roaches would fight each other for the remains. When the guard came and opened the door, I'd have to pick those dishes up with all the roaches to take them outside. The roaches would scramble to get away and some would run up my arms. After awhile I got a little smarter, and I tied off my sleeves at the wrist so the roaches couldn't get to me so easily.

One night I was awakened by my neighbor, Bill Tschudy. He was yelling and throwing things around in his room. In the morning I asked him what all the ruckus had been about. Life was primitive at Briar

Patch, and we didn't get to shave very often, maybe once a month, and baths were once a week or so. Bill had been lying on his back asleep when he was awakened by something on his chest. He looked down, and there was a rat standing on his chest eating the soup drippings off his beard. Needless to say, he went ballistic.

One day a guard snuck up on me, opened the shutter, and accused me of tapping on the wall. I hadn't been tapping, not then at any rate, but what did that matter? No one ever said this was a democracy. I was taken to a quiz, and the camp commander sentenced me to three months in "the hole." The hole was a bomb shelter about two feet deep that had been dug out beneath a bunk in each of the cells. When serving out a sentence in the hole, you would take your toilet bucket with you to serve as a stool, and you would spend your entire time, day and night, in "the hole." You were normally handcuffed, usually in back, so this wasn't a pleasant existence. Shortly after I'd started my sentence, I heard my neighbor George McKnight tapping a message to me. George was also in the hole. He'd been there a week or so. He tapped over to me, "Welcome to the UMW" (United Mine Workers).

One day, after I'd been down there for a week or so, my toilet bowl was emptied by Ralph Gaither. Ralph was one of the few POWs that had been shot down as an ensign. If you ever find yourself in a predicament like this, and I surely hope you never do, look around and surround yourself with young people. The junior officers are the ones with the most ingenuity, innovation, and aggressiveness. Older people tend to roll with the punches and devise a strategy for survival, while the younger people tend to want to fight it every inch of the way. The problem with being over-aggressive is that you can get hurt doing that, but it makes life and your everyday survival a lot more interesting.

Anyway, after Ralph had returned my empty bowl to me, he tapped over to me to check the bowl for "a present." What I found was a little piece of wire, maybe an inch and a half long, bent in a couple of odd angles. Ralph told me this was a "pick," and I could use it to open the handcuffs. I worked at it for a week, maneuvering that little pick at all angles trying to trip the lock. Working behind my back made it difficult, as well as the fact that the guards always squeezed the cuffs as tight as they could when putting them on. After awhile, my hands would swell as the circulation was cut off.

One day, while I was struggling with the cuffs, they suddenly sprang open! I'd done it—I'd actually opened the cuffs with that little piece of bent wire. Incredible. I closed the cuffs again and tried the pick again. After a short while, it worked. I'd opened the cuffs again. I'd discovered the secret of the cuffs and what a godsend it was. After that, I was usually out of my cuffs all but a couple of hours a day. If the guard did sneak up on me and open the shutter to check on me, I was under the bunk, and he couldn't see me too well down there anyway. One day I almost did get caught, though, and that would have been a disaster.

I was at my window looking through a peephole in the shutter when I saw the camp commander coming my way with a visitor. The visitor looked like a high-ranking Chinese army officer. I quickly got back in the hole and started putting my cuffs back on at the same time the guard was unlocking my door. For some reason I was having trouble getting the cuffs to close when suddenly the door swung open, and the camp commander was standing there motioning for me to come out. I couldn't—I didn't have the cuffs on! Finally, I got the cuffs to engage, but I didn't dare close them all the way because they clicked noisily as the teeth passed through the locking mechanism. I slowly crawled out of the hole, coughing and scraping my knees on the floor to make as much noise as I could as I slowly clicked the cuffs together. Finally, I stood up with the cuffs closed, and the camp commander proudly showed off one of his captured "Yankee Air Pirates" to the visiting dignitary. I don't think my pulse rate got back to normal for an hour.

During this time, the spring and summer of 1966, we were somewhat aware of the political debates going on around the world regarding the political correctness of the American involvement in Vietnam. I said there was no electrical power at Briar Patch, but this was not exactly true. Twice a day they fired up an electrical generator so we could listen to the "news" on Radio Hanoi. Every cell had a speaker, and for the entire seven and a half years I was in NVN we had to sit down, be quiet, and listen to Hanoi Hannah's propaganda broadcast to American servicemen in VN twice a day.

One of the most vociferous opponents to American Vietnam policy was the noted British philosopher, Bertrand Russell. He thought it to be totally wrong and those who waged the war should be tried as war criminals. He really pushed his thesis that the American POWs were war criminals and should be tried by an international tribunal for their crimes. The NVN latched onto his sentiments with a vengeance.

On the sixth of July, twelve of us from Briar Patch were blindfolded and loaded up in the back of a truck. There were only a couple of guards with us so we were able to do a lot of whispering among ourselves and sneak a look beneath our blindfolds now and then at our neighbors with whom we'd been communicating for months and had never actually seen. We speculated as to where we were going, and the consensus was that we were going to a war crimes trial of some sort. Little did we know what they had in mind.

The truck took us to Hanoi where we were joined by another forty of our mates from camps there. Although this made a total of fifty-two of us, the V had previously stenciled numbers on our prison shirts that were in the hundreds. I think my number was 302. We were lined up in a column of twos with guards and fixed bayonets on either side of us. We were then led through the streets of downtown Hanoi through a crowd of thousands of shouting, screaming, and very angry Vietnamese. There were "agitators" with battery-powered megaphones working the crowd. Soon, the parade turned into a feeding frenzy, and we were the food.

The crowd pushed past the guards to hit us with fists, shoes, and anything else they could find. The guards removed the bayonets from their rifles for fear of hurting someone in the melee. The women were the worst—they used their wooden-heeled shoes as hammers, and those things really hurt. The parade probably took an hour until we reached the sanctuary of a fenced athletic stadium. As I looked around at our group, almost everyone was bleeding from cuts on their faces and arms, and we all realized that we were very lucky to have escaped what could easily have become a disastrous event. Later in the evening, we trucked back to Briar Patch to end a very momentous day.

As bad and as painful as it was, the Hanoi March did accomplish some good for us. The V had overplayed their hand. Among the tens of thousands of spectators at the march were numerous foreign journalists and photographers who dutifully reported the event to the world press. In most quarters, it was met with loud indignation. President Lyndon Johnson took the opportunity to inform the NVN government in the strongest terms that if any harm befell the American POWs the retaliation would be swift and it would be forceful. Whatever he said, it worked. We never heard the threat of war crimes tribunals again.

The other thing to our benefit was that pictures of many of us, some of whom were still listed as MIA, were published all over the world. From that day forward, no one could question whether Jim Bell was still among the living. Ralph Gaither and I were the last two POWs in the parade, and we were clearly identified as participants.

During the summer and fall of 1966, my health went steadily downhill as I suffered from diarrhea that never went away. The food—green soup and rice—was not good, but what I could force down went through me like gangbusters. I'd obviously lost a lot of weight, and I was not looking forward to another winter at Briar Patch. It does indeed get cold in Vietnam in the winter—I think it got down into the low forties at night, and two cotton blankets and a low-calorie diet just weren't enough. Many nights, I'd just lie there and shiver all night. My condition had not escaped the attention of the V, for in October, I was loaded up one night, and back to Hanoi and into the Zoo I went. I ended up, still solo, in a remote room at a back corner of the former theater building.

I was given warm milk and liver with my meals for a couple of weeks; obviously, my condition had deteriorated to the point that a boost in my diet was necessary. As it turned out, I spent the next year in that remote room, separated from the rest of the camp so there was no communication, no interaction at all with any other American. The days all seemed to be forty-eight hours long. The worst thing about it was that the interrogation building was about ten feet from my window. I couldn't see anything, but I heard the cries of anguish and pain every day as POWs were forced to do things, write things, say things that they did not believe or want to do.

November 1967 was another landmark day in my VN tour. By that time I'd been a POW for over two years, all of it in solitary confinement and much of that time out of contact with my fellow Americans. Late in the afternoon, a guard opened the door and gave me the signal to "roll up." I was being moved again. Five minutes later, he opened the door to room seven in the Pool Hall and in I went. I had a roommate! Mike Lane was an air force first lieutenant F-4 back-seater, who had been captured in December 1966. Unbelievable.

My news of the outside world was going to be updated by a full year—a quantum leap—and I was going to have someone to talk to. And talk we did as he told me the news from the States, how the war was going, who'd won the World Series and the Army-Navy game. I couldn't believe my good fortune. We talked, and we talked, and we talked. Suddenly, there was the sound of the wake-up gong that went off at 5:30 every morning. It was time to get up, and we hadn't even gone to bed. We'd talked all through the night!

In the weeks to come Mike brought me up-to-date on all the happenings in the world that he could recall, and we tried to entertain each other with tales of our youth, college, the military, and anything else that came to mind. On 7 December, I asked Mike what he'd been doing on Pearl Harbor Day. He replied, "I don't know. I was only about ten days old!" Somehow, I'd never thought of Mike being younger than me.

After three or four months, though, the inevitable day came when the guard opened the door giving the "roll 'em up" sign. I guess I should explain roll 'em up. We slept on a straw mat on the wooden (usually) beds. When we moved, we rolled up all our belongings in the straw mat and off we went. In this case, my move was to the other side of the same building with a new roommate—Ray Vohden.

Ray had been an A-4 pilot shot down in April of 1965, POW number 4 in terms of longevity. After his ejection he'd landed in a pile of rocks in a high wind and ended up with a badly broken leg. He had broken the fibula, the smaller bone in the lower leg, in several places, and after a couple of operations there was a two- or three-inch piece of bone missing. Ray was one of the few prisoners that actually did receive some medical treatment in Hanoi. Most of us with broken arms, ribs, dislocations, and such were not treated. Broken legs were treated within their very limited capabilities and resources. By the time I moved in with him, Ray had been a POW for over three years, but his leg injury still seeped all the time.

Ray was on crutches and pretty much incapacitated. He spent most of the day sitting or lying on his bed. Occasionally, every three or four months, he'd make a trip to the hospital for an X-ray or examination of the leg. He'd always be blindfolded for the entire trip, and it would always be at night. Every so often, I meet someone who has a leg injury and is struggling with crutches for the first time. They always comment on the difficulty of negotiating stairs on crutches. Ray used to have to go up and down stairs at the hospital blindfolded, always in deadly fear of falling and further injuring his festering leg.

One day the V came by with a pack of playing cards. They were terrible cards from China. They were printed on a cheap grade of paper or cardboard that absorbed moisture readily in the summertime when we sweltered in our windowless rooms. After a few days of playing solitaire and double solitaire and a few other no-brainer card games that we could come up with, Ray started thinking of how we could play bridge. Ray had been an accomplished contract bridge player in his other life, and he was consumed with the thought that there were two people in our room with a deck of cards, and two more people with a deck of cards in the next room; there just had to be a way to put it all together and have a four-person bridge game.

Communicating was not a problem; we were all very proficient in expressing ourselves through the wall by this time, but devising a system for distributing the cards and playing the hands so we'd be exactly duplicating the process in both rooms was a challenge. Ray and I worked on the problem for several weeks. As it eventually evolved, Ray devised a procedure for playing the hands that was workable, and I came up with the system for shuffling and dealing the cards that would distribute four identical hands in the two rooms. We soon had our neighbors involved in our bridge games, and we played every night and frequently in the afternoon as well.

It was a godsend for Ray. Not only was he back in his favorite pastime of bridge playing, but it was a great time killer when he sorely needed a diversion to just lying on his bed. I'd sit at the foot of his bed with my back to the wall holding the cards in one hand with the other behind my back tapping out the play of the cards. We never got caught, and soon we had most of the guys in other rooms in the building playing bridge through the wall with their neighbors. A few times, on a quiet Sunday afternoon, we even tried contract bridge tournaments where we had all ten rooms in the building playing five identical hands at the same time. This was very involved, though, and it only took one miscommunication to put the whole tournament in disarray so we didn't try that too often.

The year 1969 became a momentous time for us at the Zoo, when we all became involved in an escape attempt that fell short of its goal. John Dramesi and Ed Atterbury were roommates in an area we called "The Annex," a prison area adjacent to our camp but outside the peripheral wall surrounding it. Dramesi and Atterbury had been planning an escape for months and had been squirreling away some items they could use like coolie hats and other clothing they had somehow acquired.

One stormy night in May in the middle of a heavy thunderstorm, the power went out, and they decided, "now is the time." Out they went and over the wall to a very uncertain fate. Their plan was to get to the Red River which flows through Hanoi, contrive some sort of flotation support with which they could float down the river, and eventually make it to the Gulf. They started out okay, but it didn't take long to realize the futility of their effort. By mid-morning the next day they had gotten probably ten miles from camp and had secreted themselves in some shrubbery in a large field. After awhile they heard some voices and shouting and looked out to see hundreds of V coming across the field in a line, each with a stick, prodding every bush and potential hiding place as they came. There just wasn't a chance, and they were soon discovered and returned to camp.

They were placed in separate small rooms in the auditorium, and the interrogations and beatings began. It went on for days, and we could all hear it when we were outside going to quizzes or taking toilet buckets to the latrine. Eventually, it ended, but not before Ed Atterbury was dead. Somehow in that process, the V got the idea there was a command structure in the Zoo that included the Annex, and that our leadership had masterminded the escape. With that premise, they initiated a purge in the camp that attempted to unearth the extent of the command structure, what our policies were, and how we were able to communicate that throughout the camp and to the Annex.

They gave us far more credit for our organizational abilities than we actually had, but that didn't help us as the purge went on. Their methods were brutal as they went right down the line in forcing information from the senior POWs. Many people were subjected to beatings with fan belts which quickly tore up the skin and would turn your backside into a bloody pulp. It all stopped as quickly as it had begun when Ho Chi Minh died on 2 September. Overnight, the policies seemed to change towards leniency.

In June of 1970 most of us at the Zoo were moved to a newly constructed camp west of Hanoi called Camp Faith. It had four compounds, each separated by a high wall, and each compound holding eighty to one hundred POWs. This was a big move for most of us, since it meant meeting and living with more people than we'd even seen up to that point. The first five years in Hanoi I'd been allowed to see and openly talk with five other Americans. Now, at Faith, I was living with six other guys, and every day at exercise time I mingled with another fifty or sixty out in the yard. It was a wonderful change for most of us, but it was soon going to get even better.

On the night of 20 November 1970, after we'd been at Faith only a few months, we were awakened in the middle of the night by a lot of anti-aircraft guns and aircraft noise. Within the next few days, we were all loaded up in trucks and moved back to the "Hilton," only this time to the big rooms. Initially, things were pretty crowded with seventy or eighty people in a room, but within a few weeks other rooms were emptied of SVN prisoners, and we were moved in. Eventually, we occupied eight rooms in the same compound with forty or so POWs in a room. This was where most of us were to spend the remaining two and a half years of captivity, and it was this camp, the Hanoi Hilton, which was to receive the most notoriety after the war. Called Hoa Loa, the Hilton had been the main Hanoi jail before the war.

It took us several months to piece together what had happened at Faith in November. I think we eventually got the big picture by combining inputs from new shoot-downs, as well as tidbits from guards and interrogators. We also had contact most of the time with SVN and Thai pilots who had been captured in NVN and were kept in the same camps as us. The SVN pilot, whom we called Max, spoke excellent English, and he frequently passed on bits of news he'd gotten from the guards.

The event of 20 November, which had caused the V to abandon their newly constructed camp Faith, was, of course, the infamous raid on Son Tay. This raid was intended to liberate some POWs who were thought to be confined at Son Tay. Unfortunately, they had been moved several months before that, but Son Tay was only fifteen miles or so from Faith so we were almost front row spectators at what could have been a major coup of the war. Unfortunately, our intelligence was bad or outdated, and the rescuers came up empty-handed, but in the long run it was a major morale booster for us. It was a daring demonstration by our country that we had not been forgotten, and it forced the V to consolidate us all in Hanoi, most of us at the Hilton. Life then became a lot more bearable as we were able to interact with forty or fifty POWs every day.

It was about this time, while still at Faith, almost five years to the day after my capture, that I got my first letter from home. I had started writing letters home—short, six-line, heavily censored—about a year earlier. I also started getting packages from home with foodstuffs and vitamins in early 1970. In one package, I got some pictures of my children. It was one of the few times I really lost it while I was a POW. I'm not sure I really recognized any of them after so many years. My son Tom I did recognize, of course—he'd only gotten a lot bigger. But Matt and Ann were strangers. And there was nothing to indicate where they were living or what was going on with their lives. And it would be several more years before most of those questions were answered.

Our life at the Hilton soon settled down to a routine of bridge, classes, outdoor time with a bath almost every day, and communicating with the other rooms in camp and with our senior officers who were kept separate in smaller rooms adjacent to our living area. For the first time since I'd been a POW, we were being allowed, at least tacitly, to organize our room and the entire camp with our military command structure. Every room had a room commander, executive officer, entertainment director, and an administrative officer responsible for memorizing and promulgating to everyone the camp policies dictated by our leaders.

In the evenings we had classes on any subject someone thought he knew something about—languages, history, aerodynamics, real estate, the stock market. One of our crew had been a butcher in another life, and we sat through several evenings learning how to cut up a steer. The favorite for everyone, though, was movie night. Thinking back on it,

I'm still amazed at the retention of some people of movies they'd seen three or four or more years earlier; the leading actors, the story line, and then a presentation format that would keep us entertained for an hour or more. *Gone With the Wind* was a two-nighter and was presented by a team of two or three who collaborated in putting it all together so it made sense. One of the best at this was John McCain. He had an extensive "library" of movies he could retell at the drop of a hat.

In March of 1971, thirty-six of us were loaded up one night and moved to a camp called Skid Row. We lived alone most of our time there in thirty-six small cells that extended eighteen in the front and eighteen in the back of one long building. We were adjacent to a large camp of SVN POWs, but we never actually communicated with them, only exchanged smiles and waves occasionally. Although we were in separate rooms, we could communicate easily among ourselves most of the time, talking openly to our neighbors on either side and tapping on the wall to the rooms in back of us.

The distinguishing feature of Skid Row that I remember was the water. We had one well in front of the building that we used for bathing and for drinking water. Most of the time the water we drew from the well was more mud than water. Bathing in it was a joke. The water was boiled before we drank it, but I still don't know how we got away with using it for cooking and drinking.

The other thing I remember is our taunting the guards about "Our Moon." I think we initially got word of Apollo 7 and landing men on the moon from our guards through Max. Max, actually named Dat, was a South Vietnamese pilot, who was in the camp with us. The news was confirmed when someone got a letter from home with an Apollo 7 stamp on the envelope. That news was so unbelievable we couldn't really comprehend it, but as incomprehensible as it was to us, imagine what must have been going through the minds of our Vietnamese guards.

Sometimes at night, when we'd be standing up at our doors talking to our neighbors and there'd be a big full moon up there, we'd hear a guard coming, and we'd all start saluting the moon. The guard would give us a quizzical look, wondering, *What are you guys doing?* We'd point at the moon and say, "That's our moon; that belongs to the USA." The guards would skulk away shaking their heads.

In the fall of 1972 I finally got a letter from my parents informing me that I'd been divorced for four years. As disheartening as that was to me, I also realized the affect it had on my fellow POWs. You sit there for years isolated from the rest of the world realizing initially that those very coveted orders to Empire Test School had gone down the drain, then you start lamenting the impact of the long absence on your career, and, finally, you come to the realization that all you have left is your family and their support that will always be there. Then you get a letter one day that says you don't even have that anymore, and your whole world comes apart. I was certainly not alone in meeting this challenge. The impact of the long separation was disastrous to many relationships that had been presumed as being very strong.

In October of 1972 we learned through Radio Hanoi that peace negotiations were finally close to fruition. Morale in the camp soared, and we hung on every word during the daily broadcasts to see what we could read between the lines. My friend, Art Burer, and I came up with the Bell-Burer Probability Number that measured the chances of us going home soon. We'd sit down after the news each morning and discuss the impacts of the news we'd just heard and then quantify it with a probability number. Art played the part of the pessimist, and I slanted my inputs to the optimistic side. The Bell-Burer Probability Number became an important ingredient of the daily news as it circulated between rooms every day.

Then in December the B-52s arrived over Hanoi, and we knew it was all but over. The Bell-Burer Probability Number soared to 95 percent! A couple of times, the bombs fell pretty close to us. They knocked plaster from the ceilings and shook down a lot of dirt, but we loved it all. We'd stand up at the windows, which were no longer blanked off, and yell and cheer like a bunch of kids. If only LBJ had had the fortitude to do this in 1967, it would have been a lot shorter war.

One night during a raid we were all standing on our beds rooting them on, when a very low-flying aircraft came directly over the camp. He couldn't have been over 200 feet high at 500 or 600 knots. We all dove for the floor, but he was a couple of miles on down the road by then. All we'd seen was a dark shape when it flew overhead, but our guess was it was an F-111. Whatever it was, he got our attention.

Evidently the 111s and the B-52s also got the attention of the V, for in January they returned to the negotiating table in earnest, and by the end of the month we heard that an agreement had actually been signed, and we soon would be returning home. A week or so later there was a big shuffle in camp as we were organized according to our POW longevity, which was our shoot-down date. A few days later we were issued new clothes, and we knew that release was imminent. On the 12th of February the first group to be released, of which I was one, was bussed to the airport where we were met by an American contingent and two C-141s.

How wonderful they looked! But we held our emotions in check until we were finally aboard and we got airborne. As the wheels retracted noisily and the flaps were raised, we realized that this was finally it. There would be no more delays, no more sitting in disbelief as the diplomats argued on the shape of the negotiating table or who was to sit around it. It was finally over, and we were on our way home.

A few days later I was reunited with my parents at the naval hospital in Bethesda, and the transition to my new life began. Shortly after that I flew to California to be reunited with my children at a beach house of friends in Santa Cruz. As difficult as it was for me to try and bridge the gaps that had developed during the years, I understood that it was infinitely more difficult for them. I had been gone for eight years during the most formative period of their lives, and no one had told them that they had a dad out there somewhere who would be coming home someday. It was a confusing time that would take some of them years to resolve in their minds.

In many ways this had been as difficult a period for our country as it had been for us, but we learned to accept what we had to and work at changing those things that we could. As a wise man once said, "Life goes on," and as I write this over twenty years later in 1996, that period in my life is a dim memory. I am probably reminded of some aspect of it almost every day, but it is no longer a cancer threatening to consume me. It was not a pleasant experience, but I know I learned a lot from it, not the least of which I learned a lot about myself. My hope is that none of you should ever be subjected to a similar existence.

→ 21 ←

Reunions

May 2003 Reunion of Vigilante Community in Sanford, Florida

Driving into Lake Mary in our compact rental car, I am amazed at how much the area has changed since our last visit to Central Florida some eight years ago. Where I-4 cuts across the Florida landscape, there are now huge hotels, sprawling but attractive housing developments, and new highways choked with cars. The sleepy town of Lake Mary has been swallowed up in the industrial invasion that has come to Central Florida since the arrival of the Walt Disney organization.

When we lived here in the 1960s, Walt Disney had not yet arrived. Instead, it was film star Roy Rogers who first purchased the palmetto-filled swampland southwest of Orlando. We joked about how a cowboy was going to fend off alligators to make a theme park "in the middle of nowhere." But Roy had the last laugh when a few years later, he sold out to Disney, and theme parks attracted more theme parks...and money.

We have come here to join a gathering of former members of the Vigilante community. The group that lived in Sanford during the Vietnam War and saw the changeover from a mission of "heavy attack" aviation to one of reconnaissance as the navy phased out its program of A-3Ds based here and brought in the sleek A-5s, later RA5-Cs.

We check into our hotel, about two miles away from the hotel housing the reunion. We like to save money, and by shopping through an Internet company we have been able to extend our stay in Florida by a day and pay less than we would have spent on two nights. After a rest, we drive over to the Marriott to register, and we find the lobby swarming with old Vigilante pilots, crewmen, enlisted squadron mates, and their wives. Everyone has aged some thirty-five to forty years since the days when the Viggies were a vibrant group of naval aviators. We only recognize about one out of five of the people we see. And not many people recognize us.

Thus begins a weekend of renewed acquaintances, hugs, storytelling, and a few tears. Some of the main players are absent. A former wing commander has recently died. One of the cutest Skippers' wives ever to grace a Sanford gathering is here in a wheelchair.

The next morning we drive through our former neighborhoods while making our way to the site of a new park where a Vigilante aircraft has been purchased and installed as tribute to the days when the navy was the center of activity for the area. As we turn into Pinecrest, where Jimmie and I lived among dozens of other fliers some thirty-five years earlier, we see evidence of the economic impact left when the air station moved from Sanford to Albany, Georgia in 1968. Many of the houses now are in need of paint and yards are not so manicured as when we lived here.

We have difficulty identifying the house about a mile north of Pinecrest where Jim lived with his first wife. The Spanish moss still drapes from palms and branches of water oaks. "I think there was a big tree in the backyard where Tom used to climb," he says. Now there are big trees in every yard.

A new highway slices through the residential area, and many of the homes that existed in Ravena Park, my last home in Sanford, have been razed for the construction. Finally, however, we locate the corner where the official navy car pulled to the curb in front of my house that fateful morning in 1967. The house seems smaller now. The wall enclosing the patio has been partially removed. The neighborhood is a stranger to me. None of the people I knew live there now. At my request, after circling the block, Jim drives quickly away.

We join the reunion crowd for a ceremony dedicating a park in memory of the days when community life revolved around the Sanford Naval Air Station. The sun is ruthless as it bakes the large field which has now been transformed into a park. An RA5-C, bearing the name of George Kimmons, the recently deceased wing commander who was instrumental in raising funds for the project, stands proudly in the center of a circular walk. It is surrounded by benches dedicated by various squadrons and civic groups.

We manage to sneak into one of two tents offering shelter to local dignitaries in order to sit in the glaring sunshine through the hour-long dedication ceremony held adjacent to the plane. There are perhaps 1,000 people seated in front of the dais, listening to former POW Gerry Coffee speak about the glory days of the Vigilante. Later, we make our way to the new international airport, site of the former air station, where photos and other memorabilia are displayed. There is a reception with refreshments, but we are too busy hugging and greeting old squadron mates to partake of food. Afterward, Jim and I stop and have sandwiches for lunch near the site of the old Spencer's restaurant that once was a favorite of the naval community.

We make our way back to the Marriott in the evening for the reunion banquet, and again we see many old friends. There we spend time with Al Wattay, who was Jimmie Griffin's roommate on the *Kitty Hawk* and who packed his gear to ship home to me. Al, his wife Diane, and the Recknors, who introduced me to Jim Bell in 1973, are all seated with us at dinner, along with Duffy Hutton, Jim's back-seater, and his wife, Eileen. After dinner Diane Queen and her husband Ron, a RVAH-

13 bombardier-navigator on that fateful cruise who later became one of the first BNs to command a squadron, share a scrapbook with me. Included is a speech Ron made about Jimmie Griffin after Ron retired from the navy. After all these years they still praise him.

Meanwhile, Jim is having some special memories stirred as well. The next morning we go to the Sanford Museum to look over exhibits from the Sanford Naval Air Station days, and in a base newspaper from 1965 we find a large photo of Jim's son Tom, all decked out in costume as a shepherd in a nativity scene. Jim was already a prisoner when that picture was published in Sanfly.

During the afternoon we manage visits to two of my former neighbors, both of whom were very close friends when Jimmie and I and the children lived in Pinecrest. Although both couples were civilians, we had shared the death of JFK, our children had been playmates, we had gone to church together, and the women were like sisters to me. I can see that it would be easy to pick up again where we left off if I lived here now.

In the evening we join the reunion group for a boat cruise, which turns out to be a floating dinner on the St. John's River. Sitting with us are the son and daughter-in-law of Chaplain Leo McDonald, who not only gave the group spiritual support in the sixties, but kept us all smiling as he tooled around town in his Model-A. We were also joined by Colin Pemberton, another of Jim's back-seaters who had been with him when they had to bail out of an airplane over Sanford in 1964. We leave Sanford with a feeling of having closed a chapter in our lives that needed closing. We know we will never forget the bittersweet days we spent here or the friends we made, but we are ready now to move on with our lives.

June 2003—30th POW Reunion in San Diego

It has been thirty years and four months since Jim and the 590 other POWs stepped off the planes at Clark Air Force Base in the Philippines, heading back to their homes after anywhere from a few months to seven or eight years of incarceration in Vietnam. As we gather with the others in Southern California to mark this event, I note that the men, in speaking with one another, still refer to that time as "When I was in jail…" In other social situations, some of them are more vocal about their experiences than others, but in this group, nothing is held back. They speak freely about the discomforts, the torture, and the rocks and bugs in their food as easily as other people would chat about eating a meal at McDonald's.

We gather the first evening at the main reunion hotel, some ten miles away from where Jim and I are staying, and board buses for the Nixon Library for a reception and buffet dinner. We wander through the crowd in the garden, our plates and drinks precariously balanced in one hand while we greet dozens of the other former prisoners and their wives.

Some twenty-five years earlier, when for the first time I went with Jim to a POW reunion, I had chided him for not introducing me to the others who came up to him to embrace and exchange stories. But through a half dozen or so of these gatherings, I have come to realize that what he said then at the hotel in San Antonio may still be true, "Dora, I just don't recognize them." At that time it was difficult for him to put names to faces, because when they left Vietnam they had all been emaciated and worn scraggly beards and two years later were beginning to flesh out and look "normal." Now, they all have aged and changed in other ways, but though they are wearing nametags this time, I am quick to put out my hand and introduce myself to anyone who pauses near Jim or who is wearing a nametag that I realize I should recognize.

Again, Jim seeks out the men with whom he shares special memories of Hanoi, and the next morning, during the business meeting, I spend time visiting with my own special friend, Peggy Mullen. Peggy worked with me in real estate in the Washington area in the seventies and eighties, and she found herself in a particularly difficult situation when her husband suffered a stroke at age forty-three. Her life over the next twenty years was not unlike what we went through as POW wives. She and I had shared many lunches over the years, and I had been delighted when, after her husband's death, she married Dick Mullen.

She and Dick met in San Diego at a church workshop about a year after his wife Jean had died. On learning he had been a POW when being introduced to him in San Diego, Peggy had asked Dick whether he knew Jim Bell. She said he grinned and replied, "Well, I know him pretty well. We were chained together for three weeks in Hanoi!" When they realized they had mutual friends, the relationship took off and they were married a couple of years later.

When the reunion's business meeting adjourns, the Mullens and Duffy and Eileen Hutton join us for a jaunt to Newport Beach where we spend the afternoon over a leisurely lunch. We had all been together at the Mullens' wedding in San Diego, when their children presented them with a tandem bicycle. Now, we listen with pleasure as they tell us about their recent biking vacation through Germany. We are making some new, good memories!

The reunion concludes with a banquet at the main hotel, and we gather first in the hotel garden. With so many former POW's and their families, it is difficult to find specific people. But I have to smile as I listen to them again recounting those grim days when someone awoke to find a rat nibbling on the food left in his beard, when one of them ate a roach that floated in his soup—"I heard it crunch!" These men have been to hell and back, and yet they still can laugh about it.

Wandering among the crowd is a young woman who asks questions about her father who died in Vietnam. "I know so little," she says. A few people who remember her father tell her what they recall.

At the banquet we sit with Red McDaniel, another Alexandria resident, and his family. The McDaniels have brought eighteen family members to the reunion. "I got a really good airline rate...and I figure I won't ever have a chance to bring them to another one. I wanted them to see all these guys," Red says. Red was on a bombing mission over Hanoi when Jimmie Griffin was shot down on May 19, 1967. Jimmie was to do the reconnaissance for Red's flight. Both of them ended up as POWs following that event, though Red went down in the mountains west of the city and was not captured until the next day. Jimmie, my husband, died two days later in a small hospital in Hanoi. Jim Bell had been a prisoner for eighteen months at that time. I am in the presence of heroes here, and I still have strong memories of that other hero as well. I have been fortunate to be married to two of them.

Red's son, called Chip, seated on my right, tells me he is on active duty now, stationed in Bharain, but he has managed to come home on leave to attend the reunion with his father. Chip's job in Bharain involves cataloging the historical artifacts there, safeguarding history. His is another heroic task.

We leave the reunion again with a sense of closure. Another gathering is planned next year in Charleston, South Carolina. It seems important now for the men to get together as often as they can. They are growing older, and some are dying. And this time, although many of them are still suffering with the effects of wounds from ejecting from their aircraft in Vietnam or from the incarceration, some of them are dying of "old age."

→ 22 ←

Nightmares

The night is quiet, and only a light wind outside competes with the occasional drone of a plane landing late at Reagan National Airport, just six miles from our house in Alexandria. I put aside the travel book on Singapore and Malaysia that I have been studying in preparation for our trip to Southeast Asia and touch the heat-sensitive lamp on my bedside table to extinguish the light.

Sleep does not always come easily for me, especially since we have been making plans to travel to Vietnam. I am excited, but a bit apprehensive. I close my eyes and immediately visions of Asians on bicycles fill my thoughts. While we have been told that we are unlikely to encounter any hostility from the Vietnamese people during our visit, I fret over the possibility that we might be upset by something or someone we see there. Glyn Carol told me that during her 1994 trip to Vietnam, she sometimes was very upset. She was most bothered when she toured the War Museum in Hanoi, seeing on display rows of flight helmets taken from captured and dead American flyers. The scene stirred up visions of horror for her.

I pull the duvet higher around my shoulders to get warm and slowly sink into dreams of the beautiful countryside of Vietnam. But my peaceful dreams end as I am suddenly jarred awake. Jim, sleeping beside me, is having a dream of his own, a dream that is not so tranquil.

Through the twenty-nine years we have been married, I have come to expect his occasional nightmares. Jim jerks a bit, and sometimes he cries out in his sleep, "Stop! Stop that, you son of..!" This time he seems to be dreaming of a physical encounter with Vietnamese guards. His hands are flailing about, and his fist hits the headboard, and I slide further toward my side of our king-size bed. Soon he is peacefully snoozing away again. I know that tomorrow, when I question him about the dream, he will, as always, insist that he doesn't recall any bad dreams. I wonder how many former POWs still have dreams and nightmares about the days, weeks, months, and years they suffered at the hands of their captors. And what hidden emotions does Jim still harbor about the torture he experienced during those years?

When these dreams return for him, I lie here listening, and sometimes, I am rewarded with a few words as he talks in his sleep. But always, I am reminded of that frail, shy fellow that called me from the Officer's Club in 1973 and told his story about the guy in the ill-fitting bargain suit and then slyly glanced around at his listeners to see how the story was being received.

I also remember the first time he danced with me. We were at a supper club that offered live music with meals, and when the music started, we each looked helplessly at one another, thinking, "I'm not sure I remember how to dance." But when the music became spirited I urged him onto the dance floor, insisting, "Jim, they don't really dance like they used to. I think we can just do our own thing." And to the tune of "Bad, Bad Leroy Brown" all his shyness vanished, and he quickly came up with some moves that put him at ease. It still is his favorite song.

The bad dream is over. He is snoring again. All is well.

Having breakfast at Hanoi Hilton Opera Hotel in 2003
(L. to R., seated) Vi Peterson and Dora Bell.
Standing: Dick Mullen, Peggy Mullen, "Pete" Peterson and Jim Bell.

Plaque on a corner of Lei Truc Steet in Hanoi commemorating American planes shot down on May 19 1967, depicting the RA5-C piloted on that day by Jimmie Griffin and his bombadier-navigaor Jack Walters.

Jim and Dora with Vietnamese greeter in Hanoi restaurant 2003.

Jim and Dora Bell with Peggy Mullen with their guide on boat in Halong Bay where Jim and Duffy Hutton landed after their RA5C was shot down on October 16, 1965.

Duffy Hutton and Jim Bell at the Smithsonian Institution POW exhibit 2004.

Dora and Jim on their 30th wedding anniversary in Alexandria, Virginia August 2004.

Art Burer who was captured in Vietnam in March,1966 with Jim Bell preparing to attend Air Force 560th Training Squadron Dining-In which annually honors Vietnam POWOs in San Antonio in 2005.

→ 23 ←

Vietnam Visit 2003

"Is this a pleasure trip?" a friend asks me on this October afternoon when I mention that we are planning to travel to Vietnam next week. Many people have wondered why we would want to visit that country, so far away in Asia, after the painful memories with which both Jim and I have dealt for thirty-five or more years.

Colorful leaves blow past the window as I take my time answering, because I am not ready to bare my soul to everyone about the reasons we are going to Vietnam. It has taken us a long time to prepare for the journey we are about to undertake. We have studied maps and books and tried to come to grips with emotions that are still not completely neutral.

"The trip is a sort of pilgrimage," I say and avoid explaining any more. For the journey is, indeed, a mission. I need closure after so many years. And Jim, who flew reconnaissance missions over Vietnam some thirty-eight years ago, wants to see the country on the ground, the country he could not see through the peepholes in his prison cells.

We have found an affordable airfare, and we are making plans to meet Dick and Peggy Mullen in the Malaysian capital of Kuala Lampur to make the trip to Hanoi together. Dick, whom Jim calls "Moon," shared shackles with Jim in Hoa Lo prison for three weeks in 1970, and he is on a similar mission. The Mullens will fly from Los Angeles by way of Taipei, and we will leave from Newark, stopping in Dubai, to meet them in Kuala Lampur.

In 1994 Glyn Carol and her fiancé visited Vietnam, and she has given us valuable insight about what we can expect. If the trip ahead is an uncertain challenge for me, I cannot imagine how she must have felt, visiting the place where her father died in 1967.

When she and Jeff made the trip, she met with the MIA office in Hanoi four times, and a team of State Department people assisted her in finding the sites she wanted to visit. They explained to her the procedures used in the repatriation of nine remains in 1974. And they reviewed information about live sightings of possible Americans left behind as reported through the past twenty years.

Glyn saw the place on Thuy Khue Street and Pham Chu Trinh Street where her father and Jack Walters were captured. And she learned that on the corner where the militia stood while shooting down their plane, Lei Truc Street, a plaque was erected telling about the event. She was shown film that included the recovery of wreckage of his aircraft from the lake in which it landed. She also sat through several propaganda films depicting the "pleasant life" of American POWs eating great food, playing basketball, volleyball, and guitar. There was a Christmas service, footage of Jane Fonda's visit, and scenes from the return of three POWs who came home early. How did my daughter keep her composure while viewing that film? I know I would not be so strong!

Then, the film included a scene of a prisoner whose profile looked like her Dad, struggling in the back seat of a jeep. "It could be Charles Plumb," she told me. Finally, there was the scene of a shadowy figure swathed in bandages in a darkened room, possibly a hospital room. She obtained a copy of that film and later showed it to me in her home in Palo Alto. Glyn told me she believes the obviously very ill person in that last film clip was her father just before he died. A practicing physician, she was able to see the autopsy reports on her Dad, and she seemed satisfied with the answers to her questions.

During her tour of Hanoi, she bravely visited the military hospital where Jimmie died, and she learned that he had been buried twice in Vietnam. First, he was interred at Van Diem Cemetery in Hanoi, where even local dignitaries are only allowed to remain for five years before being transferred to other locations. She was told that her father's remains were transferred in January of 1973 to Ba Huyen Cemetery in the nearby countryside. And, of course, he was again removed and brought home to Arlington Cemetery in March of 1974. In her quest for the full truth, she went to see both of them. It is not surprising that during her visit Glyn had dreams about her father's torture and about graves being dug.

As I review her notes, I decide that I am past the stage of curiosity that prompted her to seek out all those locations. Visiting the cemeteries was very important to her, but I prefer to think of Jimmie "at rest" in Arlington, and I decide not to go to the cemeteries during our visit. But there are other things that I would like to see, and so we prepare for the journey.

Paul Mather, who works in the Department of Defense POW and MIA office in Arlington, welcomes Jim Bell and I to his office and supplies us with maps and phone numbers that we will need when we visit Hanoi. As he points to the map to indicate locations of the various prison sites where Jim once lived, Paul reveals that his wife is a native of Vietnam.

He shows me where I will find the plaque marking the downing of Jim Griffin's plane in 1967, and he indicates the site of the Hanoi War Museum and the mausoleum where Ho Chi Minh's embalmed body is on display. Paul assures us that we are unlikely to experience any hostility from Vietnamese people we meet on the trip, and he tells us the American military detachment there will be available if we need further assistance.

We scan the newspaper for current temperatures in Hanoi, and we pack clothes for a warm climate. We also will be visiting Singapore on the trip, and that is very near the equator. A very long plane ride lies ahead for us, and for that reason we know that if we wait until we are older, we will never make this trip.

On the second day of November, having come by way of Kuala Lampur, we reach our goal, the city of Hanoi. Our plane lands at Hanoi Airport in a cloud of midday fog. Located some ten miles from the city, the airport has very few buildings around it. Instead, it is surrounded by small farms that are laid out with small patches of vegetables.

Our van driver repeatedly blares the horn as we make our way into the city through swarms of motorbikes. There are only a few small cars and trucks on the road, and they are competing for space on what appears to be the only major highway. There are no traffic signals, and I crane my neck to look for stop signs, but they also seem to be missing.

We see several primitive lean-tos, as well as many narrow three-story buildings in various stages of construction, and the air is heavy with dust. Some thirty years after the end of the Vietnam-American War, the city is still suffering. This country has been through two other wars, border disputes with China, since Jim and Moon left here in 1973, and Vietnam has experienced centuries of domination by other nations. Today, the country seems to be an infant in the world of free-market trade, and it appears to me that Vietnam has a long way to go to catch up with such places as Mexico, Puerto Rico, and Turkey!

We have arranged to stay in the Hanoi Hilton, the name the men gave to Hoa Lo prison during their long stay here. We had assumed the hotel would be located on the site of Hoa Lo. But the Hilton Hotel Corporation has chosen to locate their hotel, built some twenty-five years after the war's end, several blocks away alongside the Hanoi Opera House. For this reason, the hotel actually is named Hanoi Hilton Opera. On entering the lobby, we find it is much like any upscale hotel around the world today, and in this city it proves to be a welcome respite for us each time we return to it during our stay.

As soon as we are settled in our comfortable rooms, Jim decides to take a walk around the area. He spent more than seven years just a half mile away from here, but he never saw the sights that lay beyond his cell and the prison walls. Now, he is eager to see them. He is surprised when, just a few steps outside the hotel, he recognizes Pete Peterson, another ex-POW and former American ambassador to Vietnam. Pete and his wife Vi, who is of Vietnamese descent, now live in Australia, and Pete heads a charitable foundation that frequently brings him back to Vietnam. Although they are leaving the city in two days, they agree to meet us for breakfast in the hotel.

For dinner we get a recommendation from the hotel desk and then walk three blocks to the Emperor restaurant, literally risking our lives to get there. Crossing the street in Hanoi is like trying to walk across a major interstate highway! And the when we finish dinner we must face the possibility of death again, maneuvering across the paths of speeding motorbikes to return to the hotel.

Much of the northern perimeter of Hanoi borders West Lake, but there is also a beautiful small lake in the center of downtown Hanoi named Hoan Kiem Lake, often called Sword Lake. Knowing that much of the wreckage of Jim Griffin's RA5C landed in Hoan Kiem Lake, we ask our guide to take us there during our morning tour of the city. Thanh Trinh, a young man whose age I would guess to be about thirty, is sympathetic to our interests in seeing certain places since he has been guide to several other former POWs during their return visits to Hanoi.

Thanh (whose name is pronounced "Tynh") tells us that because his parents had conflicting opinions about the Hanoi government, they had separated after the war. Eventually, his father was sent to prison for his radical views, while his mother was employed by the government. As we speak, Thanh's mother is traveling in Europe, a trip she was awarded as a retirement bonus since she will soon retire from her job.

Thanh asks us about other locations around the city that are of particular interest to us. He knows we want to see the prisons, and Jim and Moon ask if they can see where the famous Hanoi March took place in July of 1966. We are driven to Nguyen Thai Hoc Street, where the march is believed to have originated, and to the stadium where the march ended. Jim tells Thanh that he was in one of the last rows of blindfolded prisoners who were paraded before the rabid crowd and that he was hit with sticks and pelted with women's wooden shoes.

"One angry man broke out of the bystanders and punched me in the nose, saying 'Take that, you American millionaire son-of-a-bitch!' It was painful, but I was a little flattered," Jim recalls. "No one ever called me a millionaire before."

"Oh, I'm sor-ree," the guide politely commiserates.

"Hey, it was wartime. That's what people do in wars," Jim replies. But I know that night will live forever in Jim's bad dreams.

Thanh takes us along the edge of West Lake, explaining that this is the place where John McCain's plane went down in the fall of 1967. Then, as we continue past Sword Lake, he tells us the traditional story of this beautiful little lake. It is said that in the fifteenth century, the emperor was given a magic sword by Heaven, and he used the sword to drive the Chinese out of Vietnam. Then, sometime later, the emperor was out boating in the little lake, and he saw a giant tortoise swimming by. Suddenly, the tortoise grabbed the sword, dived into the lake, and was never seen again. So, since that time, the lake has been known as Ho Hoan Kiem—Lake of the Restored Sword.

On a little island in the middle of the lake, there is a small tortoise pagoda which is topped with a red star, often used as an emblem of Hanoi. During early morning hours, Thanh told us, many people come to the lakeshore to jog, play badminton, or to practice tai chi. But for me it is the place where Jimmie Griffin's plane landed on Ho Chi Minh's birthday in 1967.

We drive past Thuy Khue Street where Jimmie and Jack were captured, then the guide takes us to an intersection near the stadium on Le Truc Street to see the plaque erected. As we get out of the van and walk across the street with our cameras aimed toward the plaque, a woman wearing a conical hat struggles past. She is balancing a pole on her shoulders with baskets of vegetables dangling from the ends.

Thanh has to translate for us the inscription on the plaque, which does not name Jimmie or Jack but bears the date and time, the identification number from their aircraft, and the words USS *Kitty Hawk.*

"It says that nine aircraft were shot down on this date—19 May 1967—and that the pilots from this plane were captured in the afternoon. It also says that electronic surveillance equipment was recovered from the plane when it landed in Hoan Kiem Lake," Thanh tells us. The North Vietnamese government always announced one aircraft downed for each crew member captured, so we know there were five or six planes shot down here that day. And we already know that nothing of value could have been recovered from the plane at the speed and altitude it was traveling...but if it meant erecting a plaque to mark the event, I am glad they did it.

Our next stop is what remains of Hoa Lo prison—which we have come to know as the Hanoi Hilton. What remains of the building is now a museum. Thanh seems to understand that coming to this place is a difficult experience for Jim and Moon. It is difficult for me as well. But he dutifully walks us through an exhibit, complete with mannequins which supposedly depict Vietnamese prisoners suffering at the hands of a French occupation force in 1954. "It looks very much like it did when we were housed here in one of the big rooms," Moon comments.

On this warm November day the small, dark cells seem stagnant. I cannot imagine how thick and dank the air must have been during the long summer months when Jim and Dick were locked up here. Their only view of the outside world was through small windows latticed with bamboo, and those tiny openings could not allow in much fresh air.

Since the original entry to the prison has been torn down, a painting depicting the entrance has been placed in that location, and Jim and Moon tell us it looks very much like the real thing as they remember it. Jim points out a small, dark concrete enclosure and says, "This is where we all started out. We were thrown in there when we were first brought in, for the initial questioning."

I gasp and turn away, realizing that in this cubicle, my first husband was interviewed—the interview that was broadcast around the world by Hanoi Radio. He then lay here, having received minimal medical treatment for his horrific injuries, until infection set in. Two days later, he lapsed into a coma and then was taken to the small hospital where within a few hours, he was pronounced dead. I slip out into the passageway quickly to hide my tears from the others, bruising my thigh into a rusty stock that protrudes from the wall in the darkened hall. Jim and Dick Mullen are dealing with ghostly memories as well. Their eyes mirror their memories of the two thousand plus days and nights they spent in these walls and other prison sites in the area.

A group of tourists in the museum complex watches us as we wander through the exhibits. The walls of the entry halls contain posters touting the Viets' "adequate treatment" of prisoners, the recreation and good food they claim to have provided. There are displays of clothing the men were supposed to have worn but never actually saw. We see posted statements that Jim and Dick say are "flat-out propaganda." Some of the foreign tourists standing nearby are listening closely to this exchange.

As we continue through the city to another prison the men call the Zoo, we are surrounded by what seems like thousands of people riding mopeds. Then, when we arrive at the Zoo, we are disappointed to find that only one section of the peripheral wall remains, most of the prison having been torn down for the construction of a swimming pool and apartments. Toward the rear of the property, Jim sees a small building, now occupied as housing for several poor families. He says this is the cell where he spent much of his incarceration between 1965 and 1970. The roof still has the same red tiles it had then, but inside the door is a depressing sight. There is one small dingy cot for sleeping and no other visible furnishings. "It's all right," Jim says. "I'm glad it's gone. It should be gone."

There are several pleasant parks around the lakes, and we notice a great deal of construction underway. But, as has been true in some other Third-World countries we have visited, it appears the construction was begun and then halted when the builder ran out of money.

Dutifully, Thanh takes us to a large cordoned off area, much like Moscow's Red Square, where we see Ho Chi Minh's tomb. Since the tomb was designed and built by Russians, it resembles Lenin's tomb. Fortunately, we are spared going inside to see Ho Chi Minh's preserved body, since we arrive during the hours when the tomb is unavailable for viewing. Thanh tells us that Ho is rumored to have had an illegitimate son, Nong duc Manh, who today is the general secretary of Vietnam's Communist Party.

Another prison, located in the countryside at least an hour out of Hanoi, was called Briar Patch. Jim spent some time there when he was a prisoner and had wanted to see it during our visit. But we now learn that the buildings have been bulldozed, and it is part of a military complex that is off-limits to us. I would like to think they are tearing down the prisons because, like us, they are trying to put the war behind them.

It has been a long morning, and we are all exhausted, emotionally if not physically. So we are relieved when Thanh delivers us to a shady garden courtyard adjoining the restaurant, Le Tonkin, for a delicious lunch. Back at the hotel, we take long rests in the afternoon before joining a crowd of other tourists for an early evening viewing of a water puppet show. The final act for the water puppets is a reenactment of the Hoan Kiem Lake story, complete with the emperor in a boat and a giant turtle.

We meet the Petersons for breakfast in the Hilton Tuesday morning, and they give us tips on crossing the street in Vietnam when facing an onslaught of motorbikes.

"Just never make eye contact," Pete tells us. "They will avoid hitting you, but if you make eye contact, then it is up to you to dodge them!"

Thanh is waiting for us in the lobby as we say goodbye to the Petersons. Then we board the small tourist van for our day's outing to Ha Long Bay. A beautiful area and a tourist attraction, the bay is also the place where Jim and Duffy's airplane ended up in 1965.

When Glyn Carol visited Ha Long Bay in 1994, she had to travel a rough dirt road from Hanoi, but now there is a smooth, paved highway.

Today it is buzzing with motorbikes as well as truck traffic, since the nearby Haiphong Harbor is a major shipping center. As we ride out of the city, we can make out mountains shrouded by fog in the distance, but the scenery soon turns to agricultural land. From our van we can see numerous farmers, most of them women wearing cone-shaped hats. The women are harvesting rice or hefting flat axes to dredge irrigation paths, and occasionally, we see men plowing with water buffalo. All of the farming here seems to be done by hand.

As we near the coastal area, we notice a number of three- or four-storied homes, all very narrow, each decorated with white, flowery ornaments and brightly painted banisters. Our guide tells us the government is supporting free market these days. He says this area is being promoted for tourism, so these houses may be intended as holiday rentals. Many such buildings are still under construction.

The marina is filled with boats, most of them wooden, and one of them has been hired to take us on a tour of Ha Long Bay. Aboard the boat a table has been laid with a starched, lace cloth with china and wine glasses, and we detect the aroma of lunch being cooked in the galley below. We climb to the top deck to get a better view of the harbor as the boat maneuvers among other vessels to sail toward a scattering of small islands in a misty area off shore.

"Was it this beautiful when you landed here after your shoot-down?" I ask Jim, while admiring the fairyland of small islands dotting the waters.

"I really didn't see anything beautiful that day. I was too busy trying to stay alive!"

After three days in Hanoi, we leave the Hilton behind late in the evening to board a train for Saigon, or Ho Chi Minh City as it is called today. We have booked a first class "soft-sleeper" compartment to be shared by the four of us. And in order to make the thirty-hour trip without undressing, we wear loose, comfortable attire so we can sleep in our clothes. There are several other classes of compartments on the train, and we have chosen the top of the line. It is not as rustic as we have been told to expect, but since there are no backrests and the bunks remain in the down position throughout the trip, it is not exactly comfortable either. A few years ago, the train and roadbed on this route were more antiquated, and the journey would have taken a much longer time, so we are glad we have waited until now to come here.

Rather than flying from Hanoi to Ho Chi Minh City, we decided to make the trip by rail in order to see some of the countryside. During the first few hours, we can see very little from the pitch-black window of our compartment, but the ride is fairly smooth, and there is little noise to disturb us. We are actually able to sleep. Then, when daylight arrives, we see farmland as the train moves south.

A train employee comes to our compartment with breakfast, offering boiled eggs and homemade hot dogs wrapped in banana leaves. Throughout the trip we are served other meals that include boiled rice, rough cabbage, and bony chunks of chicken. Jim and Moon say it resembles the food they received while POWs. There also is beer, but it has not been chilled. We drink it anyway.

Later in the day, we pass through the outskirts of Hue and Da Nang. We marvel at the unspoiled coastal areas of crystal blue waters, picturesque cliffs, and broad, sandy beaches. It looks much like the California coast must have appeared a century ago. The day is long as we rattle along through the country, and we find ourselves surrounded by darkness again long before we reach the city we still call Saigon. Finally, we begin to see the flicker of lights on shadows of buildings, and at about 5 a.m. of the second day, we arrive in Ho Chi Minh City.

The station is swarming with vendors and taxis, all competing vigorously for the business of the debarking train passengers. We take a van to the Rex Hotel where we have reservations. The lobby is very quiet at this early hour, but we have no other place to go and so we flop down in a group of chairs to wait for our rooms to be readied. We must look exhausted because the person manning the hotel desk makes a few calls and arranges for us to go up within a half hour.

We know many American GIs stayed at the Rex during the war, including Peggy Mullen's brother Billy. The hotel still offers some of the quaint French influence in its decor with large fan-backed rattan chairs with silk cushions placed about the lobby. There are other groups of seats made of dark ebony wood and adorned with carved animals. We find our rooms are also styled as in days gone by with satin coverlets and old maple furniture. In each room there is a lampshade topped with a silk crown—to remind us that we are at the Rex.

Having an early breakfast in the hotel's large dining room, we are surrounded by boisterous tourists from a variety of different countries. They are finishing their meals and are ready for a day of sightseeing at six o'clock in the morning! Despite our need for a good night's sleep in real beds, we soon wander out to look around the area when we finish eating. The differences between Hanoi and Ho Chi Minh City are quickly evident. Here, the streets are much wider; there are still many, many motorbikes, but the traffic is more orderly. This part of the city is still known as Saigon since it was the French sector during the Vietnam War. Here, we find retail shops more attractive than those we saw in the north. The shopkeepers seem to have had more training and experience in merchandising and display.

Again, we arrange for a tour guide, this one recommended by the company that gave us Thanh in Hanoi. A man called Zoom meets us at 8:30 the next morning, and we are appalled to learn the four of us will be touring in a sixteen-passenger Mercedes van. We ride across town past Bin Thanh, the central market, to Cholon, a gigantic Chinatown market. Zoom tells us that we probably saw few Chinese in the Hanoi area because border disputes with the Chinese are still a major problem, so any Chinese who have been in the country for a while have migrated to the south. He says there are now seven million people in Ho Chi Minh City and four million motorbikes! We have seen a million of them already, and it's not yet 9 a.m.

Everywhere we look—on the streets, throughout the market, on sidewalks outside the shops, riding mopeds—the people are eating; noodles, spring rolls, bean sprouts with meats, rice, or soups. Apparently, the Vietnamese people love to eat, and they love to cruise around on motorbikes. We decide that people in the south have more money than those in the north. And they seem full of energy and motivation, but the citizens of Saigon have had free-market experience for a longer time than the people of Hanoi.

Zoom takes us to all the usual tourist sights, including Thien Hau Pagoda in Chinatown, the Saigon Post Office, and the American Consulate which was built after the war since the American Embassy must now be located in Hanoi.

Because the Reunification Palace is not open to the public during the time we are with Zoom, we return for a tour on our own. The palace, which was the home of President Nguyen van Thieu during the Vietnam War, is maintained today as a museum. Our English-speaking guide at the palace takes us through the reception room, the war command room, the president's office, dining rooms, and part of the president's private quarters. She says that over the course of one week in 1973 President Thieu resigned turning the presidency over to his vice president, and then that man stepped down handing the reins to a general. Finally, in April 1975, the Vietcong drove a huge army tank through the gates and right into the palace to take over the government. Because the general stepped down peacefully, we are told by the guide, his life was spared and the palace was not totally destroyed.

We go down below the palace into the bomb shelter to see a room where we are told many war decisions were made. Nervously, I notice a red telephone nestled among phones of other assorted pale colors. The red phone stands out prominently. Our guide says it was the phone used by President Thieu during those perilous days.

Often during our stay in Saigon, we find ourselves crossing the street near the Rex, facing a multitude of motorbikes. This intersection is a roundabout, so there are no traffic signals to keep order. We remember the advice given to us by Pete Peterson during our breakfast meeting in Hanoi. Avoiding a glance at the drivers' faces, we start across as soon as there is a slight pause or gap in the action. Then, cautiously, we weave our way through the throng of moving bikes. Miraculously, we only have one close call during our stay.

Our mission for this trip has been accomplished. We came to see the country where the Vietnam War was fought, and we have seen the people of both sides. We know now that a kind of peace has come to these people, both in the north and the south, and they are moving ahead with their lives. We learn that regular direct air travel from the United States to Vietnam soon will begin. Here in Saigon, we have found an almost frenetic energy, people eager for what they call "free market." While they do not have all the freedoms we have in America, they now are able to keep some of the money they earn, and they seem very motivated.

We notice some of that motivation on our last day in Saigon when, finally, we go shopping. Many products from Vietnam today are exported to the United States and other countries around the world. We find great bargains as we load up our luggage with gifts to be given to family and friends during the holidays. As we leave Vietnam to return home, we realize that we have been charmed by the people here, and we are in awe of scenes from their beautiful countryside.

A few weeks after our return from our journey to Vietnam, I notice a small item in the *Washington Post* about a man in Vietnam who published an article criticizing the current Vietnamese government. He has been given a prison sentence. Despite the progress we saw when we visited Vietnam, some things have not changed as much as we had hoped.

January 2004

It is the week of the Tet, and we have come to the Fairfax, Virginia home of Dr. Khoa Nguyen and his wife Kim for a special dinner celebrating this holiday long observed by their ancestors in Vietnam. And we are joined by Khoa's brother, Dat Nguyen, a former South Vietnamese pilot who was shot down during the war and held in a Hanoi prison with our men. Called Max by the American POWs, Dat has come to visit their mother who, along with Max and Khoa, came to Camp Pendleton in California in 1973. Jim and I had met her then, as well as sixteen other family members who were refugees. Kim has prepared a feast of traditional Vietnamese food, and several other Vietnamese expatriate friends have joined them for the dinner.

For almost thirty years, since we first moved to the Washington area, a group of former POWs have gathered over dinner at a Vietnamese restaurant to celebrate Tet and reminisce about their days in prison. So, though we are to attend the Tet dinner with the other POW's tomorrow evening, we are treated tonight to an even more authentic celebration with the Nguyen family. We gather around their dining table, laden with a dozen colorful dishes of various vegetables, rice, chicken, soup, and a special Vietnamese salad. Kim has prepared a banquet!

The conversation on our end of the table soon turns to our recent trip to Vietnam, because Max is especially interested in our impressions of Vietnam today. During our trip to Saigon, we had been told that Nguyen is the name of the "king family" or rulers of ancient Vietnam, and so I comment that we are in very good company this evening.

"During the war," I say, "most Americans thought our troops were there to liberate the people. My first husband and Jim and the other American military people in the war believed we were needed to free them from communism. But the people of North Vietnam feared we were coming to, as one of our guides told us, take over their country—like the French had done earlier."

At this point, everyone at the table jumps into the conversation, all talking at once. "It is true," one of the women says. "But you *were* needed!" And she is joined by others as they describe some of the atrocities visited on the South Vietnamese by those in the north. "It was two different countries," she says. "And if we wanted to be communists, we could go to the north. It was for this reason that our family all left the Hanoi area and went to the south."

"Well, at least today it seems that the people there have some of the freedoms we were trying to give them," I reply.

"You can't trust them," the woman replies. "They are not so free as you think. The government there still tells lies."

When Jimmie Griffin first mentioned Vietnam in 1964, telling me the United States was about to be involved in a conflict there, I had to look it up on a map. I hardly knew where it was. Today, I know a great deal about that faraway land known as Vietnam. It was where Jimmie died, where Jim Bell spent more than seven years locked behind prison walls. Now, we have traveled to Vietnam. We have seen the country as it is today. And here at home, we have friends who were born there and who lived through the conflict we have come to know as the Vietnam War. All of our lives have been changed by that conflict that took place there between the United States and North Vietnam, and our friends who were natives of South Vietnam say they appreciate the sacrifices we made in that war. And that means everything to me.

Printed in the United States
69265LVS00003B/28

9 781425 926038